Generating
Theatre Meaning

D1610428

LIVERPOOL JMU LIBRARY

3 1111 01490 6554

"Eli Rozik has written a comprehensive and brilliant study of performance analysis. His book, *Generating Theatre Meaning*, joins a long tradition of scholarship on the performance codes of theatre, stretching from the Prague Linguistic School of the 1930s to contemporary writings in theatre semiotics, phenomenology, hermeneutics, and audience response theory. But Rozik is not merely adding an important book to the modern traditions of performance theory, both verbal and visual; he is also reflecting upon this heritage and offering a culminating assessment of the key issues, methods, and models of performance analysis. Chapter by chapter, Rozik provides an astute investigation of the play-script, theatre conventions, dramatic action, stage metaphor and symbol, audience response, and the fictional nature of theatrical representation. Most tellingly, the actors, who embody yet also enhance the implied intentions of playwright and director, are at the heart of his study. Drawing upon an impressive range of knowledge, from philosophy and neuroscience to rhetoric and literary aesthetics, Rozik delivers a rich and complex investigation of theatre performance, written in a clear, forceful style. He also describes and interprets several productions as demonstrations of his method of performance analysis. This is an essential book for everyone in the theatre community – scholars, directors, performers, designers, and spectators. It is a textbook for theatre study today." *Thomas Postlewait, editor of* Studies in Theatre History, *School of Drama, University of Washington*

"Eli Rozik has been at the forefront of the development of the analysis of performance for over two decades and is one of the world leaders in developing a paradigm shift within theatre studies away from the studies of play-texts to the text that is performance. His early work coincided with the dominance of semiotics as a critical tool for the analysis of performance. This new book, while situating semiotics within a range of possible theoretical tools, charts the development of the theories of performance analysis that have developed from the early semiotic applications. As co-founder of the first working group in Performance Analysis of the International Federation for Theatre Research, Eli Rozik has been continually seeking to chart a path for scholars through that problematic field that had lost its way in a sender–receiver binary. In his new book he offers the possibility of analysing performance less as a 'descriptive-communicative text' in the traditional semiotic model, and more as a phenomenological experience, using a range of analyses of actual performances to exemplify his approach." *Brian Singleton, former editor of* Theatre Research International, *and president of the International Federation of Theatre Research; Trinity College, Dublin*

Generating
Theatre Meaning

A Theory and
Methodology of
Performance
Analysis

ELI ROZIK

sussex
ACADEMIC
PRESS
Brighton • Portland • Toronto

Copyright © Eli Rozik, 2008; 2010.

The right of Eli Rozik to be identified as Author of this work has been
asserted in accordance with the Copyright, Designs and Patents Act 1988.

2 4 6 8 10 9 7 5 3

First published in hardcover 2008, printed in paperback 2010, by
SUSSEX ACADEMIC PRESS
PO Box 139
Eastbourne BN24 9BP

and in the United States of America by
SUSSEX ACADEMIC PRESS
920 NE 58th Ave   Suite 300
Portland, Oregon 97213-3786

and in Canada by
SUSSEX ACADEMIC PRESS (CANADA)
90 Arnold Avenue, Thornhill, Ontario L4J 1B5

All rights reserved. Except for the quotation of short passages for the purposes
of criticism and review, no part of this publication may be reproduced,
stored in a retrieval system or transmitted in any form or by any
means, electronic, mechanical, photocopying, recording or
otherwise, without the prior permission of the publisher.

British Library Cataloguing in Publication Data
A CIP catalogue record for this book is available from the British Library.

Library of Congress Cataloging-in-Publication Data
Rozik, Eli.
   Generating theatre meaning : a theory and methodology of
   performance analysis / Eli Rozik.
   p. cm.
   Includes bibliographical references and index.
   ISBN 978-1-84519-330-0 (pbk. : alk. paper)
   1. Theater—Semiotics. 2. Theater—Philosophy.
   3. Acting—Philosophy. I. Title.
   PN2041.S45R69 2008
   792.01'5—dc22

                                        2007032491

Mixed Sources
Product group from well-managed
forests and other controlled sources
www.fsc.org Cert no. SGS-COC-2482
© 1996 Forest Stewardship Council

Typeset and designed by Sussex Academic Press, Brighton & Eastbourne.
Printed by TJ International, Padstow, Cornwall.
This book is printed on acid-free paper.

Contents

Preface and Acknowledgements   x

Introduction: *State of the Art and Perspectives*   1
  Main schools and trends   2
    The formalist movement   2
    The Prague Linguistic Circle   3
    Roman Ingarden   4
    The semiotic school   4
    Post-semiotic criticism   5
    The IFTR Performance Analysis Working Group 6
  Main theoretical topics   7
    Textual nature of the theatre performance   7
    Descriptive nature of the performance-text   8
    Imagistic nature of the theatre medium   8
    Basic convention of the theatre medium   10
    Univocal nature of theatre units   10
    Segmentation of the performance-text   11
    The principle of acting: deflection of reference   12
    Theatrical nature of the play-script   12
    Poetic structure of the fictional world   13
    Metaphoric nature of the fictional experience   14
    Rhetoric structure of the theatre experience   15
    Role of the implied director   15
    Role of the implied spectator   16
    A phenomenology of theatre   16
  Structure of the book   17

Part I   *Semiotic Substratum*

1   **The Imagistic Nature of Iconicity**   21
  Imagistic thinking: from Nietzsche to neuroscience   23
  Iconicity: image imprinting and language mediation   25

The basic convention of theatre	27
Explanatory power of the imagistic approach	27
Typical iconic units	28
Real objects on stage	29
Stage metaphor	31
Stage convention	32
2 Segmentation of Performance-texts	**34**
Segmentation of real interaction	35
Ingarden's view of fictional verbal interaction	39
The pragmatic approach of Serpieri et al.	40
Segmentation of iconic interaction	41
Segmentation of stage objects	44
Segmentation of iconic interaction in Habimah's *The Seagull*	45
3 Stage Metaphor and Symbol	**48**
A theory of verbal metaphor	48
Stage metaphor	52
Speech act stage metaphor	56
Stylistic implications of mixed stage metaphor	57
Stage allegory	58
Personification	58
Substitution	59
Mediation by abstraction	60
Mixed praxical and allegoric discourse	61
Stage symbol	61
4 Stage Conventions	**64**
Reading principles	65
Kinds of stage conventions	66
Medium conventions	66
Imagistic conventions	67
Functions of stage conventions	68
Semiotic functions	68
Poetic functions	69
Norms and styles	76
5 Acting: The Quintessence of Theatre	**78**
Deflection of reference	79
Expanded notions of 'actor', 'text' and 'character'	82
Existential gaps between text and two worlds	84
The fundamental gap between real action and enacting action	86
Experiencing the performers' bodies	88

Contents

6   The Theatrical Nature of the Play-script   90
    Two kinds of theatre texts   91
    The literary fallacy   93
    Play-script analysis   95
    Intertextual relations between performance-text and play-script   97

Part II   Additional Strata and Disciplines

7   The Poetic Structure of the Fictional World   105
    The twofold structure of the performance-text   106
    Archetypal patterns of response   107
    The stratified structure of the fictional world   110
        Mythical layer   110
        Praxical layer   111
        Naïve layer   112
        Ironic layer   113
        Aesthetic layer   114
    Structure of the character   116
    Possible fallacies   116
    Sophocles' *Oedipus the King*   118

8   The Metaphoric Nature of the Fictional Experience   120
    The metaphoric principle   121
    The expressive nature of fictional worlds   122
    The principle of personification   123
    The apparent double reference of the performance-text   124
    The mechanism of textual metaphor   125
    Poetic implications   127
    Metaphor in dramatic practice   129
        Sophocles' *Oedipus the King* (continued)   129
        Yerushalmi's *Jephthah's Daughter*   130

9   The Rhetoric Structure of the Theatre Experience   133
    The pragmatic nature of speech interaction   134
    The pragmatic nature of stage/audience interaction   135
        Descriptive nature of the performance-text   136
        Performative nature of the performance-text   136
        Equivalence agent/director and object/spectator   137
        Notion of 'macro-speech act'   138
    Rhetoric nature of the stage/audience interaction   139
    Yerushalmi's *Jephthah's Daughter* (continued)   143

10 The Implied Director   146
Hermeneutic vs. creative interpretation   147
The mechanism of creative interpretation   149
Fidelity, creativity, and legitimacy   150
Creative interpretation and intertextuality   151
Productions of Beckett's *Waiting for Godot*   152
The play-script   152
Creative interpretations of *Waiting for Godot*   154

11 The Implied Spectator   161
Real vs. implied spectator   161
Roles of the implied spectator   163
Yerushalmi's *Woyzeck 91*   164
Framing a performance-text   164
Reading a performance-text   166
Interpreting a performance-text   168
Experiencing a performance-text   171
Dialogue between implied director and implied spectator   173

12 A Phenomenology Theatre   174
States' phenomenological approach   175
Alternative phenomenological approaches   179
Functions of actors' bodies on stage   180
Textuality   181
Metatheatricality   181
Personification   182
Characterization   183
Aesthetic effect   183
Life Class: a personal experience   184
Theatre vs. performance art   186

Part III   Examples of Performance Analysis

13 *A Transient Shadow*: A Silent Description of a Speaking   191
Fictional World
Reading *A Transient Shadow*   192
Interpreting *A Transient Shadow*   198
Principles of non-verbal description   202
Inherently non-verbal acts   202
Symbolic non-verbal acts   203
Metonymic non-verbal acts   203
Metaphoric non-verbal acts   204
Metaphoric hand gestures   204

Allegoric characters		205
Projected titles		205

14 *Suz/o/Suz* by La Fura dels Baus: Theatre at the Borderline
207

The notion of 'performance'	208
The notion of 'actual'	210
Performing an action vs. enacting an action	213
Suz/o/Suz by La Fura dels Baus	213

15 Habimah's *The Trojan Women*: A Ready-made Metaphor 222
of Unjustified War

Euripides' *The Trojan Women* and its Homeric sources	223
Sartre's adaptation: *Les Troyennes*	227
Habimah's production of *Les Troyennes*	231

16 Robert Wilson's *H.G*: Non-theatrical Space as Stage   237
Metaphor

Reading *H.G.*	238
On the legitimacy of interpretation	244
An attempt at interpretation	245
The warren – a found-space metaphor	247

17 Yerushalmi's *Woyzeck 91*: Intention   250
in Creative Interpretation

Büchner's *Woyzeck*	251
Yerushalmi's *Woyzeck 91*	257

18 Methodological Conclusions   266

Aims of performance analysis	267
Means of performance analysis	268
Theoretical focus	268
Personal experience	269
Use of video recording	269
Abridged account	270
Intuition of structure and meaning	270
Independent performance analysis	270
The disciplines of performance analysis	271
Excludes disciplines	275

List of Cited Works	277
Index	289

Preface and Acknowledgments

This book is the result of a life-long endeavor to understand theatre art. It reflects a critique of traditional semiotics, and suggests a theory of theatre that integrates semiotic, poetic, aesthetic and rhetoric disciplines. It aims at explaining the generation of performance-texts through a limited set of clearly defined principles, to make it more accessible to theatre students and scholars. In writing it, my intention has been to take into consideration major contributions to a sound theory of the performance-text and an efficient methodology of performance analysis. These contributions are presented as faithfully as possible, and ample quotation is provided to enable readers to perceive ideas in their original terminology and own logic, allowing them to take an autonomous stand. Each presentation is accompanied by my own critical comments, which attempt both to pose the problems and to suggest possible alternatives. While each chapter is illustrated by pertinent analyses of actual theatre performances, Part III is devoted to examples of full performance analyses. Excerpts from play-scripts are analyzed under the assumption that they are performed as prescribed.

I am deeply indebted to my wife Atara for her loving support and dedication, and to Naomi Paz for her constructive English editing of the text. I also thank Professors W. B. Worthen and Shannon Jackson, the Chairs of the Department of Theater, Dance and Performance at the University of California, Berkeley, for inviting me as visitor scholar in recent years – thus enabling me to complement this book in their wonderful library. The drawing on the cover is by Josef Herman RA (Royal Academy). It pays homage to my late good and admired friend.

To Atara

my bridge to the world,
with much love!

State of the Art and Perspectives

This study focuses on theatre art and reflects a fundamental need for understanding how humanity generates meaning through its various languages and media. A process of generating meaning assumedly takes place in the context of each theatre experience; i.e., in the actual encounter between a theatre performance and a spectator. The prime aim, therefore, is to suggest a generative theory of theatre and a method of performance analysis capable of revealing the principles underlying the complexity of this process.

The twentieth century witnessed a paradigmatic change in the study of theatre: in place of the traditionally rooted play-script analysis, the actual stage performance became the main object of research. Until the beginning of the last century, the study of literature comprehended drama as one of its main branches. This fallacy persists even nowadays in the form of the distinction between drama, which belongs in the province of literary theory, and the non-verbal aspects of performance, which are the concerns of theatre studies.

This paradigmatic change reflected a justified attempt to sever theatre from the bonds of literature and establish it as an independent art form. In the process, it produced a host of theories of theatre in general and theatre performance in particular. These theories have unfortunately not yielded a single applicable and efficient method of performance analysis, not to speak of any actual analyses of note. Consequently, the chapters that follow reflect a critique of the various theoretical schools, traditional theatre semiotics in particular. They also reflect a shift from sterile attempts to develop a self-sufficient semiotic method of performance analysis to a complex method that, while presupposing a semiotic substratum, draws upon several additional disciplines.

Patrice Pavis argues that '[t]heatre semiology was born of a desire to avoid impressionistic discourse on performance' (1998: 258). He probably implies that it was born in the quest for a scientific method of analysis, based on knowledge of the semiotic discipline. However, an intuitive approach is not necessarily invalid. It is even justified by the extreme complexity of the theatre performance. Nonetheless, since intuition may equally succeed or fail, theory should aim at a kind of learned intuition. In order to prevent ungrounded conclusions, moreover, even such an intuition should be controlled by a scientific method, reflecting knowledge not only of semiotics, but of all the systems underlying the generation of theatre meaning.

Pavis' remark is correct in that traditional theatre semiotics has failed to suggest a sound method of performance analysis and apply it to analyses of particular theatre performances. However, his conclusions that a scientific approach to theatre is just an illusion (1998: 255), and that only an exclusive intuitive approach is viable (*ibid*.: 257ff), are ungrounded. A fully effective method, which is perhaps hard to envisage at this stage of theoretical development, is not only possible, but also mandatory.

In contrast to traditional semiotics, this study presupposes that a constant interaction between theoretical considerations and actual performance analyses, i.e., between deductive and inductive procedures, in which the former guides the scholar in the light of general principles and the latter probes their applicability, should underpin the development of both a reliable theory and an effective method of analysis. Theory should be able to incessantly examine itself, dismiss inadequate principles and test alternative ones, in a prolonged process of self-establishment.

Main Schools and Trends

It is widely accepted that the inception of genuine performance research is intimately connected to the Prague Linguistic Circle, while also reflecting the beneficial influence of Russian formalism. This section offers an abridged historical account of the achievements and failures of theatre theory, by all schools involved in producing a theory of theatre and a method of performance analysis.

The formalist movement showed no special interest in theatre, including scripted drama. It focused almost exclusively on the verbal arts of poetry and fiction, 'imaginative literature' in Victor Erlich's terms (p. 60), despite conceiving the dramatic text as a subspecies of literature. However, it did suggest some general principles, which can and should be applied to theatre as well such as, first, viewing the text as the main object of research. Second, the notion of 'literariness' (*literaturnost*) reflects the

2

perception that language is used for both literary and non-literary discourse. In Roman Jakobson's terms, literariness is 'that which makes of a given [verbal] work a work of literature' (Erlich: 172). By analogy, it can be suggested that 'theatricality' applies to the use of the theatre medium, which can also be employed for other ends, for works of art. The notion of 'theatricality' has recently received renewed attention in theatre studies (*Theatre Research International*, Vol. 20, 2, 1995, and *Substance*, Vol. 31, 2 & 3, 2002). Third, Victor Shklovsky suggested the device of 'defamiliarization' (*priëm ostranenija*) as 'the *raison d'être* of poetry' (p. 12). In his view, defamiliarization is produced by placing the familiar in a context that restores its perceptibility (cf. Erlich: 175ff). Bertolt Brecht's '*verfremdungseffekt*' should be seen as broadening the sense of 'perception' to include rethinking and changing attitudes to reality (1987: various).

The Prague Linguistic Circle was founded in 1926, but the first work bearing on theatre, Jan Mukařovsky's 'Art as Semiotic Fact' (1986a), was published in 1934. In the 1940s Petr Bogatyrev and Jiří Veltrusky suggested a set of principles and notions, highly relevant to theatre studies, under the twofold influence of the formalist tradition and Ferdinand de Saussure's structural linguistics, particularly his intuition of a comprehensive theory of signs termed 'semiology' (Saussure: 101; cf. Erlich: 65). Saussure's distinction between '*langue*' and '*parole*', the analysis of the word into 'signifier' and 'signified', and the (relative) autonomy of the sign in regard to the referential world, have had a crucial impact not only on this Circle, but also on the way signs in other systems of signification and communication, including the theatre medium, are generally comprehended up to the present day. However, this has possibly hampered future developments of performance analysis too, due to an exclusive interest in the sign *per se*, while disregarding other structural levels, such as the sentence, which is the basic unit of a descriptive text, and reference.

The Prague Linguistic Circle is mostly known for applying the structural paradigm to literature and drama, mainly reflected in the application of basic structuralist notions, such as 'whole', 'structure', 'function', 'hierarchy' and 'dominant function'. The notion of 'structure' may also apply to a 'system', such as a language or medium, if conceived as a structured whole; e.g., the signified of a word depends on the mapping of a domain pre-established by a specific language (Saussure: 159). A system is 'a coherent whole in which all parts interact upon each other' (Cassirer – quoted by Erlich: 160).

On both the levels of single work and system, the structuralist approach has had a major influence on the development of theatre theories. Following Otakar Zich's pioneering work, *Aesthetics of Dramatic Art* (not available in English translation), Bogatyrev and Veltrusky suggested the

3

main theoretical tenets that eventually developed into full-blown semiotic theories of theatre. The idea of 'performance analysis' is an indisputable theoretical achievement of structuralism. However, they possibly also promoted some of the basic fallacies that plagued subsequent theories.

Roman Ingarden's independent and isolated contribution to theatre theory should not be overlooked. While the first edition of his *The Literary Work of Art* was published in 1938, a few years before the first writings of structuralist scholars, and contains only a few remarks pertinent to theatre theory, his seminal and highly relevant article 'The Functions of Language in the Theater' was published on 1958 (1973, appendix). Rather than following the formalist tradition (Erlich: 166), broadly speaking, Ingarden was inspired by Edmund Husserl's phenomenology. Unfortunately, his contribution was largely ignored, not only by structuralist scholars, but even by later professed phenomenologists of theatre, such as Bruce Wilshire and Bert O. States, probably due to his approach to theatre as a borderline case of literature (pp. 317–23 & 377), contrasting thereby its thrust of self assertion as an independent art form.

Nonetheless, some of Ingarden's insights are most revealing. His most important ones are: (1) his notion of 'stage-play', in the sense of conceptual matrix of particular performance-texts, which explains both their similarity and their inherent difference from the play-script that generated them (pp. 208 & 317ff). (2) His notion of 'gap' (or 'spot of indeterminacy'), usually conceived as a crucial notion in the understanding of the active role of spectators in generating the meanings of performance-texts (pp. 247ff & 331). (3) His distinction between 'main text' and 'side text' (stage directions), which underlies his felicitous intuition that in play-scripts language fulfills different functions (pp. 208ff & p. 377). And (4) his discovery that dramatic dialogue is more a form of interaction than a form of communication (pp. 382ff), thus possibly anticipating John L. Austin's theory of speech acts. Unfortunately, no serious attempt has been made to apply Ingarden's theory to actual performance analysis. Nevertheless, he should be seen as a forerunner of theatre theory mainly because of his manner of thinking and the implications of his work.

The semiotic school developed under the twofold influence of the Prague Linguistic Circle and Charles S. Peirce's semiotics. Eminent scholars such as Tadeusz Kowzan (Poland), Erika Fischer-Lichte (Germany), Marco de Marinis (Italy), Anne Übersfeld (France), Patrice Pavis (France) and Marvin Carlson (US) made substantial contributions to theatre theory and to its consolidation and diffusion. However, despite the complexity and scope of their theories, and while presupposing the centrality of the performance-text, they did not produce the expected methodology of performance analyses. The possible reasons for their failure are: (a) deduction of theories from general semiotic principles, in particular from the notion of 'sign', which cannot be the elementary unit of a descriptive text, while overlooking the pertinent notions of 'sentence' and 'reference'; (b) a disregard of the homogeneity of the theatre medium, while presupposing that it operates signs belonging in several sign systems; (c) ignoring the limitations of the semiotic method, overlooking thereby poetic, aesthetic and rhetoric disciplines; (d) a disregard of the crucial role of the spectator in generating theatre meaning; and (e) denial of the theatrical nature of the play-script.

Due to considerations of space, in the next sections refer mainly to Fischer-Lichte's *The Semiotics of Theater* (1992), which illustrates a theory that closely follows structuralist insights, and Marinis' *The Semiotics of Performance* (1993), which illustrates a theory of theatre on pragmatic grounds, under the assumption that they fairly represent the traditional semiotic school.

Post-semiotic criticism focuses on the failures of traditional theatre semiotics and marks its decline. By and large, criticism has been leveled from within the semiotic school itself. Probably the most radical and competent critic of semiotic theories is Pavis, who following an initial solid endorsement of traditional semiotics/semiology, engaged in a severe revision of his own views. His *Languages of the Stage* (1982) and *Dictionary of the Theatre* (French: 1996; English: 1998), which best reflect the state of disorientation during the last decades of the twentieth century, convey a sense of despair in regard to any attempt to create a methodology of performance analysis. His disappointment with traditional semiotics, which in his view is plagued by 'dogmatic prejudices', is conspicuously reflected in his critique of its search for 'minimal units' and attempt to 'reconstruct' performance-texts on their grounds (1998: 255; cf. Übersefeld, 1999: 15). Pavis thus renounces scientific performance analysis and suggests, instead, an intuitive approach, on the grounds that '[t]he signs of acting are often, in current practice, minuscule, barely perceptible, and always ambiguous, even unreadable: intonations, glances and gestures, more latent than apparent' (*ibid.*: 258). His key concepts are 'pace', 'rhythm' (*ibid.*: 312–316), 'musical composition' and 'energy' (*ibid.*: 257ff), which are not sufficiently developed theoretical notions, and probably suit best an intuitive approach. As suggested above, intuition is acceptable, but it requires a scientific method for probing and controlling its conclusions. The application of a scientific approach does not require a perfectly structured object.

Pavis also strongly opposes an omnipotent and 'imperialistic' theatre semiotics capable of dealing with every aspect of the theatre experience

(1998: 259; cf. States: 7). Similarly, Marinis employs 'totalitarian' semiotics (p. 11). Indeed, traditional semiotics inappropriately annexed vital disciplines, such as poetics, despite contradicting its charter as a general theory of signs, and ignored others, such as aesthetics and rhetoric. It also overlooked the spectator's vital contribution to the generation of theatre meaning, under the fallacious assumption that all is provided by the text (cf. Shevtsova).

In many a case, criticism, which is partly justified, was leveled out of sheer ignorance. Theories of theatre semiosis developed into highly complicated and voluminous tractates, which by their very complexity deterred scholars from even engaging in studying them, not to mention adopting them. Following the Okham razor principle, which establishes that scientific theories should be kept as simple as possible, a theory should not be more complicated than what it is meant to explain; i.e., a theory should explain and not be an object for explanation.

The IFTR Performance Analysis Working Group was established in 1991, within the framework of the International Federation for Theatre Research, by Sarah Bryant Bertail, Freddie Rokem and myself, and remains active until today. This initiative reflected a sense of theoretical deadlock and a genuine attempt to create a suitable method on inductive grounds, commencing from actual performance analyses. In its years of existence it has not adopted any exclusive theory of theatre but, rather, aimed at setting the conditions for its development. Its task has been to produce a vast collection of performance analyses, so that an inductive process could be set in motion. Such a process, in proper interaction with deductive theories, was expected to result in a sound theory and method of performance analysis. Moreover, the aim was to understand the mechanisms that explain the generation of their meanings. Due to the complex nature of performance-texts, and obvious recurrence of theatrical forms in diverse such texts, it was decided that each study should focus on a single theoretical issue. Because of the fleeting nature of performance-texts the Working Group also promoted analysis based on the combination of personal experience and video recording as complementary and mutually controlling devices.

This working group produced a number of actual performance-analyses, a selection of which (21 articles) were published in three issues of *Theatre Research International* – Vol. 19, 2, 1994, Vol. 22, 1, 1997 and Vol. 25, 1, 2000 – and others later in special sections devoted to such analysis. These 21 articles, which are dealt with in various chapters of this book, reveal that most of them neither approached semiotic problems, leaving the reading of texts to intuition, nor other disciplines of research considered cardinal in this study, such as poetics, aesthetics and rhetoric.

6

Unfortunately, as a group, it has not created the hoped-for method of performance analysis, not to speak of a theory of theatre.

Main Theoretical Topics

A clear distinction should be made between the study of the theatre medium and the analysis of a performance-text. Whereas the former deals with the semiotic rules underlying the generation of performance-texts, the latter deals with the generation of theatre meaning not only by its medium, but also by the nature of its described fictional worlds, and the vital complementation of the spectator. This section attempts to map the main theoretical issues that have drawn the attention of theatre scholarship since the advent of the Structuralist school, while advancing my own alternative views on them. Following Okham's principle, this study suggests a model that presupposes a common deep structure and a reduced number of rules that generate all the surface structures of performance-texts.

(A) *Textual nature of the theatre performance*: Mukařovsky suggests that a work of art is a sign structure (1986a: 3), thus advocating the autonomy of the artistic 'artifact' (*ibid.*: 3–6). Application of this concept to the 'performance-text', the theatre artifact, paved the way for considering it as a genuine object of analysis. This assumption was tacitly accepted not only by structuralist scholars, but also by subsequent schools; e.g., Fischer-Lichte claims that 'the performance can [. . .] be defined generally as a structured complex of signs' (1992: 173); and Marinis explicitly employs 'performance text' (p. 47). The use of 'text' for a theatre performance presupposes the extension of its original sense, previously confined to verbal works, literature in particular, and its application to non-verbal units of discourse. 'According to this understanding of textuality, an image, or group of images, is, or can be, a text. [. . .] therefore, even the units of theatrical production known as performances can be considered as texts, and thus become the object of textual analysis' (*ibid.*). I believe this insight to be a turning point in the theory of theatre.

The notion of 'text' presupposes the semiotic notion of 'code'. For Fischer-Lichte, a code is 'a system of rules for producing and interpreting signs or complexes of signs' (1992: 3). In other words, a code consists of all the signs and rules of combination that can generate a particular text. In this sense, 'code' is synonymous to the Saussurian notion of 'langue', and 'text' to 'parole', when applied to all sign systems and texts respectively. Since 'code' conveys connotations of secrecy and cryptic texts (cf. Pavis, 1982: 71), this study opts for 'theatre medium' instead of 'code', 'reading' (a theatre performance-text) instead of 'decoding', and 'formulating' (in the theatre medium), instead of 'encoding'. On such grounds it also distinguishes between 'theatre medium' in the sense of 'langue' and 'performance-text' in the sense of '*parole*'; i.e., *the theatre performance is a text generated by the theatre medium* (cf. Fischer-Lichte, *ibid.*: 220).

(B) *Descriptive nature of the performance-text*: In 'Semiotics of the Folk Theater', Bogatyrev contends that signs fulfill definite functions on stage: *depiction* of characters and dramatic action (1986a: 35). Fischer-Lichte conceives the function of signs in terms of 'representation' of (fictional) entities. Following Eric Bentley, she contends that 'theater occurs when a person A *represents* X while S looks on' (*ibid.*: 13; cf. 93; cf. '*impersonates*' in Bentley: 150). Since 'representation' refers to the relation between a single sign and the object it stands for in the sphere of thinking, the notion of 'description', which refers to the relation between a text and a depicted world, should be preferred. Indeed, the notions of 'medium' and 'text' imply that a performance-text is a description. Since fictional entities exist if and only if a text evokes them in the imagination of a reader/spectator, a performance-text is an evocative description.

In principle, a performance-text can describe real, fictional or fictionalized worlds. As an art, theatre usually describes worlds in which the element of fiction is dominant. Being a medium, i.e., a system of signification and communication, theatre is an instrument of thinking, employed by people due to their fundamental proclivity to think about their own world by means of descriptions of fictional worlds. In this study, it is thus assumed that *the theatre performance is a descriptive/evocative text.*

(C) *Imagistic nature of the theatre medium*: Following Zich, Bogatyrev argues that the stage presents not only linguistic signs (speech), but also a range of various kinds of non-verbal signs, such as costume, scenery, gesture, movement, posture, miming, voice and facial expression (1986a: 42–44). He terms this heterogeneity 'plurisignation' (*ibid.*: 43). Kowzan suggests 13 sign systems, including speech (pp. 182ff) and Martin Esslin expands the list to 22 (pp. 103–5). Other theories vary in between these boundaries.

Fischer-Lichte argues that since the theatrical 'code' 'is constituted by a large number of different semiotic systems' it cannot be decomposed into a set of 'homogeneous smallest signifying units', like words (1992: 224). She assumes that further segmentation is possible, but would result in leaving the orbit of the theatrical system and entering the realm of its constituent systems/codes (*ibid.*: 218ff). She defines, therefore, 'theatrical text' (the performance-text) as a 'multimedial text' (*ibid.*: 222; cf. Pavis, 1982: 15; 1998: 58ff; Marinis: 1 & Übersfeld,1999: 14). She fails to see, however, that this conclusion contradicts her own claim that '[t]heatrical signs are [. . .] not identical with the signs primarily generated by cultural systems, but rather *portray* these as iconic signs [. . .]. In other words, at the systemic level, the theatrical code contains only iconic signs [in Peirce's sense]' (*ibid.*: 16; my italics). The classification of these 'portrayed' signs, as she perceives them, is thus tantamount to the classification of everything in the world and, therefore, superfluous. I suggest instead that iconicity, which transforms 'portrayed' signs into iconic descriptions of signs, bestows homogeneity upon the theatre text. Moreover, no theory presupposing heterogeneity has produced a viable and intelligible methodology of performance analysis. Pavis' disappointment supports this conclusion.

Veltrusky endorses this alleged heterogeneity, but considers that two systems are essential, language and acting (1986a: 114–15). In terms of this study, this attitude reflects the intuition that the verbal and non-verbal systems cannot be reduced to a single common denominator. It is widely accepted that non-verbal signs are iconic, but it is difficult to ignore the fact that language is a symbolic system (in Peirce's terms) with rules of its own. However, iconicity does not rule out the replication of speech acts that conjoin verbal and non-verbal elements in indivisible units (chapter 1 thus supporting the homogeneity of the theatre medium.

Following Mukařovsky's seminal article 'Art as Semiotic Fact', Bogatyrev implies that things on stage are signs (1986a: 35ff), a semiotic principle explicitly articulated by Veltrusky, in 'Man and Object in the Theater' (1940): 'All that is on the stage is a sign' (1964: 84). Within the set of theatrical signs, Bogatyrev distinguishes between a 'sign of a material thing' and a 'sign of a sign' (of a material thing) (1986a: 33ff); e.g., a real 'national costume' is a sign of membership in a class, such as nationality and religion (*ibid.*, *ibid.*), and, when replicated on stage, it becomes a sign of a sign. In contrast, the curtain and the footlights are conceived as signs of the (material) stage (*ibid.*: 34). Signs and signs of signs, therefore, coexist on the stage.

Fischer-Lichte accepts the notion of 'sign of sign', and employs Peirce's notion of 'iconic sign' for characterizing it (1992:16). Indeed, iconic signs are signs of signs that, because of the principle of similarity underlying their formation, can replicate any kind of sign, including indexes (e.g., a laugh), symbols (e.g., a word), an even iconic signs. The problem is that, following Peirce (e.g., Vol. II, 2.247 & 2.274–2.308), 'iconic sign' is usually defined in terms of 'motivation' through 'similarity' (cf. Sebeok: 242). Such a definition does not befit all forms of theatre semiosis, in particular real objects on stage and stage conventions. Chapter 1 suggests that *the theatre medium is imagistic in nature*. Such a definition, while not contradicting the traditional one, has the advantage of connecting the stage components to the natural faculty of the brain to produce images and employ them as units of thinking. It also enables a single explanation for all forms of theatre semiosis – regular iconic sentences, real objects on stage, stage metaphor and stage convention, thus refuting the alleged heterogeneity of the theatre medium.

(D) *Basic convention of the theatre medium*: Due to their immaterial and ephemeral nature, images cannot be communicated, and because of their diffuse and uncontrolled meanings, they cannot establish reliable communication. These are made possible by (a) imprinting them on real matter; and (b) mediation of language, which is the main repository of abstractions in any particular culture. Imprinting and mediation transform an image into an iconic unit, i.e., into a unit of both thinking and communication. While all iconic media imprint their images on matter, the theatre is the only medium to do so on matter that is similar, and often identical, to that of their real or mental models. Chapter 1 suggests that *the theatre medium is iconic in the sense of imprinting images on (similar) matter and mediation of language*.

The cultural assumption that a description of a fictional world can be generated by means of images imprinted on matter, usually similar to that of their models, and mediated by language, is *the basic convention of the theatre medium*. This basic convention too contrasts the traditional semiotic presupposition that the performance-text is generated by heterogeneous codes.

(E) *Univocal nature of theatre units:* In 'Forms and Functions of the Folk Theater', Bogatyrev conceives 'transformation' as 'one of the most important and fundamental features of the theater' (1986b: 51), meaning that the same sign may carry different meanings, even within the same text; e.g., 'the famous shoes of Charlie Chaplin are changed by his acting into food, the laces becoming spaghetti (*Gold Rush*)' (1986a: 36). Bogatyrev ignores, however, that the laces actually do not become spaghetti and that the scene generates its comic effect precisely because of this gap. Similarly, Jindřich Honzl suggests that the 'changeability' of the theatrical sign is what distinguishes theatre from all other arts (1986a: 87). He illustrates this principle by Oxlopkov's directorial works; e.g., to represent a 'sea' he engaged an actor dressed in blue, wearing a blue mask and shaking a blue-green sheet attached to the floor; and to represent a 'ship's horn' he employed one actor, and to operate it an additional one. However, these examples do not illustrate changeability, but indicate that the image of something can be imprinted, in Honzl's own words, on 'different materials for its implementation' (1986a: 88). 'Changeability' reflects, therefore, a misconception of the theatre medium because, regardless of imprinted matter, the dominant factor is the imprinted image. In fact, his examples are either stage metaphors, e.g., a group of actors, enacting merrymakers for describing a storm (1986a: 82), or stage conventions (e.g., a blue-green sheet for describing a sea). Stage metaphor and convention are ruled by additional principles.

In the same spirit, Fischer-Lichte advocates the 'mobility' of a theatrical sign on the grounds that the same thing, e.g., rain, can be represented by different images, such as sounds, lighting, a wet costume, an umbrella and by the verbal expression 'it is raining' (1992: 130). However, these reflect not the principle of mobility, but the use of images of different indexes of rain for its description, with each unit conveying an unchanging meaning. Eventually, Veltrusky criticizes Honzl's notion of 'interchangeability' (1981: 231). Therefore, because of language mediation, chapter 1 suggests that *stage iconic units are univocal*, at least as much as verbal sentences are.

(F) *Segmentation of the performance-text*: Fischer-Lichte appropriately implies that the notion of 'analysis' presupposes the notion of 'segmentation' (1992: 224). Already in 1942, in 'Basic Features of Dramatic Dialogue', Veltrusky employed the notion of 'segmentation' (1986b: 131). Unfortunately, he approached the problem under the assumption that it is the play-script, conceived as a literary work, that should be segmented (*ibid.*: 130).

In *Littérature et Spectacle*, Kowzan asserts that '[t]he application of the science of signs [semiotics] to the analysis of the spectacle [performance-text] requires [. . .] first of all the determination of the significative (or semiological) unit of the spectacle' (1975: 214; my trans.). He contends that this unit 'is a slice containing all the signs emitted simultaneously, the duration of which equals that of the sign that lasts least' (*ibid.*: 215; my trans.). Presumably, such a slice consists of several overlapping signs, such as speech, intonation, facial expression, body gesture and hand gesture. The problem is that knowing which sign lasts least presupposes knowledge of principles of segmentation on a simpler level, which is the object of inquiry itself. Moreover, paradoxically, this principle, meant to segment a text into its significant units, avoids signification as its criterion, and is, therefore, purely formal. Keir Elam remarks that 'Kowzan's "slice" has not been found applicable and has produced no textual analyses of note' (p. 48).

The fundamental fallacy of the structuralist and semiotic approaches probably lies in their attempt to detect the basic unit of the performance-text on the level of sign. In principle, in itself a sign cannot be a unit of description, unless it is part of a sentence and its syntactic function is determined. In analogy to language, chapter 2 suggests that *the elementary unit of a performance-text is the iconic sentence* because of being both the most complex unit that the theatre medium can generate and the simplest unit of description of a (fictional) world. A performance-text is, therefore, a

11

LIVERPOOL JOHN MOORES UNIVERSITY
LEARNING SERVICES

finite set of iconic sentences generated by the theatre medium. Since a performance-text is usually a description of a fictional interaction, most such sentences describe fictional verbal and non-verbal acts. However, some sentences are mediated by additional principles:

(1) Chapter 3 suggests that stage metaphor, which presupposes the notion of 'sentence', is possible on iconic grounds and, like verbal metaphor it is generated by a common syntactic deep structure and shared rules of ellipsis. Stage metaphor appears in various forms, such as non-verbal metaphor, speech act metaphor, on both the verbal and performative levels, and stage allegory. Stage symbol too is possible on iconic grounds and can beneficially combine with stage metaphor.

(2) Chapter 4 suggests that although the reading of sentences embedded in stage conventions presupposes special rules, they still are images imprinted on matter, otherwise they could not be part of an iconic text.

(G) *The principle of acting: deflection of reference*: A totally neglected question regards the nature of the mechanism through which a performance-text describes a fictional world. The extension of the principle of similarity to the material level, which characterizes the performance-text, may create the illusion that what happens on stage is the fictional world itself, despite contradicting the notions of 'text' and 'description'. Although such an impression is evidently erroneous, no serious attempt to explain this phenomenon of evocative description has been made. Since the notion of description implies the existence of a referent, the question is: how is reference to a fictional world indicated and how its description effected? The problem is that (1) actors perform acts, which are indexes of actions; (2) real indexes refer to those who perform them; and (3) the enacted indexes are not meant to refer to those who perform them, but to fictional referents, i.e., to characters. The moment such indexes are attributed to characters they recover their typical self-referential function as if they were performed by characters. Therefore, the question should be: How are indexes performed by actors transmuted into indexes attributed to characters? Chapter 5 suggests that *'deflection of reference' is the fundamental principle of acting*, which solves this paradox.

(H) *Theatrical nature of the play-script*: In 'Dramatic Text as a Component of Theater' (1941), Veltrusky conceives the dramatic text as both a literary work in its own right and 'the verbal component of theatrical performance' (1986a: 95). He considers the non-verbal components of the performance-text as the result of 'not an arbitrary process, but essentially a matter of *transposing* linguistic meanings into other semiotic systems' (*ibid.*: 96; cf. Ingarden: 319ff) – such as set, music, gestures, voice, costume, facial expression and mask (*ibid.*: 97–108). Moreover, he assumes that the meanings of all these is predetermined by the dramatic text (*ibid.*: 109; cf. Übersfeld, 1999: 163). Marinis too contends that the performance of a dramatic text (play-script) is a 'transcoding' of the latter (p. 15). Similarly, Fischer-Lichte contends that the theatrical text is not a mere transference 'into another medium', but a 'translation of signs from a linguistic sign system into those of a theatrical sign system' (1992: 192). Despite differences, these notions – 'transposition', 'transcoding' and 'translation' – presuppose that the play-script is a literary self-sufficient text, and the performance-text is a result of medium translation. Chapter 6 suggests that *although the play-script is a partial and deficient text, it is generated by the theatre medium.* Therefore, it is a genuine object of theatre research. However, due to its inherent incompleteness it not only allows but also requires directorial creative interpretation.

(1) *Poetic structure of the fictional world*: A crucial aim of performance analysis is to understand how there emerges a coherent whole out of an immense number of components and utter diversity. Zich suggests that theatre reflects a 'mutual interrelationship and interaction of heterogeneous systems within a single unifying structure' (Matejka: 280; cf. Bogatyrev, 1986a: 42 & Veltrusky, 1964: 84ff). Similarly, Marinis suggests that the textual structure of a performance 'emerges from the *combination* of the various codes of the performance-text, and which assures the coherence of the code-relations' (p. 83). Yet none of them actually suggests what such a structure might be. I contend instead that a sense of wholeness cannot be produced by a structure on the semiotic level, because the sentence is the most complex unit that any medium/language can generate. I suggest therefore, that additional poetic, aesthetic and rhetoric rules structure the description of a fictional world and explain the sense of wholeness that a performance-text may produce. The aim of performance analysis is to understand how such rules too generate theatre meaning.

Pavis correctly remarks that '[p]erformance analysis cannot do without a narratological approach' (1998: 258); and Elam, who includes poetic theories in his *The Semiotics of Theatre and Drama*, de facto acknowledges that poetics is an indispensable discipline in performance analysis. Paradoxically, the Prague structuralists did not engage in the study of structural poetic principles that lend unity and wholeness to fictional worlds; otherwise they could have made a substantial contribution to performance analysis. In his rather late 'The Prague School Theory of Theater', Veltrusky quite explicitly confirms that the Prague School did not offer a structuralist theory of theatre (1981: 255). Assumedly, this shortcoming was due to the attempt, typical of his period, to sever theatre from literary approaches, under the erroneous assumption that fictional worlds are a literary matter.

Chapter 7 suggests that *poetic and aesthetic principles structure and bestow a sense of unity and wholeness on a performance-text*. It also suggests that the semiotic and poetic principles are both distinct and complementary, and that the latter basically reflect archetypal patterns of spectator response. Fictional worlds reflect a stratified fictional structure that features five layers: mythical, praxical, naïve, ironic and aesthetic. Performance analysis should thus integrate both the analyses of a describing text and a described world, by means of semiotic, poetic and aesthetic methodologies.

(J) *Metaphoric nature of the fictional experience*: Traditional performance analysis has ignored a fundamental question: the referential function of a fictional world. In 'Poetic Reference' (1936), Mukařovsky contends that an art work weakens its reference to reality in favor of attention 'focused on the sign itself' (1986b: 160). 'Focusing attention', however, is not a referential function. He also suggests that poetic reference to reality obtains only on the level of a whole work, in contrast to practical reference that is constantly renewed on the level of each of its components (1986b: 161). Unfortunately, this felicitous insight was overlooked by structuralist and semiotic scholars alike, probably because of their attempts to construct a semiotics of theatre based on single signs, with reference not being a function of such units.

In the context of the theory of possible worlds, Lubomir Doležel argues that fictional entities can be conceived as referents of descriptions (1989). Indeed, the principle of acting, which involves the principle of deflection of reference, explains the transition from an iconic description to an evoked fictional world. It could be claimed, therefore, that the referent of a performance-text is a described world of characters and their actions. This claim does not explain, however, why spectators may become strongly involved in theatre performances that describe worlds basically different from their own. Chapter 8 suggests that *the fictional world is a potential metaphor of the spectators' psychical states of affairs on the relational level of text/spectator*. In this sense, the reference of a performance-text to a fictional world is only apparent, with the function of the latter being the metaphoric predicate of an overall metaphor, thus providing the associations needed for metaphoric meaning to emerge. Such a metaphoric structure materializes already on the basic level of fictional creativity; i.e., the personification and expression of the single psyche of an author (and spectator) by means of a multiple world of characters and their actions (Frye: 33ff). It is the existential gap between a fictional world and the world of a spectator that requires the notion of 'metaphor'.

14

(κ) *Rhetoric structure of the theatre experience*: It would appear that viewing a performance-text as both a description of a fictional world and an artifact that aims at affecting an audience is incongruous, because 'description' does not necessarily imply any effect. In traditional play and performance analysis, however, expressions that refer to various kinds of effect, such as 'reaffirmation', the 'experience of the absurd', 'shocking the bourgeois (*épater le bourgeois*)'; promoting 'conformism', 'awareness' or 'defamiliarization'; and 'catharsis' – are successfully employed in attempts to understand the theatre experience.

Traditional semiotics is vitiated by the assumption that a performance-text is only a descriptive-communicative text. Such an assumption has been challenged by Marinis on pragmatic grounds: 'it is widely believed that in this relationship [between actors and spectators], in addition to speech acts, *processes of stimulation* also come into play, through which theater, rather than "saying," or communicating something, seems to act on the audience to provoke conditioned reflexes, behavioral responses of an immediate kind' (p. 143). Indeed, although the above paradox could be solved by applying a pragmatic approach, speech act theory in particular, Marinis fails to offer a pragmatic model for this relationship. Instead, chapter 9 suggests that *the theatre experience reflects a rhetoric deep structure*. In other words, on the structural level of fictional world/spectator relationship, a performance-text is a rhetoric macro-speech act, which embeds a description of a fictional world and reflects an authorial intention of changing a spectator's psychical state of affairs and ulterior purposes. It also suggests that the rhetoric aim subordinates the ironic, aesthetic and metaphoric layers of the spectators' experiences. While the description of a fictional world and its structure belongs in the spheres of theatre semiotics and poetics respectively, the intended effect on the audience belongs in the province of rhetoric that should be developed and incorporated as an additional discipline of performance analysis.

(L) *Role of the implied director*: Traditional semiotics, and even current performance analysis, has overlooked the existence and role of an implied director, which is reflected in the structure of a fictional world and its ironic conventions. The poetic and rhetoric principles that structure a fictional world imply a potential interaction between a real director and a real spectator. In parallel to this dialogic structure, it is possible to detect a dialogic structure between an implied director and an implied spectator, which constitutes the rhetoric layer of the overall deep structure of a theatre experience. Chapter 10 suggests that a basic distinction should be made between the 'implied director' and the 'real director'. Whereas the intentions and purposes of implied directors are usually not articulated in

15

performance-texts, they are implicit in their specific choices embodied in all the structural levels of a performance-text. These are particularly evident in productions based on pre-existing play-scripts that reflect directorial 'creative interpretation', which is not a form of interpretation but a form of creativity, and establish intertextual relations between them.

(M) *Role of the implied spectator.* Traditional theatre semiotics has consistently overlooked the crucial contribution of spectators in generating theatre meaning, under the erroneous assumption that all is in the text. In contrast, the spectators' contributions from their own resources are vital and cannot be ignored. Fictional texts not only require them, but also presuppose them in order to make sense. Pavis correctly maintains that 'the authority of the subjective, never neutral, gaze of the spectator [. . .] should not be eliminated altogether [from theory]' (1998: 258). Marinis too does not restrict the role of the spectator to that of semiotic competence alone: 'it requires competences of a contextual, intertextual, and encyclopedic order, involving pragmatic as well as syntactic and semantic problems' (p. 99). He considers the spectator not only as 'the target of theatrical manipulation', but also as the 'coproducer of the performance' (p. 158). This approach has been adopted by many scholars in recent years.

Wolfgang Iser presupposes a crucial distinction between 'real reader' and 'implied reader' (1974 & 1991). In the terms of the present study, the 'implied spectator' is the set of expected reading and interpretive competences and psychical functions that a performance-text needs and presupposes for theatre meaning to fully emerge. While the implied spectator, by definition, is supposed to master all these competences and fulfil all the functions prescribed by, and inscribed in a performance-text, the real spectator is limited to various extents. Chapter 11 suggests four basic functions that characterize the implied spectator: *framing, reading, interpreting and experiencing* a performance-text. It also suggests that *a dialogue between implied director and implied spectator is inscribed in the performance-text.* In other words, performance-analysis should focus on the dialogue between implied director and implied spectator, which is a crucial constituent of the deep structure of a performance-text, and reflects a directorial intuition of the dialogue between real director and prospective real spectator.

(N) *A phenomenology of theatre*: Bogatyrev implies that a basic 'duality', of actor as actor and actor as text, is irreducible: 'Despite the fact that the actor expresses regal dignity by his costume, the sign of age by his gait, the sign that he represents a foreigner by his speech and so on, still we see in him not only a system of signs but also a living person' (1986a: 48). The

16

same applies to any object on stage, e.g., a real table, which in addition to enacting a fictional table, remains a real table; i.e., retains its nature. In Bogatyrev's own terms the actor projects both 'signs of signs' (iconic signs) and 'signs' of a real object (as an actor) (*ibid.*: 33ff; cf. Veltrusky, 1964: 84ff). This duality is underscored by the fact that actors are perceived not only as living persons, but also as having lives beyond the boundaries of specific performances: 'This special artistic duplexity acquires great theatrical effect in the folk theater where the audience knows the actors well' (Bogatyrev, 1986a: 48. cf. Carlson, 2000 & 2004).

In recent years, this duality has been reformulated in terms of 'text and body' and acquired theoretical prominence. States' critique focuses on the tendency of (traditional) semiotics to overlook the materiality of the performance-text. He suggests, therefore, introducing phenomenology as a complementary method of analysis, in addition to semiotics. The question is whether or not the experience of actors' physical presence on stage deserves attention beyond their function in enacting a description of a fictional world. I suggest that their bodies indeed fulfil additional functions in the structure of the performance-text, but that apart from them other functions are of no interest for performance analysis. Chapter 12 proposes that actors' bodies on stage fulfil the following functions: textuality, metatheatricality, personification, characterization and aesthetic effect, which deserve further research.

The main question is whether or not a phenomenology of theatre should focus only on physical presence; i.e., can have such a narrow scope and ignore all the semiotic, poetic, aesthetic and rhetoric principles that structure fictional worlds. A phenomenology of the theatre experience should address, explain and integrate all its constituents. Although the traditional semiotic approach, which focuses solely on the textual function of the body on stage, is indeed reductive, this fallacy does not justify a phenomenology that focuses only on its physical presence.

Structure of the book

This study consists of three parts. Part I (chapters 1–6) is devoted to the semiotic substratum of the performance-text, i.e., to the theatre medium and its basic forms of generating theatre texts and their meaning. Since performance-texts are generated by a specific cultural medium, theory and methodology should focus first and foremost on the nature of this medium, without which additional strata are unthinkable. Part II (chapters 7–12) deals with these additional strata, which participate in the generation of theatre meaning: the basic poetic inner structure and the metaphoric and rhetoric outer structures grafted upon them. Part III contains five perfor-

17

mance analyses that apply theoretical principles suggested in this study (chapters 13–17) and Methodical Conclusions (chapter 18).

Chapter 13 is an analysis of *A Transient Shadow* by the Khan Theatre, Jerusalem, and ponders how a speechless performance-text describes and evokes a speaking fictional world. Chapter 14 is an analysis of *Suz/o/Suz*, by the Barcelona based company La Fura dels Baus (1993), and focuses on the theoretical difference between theatre performance and performance art. Chapter 15 is an analysis of Habimah's production of Jean-Paul Sartre's *Les Troyennes*, and explores the umbilical relationship between creative interpretation, actualization and universality of play-scripts. Chapter 16 is an analysis of Robert Wilson and Hans Peter Kuhn's installation *H.G.*, and contemplates the possible metaphoric function of non-theatrical found-spaces. Chapter 17 is an analysis of Rina Yerushalmi's *Woyzeck 91*, and suggests a method for conjecturing implied directorial intentions and purposes through analysis of the intertextual relations between a performance-text and its source play-script.

PART I

Semiotic Substratum

A theatre performance is a descriptive/evocative text fundamentally generated by the theatre medium. Therefore, reading such a text presupposes a spectator's basic competence: theatre medium 'literacy'. 'Reading' and 'literacy' are employed here in a wide sense that also encompasses iconic texts. A theory underlying performance analysis should, therefore, first and foremost focus on the nature of this medium. This substratum is vital, because other strata can operate only upon a fundamental act of reading. While semiotics is the relevant discipline for this structural layer, additional structural layers require other disciplines of research. This part of the study is devoted to the semiotic substratum; i.e., to the theatre medium and its principles of generating theatre texts and meaning.

1

The Imagistic Nature of Iconicity

'Iconicity' is a crucial notion in the description of the theatre medium. In the context of a modern theory of signification it was first employed by Peirce (*inter alia*, 2.247 & 2.274–2.308). From his seminal and rather obscure definitions, it can be learned that the iconic sign is defined in terms of motivation through similarity: 'Anything whatever, be it quality, existent individual, or law, is an Icon of anything, in so far as it is like that thing and used as a sign of it' (*ibid.*: 2.247); e.g., an iconic smile. 'Motivation' means here that a sign can be read through natural inference, with no need to learn the system, through either similarity or contiguity. 'Icon' belongs in a triad that also includes 'index', in the sense of a sign motivated by contiguity, e.g., a real smile that indicates a state of mind (*ibid.*, *ibid.*); and 'symbol', in the sense of an unmotivated sign based on a conventional link between signifier (e.g., the sound of the word 'smile') and signified (the notion of 'smile') (*ibid.*, *ibid.*).

Saussure intuited the existence of non-arbitrary (motivated) systems, such as mime, and suggested the possibility of '*sémiologie*', a general science of signs, for which language is one among other systems (p. 101). Since 'similarity' applies to various kinds of relationship, such as two peas, twin brothers and two books of the same edition, an iconic sign is supposed to be recognized first as a sign, and only subsequently distinguished from other kinds of signs according to motivation and similarity. The best interpretation of Peirce's insight is probably that of Thomas A. Sebeok: 'A sign is said to be iconic when there is a topological similarity between a signifier and its denotata' (p. 242). 'Topological similarity' should be understood in the sense of similarity on the level of perceptible spatial properties. However, iconic similarity is not restricted to only visual features.

Does 'similarity' refer to the real or the described (fictional) world?

21

Those who endorse similarity to real life reveal a tendency to identify 'iconicity' with '*mimesis*' in the sense of 'imitation' of reality and, therefore, with 'realism'. In 'Typography of Representation', Michal Kobialka argues that Tadeusz Kantor's productions strive to establish a kind of ('nonmimetic') performance, which does not follow 'the external order of things'. Instead, believing in the autonomy of the art work, he promotes a kind of performance that is 'always changing and fluid, negating, decomposing, dissolving, deconstructing, or destroying any promise of representation' (p. 118). Indeed, there is no reason why a performance-text should describe only worlds that resemble the real world. The iconic arts may evoke worlds that either resemble real life or differ from it to various extents. Imitation is thus only an option. I suggest, therefore, that the notion of 'iconicity' is not a synonym of '*mimesis*', but merely implies that iconic signs are read according to their similarity, however faint or stylized, to real or mental models.

The contrasting view applies 'similarity' to the relation between a performance-text and a fictional world; e.g., it is implied that actors' appearances resemble characters' looks, which explains the use of masks and make up. Reading an iconic description also means evoking a fictional image on the grounds of similarity. This should be qualified, because not all forms of theatre semiosis presuppose that all their perceptible properties should be attributed to a fictional world. Most conventions indicate otherwise; e.g., an actor who speaks in iambic pentameter.

Definition of 'iconicity' in terms of 'motivation and 'similarity' is widely accepted in theatre semiotics (e.g., Fischer-Lichte: 16 & Carlson, 1990: xiv), even by its critics on various grounds. Pavis maintains, for example, that 'the notion of iconicity poses as many theoretical problems as it solves' (1998: 175). Indeed, while providing a reasonable description of typical iconic units, its traditional definition fails to explain some basic forms of theatre semiosis such as real objects on stage and stage conventions. The problem is that these forms do not conform to 'similarity' in the strict sense of the word. Furthermore, the universality of theatre's basic forms of semiosis leads to the conjecture that their roots must lie in a primeval, elementary and vital mental faculty (Rozik, 2002a), to which the traditional definition hardly relates. I suggest, therefore, defining 'iconicity' in terms of 'imagistic thinking'. While such a definition does not contradict the principles of motivation and similarity, it does provide the ground for connecting theatre to a natural ability of the brain to employ images in an alternative biologically rooted form of thinking, and thus solving the problem of theatre's apparent heterogeneity.

This theoretical shift will be supported by examining the nature of imagistic thinking and exploring the advantages and deficiencies of each definition for each basic form of theatre semiosis. The sections presented below aim at showing that (a) *the theatre medium is imagistic in nature*; (b) *the theatre medium is iconic in the sense of imprinting images on (similar) matter and mediation of language*; and (c) *the principle of language mediation determines that stage iconic units are univocal, at least as much as verbal units are.* The definition of iconic units in terms of imprinted images and mediation of language, in addition to connecting iconic media to imagistic thinking, explains all forms of theatre semiosis by the very same principle.

Imagistic thinking: from Nietzsche to neuroscience

Sigmund Freud believes that while dreaming the brain goes into a process of regression: 'We call it "regression" when in a dream an idea is turned back into the sensory image from which it was originally derived. [. . .] *In regression the fabric of the dream-thoughts is resolved into its raw material'* (1978: 693). 'Regression' implies that a translation from verbal into imagistic description has taken place; that there is a basic correspondence between verbally formulated ideas and their respective sensory images, e.g., between the phrase 'red apple' and the image 'red apple'; and that images are not mere perceptions, but are employed as basic units of thought. 'Regression' also implies that thinking in images has been a preverbal form of thinking, characteristic of mankind in its very early stages of development (pp. 899–700). Freud thus follows Friedrich Nietzsche's insight that 'in dreams we all resemble this savage. [. . .] in sleep and dreams we repeat once again the curriculum of earlier mankind. [. . .] the conclusions man still draws in dreams to present days for many millennia mankind also drew *when awake*' (1998: I, 17–18; cf. Jung, 1974: 33). Traces of preverbal imagistic thinking are also found in daydreaming, children's imaginative play and drawings, and the iconic arts (Rozik, 2002a: 270–292).

In *Language and Myth*, Ernst Cassirer suggests the notion of 'symbolism', in the sense of coupling representations of objects and abstractions of their qualities in basic units of thought. These 'symbolic forms are not imitations, but *organs* of reality, since it is solely by their agency that anything real becomes an object for intellectual apprehension, and as such is made visible to us' (p. 8). This wide definition of 'symbolism' enables the consideration of additional forms of representation, alternative to language, including imagistic thinking. Cassirer conceives of logic and mythical thinking as mutually independent, and suggests, explicitly, that in the latter metaphor is the principle of description (pp. 94ff) and, implicitly, that the 'mythical image' is its basic element (p. 37).

Following this line of reasoning, in *Philosophy in a New Key*, Susanne

Langer states that images are 'our readiest instruments for abstracting concepts from the tumbling stream of actual impressions. They make our primitive abstractions for us, they are our spontaneous embodiments of general ideas' (p. 145). Moreover, images are 'just as capable of *articulation*, i.e., of complex combination, as words' (p. 93). Thinking is thus anchored in perception, the raw material of mental imagistic representation. In her study, which attests to a thorough reading of Freud's writings, Langer suggests the following definition of thinking:

> Man, unlike all other animals, uses "signs" not only to indicate things, but also to *represent them*. [. . .] We use certain "signs" among ourselves that do not point to anything in our actual surroundings. Most of our words [. . .] are used to talk about things, not to direct our eyes and ears and noses toward them [. . .] They serve, rather, to let us develop a characteristic attitude toward objects *in absentia*, which is called "thinking of" or "referring to" what is not here. "Signs" used in this capacity are not *symptoms* of things, but *symbols*. (pp. 30–31)

'Thinking' thus presupposes two main properties: representation of things in the mind and manipulation of them in absentia; i.e., thinking takes place when such representations are disconnected from actual experience. This definition of thinking is meant to suit imagistic representation too.

For R. L. Gregory, in *The Intelligent Eye,* the eye is not only an 'image-forming' organ, but also one of interpretation (pp. 12–15). Perception is conceived of as the prototype of thinking (p. 146): the eyes 'freed the nervous system from the tyranny of reflexes, leading to strategic planned behaviour and ultimately to abstract thinking' (p. 13). Gregory thus supports Langer's philosophical approach on scientific grounds. In her view, '[e]yes that did not see forms could never furnish it with images' (*ibid.*: 90). Furthermore,'[t]he eye and the ear make their own abstractions, and consequently dictate their own peculiar conception' (*ibid.*: 91).

Conceiving of images as fundamental units of thought is amply supported by recent findings in neurobiology. In *Descartes' Error*, Antonio R. Damasio asserts that having a mind means 'the ability to display images internally and to order those images in a process called thought' (p. 89). Moreover, whatever is not 'imageable', including words and mathematical symbols, cannot be known and, therefore, cannot be thought (p. 107). Following findings through digital methodology, in *Image and Brain*, Stephen M. Kosslyn asserts that '[i]magery [in the sense of mental representation] is a basic form of cognition, and plays a central role in many human activities – ranging from navigation to memory to creative problem solving' (1995: 1). He distinguishes between 'propositional' and 'depictive' representation, the latter being stored in the brain spatially, like the objects they represent: 'Depictive representations convey meaning via their resemblance to an object, with parts of the representation corresponding to parts of the object' (*ibid.*: 5). 'Depictive' representation is evidently a synonym of 'imagistic' representation. Damasio distinguishes between 'perceptual images' (e.g., running your fingers over a smooth metal surface); 'recalled images', which occur when one conjures up a remembrance of things; and images 'recalled from plans of the future [that] are constructions of your organism's brain' (pp. 96–97). The latter should be conceived of as images that have been disconnected from actual experience and become units of thought. Such images are not exact reproductions of objects, qualities or acts, but a combination of faint reproduction and interpretation, 'a newly reconstructed version of the original' (p. 100).

Kosslyn characterizes thinking as hinging on two properties: 'First, information must be *represented* internally; and second, [. . .] information must be manipulated in order to draw inferences and conclusions' (1996: 959). He reconfirms thereby Langer's definition of 'thinking' in general, and thinking through images in particular.

Iconicity: image imprinting and language mediation

There are two problems in defining 'iconicity' in terms of 'imagistic thinking': First, spontaneous mental images are fundamentally figments of the imagination, i.e., nonmaterial entities, which cannot be communicated. *Mental images thus require a material carrier to enable communication of their signifying function.* I suggest, therefore, that an iconic unit is an image imprinted on matter. In Saussurian terms, both the imprinted image and the imprinted matter constitute the signifier of an 'iconic unit'. 'Medium' thus refers to the kind of material carrier that enables images to be perceived by the senses, and thus their communication.

Each iconic medium is defined by the matter it employs for imprinting its images. Whereas most iconic arts use matters different from those of their models, underscoring thereby their signifying and communicative functions, the theatre medium is characterized by extending the principle of similarity, including identity, to the material level; e.g., images of human behavior are imprinted on actors' bodies, images of costume on real fabric and images of light on real light (Rozik, 1992a: 14–15). *The signifier of the theatrical unit is thus characterized by application of the principle of similarity on both its imagistic and material levels.*

Second, in contrast to words, spontaneous mental images carry diffuse signifieds. In particular, they do not determine clear boundaries between core sense and associative peripheries, making interpersonal communication problematic. *In order for any iconic medium to become an established cultural system, the mediation of language is a prerequisite*; i.e., the set of abstractions conveyed by an imprinted image is its signified. Indeed, language is the main repository of relatively controlled abstractions. Assumedly, mediation happens spontaneously, because a brain conditioned by a language naturally assigns senses to imprinted images, according to the senses that conventionally categorize their models.

Since an iconic unit conveys the set of abstractions culturally connected to the class of its models, it can be used as a univocal unit of thinking and description. It is precisely in this sense that an imprinted image of an object and the verbal sentences used to describe it are equivalent in different systems of signification. It follows that the theatre medium presupposes linguistic competence. Moreover, this equivalence implies that, in contrast to the usual perception, a word does not relate primarily to a real object but to its correspondent image. Both words and images are mentally represented in the brain, which explains the spontaneous use of one for the other.

The term 'image' is also widely employed for a word that is capable of evoking a non-verbal image. Words such as 'sunset', 'apple' and 'bird', when used within a frame that promotes the evocation of images, such as literature, are indeed capable of evoking them in the imagination of a reader/listener. The associative links between the names of material objects (or their phenomena) and their correlated visual or other images may be variously activated: a word may evoke an image or vice versa, and each of them may evoke a sensory experience with a real object or vice versa. Such verbal images are used for categorizing both percepts and their corresponding images, whether mental or imprinted. It can be claimed, therefore, that these associative links underlie equivalent functions of categorization, which is an essential function of thinking. The only qualification is that not every word can have an equivalent image. Due to the nature of the imagistic/iconic signifier – which replicates the perceptible aspects of things – only words referring to concrete entities or phenomena have imagistic/iconic equivalents. The iconic representation of abstract words concerns, therefore, non-verbal 'figures of speech', such as stage allegory and metonymy.

The description of fictional worlds through imprinted images is made possible by actually disconnecting them from their perceptual or mental models and employing them in a descriptive capacity. Since performance-texts usually describe fictional worlds, with the text functioning as a clue for imaging such worlds, such imprinted and mediated images function in an evocative capacity.

An image becomes, consequently, a cultural unit of signification and communication under two conditions: imprinting on matter and mediation of language. I contend that such a definition in terms of 'imagistic thinking' suits all forms of theatre semiosis. Moreover, it does not contradict the traditional definition because the notion of 'image' implies 'motivation' and 'similarity'. In addition, (a) *it connects the iconic unit to a natural faculty of the brain to produce images and employ them as units of thinking*; (b) *it expands the set of models of iconic units to images solely created in the mind*; and (c) *it enables all forms of theatre semiosis to be interpreted by the very same method.*

The basic convention of theatre

Against the background of the previous considerations, the basic convention of theatre semiosis should be formulated not in traditional semiotic terms, but on imagistic grounds. *The cultural assumption that a description and evocation of a fictional world can be performed through iconic units, i.e., of images imprinted on similar matter and mediated by language, should be conceived of as the basic convention of the theatre medium.* This convention underlies all forms of theatre semiosis, and contrasts the traditional claim that a performance-text is generated by several heterogeneous codes (e.g., Kowzan: 181–205; Fischer-Lichte: 13–17; Marinis: 97ff). By virtue of the principle of similarity, the theatre medium both preserves the reading principles pertinent to the replicated units and bestows homogeneity upon the entire medium.

A theatre performance is a text generated by the theatre medium, which describes a specific fictional world for a specific audience at a specific time and place. It is the actual text that a spectator is expected to read, interpret and experience.

Explanatory power of the imagistic approach

Not all iconic units on stage, employed for the description of a fictional world, are of the same kind. Such units are either purposefully produced for a production (typical iconic units), or ready-made 'real objects', which acquire an iconic function when placed on stage. Such units are used in either a 'literal' or a 'metaphoric' capacity; and either according to the principles of motivation and similarity, thus enabling natural inference, or by mediation of a 'convention'. Therefore, while the explanatory power of the traditional definition of iconicity in terms of 'motivation' and 'similarity' is restricted, the definition in terms of imprinted imagistic thinking explains all basic forms of theatre semiosis: (a) typical iconic units, (b) real objects on stage, (c) stage metaphors, and (d) stage conventions.

27

(A) *Typical iconic units*: In contrast to 'experimental director and theorist' Michael Kirby who, in 'Nonsemiotic Performance', advocates the nonsemiotic nature of his own production *Double Gothic*, and in an attempt to demonstrate the 'all-pervasive iconicity of theatre', Carlson writes:

> The actress who plays the blind woman is not, it seems, truly blind; the thunder is not real, but produced during the performance in some mechanical manner; and so on. The audience, in turn, is quite aware of these conventions, long accepted as the basis of theatrical illusion. But here again we are in the realm of the semiotic. If the thunder is not real thunder, and if the blind woman is not a real blind woman, then they appear as iconic representatives of those realities, in short as signs. (1990b: 6)

Enacting blindness is indeed a clear-cut example of typical iconicity because the actress is meant to replicate the appearances of blind behavior; i.e., to produce images of 'being blind' and imprint them on her own body. 'Iconicity' applies, therefore, to a myriad of replicated indexes of qualities, states and actions, including the sound of a thunder.

This principle also applies to any object purposefully produced for a production by imprinting an image on matter similar to its model. It would appear, however, that there is a problem in regard to possible imprinted images of speech. 'Speech' and 'image' seem to be fundamentally incompatible categories, belonging in different spheres. Whereas 'speech' is usually conceived of in terms of basically aural signification and communication, 'image' is in terms of mental reproduction of predominantly visual percepts. Even extending the notion of 'image' to all the senses does not affect this apparent notional gap. In Peirce's terms, words and images are categorized as symbolic and iconic signs respectively, requiring different principles of reading. This conceptual gap appears to be so conspicuous that any attempt to combine them seems futile. No wonder that in traditional theatre semiotics, reduction of verbal and non-verbal means to a single principle has been found to be impossible. Whether words and images are conceived of as fundamentally different or as equivalent means in different systems, there seems to be a tacit agreement that there cannot be an image of speech.

In contrast, I contend that an image of speech is not only possible, but even characteristic of theatre semiosis. Indeed, there is nothing to preclude the formation of such an image, particularly in the case of a speech that is employed in a performative capacity, i.e., for doing something, which is equivalent to a non-verbal act, and thus non-verbal in nature. If an image of a non-verbal act is possible, such as slamming a door in protest, an image of a verbal act of protest should be possible and plausible as well. Furthermore, due to the principle of similarity, being 'signs of signs' in Bogatyrev's terms, iconic units can replicate any kind of unit, including

28

verbal sentences. Assumedly, the mind naturally creates images of acts, including speech acts, as it does of any other concrete model in the world (Rozik: 1999c).

Although there is a tendency to see 'image' solely in terms of visual perception, if it is defined in terms of similarity to real or mental models, all other senses should be included as well. Furthermore, if all senses can generate images, there is nothing to preclude complex images that combine several senses, images of aural and visual properties in particular. An unqualified opposition between image and word is thus misleading. The imagistic approach to iconicity abolishes the supposed duality of the performance-text, allegedly composed by language and non-verbal media.

Complex images of speech acts, used for the description of fictional speech acts, can be communicated by imprinting their wordings on actors' voices, and their non-verbal indexes, needed for their disambiguation, on their bodies. Iconic replicas of speech acts are characteristic of the dramatic arts, such as theatre, opera, cinema and TV drama.

Theatre, which employs imprinted images of acts, including speech acts, for the purpose of describing and evoking (fictional) worlds, is thus not a heterogeneous medium but a homogeneous non-verbal medium on two accounts: on the level of iconicity and on the level of fictional interaction. In this sense, for typical iconic units (including speech acts) the traditional and the imagistic definitions of iconicity have equal explanatory power.

(B) *Real objects on stage*: It would appear that the use of real objects on stage, such as real furniture, garments and animals, contradicts the claim that theatre is an iconic medium, whether in the traditional sense of 'motivation' through 'similarity', or in the sense of 'images imprinted on matter'. The latter is not the case.

A distinction should be made between objects purposefully produced for a production and real objects produced for their practical functions and used as ready-made objects on a stage; e.g., between the replication of a table in the Louis XIV style and the use of a real antique Louis XIV table for the performance of Molière's *Tartuffe*. Whereas the former is accounted for by both definitions of iconicity, the latter is not. Since both are tables that enact fictional tables, the question is: what is the difference? Whereas the former is produced by imprinting an image of such a table on wood (an icon), it would appear that the latter cannot be said to be such an imprinted image. Indeed, it is *not similar* to a Louis XIV style table. It *is* such a table.

Bogatyrev implies that the use of real objects on stage, including bodies, suppresses their typical practical function in favor of a signifying function (1986: 35–36), what Elam terms 'semiotization of the object' (p. 8). For

Fischer-Lichte, '[a]ny random object that can function in a culture as a sign can, without its material nature being changed in any way, function as a theatrical sign for the sign it itself represents' (1992: 130). Yet, although real objects on stage can functionally be perceived as icons, they cannot be said to be iconic in terms of 'similarity', at least according to the traditional definition.

Following Plato's logic, a real object may be considered as produced through the coupling of an image (the idea of a table) and a material (e.g., wood) (*The Republic*, Book X, 419ff). For example, in making a table a carpenter lends material existence to a design, i.e., a mental image of it. In this sense there is no structural difference between an iconic and a real object, both being characterized by a combination of an image and real matter. The only difference is that whereas the former is conceived of as intentionally constructed by imprinting an image on matter, thus creating a signifying unit, the latter is expected to be deconstructed, thus marginalizing its utilitarian use and foregrounding its imagistic element. It is possible, therefore, within the intentional space of the stage, to perceive a real object as an imprinted image; i.e., as an icon.

Although actors' bodies too are real entities, there is a substantial difference between them and real inanimate objects on stage. While the latter can be conceived of as imprinted images only by deconstruction, actors intentionally and actively produce stable and changing iconic units, and imprint them on their own bodies. In other words, actors combine a performer of such units and a bearer of an imprinted text. Nonetheless, some of the real qualities of actors' bodies (e.g., hair cut) should also be deconstructed as real objects and can thus be integrated in descriptions of fictional worlds. Actors also differ from inanimate objects intentionally produced for the stage in that the latter are imprinted images produced by artists who remain offstage.

It has been suggested that the use of children or animals may contradict the iconic nature of a performance-text, because of possibly disrupting its intentional unity by going about their own affairs; e.g., an animal urinating on stage (States: 31ff). Such disruptions, which usually elicit laughter in the wrong places, indicate that actors are expected to subordinate their behavior to their enacting function. Moreover, first, both real children and animals enact fictional children and animals and, second, there is no reason why not applying the principle of deconstruction to them too.

A performance-text may, therefore, include real objects on stage that do not contradict the iconic nature of the theatre medium. They fulfil the very same function as intentionally produced imprinted images, by placing them in the intentional context of the stage, while the principle of description of fictional entities equally applies to both. From the viewpoint of the spectator, the unity of image and matter, coupled whether for the stage or for practical use, has to be deconstructed in any case. Therefore, although a real object on stage cannot be said to be iconic in the traditional sense, it is an imprinted image on matter, and its possible deconstruction attests to that.

(c) *Stage metaphor*: Given the basic equivalence between words and imprinted images, I have claimed elsewhere that verbal and iconic metaphors are generated by the same deep structure (Rozik, 1992a: 82–103). They both reflect a predicative pattern, in which at least one term identifies a referent, i.e., functions in a literal capacity as the subject of a sentence, and at least one term describes the referent in an *improper* predicative capacity. 'Improper' means here that, within a given verbal culture, such a predicate is not meant to describe such a referent; e.g., 'robot' cannot be predicated on a person, except metaphorically. It is the nature of a referent that determines whether a predicate is literal or metaphoric. The fundamental function of the improper term is to evoke verbal and induce non-verbal associations, and attribute them to a referent. The main difference between verbal and iconic metaphor is that the latter imprints the images of proper and improper terms on matter, human or otherwise.

A (fictional) character should be conceived of as the direct referent of an iconic description, and the equivalent to a real referent (Doležel, 1989). An iconic unit performed by an actor for describing a character is literal, if it is proper to its basic characterization; and improper and potentially metaphoric, if not. For example, in Eugène Ionesco's *The Chairs*, Old Woman behaves like a whore in front of the invisible photographer:

> *Old Woman*: [to the photographer, mincing grotesquely. She should become more coquettish as the scene goes on: showing her red stockings, lifting her numerous skirts, revealing a petticoat full of holes, uncovering her ancient breasts; then, throwing her head back, hands on heaps, uttering erotic cries, thrusting her pelvis forward, standing with legs apart, she laughs like an old whore.] (p. 58; in French, p. 151)

Under the assumption that this stage direction is enacted as scripted, Old Woman's behavior 'like an old whore' is clearly improper to her (apparent) literal characterization as a decent old lady, wife of a man who is about to deliver a lecture announcing a new idea, allegedly capable of redeeming the world. This image is also improper to the nature of the situation, defined as a 'scientific lecture'. To the description of her deviant behavior, Ionesco adds that it differs from anything previously seen and 'should suggest something in Old Woman's character that normally remains hidden' (*ibid.*). However, in explaining this outburst of hidden inclinations, the notion of 'stage metaphor' proves advantageous. It

31

happens while the old couple is receiving the imaginary invitees to the alleged scientific lecture, and her seductive behavior is addressed to the photographer, a symbol of public relations. It is reasonable to conjecture, therefore, that in an attempt to draw public attention and *seduce* the audience to accept her husband's idea, she behaves metaphorically 'like a whore'. This is done in order to cast an ironic innuendo on Old Man's scientific pretensions.

While both the proper images that constitute Old Lady's basic characterization and the improper image of old whore are meant to be performed by an actress and imprinted on her own body, there is nothing to distinguish between them qua iconic units, except for their literal or metaphoric functions. Furthermore, in order to evoke the relevant associations, the improper term of a metaphor functions in its original literal meaning. Therefore, a metaphoric imprinted image accords with both the traditional and the imagistic definitions of 'iconicity'. Since this is a basic form of theatre semiosis, chapter 3 expands on 'stage metaphor'.

(D) *Stage convention*: 'Stage convention' applies only to specific forms of theatre semiosis, and is thus essentially different from the basic convention of theatre, as suggested above, which underlies all its forms and applies on a more abstract level.

In general, in order to understand a performance-text there is no need to learn the theatre medium because, due to the typical motivation of iconic units by similarity, meaning is generated by what can be termed 'natural inference'. There are iconic units, however, that are mediated by a stage convention and, at least partially, unmotivated. Following the traditional definition of iconicity it can be claimed that a sentence is conventional if the principle of similarity is cancelled, thus preventing natural inference, and requiring the principle underlying a specific convention to be learned or grasped otherwise. Nevertheless, a sentence mediated by a stage convention is still part of an imprinted image, otherwise it could not be present on stage and perceived by the spectator. For example, what happens offstage can be accounted for by the image of a speaking messenger.

A stage convention thus contradicts the iconic principle, if solely defined in terms of similarity, because it produces images that do not convey what they usually stand for. Therefore, whereas the traditional definition fails, the imagistic definition applies. Furthermore, because of being imprinted images, conventions too connect to the innate capacity of the brain to produce images and their use as units of thinking. Since this is a basic form of theatre semiosis, chapter 4 expands on 'stage convention'.

The traditional definition of 'iconicity' only in terms of motivation by similarity proves deficient for both real objects on stage and theatre conventions. In contrast, the alternative definition in terms of imprinted images reveals its explanatory power for all forms of theatre semiosis. Moreover, this alternative definition does not contradict the principles of motivation and similarity, but rather supports them, while providing the ground for connecting theatre to a natural ability of the brain to operate an alternative form of thinking, which probably preceded verbal thinking, and for buttressing the homogeneity of the theatre medium.

2

Segmentation of Performance-texts

A crucial task of performance analysis is to establish the elementary segments of a performance-text. In principle, 'analysis of text' presupposes the possibility of segmentation. 'Text' should be defined as the entire set of structured verbal and/or non-verbal signs/sentences, meant to be read, interpreted and experienced by a reader, and understood in a wide sense to also include systems of signification and communication other than language. Accordingly, 'reader' too should be understood in such a wide sense. The notion of 'text' thus presupposes a language or medium that affords discrete units and rules of combination capable of generating whole texts.

Since the beginning of semiotic oriented studies, various attempts have been made to determine how performance-texts are segmented or, rather, to isolate and define their minimal units. All these attempts have been found to have no contribution to actual analyses of performance-texts, and ended in failure and even frustration. Most theoretical attempts have presupposed that such a minimal unit was a verbal or iconic sign, although no description can be composed of such constituent units. Descriptive texts are composed not of signs, but sentences. The latter imply notions such as 'syntax' 'subject', 'predicate' and 'reference', which are not pertinent to the level of sign. Unfortunately, iconic sentences have not been isolated, described and defined. Since a performance-text is a description of a (usually fictional) world – i.e., of characters and their interaction – it is sensible to conjecture that its typical minimal unit is an iconic sentence that describes a single act/action.

This chapter aims at showing that (a) *the elementary unit of a performance-text is the iconic sentence, which is a description of a fictional verbal or non-verbal act*; (b) *there is a basic difference between a real or fictional act and an iconic description of it*; and (c) *the segmentation of a description of a fictional object follows the same principles.* These theses will be supported by speech act theory, and illustrated by analysis of a scene from the Habimah production of Anton Chekhov's *The Seagull.*

Segmentation of real interaction

In terms of speech act theory, a 'speech act' is a particular kind of 'act' that employs a verbal expression for performing an action; in John Austin's terms, a case in which '[t]he uttering of the words is, indeed, usually a, or even *the*, leading incident in the performance of the act' (p. 8). Speech acts aim not at describing states of affairs, but at constituting or changing them, exactly as non-verbal acts; e.g., speech acts of command, blame, apology, threat and declaration (Austin; cf. Searle, 1979, 1985 & 1986, Leech, Levinson and Lyons, 1988 & 1981). Due to their performative nature, following Teun van Dijk, speech acts should be analyzed in terms of action theory (Dijk, 1977: 167ff & 1980; cf. Rozik, 1989a, 1992b & 1993a).

An 'action' is defined as an event brought about by a human being that aims at changing a state of affairs (Dijk, 1977: 173; cf. 1980: 178). An act is the perceptible aspect of an 'action', which is the whole unit; i.e., an act 'indicates' an action (an 'index' in Peirce's terms), and reflects an 'intention' and 'purposes' (in Austin's terms: 'illocutionary force' and 'perlocutionary effects' respectively). In this sense the performance of a verbal act differs from a verbal description, which only aims at referring to and categorizing a state of affairs, without thereby changing it. The claim that speech acts are employed with the intention of changing states of affairs thus contrasts the widespread error that words are used only for describing states of affairs. An exchange of verbal actions is basically performed by two human beings who assume the functions of agent and object of an action in turns, and are alternately referred by 'I' and 'you', following the flux of interaction. Such an interchange of functions is most evident in short and rapid dialogue (*stichomythia*), but applies even to long sequences of speech acts with the very same orientation (the same 'I' to the same 'you'), whether these speech acts are of the same or a different kind.

The performative nature of speech acts reveals the basic equivalence between them and non-verbal acts; e.g., between a verbal threat ('I warn you not to do x') and a non-verbal threat ('I' wagging the index finger in front of 'you'). This equivalence exposes the non-verbal nature of speech acts or, rather, their subordination to the non-verbal nature of action. It explains the natural exchange of verbal and non-verbal acts in a chain of interaction. Furthermore, the performance of a real act, and the action that it indicates, is an event in the world; i.e., an extra-linguistic referential entity, and only a potential object of verbal description. Although it is not

35

a verbal description, as an object of reference and categorization it can be described by words. To use an extreme example, a declaration of war is a speech act that, although merely articulated in words, actually involves a country at war. It can, therefore, be described as a 'declaration of war'. Less consequential examples materialize the same principle; e.g., performing the sentence 'I order you to leave a room'. Moreover, there is a theoretical advantage in stressing the non-verbal nature of speech acts and the fundamental equivalence between verbal and non-verbal acts, because of allowing the perception of real dialogue not as an interchange of verbal descriptions, but as a specific form of interaction (Rozik, 1992b: 62).

Since an action is defined by aiming at changing a state of affairs, 'intentionality' is part of its definition. Both speech act and action theories agree on the distinction between 'intention' and 'purpose' (cf. Dijk, 1977: 175ff; & Elam: 169). An intention is reflected in the nature of an act/action. It can be verbally articulated through a performative verb and/or conveyed by non-verbal indicators (cf. Austin: 73ff). A purpose, in contrast, reflects the aims of a given act/action beyond its nature, and refers to what is meant to be achieved by it (cf. *ibid.*: 731). Usually purposes are not articulated in words and have to be conjectured on contextual grounds.

The deep structure of a speech act features three sets of functions: *first*, a set of performative functions: 'I' (agent), 'you' (object), a 'performative verb' and non-verbal indicators (of the kind of act/action). In a speech act a performative verb may function on two levels: (a) for performing an act/action, e.g., a speech act of promise that employs the verb 'promise' in a performative capacity; and (b) for categorizing the intention of such an act/action – the verb 'promise' may categorize a speech act that either features it in a performative capacity or not: e.g., an act of promise performed with a different performative verb (e.g., 'I assure you that I'll buy x'); without a performative verb (e.g., 'I'll buy you x' with a typical intonation of promise); or non-verbally (e.g., a verbal gesture of 'trust me': the palm of the right hand on the chest) (cf. Austin: 73–76 & Lyons, 1988: 743). It is the performative function (a) that defines a 'performative verb'. The set of performative functions indicates that an agent performs an act/action upon a (usually human) object through words. *Second*, a set of deictic functions: 'I' and 'you' (their circumstantial aspects), the present indicative of the performative verb ('now') and the usually self-understood 'here'. These functions indicate that an extra-linguistic entity, categorized as 'I' (the agent), performs an act on another extra-linguistic entity, categorized as 'you' (the object), under the extra-linguistic circumstances of 'here' and 'now'. While 'I', 'you', 'here' and 'now' do not change their signifieds, their referents may change according to changing circumstances; e.g., the interchange of agent and object in the course of an interaction. *Third*, a genuine descriptive verbal sentence (p) whose ultimate meaning is determined by the intention of the action in which it is embedded. Although a speech act is not a description, it usually includes a description. These sets of functions are actually aspects of the same elementary and unitary segment of interaction.

Since the actual meaning of an embedded descriptive sentence depends on intention, the very same verbal sentence can be used to perform different acts/actions; e.g., 'I'll take you home' may indicate a promise, if it is desired by 'you', or a threat, if it is dreaded by 'you'. Consequently, non-verbal indicators and contextual clues are the only reliable indicators of intention, and their omission makes the embedded sentence ambiguous. The problem is that under conditions of real interaction, most speech acts omit the performative and deictic elements, because of being self-understood, and only the embedded sentence 'p' is verbally articulated. Austin terms them 'primary' speech acts, in contrast to 'explicit' speech acts in which all the components of the deep structure are verbally articulated (pp. 71ff). However, if the non-verbal indicators are taken into account, even a primary speech act is explicit (Lyons, 1988: 743).

I suggest five channels of non-verbal indication of intention: intonation, facial expression (Argyle: 211–50; cf. Birdwhistell), proxemic behavior (Hall: 204–9; cf. Birdwhistell), bodily gesture (Argyle: 251–71) and hand gesture. In particular, 'gesture' is a significant bodily configuration, which combines intonation, facial expression, proxemic behavior and bodily posture, while usually converging in a specific hand gesture. Hand gestures enjoy a special status due to their being both subliminal and culturally established. Within a given culture, hand gestures (whether natural or conventional) may convey symbolic and/or metaphorical meaning (Rozik: 1992b). In addition to intentions of acts/actions, the very same channels indicate other aspects of human interaction, such as feelings, emotions and even thoughts. They also indicate characteristic aspects of doers, such as social background, education and temperament, which are reflected in each act/action, but do not affect its performative nature. Together these functions constitute what is usually termed 'body language'.

The specific configuration of all these channels is probably the best indicator of the nature of an action. It should be born in mind that (a) different channels provide different means of indication and that there is a tendency to avoid redundancy; (b) some channels may be inactivated or made to fulfil other indicating functions; and (c) most non-verbal indexes are culturally conditioned.

Performative and deictic functions also characterize a non-verbal act/action, with the descriptive verbal sentence (p) obviously missing. It is also performed by an agent upon an object, human or otherwise, while the deictic functions ('I', 'you', 'now' and 'here') are self-understood. A non-verbal act too is the perceptible aspect of an action; i.e., is an index of an action that aims at changing a state of affairs. Moreover, a non-verbal act is as ambiguous as a speech act, in the sense that the same act can indicate different actions, depending on intention; e.g., 'holding somebody's face' may indicate actions such as threat or invitation to physical contact, and express anger or love, with disambiguation relying on additional non-verbal indicators and/or contextual clues. Like a speech act, a non-verbal act also activates additional non-verbal or contextual indicators of intention. Real interaction includes verbal and non-verbal acts in any possible order.

Since the specific nature of an act/action cannot be determined by its perceptible aspects, but only if its intention and purposes are adequately established, Dijk contends that interpretation is an essential phase in actual interaction:

> An essential component in the definition of action turned out to be the various mental structures 'underlying' the actual doing and its consequences. This means that actions cannot as such be observed, identified and described. We have access to them only by the *interpretation* of doings. Such observable parts of acts, however, may be highly 'ambiguous'. (1977: 182)

Interpretation or, rather, categorization of intentions and purposes is a genuine descriptive verbal activity and a necessary step prior to reaction, if addressees wish their re-actions to suit the intentions and purposes of previous acts/actions (cf. Leech: 196). A response thus features two elements: a categorization of the previous act/action and a subsequent act/action in response. For example:

Teiresias:	All of you here know nothing. I will not
	bring to the light of day my troubles, mine –
	rather than call them yours.
Oedipus:	What do you mean?
	You know something and you refuse to speak.
	Would you betray us and destroy the city?
Teiresias:	[. . .] Why is it
	you question me and waste your labour? I
	will tell you nothing.
Oedipus:	You would provoke a stone! Tell us, you villain,
	tell us, [. . .]
Teiresias:	You blame my temper [. . .]

(Sophocles, Oedipus the King: p. 120)

Oedipus' speech acts of inquiry and command, and Teiresias' speech acts of defiance and refusal, do not feature performative verbs. Still, the response of each character is preceded by a verbal categorization of previous intentions, e.g., 'refuse', 'question' and 'blame'; and purpose, e.g., 'provoke'.

Erroneous interpretation is most plausible in cases of missing performative verbs ('primary' speech acts), but is possible even if the
performative verb is explicit, because concomitant non-verbal elements
may override it, and thus determine the nature of an act/action. However,
even an error indicates that the object of an action has engaged in interpretation; i.e., there is no way to avoid intuitive categorization not only in
responding to an act, but also in delimiting and determining such a unit.
The basic structure of interaction is triadic: an action, a categorization of
a previous action and a re-action, which in turn becomes an action, thus
starting a new cycle again. For both verbal and non-verbal interaction, real
segmentation applies to these three units.

Ingarden's view of fictional verbal interaction

Ingarden distinguishes four main functions of the use of language on stage:
(a) *Representation* of characters and objects offstage through the evocative
power of words voiced on stage, in addition to the characters and objects
enacted on stage: 'Only when objects and events are only talked about and
reported, objects that are situated or take place "off" stage, is the manner
in which they are represented and depicted fully the same as in a purely
literary work' (p. 321). Indeed, the objects or events that are not present
on stage are evoked by words, like in literature, although their imagined
existence is conditioned by the concrete reality of the stage. The evocation
of these fictional entities is 'so important that without them the play would
not be only incomprehensible but would also be bereft of the moments that
are most essential for the dramatic plot' (p. 381). (b) *Expression* of experiences and psychic states of speaking characters through intonation,
gesture and facial expression (*ibid.*). (c) *Communication* between characters through what is said by them; i.e., by the descriptive function of
language (p. 382). (d) *Interaction* between characters or, rather, 'mutual
influence' in which language is used for affecting one another as in argument or conflict (*ibid.*): 'words spoken by a represented person in a
situation signify an act and hence constitute a part of the action, in particular in the confrontations between represented persons. [And through
such an act] a certain step is made in the development of the action of the
"drama"' (p. 386). Ingarden also claims that without such a verbal act the
action would develop differently. Although the words are pronounced by
actors on stage, these functions are performed by characters within the
fictional world.

Ingarden finds that the interactive function of speech (d) is typical of
both real and fictional verbal interaction (p. 388). He suggests, therefore,
that much can be learned from dramatic verbal interaction about its real

forms (p. 391). Thus, Ingarden possibly anticipated Austin's performative theory of speech by several years. The problem is that he reaches his performative conclusions from the viewpoint of the use of language in fictional worlds, and overlooks the iconic use of language in performance-texts, ignoring thereby the substantial difference between fictional and iconic forms of verbal interaction. Nonetheless, his specific conclusions should be endorsed.

The pragmatic approach of Serpieri et al.

In 'Toward a Segmentation of the Dramatic Text', Alessandro Serpieri et al. adopt a pragmatic approach for the segmentation of theatre-texts. Their main claim is that in theatre speech is 'analogous to an utterance geared toward a speaking situation in everyday language, in that it produces meaning in relation to a pragmatic context' (p. 165). '[O]ne can claim that the theatre is *entirely performative*: indeed, performativity, which is realized in deixis, makes up what might be termed the *specific theatrical language*' (p. 168). The adoption of this method of analysis marks a crucial development in theatre theory. Their approach, however, is plagued by several errors.

First, rather than focusing on the performative aspects of speech, Serpieri et al. stress their deictic elements. They aim, therefore, at identifying 'performative deictic units' as the basic segments of the text: 'The semiological unit of theatrical language seems to be a complex sign unit identifiable in a given performative-deictic orientation assumed by the speaker. [. . .] Thus the semiological unit can be defined as *a unit of performative discourse simultaneous with its indexical axis*' (p. 169). 'Deixis' is used in the usual sense of words (or morphemes) that refer to the circumstances of a speech act's performance; and 'orientation' means the axis created by a certain agent in acting upon a certain object. Their main thesis is that '*utterances can be segmented at every change of performative-deictic orientation* by one speaker with regard to the other' (*ibid.*). Therefore, rather than looking for the boundaries between performative units in changes of their performative nature, they opt for boundaries according to the duration or cessation of a given deictic orientation. The problem is that changes of deictic orientation do not necessarily coincide with the boundaries of single speech acts. A sequence of similar or different speech acts may take place without change of orientation. Consequently, while in some cases a deictic change is instrumental in detecting and isolating a speech-act segment, it is misleading in others. Their fallacy thus lies in avoiding interpretation of speech acts for detecting and isolating such units.

Second, rather than actually analyzing performance-texts, Serpieri et al. illustrate their thesis by analyzing play-scripts. Initially, they reject both the play-script and performance-text as the object of segmentation, the former 'to the extent that it remains "literary"' and the latter 'in so far as it is transient and unrepeatable' (p. 164). However, they eventually opt for the play-script because of reflecting a possible performance, in the sense that the performed dialogue is already 'stamped' in its scripted version (*ibid.*). In other words, in contrast to literary language, the performativity of 'theatrical language' is already inscribed in the play-script, under the assumption that it will be uttered by actors on stage as scripted. Therefore, consistently, they illustrate their method of segmentation by texts such as Shakespeare's *Macbeth* and *The Tempest*. However, their claim does not solve the inherent ambiguity of scripted speech acts. The problem is that most play-scripts articulate only the embedded sentences, and not necessarily their performative and deictic elements. Since the same verbal sentence can be used for performing different acts/actions a play-script is a deficient text. In contrast, in performance-texts speech acts are always performed with specific non-verbal indicators of intention; i.e., they are always explicit. Even an innovative performance-text, while preserving the words of a play-script, actually ascribes them pragmatic meaning. In order to establish the nature and boundaries of a speech act, therefore, its interpretation cannot be avoided. Moreover, disqualification of performance-texts because of their ephemeral nature, while presupposing the univocality of play-scripts, ignores the use of video recording that overcomes this technical difficulty. Their fallacy thus lies in overlooking both the deficiency of play-scripts and the absolute reliability of non-verbal indicators of intention.

Third, rather than addressing the performative units on the textual level of a performance-text, Serpieri et al. actually segment verbal interaction in fictional worlds. Indeed, in such worlds, like in real life, speech is used for performing acts/actions, while reflecting the circumstances of their performance; i.e., fundamentally, what has been suggested for real speech acts applies to fictional interaction too. However, performance analysis should address the descriptive level, because the mental existence of a fictional interaction depends on the evocative power of an iconic text. This does not preclude analysis also on the fictional level (chapter 7). Their fallacy thus lies in not distinguishing between iconic and fictional speech acts. Henceforth, I suggest principles for the segmentation of performance-texts (Rozik, 2001).

Segmentation of iconic interaction

In the segmentation of stage interaction there are three different orders: (a) the histrionic order – the actors' performance of images of verbal or non-verbal acts that they inscribe on their own bodies; (b) the textual order – the set of inscribed iconic acts that describe a set of acts/actions in a fictional world; and (c) the fictional order – the set of acts/actions described and evoked by a performance-text and assumedly performed by characters. These are the very same segments as perceived from three different viewpoints. Since segmentation is meant to apply to the performance-text, the semiotic search for minimal units of description should focus on the textual order

The basic segment of a description of a fictional interaction is an iconic description of a single fictional verbal or non-verbal act and, therefore, it is an iconic sentence whose subject is a description of a character and its predicate a description of an act. Whereas the iconic sentence is the maximal and most complex unit that the theatre medium affords, from the viewpoint of the description of a fictional world such a sentence is the minimal and simplest unit. By sequential aggregation, these units constitute a description of a whole fictional interaction.

The fact that *an iconic replica of an act is a sentence, and thus the elementary segment of a description,* does not preclude its segmentation into component units, including single iconic signs; it rather presupposes further segmentation. Since mediation of language also applies to the syntactic structure of iconic sentences, these must consist of at least two signs fulfilling two functions: subject and predicate. Since 'description' presupposes a referent, a descriptive sentence must feature a subject that fulfils a referential function: at least one sign that identifies a referent, i.e., a character; and a predicate that fulfils a categorizing function: at least one sign that describes this character (Rozik, 1992a: 30–40). Since a verbal and/or non-verbal act is transitive, the iconic description of a fictional interaction features two possible subjects that interchange on the time axis: s/he$_1$ and s/he$_2$. Like a single verbal sign, a single iconic sign cannot describe anything, unless it is included in an iconic sentence and its syntactic function is determined.

An imprinted image is, therefore, never a single iconic sign, but at least an iconic sentence, and at most an 'icon'; i.e., a 'gestalt' of iconic sentences (cf. Pavis, 1982: 15). An icon is a complex iconic unit that can be analyzed into a cluster of simultaneous iconic sentences predicated on a single referent; e.g., 'the apple is red, is ripe, is fresh and is tempting.' Each of these predicates may change on the time axis; e.g., from 'is ripe' to 'is rotten'. While reading these features on the holistic level of their configuration is equivalent to the subject of an iconic sentence, or referential function (e.g., the apple), reading it on the level of its single qualities, states or acts is equivalent to its predicates, or categorizing function (e.g., 'is red'). All the verbal predicates that can describe such an iconic apple, and are true, can be said to be an icon's descriptive meaning. The iconic sentence thus neither precludes further analysis into component units (subject and predicate), nor aggregation into a more comprehensive unit (icon).

As a real object on stage, an actor too should be conceived of as an icon, which can be read on either the holistic or partial levels. An actor presents both a cluster of unchanging imprinted images, at least during an entire performance, which aim at identifying a character (subject function), and a series of changing imprinted images of fictional acts on the time axis (predicative function). The permanent features that aim at identifying a character, being equivalent to verbal adjuncts, can also be conceived of as implicit predicates (cf. Sadock: 47). Unchanging and changing images constitute a dynamic image imprinted on an actor's body. A performance-text is predominantly a description of a complex fictional interaction, a 'plot' in traditional terms, through interchanging images of fictional acts imprinted on actors' bodies.

The principle of similarity underlying iconicity implies that some structural properties are shared by real and iconic acts. In principle, an iconic medium operates two principles of signification – that of iconicity (similarity) and that of indexality; e.g., indexes of actions (contiguity). The implication is that the principle of segmentation that applies to real/fictional interaction basically also applies to its iconic replication. Theatre iconicity, in addition to its own non-verbal nature, also reflects the non-verbal nature of described verbal or non-verbal acts.

Indeed, there is no fundamental difference between a real/fictional and an iconic act in their inner structure: I + act + you (+ p). In addition, there is usually a total overlap between the boundaries of propositional sentences (p) of speech acts, whether primary or explicit, and the boundaries of their non-verbal indicators in both the real/fictional and the iconic realms. Such an overlap corroborates from an unexpected angle Kowzan's intuition that the minimal unit of a performance-text is a slice containing all the signs emitted simultaneously (Introduction). A real/fictional or iconic act thus constitutes a discrete unit, which can be considered as an elementary segment of interaction.

Nonetheless, the descriptive nature of an iconic act determines a crucial difference: *whereas a real act is equivalent to an 'I' sentence, as all indexes are, the descriptive nature of an iconic act implies that it is equivalent to a 's/he' sentence*; e.g., whereas a real order performed by somebody is equivalent to the sentence 'I order you that x', the imprinted image of such an act is equivalent to the sentence 'S/he₁ (a character) orders s/he₂ (another character) that x.' This reflects the existential difference between being an object of description and being a description.

In contrast to David Z. Saltz, there is no need for a theory of game for determining that actors only perform semblances of acts, without committing themselves to the indicated actions (pp. 41–43). The principle of iconic description, which is characterized by replication of semblances, entails that actors are not 'pretending' or 'playing a game'. They are meant to perform, not actions but, rather, evocative descriptions of such actions, which are only clues to their evocation. There are no iconic actions; only iconic acts. Only when attributed to characters do iconic acts reacquire their indexical nature, as indexes of both fictional actions and characters that perform them.

The following are the different deep structures of real/fictional and iconic verbal and non-verbal acts:

> A real or fictional non-verbal act: I + act + you.
> An iconic non-verbal act: S/he$_1$ + act + s/he$_2$.
> A real or fictional speech act: I + performative verb + you + that (p).
> An iconic speech act: S/he$_1$ + performative verb + s/he$_2$ + that (p).

These deep structures reflect the difference between a description and an object of description.

Segmentation of stage objects

Principles of segmentation should also apply to iconic objects on stage: set objects, props and garments in particular. Fischer-Lichte suggests that 'a shirt of a nobleman' is an example of a basic segment (1992: 225). However, this is not a single sign, but an icon; i.e., a cluster of iconic sentences. An iconic medium does not afford a noun, but a recognizable configuration of features (holistic reading), which is functionally equivalent to a noun. Whereas reading these features on the level of the whole fulfills the nominal function of an icon (e.g., 'shirt'), reading them on the level of single qualities (partial reading) fulfills the predicative function (e.g., 'made of silk', 'brown' and 'embroidered'). The iconic shirt is, therefore, a set of implicit or explicit predications on the same subject, and not even a single sentence. In this case too, all the verbal sentences predicated on such a shirt, and are true, can be said to be its total meaning. It is in this sense that a picture is worth a thousand words.

In addition, a particular kind of shirt may be part of a description of a character; e.g., '[a character] wears the shirt of a nobleman'. In such a case, the character is the iconic subject and 'wears the shirt of a nobleman' its iconic predicate; i.e., by wearing such a shirt, the character indicates something about itself. Depending on characterization this may be interpreted as an index of class (if predicated on a nobleman) or of pretension (if predicated on a commoner. In each context it would convey different connotations.

44

The common denominator of fictional interactive and non-interactive icons is that all are described by iconic sentences as minimal units of description. This is in contrast to language, for both iconic sentences are 'pictorial' in the sense of spatial coexistence of subject and predicate signs, while linearity applies only to the interchange of predicates on the time axis.'Pictoriality' also applies to the simultaneous coexistence of more than one icon on stage. In most cases icons of inanimate objects remain unchanged during an entire performance, but changes may occur and be most significant; e.g., Ionesco's *Amédée*.

Segmentation of iconic interaction in Habimah's *The Seagull*

The following is an analysis of Arkadina and Trigorin's dialogue in act III of Anton Chekhov's *The Seagull*, in the Habimah production of 1992, directed by Boris Morozov, with Michail Kozakov as Trigorin, Shuli Rand as Konstantin and Jetta Monte as Arkadina.

This scene revolves around two opposing motives, but only Arkadina accomplishes what she has set out to achieve. She manipulates Trigorin's weak personality, with each change in her tactics affecting his behavior. This scene can be divided, therefore, into three parts. In the first, Trigorin confronts Arkadina in an attempt to persuade her to accept his attraction to Nina. He repeatedly asks her consent to remain with Nina after her leaving, while Arkadina, increasingly infuriated, absolutely refuses. In the second part, Arkadina changes her tactics. She flatters him until he renounces his request. In the third part, Arkadina, changing her tactics again, consents to his staying, while he refuses. Eventually she "allows" him to make the final decision, thus gratifying his male self-image. The transitions from one part to the other are marked by extreme changes of behavior: e.g., from harsh blaming to exaggerated flattery.

Although the director opted for minimal changes in regard to the verbal script, and some non-verbal components were performed according to the few stage directions, a distinct directorial interpretation could be detected: all changes were subordinated to a predominantly melodramatic mood. A comparison of the same scene in the play-script and the performance-text reveals the following: (1) that verbal and non-verbal acts are equivalent and may be exchanged in a chain of interaction. For example,

> *Trigorin:*   [. . .] Let us stay one more day!
> *Arkadina:*   [*shakes her head.*]   (p. 160)

While speaking, Trigorin puts his hands in his pockets, thus indicating that his is determined to leave and that it is not a speech act of request but of firm suggestion. Arkadina, accordingly, responds by performing a non-verbal act of refusal. Moreover, in contrast to the play-script, Trigorin's speech act features all its structural elements, the non-verbal indicators in particular; i.e., is explicit, like in real life.

(2) Most of the speech acts in the play-script do not feature a performative verb. The following is an exception:

> *Trigorin:*   You must try to be sober, too – and sensible and reasonable.
> /Do try to see all this like a true friend, I implore you . . . [*Presses her hand.*]
> /You are capable of sacrifice. . . . .
> /Be a friend to me, release me . . .   (p. 160)

This set of speech acts includes only the explicit performative verb 'implore'. Being an exception, this example emphasizes the extensive use of primary speech acts. The use of non-verbal indicators is thus made indispensable. Although Chekhov's few stage directions illustrate this need, most underlying intentions were specified in the directing process.

(3) In contrast to Serpieri et al., a series of different speech acts can be performed without changing deictic orientation. For example,

> *Arkadina:*   Am I really so old and ugly that you can talk to me about other women without embarrassment? [blame]
> / [Suddenly, calmly, head up; tapping her nose and slightly smiling; goes over to him, folds her sleeves; raises his head embraces him from behind, and kisses him]
> Oh, you must have gone mad! [soft blame]
> /My beautiful, my wonderful. . . . You – the last page of my life! [flattery]
> /[Kneels before him.] my joy, my pride, my happiness! . . . [flattery]
> /[Embraces his knees.] If you leave me even for a single hour I shall never survive it, [entreaty]
> /I shall go out of my mind [threat] – my wonderful, magnificent man, my master. . . . [flattery]   (p. 161)

Arkadina performs speech acts of blame (twice), flattery (thrice), entreaty, and threat without change in deictic orientation.

(4) Whereas on the verbal level most speech acts seem to be self-explanatory, the kinds of actions that these words can indicate may vary; e.g., if both characters make use of irony throughout the scene. For example, in the previous quotation, Arkadina's gesture of tapping her nose, while slightly smiling, indicates her ironic intention to deliberately manipulate Trigorin. Without it the entire sequence would have conveyed a different meaning.

(5) As suggested above, the same wording can be used for different speech acts. For example,

Trigorin: I have no will of my own. . . . I've never had a will of my own. [acceptance]
/Sluggish, flabby, always submissive – how can any woman like that sort of thing? [self-blame]
/Take me, carry me off, but don't let me ever move a step away from you. . . . . [soft warning]   (p. 161)

In the Habimah production, although the actor pronounces the last words with an intonation of warning, they could have equally been performed as an act of entreaty.

Another example:

Arkadina: [to herself]. Now he's mine!
/[Affecting an easy manner as if nothing had happened.] But, of course, you can stay if you want to.
/I'll go myself, and you can come on afterwards, a week later.
/After all, why should you hurry?
Trigorin: No, we may as well go together.   (p. 162)

In the Habimah production, in his last words, Trigorin drinks a glass [of vodka] in one gulp – thus creating an image of manliness, as if the final decision was his own. This non-verbal act is equivalent to a speech act of determined decision.

All these speech acts reflect a common perlocutionary effect: to persuade one another. Trigorin strives to get her consent and Arkadina to dissuade him. Only she succeeds, at least momentarily, by manipulating him into making him believe that it had been his own decision. It is known that subsequently Trigorin will join Nina, and eventually return to Arkadina.

In most of these examples the syntactic unit of the verbal component overlaps the duration of the non-verbal indicators of intention. In a few cases, non-verbal indicators were performed before the beginning of a verbal utterance, but there was total overlap at the end. This may imply that psychological reaction begins before actual response.

The analysis of this scene illustrates the main theses of this chapter; especially, that the segmentation of a performance-text is not only possible, but also overcomes the deficiency of the play-script.

3

Stage Metaphor and Symbol

Traditional theatre semiotics has neglected the study of non-verbal stage metaphor and symbol. This chapter aims at making up for these short-comings, and focuses first on verbal and stage metaphor and subsequently on stage symbol.

Performance-texts feature several types of metaphor: verbal metaphor, stage metaphor, speech act metaphor and allegory. I suggest that the structure of the theatre experience too is metaphoric and devote chapter 8 to this singular phenomenon.

The following sections offer a theory of metaphor that has been designed to suit all forms of metaphor in language and iconic media. Although this theory reflects my own approach, other approaches to non-verbal metaphor may suit the aims of performance analysis as well. Since I have published my views on verbal and non-verbal metaphor extensively, the following considerations are restricted to aspects pertinent to the present study.

This chapter aims at showing that (a) *verbal and stage metaphors are generated by the same deep structure and rules of ellipsis, with differences deriving from the nature of either language or theatre medium*; (b) *stage speech act metaphor is possible on iconic grounds*; (c) *stage allegory is a particular case of stage metaphor*; and (d) *stage symbol is possible on iconic grounds and can beneficially combine with stage metaphor*. These theses are illustrated by excerpts from Ionesco's *The Chairs*, under the assumption that they are performed as prescribed by the stage directions, and from Rina Yerushalmi's production of this play-script, 1990 (Rozik, 1994b).

A theory of verbal metaphor

In a performance-text, a verbal metaphor is voiced by an actor and attributed to a character, usually in a dialogic situation. Most modernist theories of verbal metaphor (e.g., Beardsley; Black, 1962 & 1988 and Searle, 1988) share the following claims:

(A) Metaphor is a standard means of description of objects and/or their phenomena (referents) and alternative to literal description. Metaphor requires a distinct form of reading and interpretation, according to its specific rules.

(B) Literal and metaphoric sentences have some features in common: First, there is no difference in their syntactic structure, which reflects the basic relationship between a subject (referential function) and a predicate (categorizing function) (Searle, 1985: 72ff); for example: 'Richard is violent.' and 'Richard is a gorilla.' (Searle, 1988: 102). Second, although metaphor features an 'improper' term, its subject is modified by an explicit or implicit literal modifier that makes sense with the subject on the literal level exactly as in a literal sentence. Therefore, there is no crucial difference in their categorization of the referent (description); e.g., the predicate 'is a gorilla' is meant to evoke 'is violent', which is a possible literal modifier of Richard (+ human). Third, therefore, there is no difference between them in regard to their truth conditions.

(C) The definition of 'metaphoric' depends on the definition of 'literal' that presupposes a convention that connects a word with a set of referents. Any use in accordance with such a convention is 'literal' ('proper'), and any use that breaches it, is potentially metaphoric ('improper'). 'Improper' means here that, within a certain verbal community, such a predicate is not meant to describe such a referent. For example, whereas the use of 'man' (+ human, + male) for a set of referents 'male human beings' is 'literal', the use of 'gorilla' (– human + animal) for such a set is 'improper'.

(D) Since metaphor is characterized by the use of an improper predicate in the description of a referent, it is implied that the latter must be known for identifying a case of improperness. It is also implied that the subject is always literal, otherwise it could not fulfill its referential function: identification of the referent.

(E) Whereas the age-old theory of comparison presupposes a predicative deep structure of double reference, i.e., to two syntactically equivalent subjects, modernist theory suggests a predicative deep structure of single reference, to the object represented by the literal subject. Whereas the comparison view implies that reversing a metaphor does not change its meaning, for the modernist view it is not the case.

These claims and their implications should be seen as reflecting the main achievements of the modernist theory of metaphor, particularly the 'interaction view' (Rozik, 1994d). This approach, however, does not explain the use of such an oblique literal description, while a straightforward version is readily available, if they are fully equivalent; e.g., the use of 'Richard is a gorilla' in place of 'Richard is violent'. Modernist theory is aware of the problem, but fails to account for the specific difference of metaphor and its preference under certain conditions (cf. Black, 1962a: 234; 1962b: 46; & Searle, 1988: 97).

Modernist theory conceives of metaphor as an elliptic structure, with the function of the improper term being to evoke a literal modifier capable of making sense with the literal subject. Ellipsis, however, does not explain the necessity for such a circuitous predication. 'Ellipsis' applies to missing words that can be evoked through knowledge of the common deep structure and a thematic context, and should thus be conceived of as 'elliptically present'. Therefore, whether a component is actually present or elliptically present makes no difference. Ellipsis is thus not an essential component of metaphor. Indeed, most surface structures of metaphor reflect elliptical processes that may reduce them to a minimum, even to a single word (Rozik: 1998a). Still, their mechanisms of generating meaning are the same; e.g., 'Richard is a gorilla' and 'Richard is violent like a gorilla' are equivalent metaphors.

I suggest, therefore, that the problem focuses on the difference between two modifiers that on the verbal level would appear to be the same; e.g., the straightforward literal modifier 'violent$_1$' and the indirect literal modifier 'violent'$_2$, which may be either explicit or evoked by the improper term; i.e., elliptically present. The difference lies in the distinct ''non-verbal associations or, rather, 'referential associations' induced by each of these literal modifiers, 'violent$_1$' and 'violent$_2$', with the latter being mediated by an improper term (Rozik, 1994d).

'Referential associations' are non-verbal recollections of actual experiences resulting from the use of words for *referring* to and categorizing real or fictional objects. Such associations may be classified as sensory, emotional, ethic, aesthetic, modal (tragic, comic and grotesque) and the like. Such a classification is necessarily reductive: there is a fundamental difference between inducing referential associations and verbally describing them. The vitality of such associations is clearly revealed by what is usually called 'trite' metaphor, which can be defined by their dwindling nature, so that it becomes synonymous with its verbal components. I abstain here from 'connotation' because it does not distinguish between verbal and non-verbal associations.

Modifiers are too abstract to induce referential associations by themselves. Since they usually modify various nouns, for fulfilling their typical function they have to relinquish any reminiscence of previous particular referents. Therefore, referential associations can be evoked only when a modifier is coupled with a specific noun (e.g., violent and man, or violent and gorilla). A basic 'triangular' relationship between a literal modifier, a literal subject and their correspondent referential associations is thus generated. This triangular model is valid for both literal and metaphoric descriptions. However, the metaphoric mechanism creates an alternative kind of literal modifier that involves two principles: (a) the literal modifier is connected to two nouns, the literal subject of predication and the improper noun, thus creating two potential sources of referential associations (e.g., 'violent' and Richard (+ man); and 'violent' and gorilla (+ animal)); and (b) preference is given to the referential associations originating in the improper term (gorilla) (Rozik, 1994d).

This implies that the improper term must be used in its literal capacity, as otherwise it could not be improper to the literal subject and induce improper referential associations. For example, in *The Chairs*, Old Man's replica 'Your Majesty! . . . I'm here! [. . .] Your servant, your slave, your faithful hound, aouh! aouh!' (pp. 72–3; in French: p. 168) The common modifier 'faithful' potentially induces two specific sets of referential associations due to previous experiences with either human or canine faithfulness; and the metaphoric structure determines preference for the referential associations originating in the improper 'hound', which are instinctual and degrading, and do not compare at all with those originating in the human sphere. Whereas the word 'faithful' accounts for the common traits of all 'faithful' creatures, the 'referential associations' of 'faithful' in the context of 'hound' account for its singularity.

In some types of surface structure, preference for improper referential associations is marked by particles such as 'like' and 'as', which do not indicate a relationship of comparison, but are kinds of shifters that trigger the induction of referential associations originating in improper terms (e.g., 'is faithful *like* a dog'). This convention is optional, since preference is marked in any case by the mere presence of an improper term; i.e., there is no fundamental difference between 'he is a dog' and 'he is like a dog'.

Two metaphoric predicates having the same literal modifier in common, but differing in their referential associations, can be said to have different truth conditions. For example, when predicated of a particular person, while 'faithful like a dog' may be false, 'faithful like a slave' may be true. In general, in contrast to modernist theory, an improper predicate (e.g., dog), since it cannot be true, cannot be false either (cf. Austin: 70). Only after a metaphor is read and interpreted, can it be true or false. Moreover, it can be true even if the activated associations are false, on condition that they are believed to be true; e.g., a gorilla is not a violent animal.

The deep structure of verbal metaphor thus includes five verbal components: (1) a subject–predicate syntactic pattern; (2) a literal subject of a predication (Old Man); (3) an improper term (dog); (4) a common literal modifier (faithful); and (5) an optional preference marker (like). There are also four extra linguistic components: (6) the set of objects referred to by the literal subject; (7) the set of objects only apparently referred to by the improper term; (8) the overlooked referential associations of the common modifier originating in the literal subject (x); and (9) the preferred referential associations of the common modifier originating in the improper noun (y). This deep structure is realized by readers or listeners, whether these components, excluding the improper term, are explicit in the surface structure of a certain metaphor or not. The improper term should always be present as otherwise no associative process typical of metaphor can be set in motion. This deep structure applies to metaphor of any scope: phrase, sentence, motif or full text.

Stage metaphor

I suggest that *the same deep structure and the same rules of ellipsis generate verbal and stage metaphor, with differences stemming from the nature of either language or iconic medium.* Moreover, due to language mediation, verbal and stage metaphors generate the same kind of meaning; i.e., are basically equivalent (Rozik, 1998a & 1989b). Within the set of iconic media, the specific difference of the theatre medium lies in that it imprints images of improper terms on materials similar to those of their models.

Because of language mediation, stage metaphor also reflects the ability of the theatre medium to generate sentences. A stage metaphor thus reveals a predicative structure in which at least one iconic sign indicates a referent, i.e., functions as the literal subject of a metaphor; and at least one iconic sign, also in a literal capacity, functions as its improper predicate. It is thus the syntactic relation between the two terms that is improper. The relation between literal subject and improper predicate presupposes a common literal modifier, which is either iconically explicit or elliptically present. Preference for referential associations originating in the improper term is marked by its mere presence (Rozik, 1989b).

A conspicuous difference between verbal and stage metaphor is that iconic syntax is pictorial; the subject and predicate signs are simultaneously present in the performance-text. The linearity of verbal metaphor is thus not an essential property of metaphor, but derives from the nature of language. Additional differences are: first, the iconic system does not provide names for referents, but clusters of iconic sentences, that can be read either on the holistic level (subject function) or on the partial level (predicative function). Second, it does not provide common modifiers on an abstract level, although these can be evoked by mediation of language. These differences do not impinge on the metaphoric mechanism of generating meaning.

Whereas all surface structures of non-verbal metaphor have their equivalents in verbal metaphor; the opposite is not the case: since language is the most articulate system of signification and communication, it can generate surface structures that feature all the components of the deep structure, except for the non-verbal associations (Rozik, 1998a). This asymmetry reflects the limitations of the theatre medium, which reduce the generation of possible surface structures. However, like in language, all the functional components of the deep structure of stage metaphor that cannot be articulated can be elliptically evoked. Activation of rules of ellipsis thus enables abridged forms of stage metaphor to convey the same meanings as more articulated ones (*ibid.*).

A character should be conceived of as a fictional referent (chapter 1; cf. Doležel, 1989: 230 & 1998: 16). Although a character is devoid of existence, being a figment of the imagination, on the fictional level it is assumed that it is a human being. In this sense a character functions as an extra-linguistic entity and, therefore, as an object of literal or metaphoric description. Consequently, 'stage metaphor' applies to a quality, state or action that is improper to a character's basic characterization. For the moment, it is assumed that this basic characterization is literal, although on a more complex structural level, as shown below, this may not be the case. A stage metaphor may reflect a self-image of a character, but usually describes a character from an authorial viewpoint. In principle, since the intention is to make sense, any improper term in the context of any specific characterization should be conceived of as a potential stage metaphor. For example, in Rina Yerushalmi's production of *The Chairs* (cf. Rozik, 1994b), Old Man cried like a baby:

> *Old Man:*   (sobbing, with his mouth wide open, like a baby) I'm an orphan . . . a norphan.   (p. 44; in French, p. 136)

Although a live actor enacted Old Man, it is the fictional character, the actual referent of the metaphoric description, who was 'sobbing like a baby'. Old Man was characterized as an octogenarian, and this age was depicted on stage by a set of iconic signs such as gray hair, wrinkled face, tremulous voice and shaky movements. These steady modifiers were literal because of conforming to his being an old man. Since Old Man's actual 'baby-sobbing' did not conform to his basic characterization, it was potentially metaphoric. Namely, if he had sobbed like an old man, the predicate would have been literal, but since he sobbed like a baby the predicate was metaphoric. Moreover, the actual crying of Old Man evoked the image of a baby (improper noun) and, on a more abstract level, 'sobbing like a baby' evoked an abstract 'sobbing', capable of modifying both 'old man' and 'baby', with the deep structure of metaphor determining preference for the referential associations originating in 'baby'. This metaphor explains the subsequent verbal metaphor 'I'm an orphan'. In this sense also the barking of Old Man in the previous example ('aouh!') is a stage metaphor. These metaphors were meant to lend a ludicrous innuendo to Old Man's behavior.

Old Man and Old Woman in Yerushalmi's *The Chairs*. Courtesy of the Cameri Theatre Archive. Photo: Israel Haramaty.

The fundamental function of the improper iconic predicate, e.g., the actual kind of sobbing, is to induce alternative referential associations. The specificity of the referential associations can be discerned by comparing possible different stage metaphors that may evoke similar modifying images; for example:

Old Man sobs like a baby   ⇒ referential associations 'a'
Old Man sobs like an old lady   ⇒ referential associations 'b'
Old Man sobs like a crocodile   ⇒ referential associations 'c'

The same modifier 'sobs' is expected to be experienced distinctly in the context of each improper image. Whereas 'sobs' accounts for the common traits of different images of 'sobbing', the distinct referential associations account for their singularities. These various kinds of 'sobbing' form a paradigm of the same modifier, which only differ in their induced referential associations.

Stage metaphor is not confined to human characters; e.g., in Ionesco's *Amédée*, in the context of a set described as 'a modest dining room-office', Amédée finds poisonous mushrooms growing out of the floor (p. 239). The improper behavior of the floor indicates a potential stage metaphor, which clearly conveys verbal and referential associations of festering soil and putrefaction. These associations fit that in the next room a hidden corpse is 'mushrooming' in size. Since the author is possibly describing some mental aspect of marital life, the metaphoric meaning of 'festering soil growing poisonous mushrooms' is self-evident.

The theatre medium also enables mixed stage metaphor, as in the following example:

[*When the* Orator has reached the back of the stage, he removes his hat and bows in silence; he greets the invisible Emperor with a flourish of his hat, like one of the Musketeers and a little like a robot.] (*The Chairs*: 79; in French p. 174)

The orator greets the invisible Emperor both like a 'musketeer' and an 'automate'. If 'orator' (+ human, – musketeer, – automate) is his literal characterization, the images of 'musketeer' and 'automate' are improper terms. As in language, more than one improper source of referential associations, improper to one another, may be predicated on a single literal subject, even within the same overall image. The Theatre of the Absurd abounds in mixed stage metaphor (Rozik: 1996b).

The extension of the principle of similarity to the material level, typical of the theatre medium, may lead to the conclusion that the spectator actually experiences the referential associations of an improper image; in contrast to verbal metaphor that evokes them only in the reader/hearer's mind. However, this reflects a misconception of stage reality: a performance-text may convey a sense of reality, but only on the sensory level, and not all referential associations are of the sensory kind. They also include emotional, ethical and aesthetic recollections of experiences. Therefore, the basic function of an improper term of a stage metaphor is to induce improper referential associations, just like verbal metaphor. Nonetheless, due to the material nature of its icons, one should not underestimate the ability of performance-texts to shape some non-verbal associations on the sensory level.

A stage metaphor, designed for a performance-text, is usually described by an equivalent verbal metaphor in a stage direction. Since a stage direction is a directive speech act, instructing a potential performer how to perform a non-verbal aspect of a possible performance-text, the description of a stage metaphor should have been literal. It is difficult to conceive, however, of a literal verbal description of a stage metaphor. It follows that both metaphors are parallel and equivalent descriptions of a single fictional referent, and that a stage direction may combine directive and descriptive functions.

Speech act stage metaphor

The theatre medium is not confined to imprinting images of non-verbal qualities, states or actions. It also generates images of speech acts, and as such they can be either literal or metaphoric.

In regard to metaphor there is a crucial difference between the performative nature of a speech act and its embedded descriptive verbal sentence. As suggested above, it is widely accepted that a descriptive verbal sentence may be either literal or metaphoric. Unfortunately, speech act theory has not contemplated the possibility of having a kind of real or iconic speech act, whose performative component is metaphoric in itself (Rozik, 2000c). If this is the case, there should be a structural and semantic equivalence between non-verbal and speech act metaphor.

The existence of 'speech act stage metaphor' seems to be precluded because it would presuppose, within a single structure, the integration of the performative nature of speech act, which is an object of description, and 'metaphor', which is a standard form of description of referential objects. Such a combination would appear to blur the existential boundaries between a referential world and its description or, in other words, between the extra-linguistic and the linguistic/semiotic spheres. It would seem, therefore, that this line of inquiry leads to a dead end.

This apparent contradiction, however, does not apply to a stage speech act, which is a genuine description of a fictional one, generated by the theatre medium. The iconic principle implies that anything that is an object of description in a world, when replicated on stage is transmuted into an iconic description. On such grounds, *stage speech act metaphor is possible*. An enacted speech act is thus an iconic description of a fictional speech act, a s/he sentence, which is predicated on a character whether it is literal or metaphoric. Such a speech act reacquires its indexical (self-referential) nature, i.e., its 'I' sentence property, when attributed to a character.

In the so-called Theatre of the Absurd, there are sentences that cannot be understood unless it is assumed that speech act metaphor is employed (Rozik: 1996b). For example, in *The Chairs*, the old couple is preparing the place for a scientific lecture, in which Old Man is supposed to deliver a message announcing a new idea capable of redeeming the world. Suddenly, Old Woman offers choc ices in a way that evokes a vendor of sweets:

Old Woman: [. . .] Programme, would you like a programme, choc ices?

(p. 68)

In French: *Demandez les programmes . . . qui veut le programme?* Chocolat glacé, caramels . . . bonbons acidulés . . .

(p. 162)

Her behavior is improper to both her basic characterization as an old lady and wife of a scientist, and to the nature of the situation, which is defined as a 'scientific lecture'. Instead, she performs a speech act of vending sweets in the typical manner of events of popular entertainment, such as a soccer game or a circus performance, which is done for casting an ironic innuendo on the Old Man's scientific pretensions. Like a metaphoric iconic non-verbal act, this metaphoric iconic speech act evokes an alternative source of referential associations, e.g., a circus performance, and should be seen, therefore, as a particular case of stage metaphor (Rozik, 1989a).

Since both the speech act and the embedded sentence can be metaphoric, whether their improper sources of referential associations are proper or improper to each other (mixed metaphor), there is nothing to preclude the combination of both in a single speech act.

Stylistic implications of mixed stage metaphor

The profusion of stage metaphors, whose improper terms are improper to one another, has far-reaching stylistic implications. For the non-initiated this may create the impression of a chaotic or, rather, an absurd fictional world (cf. Esslin: xixff.). Such an impression may be produced also by mixed verbal metaphor in a literary text, poetry in particular. However, in principle, after evoking the expected set of associations, verbal and non-verbal, the improper terms should be disregarded and not attributed to a fictional world. This may difficult in the case of stage metaphor, whose improper terms enjoy material existence on stage, because of being images imprinted on real matter, thus introducing a strong element of distraction. It is indeed easier to overlook improper words than improper imprinted images. However, if this concrete existence is understood as a feature of the medium, in contrast to Esslin, an initial sense of absurdity should vanish (Rozik, 1996b). It follows that such an impression is not inherent in mixed stage metaphor, and is fundamentally erroneous. This conclusion does not contradict the possibility of creating an image of absurdity on different grounds.

The way to read and interpret mixed stage metaphor is, first, to induce the referential associations originating in each improper term; then, to link these associations to common modifiers; subsequently, to attribute them to a fictional referent; and finally, to disregard all improper terms despite their concrete presence on stage.

If interpreted adequately, mixed stage metaphor is definitely not absurd in itself. However, the creation of an absurd stage metaphor is possible; e.g., in comic and grotesque fictional worlds. It should be noted, however, that this is not of recent invention; e.g., in Aristophanes' *Frogs*, the god Dionysus is scared to death and craps in his pants like a cowardly human being (479–92). The main innovation of modernist drama probably lies in the operation of absurd stage metaphors in comically handling deadly serious themes, such as human frustration and death, while aiming at producing a grotesque image of the human condition. Although the grotesque mood does not depend only on the use of stage metaphor *per se*, the proliferation of absurd and mixed stage metaphor certainly creates a distinct type of theatre style.

Stage allegory

Traditionally, 'allegory' in general, and *'stage allegory' in particular, is conceived of as a kind of complex metaphor – 'symbol' in dated terms – which may expand up to an entire text.* It is usually defined in terms of 'personification' and 'substitution'.

(A) *'Personification'* is a specific kind of metaphor that reflects a classification of metaphors according to the semantic domains of the improper terms, such as 'human', 'animal' and 'vegetal'. Consequently, the literal subjects of personification can be anything but human. Indeed, the usual referents of personified descriptions are abstract entities, described by human characters; e.g., the various human qualities/drives personified in anonymous *Everyman*. The old couple of *The Chairs* too illustrates this principle by splitting up a human entity, following the confidant convention, to create an image of dramatic interaction. Through their grotesque games the old couple possibly describes metaphorically and ironically the playwright's own tragic quest for meaning and redemption of the world. The split of this human entity and its description by two human characters pervades the entire fictional world, and its enactment by two flesh and blood actors substantially supports personification. Since anything that reinforces the human-like nature of characters is akin to personification, naturalistic allegory is possible.

The tendency of traditional theory is to equate stage allegory with personification. However, there is no reason for such a restriction. The allegoric principle equally applies to 'animal metaphor' (e.g., humans becoming animals in Ionesco's *Rhinoceros*); 'vegetal metaphor' (e.g., the huge 'tree' in Federico García Lorca's *Blood Wedding*); 'inanimate metaphor' (the growing mound in Samuel Beckett's *Happy Days*); and 'mechanical metaphor' (the tape recorder in Beckett's *Krapp's Last Tape*). The tape recorder is probably an imprinted metaphoric image of human memory: by listening to his old tapes, in which he also finds himself listening to yet older tapes, Krapp confronts various levels of his own past. Consequently, the equation allegory–personification is unsustainable. Just as non-human entities may be described by human images, so too may the latter be described by non-human ones. The principle should thus be expanded to 'metaphorization'. The classification of metaphor according to meaning domains is rather pointless.

(B) '*Substitution*' means the total or almost total replacement of the literal subject of a (usually whole) text by a set of improper imprinted images, which usually belong in a single semantic domain. However, even total substitution does not cancel the elliptic presence of the literal subject, and the actual improper set still maintains a predicative relationship to it. The more consistent the substitution, the more difficult it is for the spectator to detect the implied subject of predication. It is the task of the spectator/scholar to intuit improperness, conjecture the implied literal subject, restore the entire network of relations as required by the deep structure of metaphor, and interpret the metaphor as if all the elliptic elements were actually present in the text.

Most stage allegories opt to disclose, through verbal or non-verbal hints, their literal subjects. In *Everyman*, for example, the literal subjects of predication are revealed by introducing the characters by their abstract "names", before they speak:

> *Everyman:*   Where art thou, my Goods and Riches?
> *Goods:*   (within) Who calleth me? (1. 392)

These characters probably carried metaphoric or symbolic attributes as in allegoric art. A modern example of such a disclosure is found in Beckett's *Waiting for Godot*:

> *Vladimir:*   To all mankind they were addressed, those cries for help still ringing in our ears! But at this place, at this moment of time, *all mankind is us* whether we like it or not.   (p. 79; my italics)

This clue indicates that the two characters are meant to represent and describe abstract humanity, for grotesque purposes. The play-script clearly formulates a metaphoric description of Beckett's abstract concept of the human condition.

A playwright may opt, however, to deny disclosure altogether and give no clue to the identity of the overall literal subject. In such a case, the audience is left with a text that only presents an overall improper image. Since the structure of metaphor requires a literal subject, it is the task of the audience to speculate regarding this missing element; for example, in *The Chairs* the substitution of the playwright's mind by the old couple. In fact, by choosing this option, unless being deliberately ambiguous or obscure, a playwright increases the set of possible referents of a fictional world, thus widening the applicability of its message. The result is a kind of ready-made metaphor capable of describing even unforeseen referential social and political constellations. However, since a metaphor does not make sense unless there is a possible modifier, common to both the literal subject and the improper term, the options are drastically reduced.

Identification of the literal subject of predication does not complete the process of interpretation. The aforementioned interpretation regarding the old couple in *The Chairs* only goes part of the way. The next steps, like for stage metaphor, are: to establish the common literal modifiers and respective referential associations that are activated by the metaphoric description and, eventually, to determine how they actually describe the referent (the playwright). For example, in interpreting the main metaphor in Ionesco's *Rhinoceros*, the verbal and referential associations of these animals are meant to be attributed to human nature. As suggested above, what matters is not a true knowledge of real rhinoceroses, but the widespread belief that they are wild and dangerous, especially in herds (although usually they are not). In other words, in the metaphoric description of this human tendency it is their commonplace associations that are activated.

(c) *Mediation by abstraction*: Since a stage metaphor may also describe

60

a praxical fictional world, I suggest that the specific difference of a typical allegoric fictional world is that it refers to the spectator's psychical state of affairs by mediation of an idea. 'Praxical' is employed here in the sense of 'non-allegoric' fictional world. In other words, an allegory is relevant to an audience only by mediation of a specific set of religious, philosophical or ideological ideas, which are its mediating literal subject. *Stage allegory is thus a special case of stage metaphor, featuring the substitution of an idea by a metaphor of possibly textual scope, whose sources of referential associations are not necessarily human.*

(D) *Mixed praxical and allegoric discourse*: The usual assumption is that performance-texts are either 'praxical' or 'allegoric'. In fact, many descriptions of fictional worlds combine praxical and allegoric characters; e.g., the villagers and the denizens of the forest in García Lorca's *'Blood Wedding'*. Other examples readily come to mind, such as the masks in García Lorca's *Yerma*, the necrophiliac in Fernando Arrabal's *Solemn Communion* and Matchseller in Harold Pinter's *A Slight Ache*. Such a mixture has become common practice in modern and postmodern theatre.

Stage symbol

In this study, 'symbol' has already been mentioned in Peirce's sense of a sign characterized by an unmotivated relation between signifier and signified (sense 1); e.g., a word. This is not, however, the typical sense of 'symbol' in various disciplines such as psychoanalysis, religion studies and theories of the arts, theatre in particular. In these domains it is employed in the sense of a figurative use of a sign (sense 2). Accordingly, I suggest the following definition of verbal 'symbol': a word capable of evoking, in addition to its basic signified and correlated connotations, a verbal and non-verbal contextual associative periphery; e.g., the word 'owl' as a symbol of wisdom, in addition to its zoological meaning (1992a: 64–81). Consequently, a word, a symbol in sense (1), may or may not be employed as a symbol in sense (2).

The same definition applies to equivalent mental images or icons; e.g., the imprinted images of 'owl' (wisdom), 'scales' (justice), 'Cross' (martyrdom and redemption), 'hammer & sickle' (communism) and 'flag' (nationhood). The paraphrases within the brackets are obviously reductive because their referential associations can not be made explicit. Associative peripheries attached to verbal and equivalent iconic units are similar because they represent the same objects, real or fictional, and associations are fundamentally attached to objects; they are attached to signs by recurrent experiences with them in real or textual contexts. This process

61

of symbolic loading may take place either in the context of a culture (a symbol may exist prior to its inclusion in a text), or in the context of a work of art; e.g., the word and image of 'seagull' in Chekhov's *The Seagull* (Rozik, 1988b). In this sense a motif is a symbolic phenomenon.

In contrast to Ricoeur (pp. 21ff) and Todorov (pp. 9–38), within the symbolic associative periphery a distinction should be made between associations controlled by the sense of a sign and additional uncontrolled diffuse associations. In such diffuse peripheries, which include unconscious and culturally conditioned associations, non-verbal associations reign supreme. Therefore, their meaning cannot be exhausted by words. This is also manifested by the fact that the same signs may convey different and even conflicting peripheries in different cultures; e.g., whereas the 'star of David' bears positive emotive and value associations of Messianic redemption for the Jews, it was employed as a symbol of contempt and degradation by the Nazi regime.

Like a metaphor, a symbol is 'trite' if its associative periphery has dwindled to the extent that its meaning is easily translated into words, which is not the case with vital symbols. A symbol can lose its associative power, under at least two conditions: when it is used too frequently and/or when it ceases to be part of a reloading context (Rozik, 1992a: 64–81); e.g., the symbol of 'pelican and young' was probably based on the belief that pelicans, wounding their own breasts, nourish their chicks with their own blood. Plausibly it was on such grounds that it became a metaphor of Christ, which by mere reiteration became His symbol. The word or image 'pelican', which had formerly attached a sense of devotion for a fervently believing community, probably lost its vitality following the decline in the belief of pelican's self-sacrifice. Its inclusion in a dictionary of symbols was evidently the last nail in its coffin. Such dictionaries list paraphrases of symbols (e.g., Cirlot; and Vries). Dwindling associative peripheries attest to the inducing power of vital symbols.

Like words, icons may be used either symbolically or not; e.g., an imprinted image of 'traffic lights' either in a thriller film or in a book for new drivers. The problem is that signs do not feature markers that distinguish between symbolic and non-symbolic uses of a term, and prescribe a specific form of reading and interpretation. Assumedly, a symbol will make sense in either a literal or figurative interpretation. How should readers/spectators know when to engage in symbolic interpretation? First, certain cultural domains promote symbolic reading and can be seen as domain markers. Second, some texts may generate intentional gaps, and even not make sense at all, if not interpreted symbolically. Third, in some cases there is a clear advantage in such an interpretation. For example, in Sophocles' *Oedipus the King*, while the act of blinding himself can be read only on a literal level, as Oedipus' sheer self-punishment, reading 'eyes' as symbols of the limitation of human understanding opens the text to additional and crucial dimensions.

Both metaphors and symbols evoke associations, non-verbal in particular, which are essential to the process of textual interpretation in the arts. Their main difference is that while metaphor is a predicative phenomenon, linking at least two terms, symbol concerns the relation between a single term and its additional associative periphery. *The combination between them, therefore, is possible and even beneficial*: due to its rich associative periphery a symbol may make an excellent improper term of a metaphor, and a recurrent metaphoric predicate can eventually become a symbol; e.g., the lamb is a typical metaphor of Jesus, which by recurrent use it became His symbol.

Stage symbol should not be confused with 'stage metonymy', which like verbal metonymy is an elliptical 'figure of speech' in which a present term evokes an elliptic term to which it has been usually associated in previous contexts. For example, in Ionesco's *The Chairs*, the empty chairs are iconic metonymies of sitting people. In contrast, again, 'symbol' relates to a single term that induces associations beyond its basic sense. Furthermore, whereas metonymy evokes elliptically missing terms, symbol induces diffuse and less controlled associations. A symbol can be a metonym or not.

Because of their built-in tendency to abstraction, cognitive disciplines reflect a tendency to intentionally ignore additional associative peripheries, which is most conspicuous in philosophy and science. This proclivity paradoxically reveals the existence of such associative peripheries. Therefore, in the context of a verbal culture, it must be presupposed that some domains, as mentioned above, enjoy a cultural permit to engage in metaphoric and symbolic formulation and interpretation. In preverbal culture a distinction between core and additional associative peripheries is inconceivable. It may thus be assumed that the mind naturally operates metaphors and symbols.

4

Stage Conventions

Traditional theatre semiotics has quite consistently ignored the entire domain of stage conventions despite their crucial function in generating theatre meaning.

In the social sciences the notion of 'convention' is usually defined in terms of 'social agreement' (Bradbrook: 4). Since for most conventions it is very difficult to determine the social circumstances of their establishment, their definition is usually put in terms of 'tacit social agreement' (Hauser: 371; Lewis: 83ff; Burns: 28). In linguistics 'convention' applies to a word (a 'symbol' in Peirce's terms) that reflects a non-motivated link between signifier, the perceptible sound sequence, and signified, the set of abstract features that it conveys (Saussure, 1972: 99–101; cf. Lyons, 1969: 63). In this context, 'non-motivation' means that the signified cannot be inferred from the signifier through either contiguity (an index) or similarity (an icon). A non-motivated link between signifier and referent may be added. This sense of 'convention' is a particular instance of the sociological one.

A similar sense of 'convention' applies to the theatre medium. In principle, the typical theatre unit is motivated, due to the principle of similarity underlying iconicity; meaning that a signified can be inferred from a signifier because of similarity to its real or mental model and mediation of language. Since language assigns a word to such a model, an iconic signifier can evoke its correlated signified. Therefore, in order to understand a performance-text there is no need to learn the theatre medium, which is, fundamentally, transparent. Meaning is thus generated by 'natural inference'.

However, not all theatre segments are transparent. There are verbal or iconic sentences that are mediated by stage conventions. In principle, a theatre unit is conventional if the principle of similarity is at least partially cancelled, thus either preventing or impairing natural inference, unless its reading principle has been learned or otherwise grasped; i.e., 'stage convention' means that such an iconic unit has no real model, or that its reading differs from that of its real model; i.e., a stage convention conditions the way of reading a stage unit; e.g., the reading of the image of an actor speaking to himself in soliloquy differs from that of its real model (cf. Elam, 1980: 87).

'Stage convention' does not refer here to a theatre signs/sentence that replicates a convention in social intercourse. 'Shaking hands', for example, is a social convention that conveys a sense of 'friendship' and/or 'good will', although the gesture itself does not attest to such a meaning in a natural manner. Nevertheless, an imprinted image of this convention transforms it into a regular motivated and univocal iconic sentence, whose meaning is inferred on the grounds of similarity; i.e., as it is inferred in the real world. A distinction should also be made between the basic convention of theatre (chapter 1) and 'stage convention' in the sense discussed here. Whereas the former applies to all forms of theatre semiosis, the latter applies to a specific subset of such forms on a different level. In this sense a stage convention materializes both principles.

More than any other form of theatre semiosis, conventions indicate the existential gap between stage reality and fictional world, because the unmotivated features that establish each convention are not and cannot be attributed to a fictional world; e.g., a soliloquy does not entail that a character speaks to him/herself in its fictional world. In this sense they clearly convey the message 'this is a text'.

This chapter aims at showing that (a) *stage conventions depart from the principles of similarity and motivation, despite being images imprinted on matter*; (b) *since stage conventions depart from these principles, they require special reading rules*; (c) *kinds of stage conventions are defined by their specific departures from similarity either on the material or imagistic levels*; (d) *functions of stage conventions are determined by both the limitations of the theatre medium that they overcome and the contributions they make to the description of a fictional world*; and (e) *most stage conventions fulfil an ironic function*. Since play-scripts reflect the typical conventions of a contemporary theatre, the above principles will be illustrated by specific conventions in both performance-texts and play-scripts.

Reading principles

'Stage convention' impairs the principle of similarity that defines iconicity, thus implying its definition in terms of 'non-motivation'. However, although similarity is diminished, distorted or borrowed from dissimilar models, stage conventions are still imprinted images, otherwise they could not enjoy stage presence. The element of dissimilarity, which impairs their motivation, requires that the reading principle of each convention has to be learned or otherwise grasped on the grounds of recurrent experiences with it and/or its functions in the description of fictional worlds. *Reading stage conventions is, therefore, like operating shifters that instruct the audience to change from the typical reading of verbal or iconic sentences to readings according to their particular rules.* As suggested above, a stage convention requires that the elements of difference that establishes it as such should be overlooked; e.g., by the very pattern of their movements actors may create spatial images, such as angular or circular grids, but these do not imply that characters behave so in their own worlds.

The adequate reading of a convention requires the following questions to be answered: what is its kind; what is its function; what is its degree of authority; and what should be attributed to the fictional world or ignored? For example, in regard to the chorus it can be learned that (a) it is a collective stage convention (kind); (b) it usually interprets the action from an ironic viewpoint (function); (c) it usually commands a higher degree of authority than that of the characters' naïve viewpoints (authority); and (d) its speaking in unison should not be attributed to a fictional world. These are prerequisites for the correct reading of the verbal information conveyed by a chorus.

Kinds of stage conventions

The theatre medium materializes the principle of similarity on both the imagistic and material levels; therefore, stage conventions can depart from this principle on each of these levels or on both. A distinction should be made, therefore, between medium and imagistic conventions:

(A) *Medium conventions* are defined in terms of *departure from similarity on the material level,* which leads to a transition from the theatre medium to another iconic medium that imprints images on materials dissimilar to those of their real models; e.g., a street set painted on a backdrop. Such a departure does not impair the spectators' inferential capacity, since the imagistic component remains intact. While an image on a backdrop should be attributed to a fictional world (e.g., an imprinted image of a street), the fact that it is painted on a backdrop should be overlooked.

Some stage conventions resort to language for the description of various aspects of a fictional world. In many a case, the relevant reading principle relies on the semantic equivalence between verbal and iconic descriptions. Because of their evocative power, words are capable of evoking images, which do not contradict the ultimate aims of a performance-text. In this case too the reading capacity of the spectators is not impaired due to their

66

familiarity with the evocative use of language in literature. In such a case, a descriptive sentence conveyed through a convention should be conceived of as an embodied image of an assertive speech act (Searle, 1986: 12–13).

Medium conventionality thus resides in the borrowing from another medium/language and the mixing of two media within a single work of art. However, the predominance of human acting indicates the actual subordination of any other medium/language to the theatre medium.

(B) *Imagistic conventions* are defined in terms of *departure from similarity on the imagistic level*, which may impair natural inference, because the iconic reading principle naturally granted to the audience is totally or partially abolished. Actually, in the European tradition at least, total cancellation of similarity is never absolute, and usually stage conventions allow inference on reduced iconic grounds. I suggest the following kinds (while noting that this list may not be exhaustive):

(1) Partial cancellation of imagistic elements
(2) Distortion of imagistic elements
(3) Borrowing of imagistic elements

(1) *Partial cancellation of imagistic elements*: many imagistic conventions reveal a partial cancellation of similarity; for instance, when a symbolic set describes a certain location by a single object, metonymically associated with it in the minds of spectators; e.g., an image of a single gondola representing Venice. In such a case, the correct reading relies on the existent elements of similarity, and complementation relies on spectators' associations. Another example: a constructivist set may describe a fictional place through the spatial relations among its various levels. In such a case, the correct reading depends on the iconic behavior of the actors, or the verbal descriptions that evoke the missing elements of the set. Therefore, the fact that elements are missing should not be attributed to the fictional world, they are metonymically present.

(2) *Distortion of imagistic elements:* Some stage conventions feature images distorted to various extents and for various reasons; e.g., actors speaking extra-loudly or performing exaggerated gestures for facilitating aural or visual reception in large theatres. Another example: a dialogue in alexandrines distorts the prosaic character of real dialogue, with the intention being to produce a particular aesthetic impression. These examples do not imply that in the fictional world characters speak extra-loudly, perform exaggerated gestures or speak in this meter. In such cases too, the remaining elements of similarity on the imagistic and material levels enable the reading on iconic grounds. While the undistorted elements should be attributed to a fictional world, the distorted ones should be overlooked.

(3) *Borrowing of imagistic elements*: Some stage conventions borrow their

images from models of behavior or situations that are not supposed to be part of a fictional world, e.g., the use of signposts for places, such as 'the court' or 'the living room', usually not used for indicating such locations. The borrowed image should be overlooked and the key for its reading is usually provided by the function of the information it provides.

A stage convention may depart from the principle of similarity on both the medium and imagistic levels; for example, a nonexistent door (a '0' icon) can be acted upon as if it was where it is assumed to be, opened or closed whenever an actor approaches the place. Another example: a stage prop that is meant to evoke different fictional objects, such as the Japanese fan that, in addition to describing a fictional fan, may evoke a sword, a cup of tea, or a shield, depending on the way it is manipulated. Such twofold conventions should be viewed primarily as imagistic conventions, because they impair the reading competence of the audience.

Despite departures from similarity on the imagistic level, all such conventions maintain the principle of 'imprinted image', as otherwise they could not be part of the performance-text and perceived by the audience, which makes them integral to the theatre medium.

Functions of stage conventions

In principle, although fictional worlds can be described solely through the theatre medium in its basic motivated guise, various constraints prevent their full descriptions. I suggest, therefore, that *the main function of stage conventions is to compensate for these limitations; and that their functions are determined by both the limitations that they overcome and the contributions they make to the description of a fictional world* (Rozik, 1992a: 104–25; cf. 1992d). Theatre cannot do without stage conventions, unless it relinquishes the purpose of fully describing fictional worlds. Even naturalist drama disguises but not disposes of them.

Whereas a 'stage convention' is defined in terms of its particular departure from the principle of similarity, its functions are defined by both the kind of medium limitation that it overcomes and the kind of meaning that it provides to a description of a fictional world, which are two sides of the same coin.

(A) *Semiotic functions* are defined by the type of medium limitations that they overcome; e.g., the inability of the iconic medium to describe what happens in the mind of a character, which is overcome by soliloquy. In principle, the same convention can fulfil different functions and the same function can be fulfilled by different conventions. However, most conventions specialize in a specific semiotic function; e.g., the chorus may

68

overcome the limitation of iconic media in rendering the meaning of events from an ironic viewpoint. Because of this propensity, the intuition of a semiotic function may assist in reading a stage convention. Semiotic limitations can be classified under the following headings:

(1) *Medium constraints* concern limitations of the theatre medium in conveying certain types of information; e.g., the confidant convention makes up for its inability to describe the non-perceptible aspects of a character's behavior.

(2) *Performative constraints* regard the technical constraints in performing some iconic descriptions; e.g., the imprinting of images of 'sea', 'woods' and some 'animals' on materials similar to their models. They also regard phenomena such as invisibility and nakedness (Bradbrook: 15).

(3) *Physical constraints* relate to the limitations imposed on spectators by their physiology; e.g., the use of *coturnoi* and *onkos* on the ancient Greek stage to prevent the dwarfing effect of distance in a huge amphitheatre.

(4) *Decorum constraints* concern the restrictions imposed on a performance-text by the ethos of an audience; e.g., the use of an *ekkyklema* for the description of an off-stage event that may upset the culturally conditioned sensibilities of spectators.

(5) *financial constraints* relate to the impossible cost of an imprinted image.

(B) *Poetic functions* contribute vital information to descriptions of fictional worlds. In principle, the same convention can fulfill different poetic functions, and the same poetic function can be fulfilled by different conventions. Nonetheless, certain affinities between some conventions and functions can be detected. Furthermore, the set of stage conventions that can fulfill the same function can be seen as a paradigmatic set, from which an author may choose or to which s/he may add newly created ones.

From the perspective of poetics, since its rules apply to the described aspects of a fictional world, a function is defined by the kind of meaning it contributes to its description. However, most poetic functions specialize in conveying dramatic irony from author to audience. In principle, the theatre medium poses a serious problem for an author who wishes to promote 'dramatic irony', in the sense of an understanding of a fictional world better than that of the characters (cf. Sedgewick: 49 & Styan: 48ff). The problem is that a fictional world is basically presented by the actual behavior of its denizens, who conceive of their world from their own naïve perspectives, independently of their author. It is usually assumed, therefore, that directors are not represented in performance-texts. I contend, in contrast, that the absence of their viewpoints is only apparent. It is not only that a director's presence is reflected in the structure of a fictional world, but it is also represented on stage by functional characters and/or interactive characters in functional situations. This is conspicuous in the case that such an ironic agent is missing, or used to the spectators' detriment – thus revealing a directorial intention to position the audience as an object of dramatic irony.

Most stage conventions thus reflect the author's need to produce an expected attitude in an audience to an independent fictional world; i.e., to create an ironic perspective. A higher degree of authority should thus be assigned to such stage conventions, therefore, than that of the characters' perspectives. They convey more information and/or advantageous conceptual frames, as understood by directors, in comparison to characters in non-conventional speeches. For example, what Hamlet says in his soliloquies is more consequential than what transpires from his words in front of Polonius or Rosencrantz and Guildenstern. *Most stage conventions reflect a directorial need to circumvent the characters, thus establishing a non-mediated channel of communication with the spectators.* Consequently, the direct address to an audience, which characterizes some conventions, should be seen as the basic form of fulfilling this ironic function.

Ironic functions are usually carried out by functional characters, whose images apparently have nothing to do with representation of directors; e.g., a messenger may insert a verbal description of an offstage event into the flow of events iconically described on stage, because of an author's need to share a non-iconically described part of the action with the spectator. While the image of a messenger imprinted on an actor has nothing to do with the image of a director, what he says should be conceived of as uttered on the latter's behalf. This incongruity is paradoxical: while the presence of an author's image may upset the spectators' sense of experiencing an independent fictional world, this intervention is indispensable for guiding spectators to a desired interpretation and experience. However, a verbal categorization from an author's viewpoint could never become part of an iconic text, unless in the guise of an imprinted image; i.e., unless voiced by an actor enacting a functional character or an interactive character in a functional situation. Therefore, these should be seen as personifications of a director's ironic perspective.

Ironic conventions pose an additional dilemma: on the one hand, they play a crucial role in the communication between author and audience, fundamentally different from that played by interacting characters; on the other hand, they tend to depart from the motivated nature of the theatre text. Consequently, different styles may reflect different solutions to this basic tension, on a continuum from straightforward presentation of conventions to extreme disguise or concealment, as in naturalistic theatre.

The latter, however, may confuse spectators as to their ironic function. This should lead to the conclusion that the overt foreignness of conventions is advantageous.

However, functional characters are designed to be at least apparently akin to interacting characters: authors usually assign human characterization to functional characters to various extents, thus enabling them to generate human-like behavior, and facilitating their apparent integration into the human fabric of a fictional world. For example, the chorus is characterized as 'the old men of Thebes' in Sophocles' *Oedipus the King;* or the confidant as a 'teacher' in Jean Racine's *Phaedra.* They may also be assigned parallel actions, such as final marriage, or parallel catastrophe; e.g., in Molière's *Don Juan.*

In some cases, this function is carried out by interacting characters in conventional situations, i.e., 'out of character', in contrast to their characteristic behavior 'in character' (cf. Bradbrook: 111); e.g., soliloquy. In such a case, there is a borrowing of a foreign image (speaking to oneself usually indicates a mental condition), which may affect the spectators' ability to read a performance-text, unless they are acquainted with the principle underlying this convention.

The reading principles that apply to ironic conventions presuppose that what is verbally described by their means should be regarded as integral to a description of a fictional world, and even assigned higher authority, while their distinguishing features should be ignored. For example, the fact that in Racine's *Phaedra* each main character has a confidant does not entail that this is the case in the fictional world. If the poetic function of a confidant is to provide genuine information on what is occurring in a character's mind, a function that the iconic medium cannot provide due to its ability to replicate only the external appearances of things, its existence should not be attributed to the fictional world.

Consequently, it is convenient to see a performance-text as a complex mechanism of description, in which the main task of description is performed by actors enacting interactive characters and their actions, as they naively conceive of their own worlds (direct channel), and the task of conveying an alternative ironic viewpoint is carried out by actors enacting functional characters or interactive characters in functional situations, which are meant to circumvent the interacting characters (indirect channel). The ironic functions of stage conventions may be classified as follows:

(1) *Description of the non-iconically represented parts of an action*
(2) *Description of the non-perceptible aspects of an action*
(3) *Conditioning the 'expected' cognitive or value meaning of an action*
(4) *Conditioning the expected aesthetic effect*

LIVERPOOL JOHN MOORES UNIVERSITY
LEARNING SERVICES

This list may not exhaust all the possible ironic functions of stage conventions, and additions can be expected.

(1) *Description of non-iconically represented parts of an action*: The authorial need to convey full information to spectators is often limited by two constraints: (a) the spectators' physiologically limited ability to concentrate over a long period and/or the socially limited time that they are willing to devote to theatre; and (b) the limited ability of the iconic medium to provide telescopic formulation, such as compressing a description of events into a few sentences through language. These constraints are, for example, easily overcome in television 'series' due to their extended scope. Under typical circumstances, however, time is restricted and, therefore, two complementary functions operate in performance-texts: (a) the exclusion of certain events from iconic description; and (b) the inclusion of these off-stage events or episodes in telescoped verbal guise within the sequence of an iconic description. Such episodes, which are temporally and/or spatially off-stage, are not necessarily inserted into the iconic sequence at their right time or space. The ironic function of these conventions is evident when the information conveyed by them is already known to some characters, with their aim being to provide the same information to the spectator.

Telescopic formulation is provided only by language in its storytelling and depicting functions. Verbal descriptions aim at evoking corresponding images of events in the minds of the spectators. According to the principle of equivalence, what is verbally told or depicted should be seen as an integral part of the description of a fictional world. However, despite equivalence, differences between iconically and verbally described parts of an overall action should not be overlooked. It can be conjectured that iconic scenes provide a perspective from which the audience is invited to approach the verbally evoked ones. However, such considerations do not imply that verbally described scenes are less important than iconic scenes. Crucial scenes are frequently placed off-stage for various reasons, such as constraints of decorum.

This ironic function should also include the verbal characterization of *dramatis personae* through a verbal exposition, which is imposed by the short scope of the performance-text. Verbal characterization is alternative to presentation of characters in various situations, prior to the iconically described action, from which characterization is supposed to be abstracted. Verbal characterization differs from verbal description of offstage events in their organization of data: a-temporal in the former and temporal in the latter. Moreover, characterization and telescoped storytelling prior to action are indispensable because they condition the meaning of iconically described events and the expectations of possible future ones.

The 'exclusion conventions' include the following: chorus (e.g., in Greek drama); interludes (e.g., in Spanish Golden Age drama); music (e.g., in French Classicist drama); emptying the stage (e.g., in Elizabethan drama); curtain (e.g., in modern proscenium stage); blackout, spotlight, mechanical changes and freeze (e.g., in modern theatre). Lope de Vega relates to the interval as a convention, in the sense that time is not iconically described in it and can be attributed different spans (1965: 91; cf. Corneille: 253). In fact, it should be seen as an exclusion convention.

The 'inclusion conventions' include the following: chorus (e.g., in Sophocles' *Antigone*); prologue (e.g., in Shakespeare's *Romeo and Juliet*); epilogue (e.g., in Plautus' *The Prisoners*); servants' exposition (e.g., in García Lorca's *The House of Bernarda Alba*); characters' exposition (e.g., Ibsen's *Hedda Gabler*, I); messenger (e.g., in Euripides' *Medea*, 1138ff); over-the-wall account (e.g., the description of the race in Synge's *The Playboy of the Western World*, III); *ekkyklema* (e.g., the revelation of Jocasta's corpse in Sophocles' *Oedipus the King*).

The change of sets is not a convention in the sense suggested here. It rather derives from the basic convention of theatre, which presupposes that a stage can enact whatever time and place is required after each break in the continuity of a performance-text; i.e., after intervals between acts or scenes. In contrast, 'simultaneous settings' (mansions) are a convention because they telescope space. Such a contraction of space does not impair the spectators' reading because the imprinted images retain spatial relations intact. The same applies to conventionally telescoped time, as in Shakespeare's *Othello* (II, i), because it does not abolish the natural sequence of time.

(2) *Description of non-perceptible aspects of an action*: The theatre medium is limited to replication of perceptible aspects of objects and phenomena. While simple intentions, purposes, thoughts and feelings are usually properly inferred, fictional actions often reflect more complex states of mind. This is particularly conspicuous when a character's external behavior is deliberately designed to mislead other characters by concealing its true disposition (e.g., Hamlet). In such a case, a character's behavior may also mislead the audience and, therefore, there is a directorial need for communicating the true verbal description of an inner state of affairs; e.g., through soliloquy. All the conventions that fulfill this function depart from the principle of similarity on the imagistic level. They usually resort to verbal description but, in cases, to background music.

These stage conventions tend to present an event from at least two perspectives, their (external) iconic description and the verbal description of its inner reflection, thus creating two types of scene. This duplicity, which deploys two aspects of the same behavior on the time axis, should

73

be overlooked. The unmotivated features of these conventions should also be discounted from characterization; e.g., the fact that a character soliloquies does not mean that it soliloquies in the fictional world; it does not imply qualities such as frankness, self-awareness or poetic eloquence.

The set of conventions capable of fulfilling this function include the following: soliloquy to audience (e.g., Iago in Shakespeare's *Othello*, I, ii); soliloquy to self (e.g., Hamlet in Shakespeare's *Hamlet*, III, iii); aside, (e.g., Macbeth in Shakespeare's *Macbeth*, I, iii); reading of a personal document, such as a diary or letter (e.g., Lady Macbeth in Shakespeare's *Macbeth*, I, v); confidant (e.g., Œnone in Racine's *Phaedra*, I, iii); dialogue with *coryphaeus* (e.g., Creon and *coryphaeus* in Sophocles' *Antigone*); confession (e.g., Masha and Trigorin in Chekhov's *The Seagull*, III, p. 152); mask (e.g., happy and sad masks in Greek tragedy); aria (e.g., Victor and Yerma in García Lorca's *Yerma*: 'Why, shepherd, sleep alone?' (p. 112); and background music (e.g., in Arthur Miller's *Death of the Salesman* (e.g., various). A distinction should be made between background music in an ironic interpretative capacity, such as indicating the feelings of a character or conditioning the feelings of an audience, and music as part of the fictional world, as when music is heard from a fictional street or a radio. Transitions to concealed levels of experience, such as memory, dream and vision, are usually indicated by changing lights. Since these spheres reflect the innermost contents of the characters' psyches, they too should be seen as fulfilling an ironic function.

(3) *Conditioning the expected cognitive or ethical meaning of an action*: The theatre medium is limited in its capacity to convey the cognitive and/or ethic meaning of an action. Furthermore, neither real nor fictional actions indicate such meanings in themselves. In principle, the same event can be categorized in such terms differently from distinct viewpoints. Therefore, fictional actions need to be ascribed such meanings by characters in their verbal descriptions from their own (naïve) viewpoints, and for the very same reason, by playwrights/directors from their alternative ironic viewpoints; in particular if the rhetoric intention is that spectators adopt them. It is the independence of fictional characters, whose viewpoints should be consistent with their characterizations, that requires these conventions. This is imperative in cases of a clear gap between the conceptualization by the characters and that expected from the audience; e.g., the pagan fictional world created for a Christian audience in Racine's *Phaedra*.

Authorial conceptualization is usually conveyed by functional characters or interacting characters in functional situations, which couple images of human-like behavior and use of language. Since all of them reflect an authorial need, they should both be seen as personifications of the ironic viewpoint of an author. Spectators too spontaneously categorize fictional characters and events independently in the terms of their own culture. It would appear, therefore, that this textual function is superfluous: due to the synchronic nature of performance-texts, terms of reference are shared by directors and audience. In fact, however, these terms are never completely absent.

The paradigm of stage conventions capable of fulfilling this function includes the following: chorus (e.g., in Sophocles' *Antigone*, 331–384); honest man (e.g., Cleante in Molière's *Tartuffe*, I, v); God (e.g., in *Everyman*); prophet (e.g., Teiresias in Sophocles' *Oedipus the King*); king (e.g., in Lope de Vega's *Fuenteovejuna*); doctor (e.g., in Shakespeare's *Macbeth*; wise person (e.g., Clotaldo in Calderón de la Barca's *Life is a Dream*); ballad singer (e.g., in Brecht's *The Three Penny Opera*); servant (e.g., Catalinón in Tirso de Molina's *The Trickster of Sevilla*); main character (e.g., Segismundo's final conclusions in Calderón de la Barca's *Life is a Dream*); metaphoric leitmotif (e.g., the seagull motif in Chekhov's *The Seagull*); symbolic leitmotif (e.g., the cherry orchard in Chekhov's *The Cherry Orchard*). An author may employ such conventions for conveying the opposite of the expected categorization, which in itself should be the object of theatrical irony, such as a god (e.g., Aphrodite and Artemis in Euripides' *Hippolytus*); and a chorus (e.g., the laundresses in García Lorca's *Yerma*).

(4) *Conditioning the expected aesthetic effects of an action*: A performance-text aims not only at describing a fictional world and conditioning its perception in cognitive and ethical terms, but also at bringing about the experience of such a world as an aesthetic object. In this sense aesthetic conventions also reflect the ironic intent of authors, although on a different level.

Aesthetic properties can be found on both the signified and signifier levels of a performance-text. On the signified level, the poetic structure of a fictional world may create an experience of harmony or disharmony with the spectators' expectations in regard to the results of characters' motives and actions (chapter 7). On the signifier level a performance-text, due to its materiality, may produce an aesthetic experience of harmony or disharmony through configurations of color and shape on the visual level and/or sound on the aural level. Usually, there is a correspondence between the aesthetic properties of both the signified and signifier levels.

Aesthetic conventions do not derive from any limitation of the theatre medium or any other constraint, but rather impose their own properties on a performance-text. They usually distort or, rather, stylize iconic units on the signifier level, thus affecting similarity as a reading principle, for the purpose of an aesthetic experience. Basically, such a distortion does not preclude comprehension of the text, as movement in dance or singing in opera. Moreover, the properties of such conventions qua conventions should not be attributed to a fictional world; e.g., the fact that in opera characters sing their parts in the action does not imply that in the fictional word the characters sing. Another example: in ancient Greece tragedies were probably performed by declamation with a minimum of body language. In general, aesthetic elements, such as attributing poetic nature to a character that excels in the prosodic aspects of his soliloquies, should be discounted from characterization. Since the aesthetic function also applies to disharmony, no performance-text is free from aesthetic conventions.

The aesthetic function underlies the following sets of conventions on the signifier level: (a) visual harmony (static pictorial harmony in setting, costume and lighting; and dynamic harmony in rhythmic movement in dance); and (b) aural harmony (rhythmic and rhymed speech or musical background). Chapter 7 expands on the sets of conventions that underlie harmony and disharmony on the poetic level.

Norms and styles

In the context of theatre conventions, a 'norm' is a culturally governed criterion for determining and explaining the preference for a specific convention for the fulfillment of a specific function, out of a set of possible conventions that can fulfill the same function. Such a norm also underlies the preference of a group of conventions, fulfilling different functions, which reveal a kind of affinity among them; e.g., the conventions of classic theatre. Such a preference derives from a broader aesthetic approach that becomes a trend in the context of a specific culture or period (cf. Ross; and Burns: 28); e.g., a preference for the confidant convention for the formulation of the inner thoughts and feelings of a character in classicist drama. A norm also explains the creation of new conventions for functions already fulfilled by established ones; e.g., the invention of the 'confession' of an interactive character in front of another such a character in naturalist theatre, instead of soliloquy, particularly in Chekhov's drama. It is possible, therefore, to characterize a specific style according to its underlying norm and the set of conventions it promotes.

The *in absentia* links between conventions that can fulfil the same function and the *in praesentia* links among conventions that fulfil different functions explains the possibility of adaptations of works from one stylistic practice to another; e.g., Corneille's translation of Euripides' *Medea*. Such a possibility is usually taken into consideration when basing a new production on a dated play-script.

Theatre styles form a continuum from an extreme degree of implementation of the principle of similarity, on both the imagistic and material levels, to an extreme degree of conventionalization; e.g., from naturalism to constructivism in set design. Directors may opt for disguising conventions to various extents, but in principle they cannot abstain from them.

5

Acting:
The Quintessence of Theatre

Traditional theatre semiotics has ignored a fundamental question: what is the mechanism through which a performance-text refers and describes a fictional world? 'Description' implies 'reference', a notion that has also been neglected. Theatre complicates the question due to the extension of the principle of similarity to the material level, which may produce the impression that what happens on stage *is* the fictional world, despite contradicting the notions of 'text' and 'description'. Even if such an impression is erroneous and discarded, no serious attempt to explain this peculiar mechanism of description and reference has as yet been made.

This descriptive mechanism is anchored in the nature of stage 'acting', which seemingly presupposes two contradicting properties: (a) actors perform indexes of qualities, states or actions that by definition refer to those who perform them; and (b) these indexes are expected to be read by spectators as indexes of characters. The question should, therefore, be reformulated: How are indexes performed by actors transmuted into indexes attributed to characters? I suggest that this is given an explanation by the principle of 'deflection of reference' (Rozik, 2002b).

This chapter aims at showing that (a) 'acting', in the sense of *'deflection of reference' is the fundamental principle of theatre*; (b) *deflection of reference makes possible the description of fictional entities*; (c) *deflection of reference characterizes both human and non-human acting*; (c) *the triadic distinction actor/text/character is more appropriate than the usual dyadic distinction actor/character*; (d) *the mediation of a performance-text creates two existential gaps: between the enacting mechanism and the text, and between the text and the enacted fictional world*; and (e) *whereas the affinity between theatre and other dramatic arts is fundamental, the similarity between it and other performative arts, based on bodily experience, is marginal.*

Deflection of reference

Iconic sentences and icons couple immaterial images, which otherwise cannot be communicated, with material carriers. Whereas in most iconic media such material carriers have nothing in common with the real models of their images, typical theatrical sentences/icons are characterized by similarity on both the imagistic and material levels. This principle obviously applies to human actors, because they usually imprint human images on their own bodies. Whereas in most iconic media lack of similarity on the material level underscores the significative and communicative function of iconicity, e.g., puppet theatre, design and sculpture, in theatre the extension of the principle of similarity to the imprinting matter may make its iconic sentences/icons identical to their models, thus blurring their semiotic nature. Furthermore, in enacting an action, actors imprint images of acts; i.e., reproduce indexes of actions that, by virtue of the aforementioned principle, may not differ from real indexes. This may contribute to the fallacy of identifying what happens on stage with the fictional world. I maintain that this possible mistake is dispelled by the principle of 'deflection of reference'.

A performance-text is a set of imprinted images that usually describes a fictional interaction. A description presupposes a referent; i.e., an object of description. Such a referent is represented by a subject, which reflects a reading on the holistic level, and is thus established as the object of description. The descriptive function is fulfilled by the predicate, whose function is categorization of the referent, its changing aspects in particular. Actors describe a fictional interaction by enacting indexes of characters and their actions.

The problem is that, in principle, indexes only refer to those who perform them, i.e., are equivalent to 'I' sentences, and actors are supposed to perform indexes that refer to entities other than themselves, i.e., to characters, which supposedly perform them. In other words, somehow actors deflect reference to characters. *The mechanism of 'deflection of reference' is made possible by performing iconic indexes that, on the level of the iconic sentence, fulfill two distinct functions: subject and predicate.* The set of unchanging imprinted images of indexes aims at singling out a human entity, which assumedly performs such indexes, other than the actor (subject signs). Subject indexes describe a character, distinct from the actor, as an unchanging entity throughout a performance. Although mask or make up can fulfill this function, even enacted idiosyncratic physical or behavioral qualities of an actor may do as well. The set of changing imprinted images of indexes aims at describing the singled out character, mainly in its interaction on the time axis, and thus perceived as its acts (predicate signs). The moment such enacted indexes are attributed to a character they recover their self-referential nature; e.g., an actor that employs a costume, make-up and a slight limp to indicate that he is enacting Harpagon (subject signs), while performing interchanging acts and gestures that indicate his share in the action (predicate signs). *'Deflection of reference' applies, therefore, to the mechanism that enables actors to iconically describe fictional entities, thus making possible the description of fictional a fictional world.* Moreover, it is an evocative device; i.e., an inversion of the process of reference, because the description itself creates the referents in the spectator's imagination through the evocative power of the performance-text.

'Deflection of reference' thus explains the transition from a descriptive iconic text to a described fictional world, and establishes *'acting' as the basic mechanism of theatre description*: (a) an actor performs an apparent index – equivalent to an 'I' sentence – because indexes are predicated only on their performers; e.g., 'an actor is smiling'; (b) since the actor is perceived as operating an iconic medium, such an imprinted image is interpreted as a 's/he' sentence; i.e., as a description of another entity, either real or fictional; e.g., 'an actor describes a character that is smiling'; and (c) the moment such an imprinted image is attributed to a character it resumes its indexical nature, as if it were performed by it, becoming a genuine 'I' sentence; e.g., 'the character is smiling'.

This principle equally applies to verbal and non-verbal acts, in the sense of indexes of actions: actors perform images of such acts by imprinting them on their own bodies, i.e., by uttering the words of speech acts in their own voices and performing concomitant bodily indicators, while deflecting reference to a character; e.g.:

An actor performs an act: 'I promise you that "p".' (*apparent index*)

A text describes an act: 's/he promises him that "p".' (*deflection of reference*)

A character performs an act: 'I promise you that "p".' (*genuine index*)

Because of its iconic and descriptive nature, an actor does perform the semblance of an act, while not intending to perform the indicated action. In contrast, a character is supposed to actually perform such an action (chapter 1). Since a speech act also includes deictic elements, their reference too is deflected to a character, so that the 'I', 'you', 'here' and 'now' are also referred to the fictional circumstances of a fictional interaction; e.g., when an actor says 'now', it is the 'now' of the character.

Deflection of reference also characterizes the function of children and animals on stage. This principle applies even if their behavior is not entirely subordinated to the textual intent; e.g., an animal may urinate in the midst of a melodramatic scene and give rise to laughter (in contrast to States: 32). Moreover, like other real objects on stage, children and animals are not meant to be exhibited for themselves, but for enacting similar children and animals in a fictional world. In this sense a child or animal on stage should be conceived of as an actor that imprints an image of a child or animal on his or its own body, and deflects reference to a fictional child or animal.

Deflection of reference also applies to verbal descriptions, embedded in speech acts, which refer to characters whether enacted on stage or not; i.e., they are not perceived as indexes of the actors on stage, despite uttering them, but of characters in a fictional world. Moreover, verbal descriptions and enacting objects on stage co-describe and co-refer to fictional entities. For example, when Trigorin notices the dead seagull at Nina's feet and says: 'What a beautiful bird!', the adjective 'beautiful' refers to the fictional seagull and not to its actual embodiment on stage (Chekhov: 151). Similarly, whatever enacts the seagull – a stuffed seagull, a puppet or other – also refers to the fictional seagull.

Deflection of reference also applies to medium conventions (chapter 4). While the theatre medium typically applies the principle of similarity to the imprinted matter (e.g., the image of a window is usually imprinted on real glass and wood or iron), the contribution of such an image imprinted on a different matter (e.g., such as paint on canvas) to the meaning of a performance-text is the same. Despite difference, both imprinted images equally enact a fictional window, thus materializing the principle of 'deflection of reference'.

Deflection of reference also applies to the time and the place of a performance. Real time enacts fictional time and real place enacts fictional place (Rozik, 1994e: 87–9).

Deflection of reference does not contradict self-reference. The very same indexes performed by actors on stage also function as indexes of their own acting, for which they are eventually applauded or criticized. Furthermore, these indexes connect them to their professional and private personalities, as referred in terms of 'ghosting' by Carlson (2004). In other words, in acting the very same behavior on stage constitutes both indexes of the characters they enact, by deflection of reference, and indexes of the actors themselves (self-reference). This stands in contrast to the performance of pure 'actuals' (Schechner: 35–67), which are only self-referential.

Is it possible for a theatre performance-text not to describe characters by deflecting reference to them? The answer is negative by definition. Alfred Nordmann argues that, in the production of Peter Handke's *The Hour We Knew Nothing of Each Other*, director Hartmut Wickert took up the playwright's challenge to actors not to enact characters. This claim, however, is grounded on a narrow definition of 'character', which is betrayed by Nordmann's own naturalistic presuppositions: 'there is no before and after, the characters are not coming from nor are they going anywhere, they have no biography or destiny' (1997: 42); and '[b]efore a character can develop or grow, the actor already shifts to another character' (*ibid.*: 44). In fact, the entire performance-text presents actors crossing the stage (probably enacting a city square), one by one or in small groups, each time enacting different people, in various attires, ignoring each other or just making formal friendly gestures. These images do not contradict the claim that these actors describe fictional entities, different from themselves. Furthermore, the mere fact that each actor enacts different fictional entities, stresses their being enacted characters. The use of an actor to enact various characters in the same performance-text is common practice. Even the shallow characterization of these characters does not impinge on their fictional nature. Nordmann presupposes a naturalistic style, while ignoring most chapters in theatre history. His claim that this text creates a meeting place for actors and spectators without mediation of characters, therefore, is ungrounded. Deflection of reference takes place even on such minimal grounds.

Expanded notions of 'actor', 'text' and 'character'

Deflection of reference also applies to inanimate objects on stage, whether real or intentionally produced for a production (chapter 1). Performers of such objects also imprint images of particular objects on matter similar to their real models (chapter 1). For example, a carpenter imprints the image of a bench on a typical matter, such as wood or iron; a costume maker imprints the image of a costume on real fabric; and a light operator imprints the image of sunlight on artificial light. However, despite extreme similarity such objects do not refer to themselves, but enact objects in a described (usually fictional) world, i.e., deflect reference to them. In principle, therefore, the term 'actor' may be employed also for a performer of such an imprinted image, because of fulfilling exactly the same imprinting function as a human actor, the term 'text' for such an object on stage, and the term 'character' for the evoked fictional object.

As suggested above, the use of real objects on stage may pose a problem. Following Veltrusky, Elam speaks in terms of 'semiotization of the object' (pp. 8 & 20), in the sense of real objects dropping their practical function and assuming a descriptive and communicative function (cf. Bogatyrev, 1986a: 35–6; cf. Veltrusky, 1964: 83ff & Brušák: 62). In contrast, I have claimed that such a real object can be deconstructed into image and matter, becoming thereby structurally similar to an icon purposefully made for a stage (chapter 1). For example, even an antique table, contemporary of Molière, used in a modern production of *Tartuffe*, enacts such a table in the fictional world. Whatever the explanation even a real table on stage describes and deflects reference to a fictional table. Even Molière himself, enacting Molière in *L'Impromptu de Versailles*, materialized the same principle, because he enacted a fictionalized Molière.

It may be argued that if a real table is put on stage, the attitude of the spectator would not be one of reading, but of recognition and categorization; i.e., it would be considered as a real table and not as a description. This is in fact the meaning of 'ostension' in Umberto Eco's terminology. His example of ostension is a drunk in a Salvation Army parade:

> What is our drunken man referring back to? To a drunken man. But not to the drunk who he is, but to a drunk. The present drunk – insofar as he is a member of a class – is referring back to the class of which he is a member. He stands for the category he belongs to. There is no difference, in principle, between our intoxicated character and the word 'drunk'. [. . .] Ostension is one of the various ways of signifying, consisting in de-realizing a given object in order to make it stand for an entire class. But ostension is, at the same time, the most basic instance of performance. (p. 110)

Eco considers ostension, therefore, as the principle underlying acting. Ostension, however, is indexical and self-referential and, therefore, contradicts the principle of deflection of reference. Eco's 'drunk' does not enact a (fictional) drunk but, because he refers to himself, he also represents and refers metonymically to the entire set of (real) drunks, and to (real) drunkenness in general. Although Eco is aware that his drunk is a case of stage metonymy (p. 116), on the grounds of *pars pro toto*, metonymy cannot explain acting. An actor is not expected to be drunk while enacting a drunk. Furthermore, even if a drunken actor enacts a fictional drunk, the principle of deflection of reference still materializes.

There is nonetheless a substantial difference between human actors and makers of stage objects, who also fulfil the imprinting function of acting. While actors perform interchanging iconic acts through actually inscribing them on their own bodies in front of audiences, stage objects are put on stage and remain unchanged throughout the performance and dissociated from their makers who usually stay offstage. While designers are mentioned in programs, makers of stage objects are usually not. Directors may decide to lay bare the production mechanism of signs, for aesthetic reasons, and make the performers appear on stage, but usually they do not. Such objects too may change during a performance, but again these changes depend on the abilities of their makers. Moreover, due to dissociation, such icons emphasize the distinction between performer of text (enacting function) and text (describing function).

Since by definition a character cannot be on stage, the ultimate implication of 'acting' is that the necessary and sufficient condition of theatre is the existence of an imprinted text, in the wide sense of everything on stage that enacts a fictional entity. The 'enacting' function, in the sense of referring to and describing a fictional world, is thus the common denominator of human actors, animals, and objects on stage.Consequently, the co-presence of a performer of signs and the material existence of a text on stage, as in human acting, is not a necessary condition of theatre. In principle, coexistence only happens in human acting, which is a *sui generis* kind of acting that derives from the property of the human body as a medium for imprinting imagistic texts.

Since 'acting' means inscribing an iconic description of a (usually fictional) entity on matter, and deflection of reference to it, the implication is that instead of the usual dyadic model of 'actor/character', *the triadic model 'actor/text/character' is more adequate*: (a) 'actor', the human or other entity that performs a descriptive text by inscribing a set of images on matter; (b) 'text', the set of imprinted images describing a set of human or other fictional entities; and (c) 'character', the fictional entity evoked in the imagination of the spectator. In a late contribution, Veltrusky already suggests such a triadic distinction: actor, stage figure and character (1981: 232; cf. Carlson, 1994: 111). The relationship between actors and characters is thus mediated by descriptive performance-texts, which are inscribed on the bodies of such performers.

Existential gaps between text and two worlds

In terms of the theory of possible worlds, *the triadic distinction actor/text/character implies two existential gaps: first, between a descriptive performance-text and actors (in the wide sense) as both performers of descriptions of fictional entities and denizens of the real world (W_0); and second, between such a text and characters (in the wide sense) as both fictional referents of textual descriptions and denizens of a fictional world (W_1).* These gaps are inherent in any description of a world generated by any language/medium in regard to both the real world that generates it and the real or fictional world that it describes. This twofold gap deserves detailed attention.

'Acting' implies a clear distinction between 'enacting an action' and 'a textual action'. 'Enacting an action' is a real action in the real world (W_0). It reflects the intention of performing not the indicated action, but a description of a fictional act; e.g., an actor who performs an act of promise. In contrast, a 'textual act' is an imprinted image of an act that reflects the intention of describing and evoking associatively the indicated action in the spectators' minds; i.e., there is no pretension of performing an action, but a genuine act of description through an evocative textual act. Such an act deflects reference to an act/action in a fictional world; e.g., an imprinted image of an act of promise that evokes both a fictional act and a fictional action of promise.

The claim that a fictional world is the immediate referent of a theatre text stands in contrast to the commonplace assumption that what actually happens on stage is a fictional world. However, actors do not create fictional worlds on stage, but produce texts, i.e., iconic descriptions imprinted on their own bodies, capable of conjuring up fictional worlds in the spectators' imaginations. If indeed, what is present and happens on stage is a text or, rather, a description of a world (W_0), it follows that there is an existential gap between such a description and the described world (W_1). This gap is best indicated, first, by the lack of correspondence between what is present and happens on stage and what is supposed to be and happen in a fictional world, which is most conspicuous for stage conventions; e.g., an actor using a flesh-colored leotard to enact nakedness does not indicate that the described character is not actually naked. Even 'illusionist' styles of theatre employ conventions, and maintain such a non-correspondence. Second, this gap is also indicated by the fact that verbal descriptions refer not to their correlate objects on stage, but to their correlate objects in a fictional world; e.g., an actor may relate to a wooden sword on stage in terms of 'steel', without the sentence necessarily being false. Moreover, by convention, even a wooden sword is not a false iconic description of a fictional steel sword either. In both cases the fictional world is the direct referent of such descriptions.

The existential gap between stage reality and fictional world derives from the very fact that the former is a description employing a cultural medium, whereas the latter is only imagined to be a world. The apparent reality of the stage derives not from being a world, but from the iconic nature of the theatre text, which is a structured compound of images imprinted on real materials. In contrast, the fictional existence of the characters derives from the evocative nature of theatre descriptions.

A commonplace fallacy in understanding 'iconicity' is that a performance-text aims at an 'imitation' of reality, which is not a necessary implication of this principle. 'Iconicity' means that a medium, based on imprinted images of models, is employed for describing worlds, and that in reading an iconic text the spectator is expected to rely on elements of similarity to real or mental models. Therefore, there is no necessary commitment to the effect that the described world be similar to any extent to the real world. Indeed, there are fictional worlds that are strikingly dissimilar to the real world, as in science fiction. Furthermore, since the performance-text is a description and not a world, the claim that theatre aims at an illusion of reality is ungrounded. The theatregoer should perceive, as he actually does even intuitively, that what happens on stage is not a world.

The synchronic experience of the enacting and enacted worlds, mediated by a performance-text, emphasizes the autonomy of theatre as an art, in contrast to non-initiated audiences who may blur the boundaries between the real world (W_0) and a fictional world (W_1). Indeed, for the initiated spectator this sense of duality underlies every theatre experience, and is felt whether it is made prominent or blurred. The experience of human or otherwise actors enacting fictional entities underlies the insight, not necessarily conscious, that it is an artifact, purposefully produced to be read, interpreted and experienced.

Performance analysis should, therefore, focus not on the inscribing function of actors, but on the inscribed text; i.e., on the textual function of bodies and objects on stage or, rather, on the textual mechanisms of generating meaning that presuppose the interaction between text and spectator.

The fundamental gap between real action and enacting action

Some theories stress the possible analogy between performing a real action and enacting an action, due to their shared performativity in the real world. In English this analogy is even fostered by language: the morpheme 'act' is employed for real 'action' and 'interaction', for 'acting' and 'enacting an action', and for fictional 'action'. This trend is prominent in Erving Goffman's theory, particularly as interpreted by Richard Schechner (1988: 166). Goffman, whose interest lies not in theatre, but in social mechanisms of interaction from a sociological viewpoint, uses a consistent analogy to theatre for describing a typical behavioral pattern in the self-presentation of people in front others: the promotion of their improved self-images (1959). In contrast, being a theoretician of theatre, Schechner relies on Goffman's theory to promote his all-inclusive category of 'performance', which comprehends traditional performative arts, performance art and even interaction in social life, while striving to *reintroduce* a ritual dimension into theatre in his directorial practice (pp. 187ff). Because of the wide appeal of these theories, I am compelled into the awkward position of having to make a distinction between phenomena that are obviously different.

First, despite both being real – whereas performing a real action is non-descriptive, and at most an object of description, i.e., is fundamentally indexical – enacting and action is both the performing of an act of description and a description of a fictional action; i.e., both indexical and iconic (chapter 2). Whereas a real act indicates an actual action, an iconic act is not meant to indicate an actual action, but to evoke a fictional action. It is not in the textual level, but on the fictional level that characters may or may not promote improved images of themselves in front of other characters. It is on this level, therefore, that a real act can be compared to a fictional act. In contrast, on the level of the performance-text, textual acts can only be compared to descriptions of fictional acts in literature or other iconic media.

Second, the ways real acts and textual acts refer to their respective worlds are fundamentally different. Being indexes, real acts present a double relationship of contiguity: first, an act is part of an action and indicates it on a part–whole basis, and second, an action is a reflection of its doer on the same grounds. The fundamental characteristic of 'self-presentation', to use Goffman's term, is that whatever is indicated by actual behavior, whether true or false, is predicated on the presenter him/herself; i.e., it is self-referential and, therefore, equivalent to an 'I' sentence. In contrast, in enacting acts, actors perform indexes that refer not only to themselves but also, by deflection of reference, to characters and, therefore, are equivalent to 's/he' sentences.

In enacting characters, primarily, actors do not engage in promoting self-images, but create descriptions of characters. Actors may concomitantly promote their own improved self-images, but this is done through the quality of their acting. Whereas self-reference may only promote self-images of real people, deflection of reference can only describe promotion of self-images of fictional entities. In contrast to a widely accepted view, actors are not 'impersonating', in Bentley's terms ('A *impersonates* B while C looks on' – p. 150; cf. & Eco: 115), or 'pretending' (cf. Searle, 1986: 65ff), but honestly employ their crafts and the underlying rules of their medium to the best of their capabilities to describe characters, which is their professional task. Indeed, people who impersonate or pretend imprint images that do not correspond to them, while intending that those be grasped as self-referential, are thought to be dishonest.

Third, it is not at all surprising that spectators may perceive an analogy between real acts and textual acts, because the latter are usually iconic replicas of the former (their models) on two levels, image and matter. This apparent analogy, however, reflects not the nature of the fictional world, but the nature of the theatre medium. Indeed, the extension of the principle of similarity to the imprinting matter is probably responsible for occasionally blurring the borderline between theatre and life. For example, street theatre may create the impression of a real social event, leaving people to wonder whether it is a real or an enacted situation. In street theatre, moreover, the stage, which should be seen as a domain marker of theatricality, is missing. Although bystanders may hesitate between these possible framings, once they are certain that they are observing an instance of theatre, their different attitude becomes evident: they allow themselves to apply the principle of acting or, rather, deflection of reference, and thus effectively read the event as a description of a fictional situation.

Experiencing the performers' bodies

Within the category of 'dramatic arts', theatre is 'performative' in the sense of producing an unmediated encounter between live actors and live spectators. It is such an encounter that produces the distinctive experience of theatre. No other dramatic art, such as cinema, TV drama, radio drama and puppet theatre, provides such an experience. Whereas imprinting images on matter is shared by all these media, the experience of concrete bodies only characterizes theatre, including opera.

On the other hand, such a bodily experience is shared with other performative arts, such as music, recitation, oral storytelling, and performance art in particular. However, among these arts, theatre is unique in iconically describing fictional worlds. Therefore, such a common denominator is even confusing: *whereas there is an umbilical kinship between theatre and other dramatic arts, such as cinema,* TV drama, radio drama and puppet theatre, there is no necessary affinity between theatre and the other performative arts. I contend, therefore, that *whereas the affinity between theatre and cinema is intrinsic, the similarity between theatre and other performative arts, based on bodily experience, is marginal.*

Whereas there is nothing to prevent performance artists from enacting fictionalized versions of themselves and occasionally enacting characters, i.e., from employing the theatre medium, acting is essential to theatre: only by imprinting images of human behavior on the actors' bodies, and deflection of reference to characters, is a theatre description of a world made possible; i.e., only by generating such descriptions does theatre exist. The performance-text is the use of the theatre medium for the purpose of art. This principle underlies the notion of 'theatricality' (Rozik, 2002b).

E. T. Kirby views an entire group of performers, such as ventriloquists, magicians, escape artists, sword swallowers, fire walkers, rope walkers, fire eaters, jugglers and acrobats as 'paratheatrical' artists, in the sense of sharing some essential features with actors (Kirby, 1974: 5–15 & 1975: 14ff). These artists perform their own skills in front of audiences, while seeking to command their admiration. None of them, however, engages in producing descriptions of fictional entities that are inscribed on their own bodies; i.e., in 'enacting' characters and deflecting reference to them. The exhibition of their skills is purportedly meant to project improved images of the performers themselves; i.e., to be indexical (self-referential). Actors may even enact such performers in a fictional world.

I agree with Schechner that such 'paratheatrical' artists are performers of actuals: 'Athletes, like circus performers, display their skills. The rules of games are designed to show prowess, quick judgment, finesse and grace, speed, endurance, strength and teamwork' (1988: 50). In other words, there is nothing in their displays beyond what is done and achieved: they do not describe anything. Furthermore, circus performers take pride in not being actors, while insisting on their performing real acts that impress spectators because of being beyond their own abilities (cf. Carmeli: 93–109). These acts reflect solely on their performers, and are praised or jeered accordingly. Consequently, they cannot be said to employ the theatre medium. Kirby also conceives of the shaman as the prototype of the actor. However, again, the shaman does not enact anyone else. Whatever he does is self-referential (to the shaman); and, even if the shaman's skills are attributed to a spirit, its alleged doings remain self-referential (to the spirit) (Rozik, 2002a: 69–89).

In contrast to Marinis (pp. 48ff), therefore, the broadening of the category of theatre to encompass both representational and nonrepresentational arts on performative grounds cannot be maintained: while creating a spurious affinity of theatre to other performing arts, it forsakes the genuine affinity to other dramatic arts, such as cinema and TV drama, which are not performative in the above sense, but engage in enacting characters. These arts are representational by definition.

In theatre, the main function of the actors' bodies is to perform and imprint texts on their own bodies. The beautiful body of an actress, a frequently used example, is definitely an index of herself, but is mainly subordinated, on iconic grounds, to the stage image that she is meant to convey and to the fictional character she is meant to describe. Although there is a limit to the application of this principle, and it is difficult to stretch it beyond a certain point, the boundary is marked by what can be assimilated by a 'character'. Beyond that it is a matter of convention, which does not contradict the principle of deflection of reference.

On the grounds of an expanded notion of 'acting', which also applies to non-human objects on stage, *the fundamental principle of theatre is not the presence of the human body on stage, despite being typical of theatre, but the principle of acting, in the sense of describing fictional worlds through images imprinted on real matter similar to their models, and deflection of reference.* This conclusion by no means implies that human actors are relegated to a secondary rank and that their bodies have no additional functions (chapter 12). The concrete materiality of all these imprinted images may be experienced by non-initiated spectators as if they constitute a world, but this contradicts the descriptive nature of the performance-text.

6

The Theatrical Nature of the Play-script

In the course of the last century, in striving to create the new discipline of theatre research and clearly distinguish it from literary research, theatre scholars have evinced a strong tendency to renounce play-script analysis. By doing so, they sustained the commonplace fallacy of seeing play-scripting as a specific form of literary creativity. I suggest, in contrast, that play analysis should not only be reintegrated into theatre research, but also be perceived as one of its cornerstones, of performance analysis in particular. The question is under what conditions and for what aims.

A play-script is definitely a text, but not a literary text. First, it would appear that similarly to a novel or short story it is a description of a fictional world by verbal means. However, it is in fact a kind of score of a particular constituent for a more complex text generated by the theatre medium: the theatre performance-text. In other words, despite being formulated in a language, a play-script presupposes its possible performance. Second, in contrast to the performance-text, the play-script is a deficient text: it is only a notation of the verbal components of the eventual dialogue, lacking all the additional non-verbal components necessary to disambiguate its component speech acts. Deficiency thus characterizes the play-script as a *sui generis* kind of theatre text.

Despite deficiency, therefore, play-scripts should be viewed as genuine objects of theatre research. Since the fictional world is the main mechanism through which an author affects an audience, it can be claimed that, in creating even a deficient description, a playwright already has in mind not only an image of its possible performance, but also an idea of the nature of such a world and its possible impact on a synchronic audience. It is this virtual performance that, in reintegrating play analysis, should be conceived of as a major object of theatre research. Therefore, taking into account deficiency, play analysis should speculate on the following: (a) the nature of the descriptive (verbal) apparatus; (b) the possible nature of its described fictional world; and (c) the kind of expected effect on its synchronic audience.

This chapter aims at showing that (a) *the play-script is a deficient text generated by the theatre medium*; (b) *the play-script is not only a design of the verbal components of a performance-text, but also reflects the intention of creating a full description of a fictional world for a synchronic audience*; (c) *due to its deficiency the play-script requires directorial interpretation*; (d) *the typical relationship between performance-text and play-script is one of intertextuality*; (e) *departures from an established interpretation of a play-script are major clues to the appropriate hermeneutic interpretation of a performance-text*; and (f) *play-scripts are, therefore, genuine objects of theatre research.*

Two kinds of theatre texts

From a semiotic viewpoint, despite significant differences, play-script and performance-text share the property of 'text'. I suggest the following working definition of 'text': the whole set of structured sentences/icons that an addressee is meant to read, interpret and experience. Both play-script and performance-text are definitely descriptions of fictional worlds; i.e., artifacts that employ semiotic units and syntactic rules of at least one system of signification and communication for the purpose of describing a world.

The fact that both play-script and performance-text are descriptions of (usually fictional) worlds means that, in addition to their specific language or medium, they are further organized by a set of poetic rules. Moreover, the notion of 'description' implies that, like a performance-text, there is an existential gap between a play-script and the fictional world it refers to and describes.

Against the background of sharing the property of theatre-text and the function of describing fictional worlds, it would appear that the main difference between play-script and performance-text lies in the use of different systems of signification and communication, language vs. theatre medium; i.e., whereas the play-script exclusively employs language for its dialogue and stage directions, the performance-text is generated by the theatre medium, which includes verbal and non-verbal means. Instead, I contend that albeit partially, a play-script too is generated by the theatre medium on the following grounds: dialogue is not a verbal phenomenon, and cannot be conducted solely on the verbal level, because it is not an exchange of verbal descriptions, but an exchange of act/actions; i.e., a kind of interaction (chapter 2; cf. Dijk, 1977). Unless all its concurrent non-verbal elements are taken into account, a verbal sentence spoken by a character is ambiguous; i.e., the very same verbal sentence may acquire different meanings or, rather, be used for different actions, depending on intention and/or purposes (Austin: 67–82); i.e., a verbal sentence is only the perceptible part of a speech act. Such a speech act can be disambiguated only by concomitant non-verbal indicators (cf. Austin: 76; Lyons, 1988: 743). This entails that these indicators actually determine the kind of action indicated by a speech act. Since a play-script features dialogue as a set of ambiguous sentences, there is no point in viewing it as a verbal text. It is more sensible to see it as a partial notation of a full dialogue in a possible performance-text. Play-scripts should be seen, therefore, like performance-texts, as being generated by the same medium. This is even more conspicuous in their reflection of contemporary stage conventions (Rozik, 1998d).

In literary works disambiguation of speech acts is achieved by additional verbal descriptions of non-verbal indicators. In a performance-text, in contrast, each imprinted image of a verbal sentence is set in the context of explicit non-verbal indicators of intention, such as intonation, facial expression, body gesture and hand gesture. It is the configuration of all these that determines the kind of action that is performed by each verbal sentence, to such an extent that, in principle, a fictional speech act is basically not different from the performative use of language in real life. In contrast to both, the play-script typically notates only the verbal components of dialogue, while presupposing the eventual (non-verbal) fullness of the performance-text. This is the main reason for asserting that *the play-script is a deficient text*. In this sense a play-script is not a piece of literature, not even a borderline case in Ingarden's sense (pp. 317ff), despite its use of language, but a deficient theatre text. It should be conceived of, therefore, as an ineffective attempt at notation of a dialogue in a medium that, although easily available, is inherently inadequate. This ineffective notation should nonetheless be granted the glory of preserving a substantial part of humanity's cultural heritage.

Stage directions may disambiguate speech acts, but these are usually scanty and do not necessarily refer to the non-verbal aspects of a dialogue. In general, stage directions are instructions for performing the non-verbal components of a theatrical production, addressed to a performer team; e.g., designers, makers, operators, directors and actors (cf. Ingarden: 377). These are further indications that playwrights have performance-texts in mind. If the scripted dialogue is viewed as a set of instructions to actors and directors ('directives' in Searle's terms: 1986: 13ff) about what should be said, how and in what order, the notion of playwrighting as scripting a virtual performance-text is reinforced. The fact that directors often disregard stage directions is an additional indication of their 'directive' status. Although Searle's analogy of a play-script to a recipe for baking a cake is quite offensive, there is a pragmatic truth in it (1986: 70).

A play-script is usually written having in mind the typical style of its contemporary theatre, which also supports the claim that it is a set of instructions. This is very clear in regard to theatre conventions; e.g., playwrights in ancient Greece wrote their play-scripts having in mind the presence and performance of a chorus, and naturalistic playwrights having in mind the self-imposed need to disguise conventions as much as possible. In this respect, the difference between play-script and performance-text lies in that while the former presupposes a set of theatre conventions, the latter is free to either implement or change them. Since such conventions depend on contemporary artistic trends, in using existing play-scripts directors tend to update their means of description and, in particular, to employ conventions more akin to contemporary norms (chapter 5). Consequently, a play-script should be conceived of as a design-text, in the sense of a set of instructions for its possible production, which presupposes a contemporary stage dialect and a synchronous audience; in short, as a script. The performance-text is, therefore, the only genuine and full description of a (fictional) world by means of the theatre medium, which is addressed to the spectator for reading, interpreting and experiencing. Only the performance-text is a self-sufficient text.

'Self-sufficiency' does not mean that a performance-text provides full information on all the aspects of a fictional world. No fictional text does so. It is not a matter of filling all the 'gaps' ('spots of indeterminacy') of a play-script through stage concretizations, in Ingarden's spirit (pp. 246–54): a self-sufficient text features all the clues needed for spectators' to provide all the expected associations through hermeneutic interpretation and psychical mechanism of experience. Whereas a director may either remove certain gaps or not, spectators must always complement a text from their own resources. A fictional world should be constructed by spectators from what actually exists in a performance-text. What is not determined by a director should not be of their concern (cf. Knights). The problem is that the intrinsic deficiency of the play-script precludes interpretation and experience on firm grounds.

The literary fallacy

The literary fallacy lies in the assumption that a play-script is a full verbal text, which includes all the necessary elements for the description of a fictional world, like a genuine literary text. Indeed, in literary theory, various approaches have been developed whose main aim is to reveal and explain the rules that enable competent hermeneutic interpretation of a play-script. Although the critique of such theories is not of our concern here, some of them are quite sophisticated (e.g., Ricoeur, Foucault and Gadamer). According to this approach, it is a reader who is supposed to engage in interpreting a play-script. However, while a reader of a novel is provided with all the clues needed for its adequate interpretation, and is given ample latitude that allows for personal readings, the reader of a play-script is extremely restricted, because crucial non-verbal clues are missing. *The claim that play-scripts are deficient texts generated by the theatre medium thus characterizes the theatrical approach and distinguishes it from the literary approach.*

Ingarden views drama as a borderline case of literature. He distinguishes between 'main text' (*Haupttext*) and 'side text' (*Nebentext*) (pp. 319 & 377). 'The main text of the stage-play consists of the words spoken by the represented persons [characters], while the stage directions consist of information given by the author for the production of the work' (p. 377). In other words, the main text consists of the verbal elements of dialogue and the side text of the stage directions. Therefore, '[w]hen the work is performed on stage' the stage directions 'are totally eliminated' and in their place 'another medium of representation' is used (*ibid.*). Ingarden incorrectly implies that whereas the performed dialogue preserves its verbal nature, only stage directions are translated into non-verbal means. However, he is also aware that in theatre dialogue is transferred to actors to enact, and language is used not in its descriptive but in its interactive capacity. However, this implies that actors cannot avoid enacting non-verbal indicators for disambiguation of verbal acts (chapter 2). In other words, Ingarden ignores the fact that the entire play-script is transposed into a non-verbal medium, which contrasts his dictum that drama is a borderline case of literature.

Only under the assumption that the verbal elements of a dialogue are perceived in the context of all their concomitant non-verbal elements, i.e., only under conditions of actual performance, can a play-script become univocal. It can be claimed, therefore, that at most, in analyzing play-scripts literature scholars analyze their own mental performances, under the erroneous assumption that these are the only possible performance-texts that specific play-scripts can generate. In contrast, it should be assumed that, due to its inherent ambiguity, the very same play-script *must* generate different performance-texts, reflecting what I have termed elsewhere the 'creative interpretation' of directors (Rozik, 2000a), as indeed happens in theatre practice.

In contrast, States contends:

> In one respect, a play read and enacted in the mind's eye is more 'real' than one seen on stage [. . .] in the sense of its springing to an imagined actuality.

Whereas a theatrical presentation of the text is precisely marked by the limits of artifice: the frontal rigidity of our view, the positional determination of everything on stage, the condensation of Macbeth [the character] into a real form, the fact that the play has already passed through the screen of an interpretation by directors and actors. (p. 28)

In terms of this study, States sees the human imagination as feeding on the indeterminacy of the play-script. He not only acknowledges that 'what literary critics study so assiduously is their own dreamed text of the play' (*ibid.*), but also lends legitimization to it. He overlooks, however, that while literary works are self-sufficient descriptions of fictional worlds, albeit by other means, play-scripts are not. In practice directors proceed from the textual indeterminacy of a play-script to the determinacy of a performance-text. They do so for a good reason: it is virtually impossible for spectators to react to a deficient text, except for free mental interpretations of their own. A certain performance-text may deliberately remain ambiguous for activating the audience's participation; but intentional ambiguity is a form of determinacy, which is usually not the case in theatre. Due to the indeterminacy of play-scripts, theatre's preference for unambiguous performance-texts implies that different stage interpretations are equally valid. States' approach reflects a personal value judgment unsupported by actual theatre practice. A preference for play-scripts does not change their deficient nature.

In contrast to the deficiency of play-scripts, performances – which are the genuine theatre texts – are full texts, to a degree similar to that presupposed for a literary work. They can therefore be seen as maintaining a reasonable equilibrium between textual clues and spectators' complementation.

Play-script analysis

Because of the deficiency of a play-script, it would appear that play analysis is a hopeless and even futile undertaking. However, it is not only a partial design and a set of instructions for a possible performance. In most cases it reflects a playwright's intention to create a definite and complete description of a fictional world, especially when the verbal component is of crucial importance. Since the fictional world is the main mechanism through which an author affects an audience, it can be claimed that, *in creating even a deficient description of such a world, a playwright already has in mind not only an image of its possible performance, but also an idea of the nature of a fictional world and its plausible impact on a synchronic audience.* Moreover, a play-script also reflects the typical stage dialect (style) of a contemporary theatre, such as conventions and functional characters (cf. Arnott: 5ff), and presupposes the cultural competences and psychological mechanisms of response of an expected synchronic audience. Therefore, engaging in play analysis only for its potential synchronic audience does make sense. Any attempt to analyze a play-script for any possible readership/audience, under conditions of cultural change, would be absurd.

Not all play-scripts are incomplete to the same extent. In some styles of playwriting, play-scripts feature more information than what could have been anticipated on theoretical grounds. Furthermore, complementation on condition of contextual coherence is a vital factor in determining the reading of such texts.

Play analysis can have at least three appropriate aims: (a) to understand the mechanisms of generating meaning through the partial notation through language, which is subordinated to its potential performance; (b) to conjecture a playwright's original design, particularly the nature of a specific fictional world on the poetic, aesthetic and rhetoric levels; and (c) to speculate on the possible effects of such a fictional world on a synchronic audience within its socio-cultural context. On all these levels the deficiency of play-scripts plays a crucial role. This incompleteness undermines any serious effort to capture the exact nature of an original fictional world and its possible impact on a synchronic audience. One can never be absolutely sure about any conclusions. In comparison to both performance-texts and literary works, there is an essential gap between them as full texts and a deficient play-script, beyond the degree of interpretive latitude they may allow.

These claims stand in overt contradiction to the deep-rooted tradition that considers interpretation of play-scripts as being done on firm grounds. This tradition does not preclude directors' efforts to create innovative performance-texts based on play-scripts, written in other cultures, reflecting thereby their indeterminacy. On the other hand, the efforts invested in understanding play-scripts are more than justified, because for most periods in theatre history play-scripts are the only primary sources left. Such efforts yield invaluable information and give the opportunity to glimpse at insights of playwrights of bygone cultures. In principle, *the fundamental indeterminacy of play-scripts not only facilitates directorial creative interpretation but, in fact, necessitates it*. Directorial interpretation not only transforms a deficient text into a full text, but also enables the recycling of dated texts for the purpose of expressing new visions. Chapter 10 expands on this principle.

Intertextual relations between performance-text and play-script

Several theories have been suggested on the relationship between performance-text and play-script. Following Veltrusky, for example, Übersfeld suggests a dialectical relationship between 'text' (play-script) and 'performance' (performance-text). In her view, the text is present within the performance, but can be read independently 'as if it were non-theatre' (p. 8); i.e., as if it was literature. They are conceived of as two distinct and even 'opposite' entities (p. 4), reflecting two different sign systems and, therefore, each should be analyzed on its own, by different tools (p. 5), as otherwise no relation can be established between them (p. 6): first, a theatre text [play-script] presents gaps that only a performance [performance-text] can fill in, while the latter bears the responsibility for doing so (p. 10); and second, 'within the theatrical text there are matrices of "performativity"' (p. 8), probably meaning that it contains or implies instructions as to how it is to be staged. Übersfeld thus views the play-script as a set of directives for the performing team to follow. These are of two kinds: they regard either what an actor should say (dialogue) or what non-verbal signs or objects actors or other performers should do on stage (*didascalia*) (p. 8ff). It is through these instructions that the play-script may determine the signs of a performance. On the other hand, she also argues that 'meaning in theatre does not exist before performance, before what is concretely said and shown; moreover it cannot exist without the spectator' (p. 192). However, Übersfeld is not aware that viewing the play-script as a set of instructions to be followed contradicts the alleged mutual independence of both play-script and performance-text and, therefore, the dialectical relationship between them. She thus establishes the primacy of the play-script and, therefore, her theory should be seen as an instance of the literary fallacy. In contrast, Pavis correctly advocates the predominance of the performance-text over the play-script, with the former lending specific meaning to the latter: 'The *mise-en-scène* is not the putting into practice of what is present in the text [play-script]. On the contrary, it is the speaking of the text in a given staging [. . .] that will confer on it a particular meaning' (1982: 18).

Another example: Pfister sees the performance-text against the background of literary fiction, and finds that its specific difference is the absence of 'the mediating communication system'; namely, dramatic texts 'lack the fictional narrator as an overriding point of orientation' (p. 5). This alleged handicap is compensated by 'access to non-verbal codes and channels which are able, in part, to take on the [missing] communicative functions' (p. 4). In other words, Pfister detects a qualitative difference between theatre and literature on the grounds not of their different media, as suggested above, but of the existence or lack of a fictional narrator; i.e., of deficiency in regard to literature. However, whereas there is equivalence between literary author and theatre director, a fictional narrator is not a necessary character even in fiction. In principle, the existence of a fictional narrator, different from the author, may create double dramatic irony (the director on a narrator; and the latter on characters), which is not a necessary condition of either literature or theatre. Pfister also overlooks productions that do feature fictional narrators; e.g., Lee Breuer's *The Gospel at Colonus* (1988) and the Garrick Theatre production of Brian Friel's *Dancing at Lughnasa* (1991). Moreover, he is not aware that non-verbal elements are not meant to and cannot compensate the author's or fictional narrator's ironic function; and that aspects of this missing function cannot 'be transferred to the internal communication system', namely, to dialogue within the fictional world (p. 4). These are functions on different structural levels. Furthermore, functional characters and fictional characters in functional situations (out of character) should be seen, not as an integral part of a fictional world, but as representing an author on stage, in the semblance of a character; i.e., as providing an ironic perspective on the fictional world (chapter 4). This entails that the authorial narrator of a fictional action is not missing, but represented differently. Consequently, although Pfister integrates elements of semiotic theories, his approach too is an offspring of the literary fallacy.

A few years before Übersfeld and Pfister's theories, Ingarden already suggested a more sensible approach. For him, 'the drama that is *read* cannot be identified in every respect with the one that is *staged*, i.e., with the "stage play"' (pp. 208 & 318ff). He thus introduced the notion of 'stage-play' for the intermediate phase between a 'play' (play-script) and the 'individual stage performance' (performance-text) (p. 318); and contrasted the stage play to both the play (as a piece of literature) and the individual performance, as a mixed text, which includes means other than language (pp. 318–23). In contrast, 'stage-play' should not be seen as a text, but as reflecting a directorial concept, a planning phase, mediating between the two kinds of text (play-script and performance-text); and as the matrix of all performance-texts generated by such a concept; i.e., what is currently and widely termed 'production'. In this sense this generative construct is meant to explain both the similarity among performance-texts generated by the same play-script and their differences. Moreover, Ingarden contends that it is not the play but the stage-play that lends unity to the entire set of individual performances, which derive from the same directorial concept.

He also claims that 'the stage play differs from a *purely* literary work [. . .] in that entirely new means of representation [. . .] appear in it' (p.

320). Moreover, the removal of indeterminacies is 'fully dependent on [. . .] the director's discretion' (p. 253). Ingarden explicitly argues that a stage play is not 'a realization of a corresponding purely literary work', but is a different kind of work (pp. 321–2), based on concrete determination of undetermined aspects in the play-script. The implication is that if such determinations depend on the directors' discretion, different determinations are possible, reflecting thereby the principle of creative interpretation. This is a sound argument. Chapter 10 expands on this matter.

Against the background of the fundamental difference between play-script and performance-text, I suggest that *the relationship between them should be examined in terms of 'intertextuality'; the former being the source-text and the latter the target-text*. Bearing in mind this principle, an analysis of the specific nature of their intertextual relationship should be carried out. Specific intertextual relations can be established only under the assumption of something in common. It would appear, however, that any kind of comparison between a play-script and a performance-text is precluded, due to the basic asymmetry between a deficient text, whose interpretation heavily depends on speculation, and a full text, whose interpretation rests on firmer grounds. I suggest, in contrast, that comparison is possible and even convenient, if some methodological precautions are taken.

In principle, each performance-text can be conceived of as correlated to a synchronic script (such as a director's stage book), whether such a script exists or not. Although a performance-text does not require the pre-existence of a play-script, it does presuppose a scripting phase: the crystallization of a concept and a plan, even in the schematic manner of a *Commedia dell' Arte* 'scenario'. Due to their extreme complexity, therefore, assumedly, all theatre performances are scripted (cf. Schechner: 68–105). Usually, such a script only partially overlaps a correlated play-script, because it integrates all the verbal and non-verbal components of a possible performance-text on a conceptual and planning level; what Ingarden termed a 'stage-play'.

Each play-script can also be thought of as correlated to a possible synchronic performance, whether there is documentation about it or not, and whether such an event took place or not. However, such correlated texts cannot always be seen as referring and describing the same (fictional) world. Two (fictional) worlds may be considered the same if the characterization of characters, the definition of situations and actions, the structure of the main action and the nature of interaction between performance-text and audience, are the same; a possible example is a play-script staged by its playwright. The problem is that directors, in principle, cannot be faithful to synchronic playwrights, due to the indeterminacy of play-scripts, not to mention diachronic productions of them. Directors necessarily attach specific qualities, intentions and purposes to acts, even when they try hard to be faithful to a play-script; even minor changes or additions generate distinct fictional worlds. This is evident in productions that professedly intend to be original; i.e., unfaithful. Even playwrights are not always faithful to their own designs; e.g., Samuel Beckett's production of *Waiting for Godot* at the Schiller Theatre, 1975 (Ben Zvi: 145).

Still, correlation is possible on the grounds of partial similarity, which from a methodological viewpoint can highlight specific intertextual mechanisms. A widespread form of correlation is the partial overlap of narratives; e.g., known mythical characters and their actions. Even adaptations fall into this category, because of preserving fictional elements to various extents. In such cases, intertextuality is based on the borrowing of preexisting characters and narratives or patterns of narratives; e.g., *Les Troyennes*, Sartre's adaptation of Euripides' *The Trojan Woman*, produced in 1965, after the end of the War in Algeria (1962). While the characters and their actions are the same, Sartre's play-script foregrounds the absurdity of colonial wars against the background of modern imperialism, in contrast to the source play-script that focuses on the absurdity of war against the background of current myths and religious beliefs (chapter 16).

In the typical form of correlation, shared by both a 'faithful' and 'creative' interpretations of a play-script, performance-texts preserve, if not all, at least most of the characters and their actions, including the verbal text; in some cases, they even implement some of the stage directions. *Against the background of partial similarity, and intertextual relations, departures from a play-script are reliable clues for revealing the nature of a specific fictional world described by a performance-text.*

The inherent ambiguity of the play-script requires the specification of the nature of a verbal interaction, and thus its creative interpretation. The implied directive of a play-script is to attribute specific qualities, intentions and purposes, reflected in the concomitant non-verbal indicators, to the ambiguous verbal and non-verbal acts. Moreover, due to the deficiency of a play-script, only departures from a certain hermeneutic interpretation can be detected, despite their speculative nature. Such departures may range from minor differences to the expression of a coherent innovative concept. Furthermore, not only changes in the perceptions of directors, but also in the perspectives of ever changing audiences, and the need to accommodate to their concerns and terms of reference, require and underlie such departures, as illustrated by the Habimah production of Sartre's *Les Troyennes* (chapter 15). 'Actualization' of play-scripts is the name of the game. *Play-scripts are not universal, but become universal by the constant creative reinterpretation of directors in different cultural circumstances.*

Departures from a source play-script may provide crucial clues to a directorial intention and purposes and to the specific meaning of a target performance-text. While spectators can perform such a comparison intuitively, on condition that they are familiar with at least a widely accepted interpretation of the source text, theatre scholars should perform it deliberately. Moreover, if the audience is familiar with the original play-script, as mediated by a culturally accepted interpretation, such an intertextual relation should be seen as an integral part of the performance-text, as if the latter is a complex allusion to the former; e.g., any production of Shakespeare's *Macbeth* for an English audience. Knowledge of the source play-text is a precondition for any intertextual relationship. Nonetheless, even if the audience is not familiar with the source-text, intertextual analysis is a valuable tool for the scholar.

This kind of intertextual relation between a performance-text and its source play-script is only a particular case of intertextual relationship reflecting creative interpretation; e.g., the intertextual relation between Trevor Nunn's production of *Macbeth*, Royal Shakespeare Company, 1978 (Nunn) and Shakespeare's *Macbeth* is analogous to that between the latter and Holinshed (Muir: 164–83), or between Ionesco's *Macbett* and Shakespeare's *Macbeth*.

Intertextual analysis for the purpose of singling out meaningful differences can also be applied to certain intertextual relations between two or more productions based on the same play-script, especially in cases where directors react to a previous paradigmatic production of it. Egil Törnquist clearly demonstrates the advantage of such a procedure by his multiple comparison of Nora's exit scene in six productions of Henrik Ibsen's *A Doll's House*, which presupposes both the intertextual nature of the relation between performance-text and play-script and among productions of it (pp. 156–64). The principle that, from the viewpoint of the spectators, effective intertextuality depends on the clarity of the allusions to the source-text and their previous knowledge of it, applies in this case as well. The fact that Törnquist analyzes theatre, cinema and video productions by the same tools reflects the correct intuition that there is no essential difference among these media in describing fictional worlds through actors imprinting human images on their own bodies.

It is indeed worthwhile engaging in play analysis despite the indeterminacy of play-scripts. Intertextual analysis presupposes that each text should be analyzed independently; i.e., the analysis of intertextual relations between a source play-script and a diachronic target performance-text should be based on previous separate synchronic analyses of them as theatre texts. It should be borne in mind that in some styles play-scripts are less deficient than in others. To conclude, *intertextual analysis reinforces the crucial importance of play analysis for theatre research.*

PART II

Additional Strata and Disciplines

The performance-text presupposes not only the role of the theatre medium in generating its meaning, which requires a semiotic approach, but also other structuring strata, which require additional poetic, aesthetic and rhetoric disciplines of research. In contrast to theatre semiotics, these disciplines are capable of explaining the poetic/aesthetic inner structure of the fictional world and the rhetoric outer structure on the level of relationship between performance-text and spectator. Part II is devoted to these additional strata and disciplines.

7

The Poetic Structure of the Fictional World

A performance-text is an integrated macro-unit composed of a describing text, generated by the theatre medium, and a described fictional world, fundamentally generated by poetics rules. These components can be distinguished from each other only through analysis. Whereas the describing text is a finite set of iconic sentences, structured only on the syntactic level, on the textual level the described world is structured by a set of poetic rules that lend a sense of unity and wholeness to a performance-text. A 'structure' is an abstract pattern of relations that organizes various functions underlying a unit of any extent. It is a kind of complex syntactic principle on the textual level.

The notion of 'structure' implies the notion of function, and *vice versa*, so that a whole fictional world is conceived of as a complex unit of organized functions. The notion of 'function' presupposes that different components may fulfill the same function, and the same component different functions. A structure determines the hierarchical contributions of its thematically specified functions, thus conferring specific meaning on them; i.e., the whole determines the meaning of its parts. It follows that *not only determining the exact function of each thematic component is vital to the interpretation of a whole performance-text, but also that this must be done in the context of at least an intuition of a fictional world's overall meaning and its possible impact on a spectator.*

It is widely assumed that, whereas play analysis should focus on the nature of a fictional world (characterization, action and structure of action), performance analysis should focus only on aspects of its performance. This dichotomy is misleading, since it perpetuates the 'literary fallacy', which presupposes that fictional worlds belong in the realm of literature and literary analysis. The study of fictional worlds, however, is definitely not an exclusive privilege of literary theory. Since described fictional worlds are integral parts of performance-texts, performance analysis should also apply to them. Likewise, any theory of an art that describes fictional worlds, such as cinema, opera, puppet theatre and animated cartoons should also engage in their analysis. Understanding the rules that structure fictional worlds and generate theatre meaning is not only a legitimate object of a theory of performance analysis, but also its essential complement.

This chapter aims at showing that (a) *the semiotic and poetic principles are distinct and complementary*; (b) *poetic principles bestow a sense of unity and wholeness on a performance-text*; (c) *poetic structures reflect archetypal patterns of response*; (d) *the fictional world reflects a stratified poetic deep structure*; and (e) *the stratified structure features five layers: mythical, praxical, naïve, ironic and aesthetic* (Rozik, 1990).

The twofold structure of the performance-text

Theatre authors (playwrights or directors) express themselves not in a 'thematic' or, rather, discursive mode (*ibid.*: 52ff & 367) but in a 'fictional' mode, i.e., through worlds of characters and their actions (Frye: 33ff & 365). Bruce Wilshire defines 'fictional' 'in a generic sense to refer to all works of fine art in respect to their being embodied by beings which have a reality distinct from whatever actual things *or* inactual things are depicted by them' (p. 28). 'Fictional' means here the whole set of imagined characters and their actions (including the circumstances of these actions), their temporary and final successes or failures, and the meanings of their worlds.

It is widely accepted that the human psyche spontaneously creates fictional worlds that reflect its innermost thoughts and feelings, e.g., in dreaming, daydreaming and children's imaginative play. Moreover, there is a vast body of literature that connects this spontaneous creativity to mythology, and conceives of it as a primeval form of thinking (Rozik, 2002; 247ff). In this sense each fictional world embodies a thought, which refers to its author and potentially to a reader/spectator.

Fictional worlds created by the human imagination cannot be communicated without descriptions capable of evoking them; i.e., they are dependent on a language or medium, although not on a specific one. Whereas the common denominator of literature is the use of language, capable of describing such macro-images through the evocative power of words, the common denominator of iconic fictional arts, such as theatre, is the use of an iconic medium.

In contrast to literature, iconic media afford a particularly suitable method for describing fictional worlds because of conveying the spontaneously created images in the mind through their imprinting on matter. In contrast to its spontaneous forms, such as dreams and children's imaginative play, cultural forms of description employ an established language/medium and contextualization in terms of the audience's culture. The aim of performance analysis is, therefore, to grasp the nature of such an embodied thought and its referent.

From a semiotic viewpoint a performance-text is an unstructured string of single sentences/icons, which is structured by additional poetic principles. Whereas the iconic sentence/icon is the most complex unit that an iconic medium affords, its thematic aspect is the basic unit of the poetic system in structuring a fictional world. In other words, *the semiotic and poetics systems are different and complement one another*. Sets of iconic sentences/icons are not only structured according to poetic rules, but ultimately subordinated to the effect that authors intend to produce in their target audiences. *A poetic structure thus lends unity and wholeness to a theatrical fictional text*. This twofold structure of the performance-text, generated by two complementary systems, is shared by literary texts that generate fictional worlds through verbal and poetic systems.

This duality also characterizes non-fictional texts. From a linguistic viewpoint, a scientific article is a chain of verbal sentences whose organization as a whole is imposed by the logic of a scientific structure of demonstration; e.g., the presentation of a problem, the discussion and rejection of previous solutions, the suggestion of a new thesis and its demonstration. In other words, *the rules of a medium and the rules that constitute a whole are different and complement one another*. In contrast to Elam, the inclusion of poetic structures in semiotic theory is, therefore, as absurd as the inclusion of scientific structures of demonstration in linguistic theory (pp. 98ff).

Archetypal patterns of response

Theoretically, different languages/media can describe the same fictional world (chapter 6). I conjecture, therefore, that it is not the principles of signification and communication, but the nature of a fictional world that fundamentally affects the audience. Moreover, the collective nature of the theatre experience explains the rigorous structuration of fictional worlds. Such a world requires that the imagination of a heterogeneous group of spectators is captured at once. Following Aristotle, it can be assumed that beyond the amazing diversity of fictional worlds there is a finite set of (surface) structures that underlie the creation of such worlds, and explain the spectators' experiences. I suggest, therefore, that the basic structures suggested in his *Poetics*, particularly in chapter 13, *reflect the spectators' archetypal patterns of expectation and response.* The numerous interpretations of this tractate are excellent examples of analysis of poetic structures.

What are these structures? Aristotle suggests four factors that constitute the structure of a tragic macro-action: the nature of a character and/or its motive; its ultimate success or failure; the 'ethical sense' (*philanthropon*) of the audience (probably in the sense of 'value guided assessment of behavior'); and the arousal of fear and pity (*Poetics*, XIII). He also suggests five types of structure, which reflect the combination of these factors:

Nature of character	ultimate success or failure	ethical sense	fear and pity
1. 'A virtuous man'	'from prosperity to adversity'	[satisfies not the ethical sense]	'it shocks us'
2. 'A bad man'	'from adversity to prosperity'	satisfies not 'the ethical sense'	[it shocks us]
3. 'An utter villain'	his 'downfall'	'satisfies the ethical sense'	[none]
4. [A virtuous man]	[his success]	[satisfies the ethical sense]	[none]
5. An error or frailty	failure	[satisfies the ethical sense]	fear & pity

Since in Aristotle's view the main purpose of tragedy is to produce tragic catharsis, a fictional world should arouse fear, in addition to the anxieties that spectators harbor prior to their theatre experience. He also presupposes that catharsis cannot be produced unless a fictional action satisfies the ethical sense of the spectators, which probably means a sense of harmony between the ethical nature of a character/motive and its success or failure. These two conditions (fear and ethos) are not completely satisfied if the characters are characterized on the extremes of the ethical scale, utterly good or utterly bad. Therefore '[t]here remains, then, the character between these two extremes, – that of a man who is not eminently good and just, yet whose misfortune is brought about not by vice or depravity, but by some error or frailty' (*Poetics*, XIII, 3).

Out of five possible structures, Aristotle singles out only three that can generate tragedies. First, he implies that the best is the structure based on 'some error or frailty', i.e., *hamartia* (No. 5), in which '[t]he change of fortune should be not from bad to good, but, reversely, from good to bad. It should come about as the result not of vice, but of some great error or frailty, in a character either such as we have described, or better rather than worse' (*Poetics*, XIII, 4). These conditions indicate that the change of fortune from prosperity to adversity *balances* a severe *hamartia* which, to be detected, should be characterized against the background of a rather positive character, otherwise its distinction from 'utter villainy' would be impossible. The *hamartia* must be, therefore, so severe as to justify catastrophe, which means that, for Aristotle, satisfying the ethical sense of the audience is a condition of catharsis.

'In the second rank comes the kind of tragedy which some place first. Like the Odyssey, it has a double thread of plot, and also an opposite catastrophe for the good and the bad. It is accounted the best because of the weakness of the spectators; for the poet is guided in what he writes by the wishes of his audience' (*Poetics*, XIII, 7). This kind of tragedy combines structures 3 and 4, which also satisfy the ethical sense of the audience and, in my view, enable catharsis. Although Aristotle scorns this double structure, he still perceives it as tragic. Such a structure can be and has been employed for single actions that involve single characters, either positive or negative.

The common denominator of these three structures is that they satisfy the spectators' ethical sense, i.e., they harmonize with their expectations, and thus may produce catharsis. It is sensible to conclude, therefore, that Aristotle conceived of the satisfaction of expectations as a precondition for catharsis. In reflecting the spontaneous expectations of spectators, all these structures should be conceived of as 'archetypal' structures, and the worlds structured by them as 'archetypal' fictional worlds.

The common denominator of his excluded structures (1 and 2) is, consequently, that they do not harmonize with the spectators' archetypal expectations. Indeed, he disqualified 'shocking' or, rather, absurd structures. Paradoxically, Aristotle did not envisage the possibility of absurd tragic structures despite knowing Euripides' tragedies. He also did not envisage the possibility of absurd structures aiming at conforming to the ethical sense of absurdist audiences. Nonetheless, structures leading to the experience of the absurd can be derived from Aristotle's harmonizing structures by simple inversion, because of contrasting archetypal patterns of expectation. One should also consider the principles underlying modern and post-modern dramatic structures, which as yet have not been sufficiently studied; e.g., Ionesco's *The New Tenant*.

Although Aristotle's approach is limited in various senses, the inclusion of the spectators' value judgments and archetypal expectations as decisive structuring factors is a major theoretical achievement. His presupposition is that the spontaneous expectations of the spectators are umbilically linked, not to instinctual drives (e.g., marry a mother), but to ethical considerations (e.g., hubris). His line of argumentation leads, therefore, to the conclusion that although each culture cherishes different values, which condition synchronic audiences' judgments and expectations, different cultures share the same archetypal patterns of response based on either ethical harmonization or not. Such expectations can be either fulfilled, leading to a sense of harmony and catharsis, or thwarted, leading to an experience of the absurd.

The implication is that all structures of fictional worlds reflect such archetypal patterns of expectation and response. Knowledge of patterns of expectation and response amounts to a kind of technology of theatre, since the principles underlying them are still a matter of speculation, and only occasionally are verified scientifically *a posteriori* (cf. Kreitler on

109

'catharsis'). Experience probably teaches playwrights and directors to anticipate possible reactions of audiences, although not always being able to explain them.

The stratified structure of the fictional word

Most approaches to performance analysis presuppose that a fictional world is not a mere admixture of characters and actions, but an organized macro-unit that reflects an intuition as to the most efficient structure for embodying a fictional thought. However, although such approaches presuppose the existence of such structures, and provide valuable insights about them, none offers an adequate account of their complexity. I suggest that a fictional world that embodies a thought and thus determines the response of the audience reflects an archetypal deep structure.

The poetic deep structure is a complex set of organizing principles, which underlie the generation of particular surface structures of fictional worlds. The following model is basically rooted in the Aristotelian tradition, although further developed along its own premises and enriched by later archetypal theories of fictional creativity. This model takes into account that there are structures not anticipated by Aristotle, and ways to depart from his archetypal surface structures, as demonstrated by modernist and postmodernist theatre. I suggest that any departure from them also presupposes archetypal expectations. *This model comprises five stratified functional layers – the mythical, the praxical, the naïve, the ironic and the aesthetic – with each one being grafted on the previous one and restructuring it, thus constructing the entire fictional world.* The aim of a performance-text is to bring about the experience not a blank structure, but of structured specific thematic material.

(A) *Mythical layer.* The deep structure of the fictional world presupposes the existence a fundamental layer of fictional material that is minimally organized and features elementary characterization of *dramatis personae*, neutral categorization of motives and actions from any ethical viewpoint, and simple temporal order. Despite minimal characterization and value categorization, this material is of profound psychical meaning for the spectator, possibly on an unconscious level, and capable of arousing a great deal of anxiety (in addition to the anxiety that the spectator harbors anyway); e.g., a son killing his father or marrying his mother. Freud explains the spectators' deep involvement in such elementary actions and the extreme anxiety they may arouse: 'It is the fate of all of us, perhaps, to direct our first sexual impulse towards our mother and our first hatred and our first murderous wish against our father' (Freud, 1978: 364). If this is indeed the case, the fact that Oedipus fulfils these suppressed wishes would be most disturbing for any spectator who has managed to suppress them. This coincides with Aristotle's claims that a tragic action should produce fear, and that it is best when suffering is inflicted on 'those who are near or dear to one another' (*Poetics*, XIV, 4). Even in this embryonic guise such an action conveys a sense of absurdity because of being perceived as contrary to human nature (cf. Corneille: 219). Not every dramatic action is built upon the violation of a taboo; but even the most trivial fears may constitute the nucleus of a meaningful fictional world, as in many a melodrama. Fear is the fundamental stuff of drama, including comedy.

'Mythical' does not necessarily refer to 'myth'. A myth never comes in a schematic and neutral form as suggested above, but is further organized by additional layers, as in any cultural rendering of a narrative. Usually, the basic and neutral core of a myth is termed 'mythos' and these additional layers 'logos', with 'mythology' applying to the combination of both. It is the element of mythos that corresponds to what is termed here 'mythical'. I suggest that not only are myths built upon such an elementary layer, but also meaningful narratives generated by a culturally established language or medium.

The way to reveal the mythical layer of such a narrative is to strip off all the additional layers, the logos, until reaching the level of elementary characterization and neutral categorization; e.g., on this level, the fact that Laius is a king and Oedipus a born prince should be disregarded, but not that they are umbilically related as father and son. A commoner and his son too could embody the same mythical core, possibly with quite a similar impact on the audience. Even the question of whether or not Laius was 'murdered' should be overlooked, but not the fact that he was 'killed'. Further stripping would change the nature of this fictional nucleus. It is the minimal narrative 'son kills father' that is most meaningful for spectators, whatever the logos. In this sense the mythical is the simplest and most distressful narrative layer. How can such deeply disturbing material be transmuted into a possible enjoyable experience? This is the function of the logos.

(B) *Praxical layer*: The mythical layer is further structured by the praxical layer that attributes a specific macro-motive to a character's action (e.g., to avoid killing a father), and a definite and related outcome (e.g., a catastrophe). The term 'praxical' is taken from Aristotle's term for action: '*praxis*'. The same mythical motif 'son kills father' can be attributed different motives and outcomes. The assumption is that the same action may reflect different motives, and the same motive can be reflected in different actions. Such a macro-motive supposedly underlies most actions of a character; e.g., gaining the crown in Shakespeare's *Macbeth* and avoiding death in Ionesco's *Exit the King*. The existence of such an overall motive produces two simultaneous expectations: to either succeed or fail. These concurrent and contrasting expectations lie at the heart of 'suspense', with one possibility being desired and the other dreaded by spectators.

The existence of a specific and consistent macro-motive that leads to a definite outcome – either success or failure – endows the action with a sense of unity. It also determines the temporal boundaries of a fictional world, from its inception to its consummation or frustration, and thus also imbues the action with a sense of wholeness. These are the main reasons for the paramount importance of the final scenes of a performance-text. Aristotle stresses the centrality of this layer: 'on actions [. . .] all success or failure depends' (*Poetics*, VI, 5) and 'it is by their actions that they [the characters] are happy or the reverse' (*ibid.*: VI, 10). He implies thereby, not necessarily, that happiness derives from success and unhappiness from failure.

This method of analysis presupposes that, fundamentally, a single macro-action reflects a single macro-motive and corresponds to a single character. The advantage of isolating a single action lies in that complex actions can be analyzed in terms of simple ones; e.g., two characters having a common end or pursuing ends that exclude one another; i.e., being in conflict.

(C) *Naïve layer.* The praxical layer is further structured by the specific cognitive and/or ethical categorization of the characters' motives and actions, from their own naïve viewpoints. A 'viewpoint' is reflected in the actual terms through which a motive or act/action is perceived, whether these are anchored in established epistemic or ethical (religious, philosophical or ideological) value systems or not; and whether these are shared by the audience or not. Usually there is no need for a full and orderly exposition of such a system because of being part of the audience's cultural baggage. It is rather represented by key terms, which should be conceived as its metonyms based on a part/whole relationship. Through them an entire system thus becomes an integral part of a performance-text. The cognitive and/or ethical neutrality of the mythical and praxical layers are thus lent a dimension of cultural meaning; e.g., Antigone's notions of family loyalty. From a naïve perspective, characters not only categorize their own motives, acts/actions and their outcomes, but also determine whether these observe or contravene their own values. Since characters tend to justify their motives even if negative, the naïve layer may add to the sense of absurdity induced by the mythical layer.

(D) *Ironic layer.* The naïve layer is further structured by the ironic layer in terms of the author's and audiences' cognitive and/or ethical value systems. The gap between the ironic and the naïve layers defines 'dramatic irony', which is the sense of advantage that spectators experience over characters in knowing, understanding and evaluating their own worlds. Since a fictional world is pre-structured to suit its expected perception by an audience, an ironic viewpoint is embodied in its structure.

Although independent categorization is made by spectators in any case, most performance-texts feature key terms (metonyms of epistemic and/or ethical value systems), that aim at guiding them towards the expected categorization. These are conveyed by ironic conventions – functional characters and interacting characters in functional situations – which represent the author within the performance-text (chapter 4). In some cases, key terms that connote the value system of a prospective audience are found even in the words of interacting (naïve) characters; e.g., 'le Dieu' (in contrast to 'Dieux') and 'père' in Racine's *Phèdre* (1401–2). The analysis of this layer requires, therefore, knowledge of the synchronic cultural background.

In the structure of a performance-text two basic perspectives can be discerned, that of the interacting characters and that of the author/audience. While the characters reveal their own concepts of their worlds, the author conditions how these characters should be perceived by the spectators. While both perspectives converge on the praxical level, the latter enjoys authorial authority. The performance-text may be seen, therefore, as a mechanism that manipulates the audience into a preconceived perspective on a fictional world. A character's perspective is thus naïve only from an ironic point of view. The ironic layer is thus the heart of the logos.

If the fictional world is pre-structured to suit the author's design, it is not surprising that whoever adopts the authorial perspective enjoys dramatic irony. When the spectator commands such a viewpoint, a character's viewpoint becomes an object of irony. This can be reversed at will, as in modernist and postmodernist drama, with the spectator becoming the object of dramatic irony. Ultimately, the spectators make the concluding value categorization, which determines the nature of their experience.

The mood of an entire fictional world, such as serious, comic or grotesque, should also be seen as fulfilling an ironic function, because of circumventing the characters' viewpoints, and betraying the author's perspective. Such a mood aims at producing a unified effect and, in particular, indicates the intention to condition the audience's attitude to a world as a serious, ludicrous or grotesque object of contemplation.

Against the background of archetypal expectations, a character may initially endanger an audience's value system, due to success despite of evil or *hamartia*. The eventual reversal of such a situation may then produce a sense of reaffirmation of the value system, even at the cost of the character's catastrophe (Hegel: 1195ff; Bradley: 80; cf. Krook: 8–9). A catastrophe thus becomes a metaphor of order. Similar considerations apply to the temporary suffering of a character who observes the contemporary value system and eventually succeeds, or the temporary success of a character who does not and eventually fails. In contrast, the eventual frustration of these archetypal expectations is meant to subvert established values and beliefs.

(E) *Aesthetic layer*: On this level, the ironic layer is further structured by the aesthetic layer in terms of 'harmony' and 'disharmony'. The experiences of unity, wholeness, proportion, rhythm and tempo are particular instances of harmony. As suggested above, the praxical level conditions the experiences of unity and wholeness.

Endings are reconsidered in terms of 'proportion or 'disproportion'. 'Proportion' presupposes that the audience exercises a sense of harmony or disharmony (absurdity in Esslin's terms; p. xix) regarding the relation between two different aspects of the human experience: value and happiness. Even real outcomes are examined in these terms. For example, an ending in catastrophe that gratifies the archetypal expectations of the audience is reexamined in terms of proportion between *hamartia* (infringement of value) and catastrophe (unhappiness). Whereas on the cognitive level a sense of proportion leads to the reaffirmation of the audience's value system, 'disproportion' may lead to questioning it. On the aesthetic level, the archetypal expectation of spectators is for harmonious structures that reaffirm their own value systems. Whereas each culture has its own value system and its own standards of harmony and disharmony, the application of such standards is universal. Seemingly there is no textual indicator of this layer, but a fictional world is actually structured to either suit aesthetic expectations or not.

The Aristotelian notion of 'catharsis' (*Poetics*: IV, 2) should be conceived of as umbilically related to the experience of harmony, and as its emotional counterpart. While initial disharmony is experienced as anxiety, eventual harmony produces pleasure, due to the sudden release of 'tension', a euphemism for 'fear'. It is in this sense that a poetic logos transmutes the initial anxiety aroused by the mythical and naive layers into an experience of pleasure. In contrast, an absurdist structure leads to a final experience of increasing anxiety.

Unity of rhythm and tempo too, despite their elusive nature, may produce an aesthetic effect. The notion of 'rhythm' applies to the regular recurrence of units of the same kind, which reflects a physiological basis, such as heart beat and breathing (Pavis, 1998: 314), and assumedly echoes in the spectator. A specific rhythm is generated not only by metre (iambus, anapest and the like), but also by other forms of regular interchange of units such as fast and slow, speech and silence, and action and reaction. A

114

rhythm is discerned not only on the temporal axis, but also on the spatial one; e.g., the regular distribution of colors and shapes. A rhythmical pattern produces expectations of recurrence that can be harmonized with or not. A certain rhythm can characterize the behavior of a character and, on the level of the whole text, it should be seen as an interpretive convention that reflects the ironic perspective of a director (chapter 4).

The notion of 'tempo' applies to the sense of pace produced by a certain behavior. It presupposes various intuitive models that characterize different personalities, occupations and activities. These models can be harmonized or not; i.e., a particular enacted behavior can be faster or slower than expected. Similar considerations apply to a whole fictional world, particularly on the generic level; e.g., a farce is usually characterized by a tempo that is faster than usual and tragedy by a tempo slower than usual, as befits sublime behavior. In this sense it also creates definite expectations that can be harmonized or not. Change of rhythm and/or tempo, in regard to previous productions of a certain play-script, may radically change the perception of a fictional world (Pavis, *ibid.*). Overall tempo too should be seen, therefore, as an interpretive convention that reflects the ironic perspective of a director.

The material nature of the theatre medium provides an additional aesthetic dimension. The pictorial elements of set, costume and light can create a sense of visual harmony or disharmony, and the elements of speech – a sense of aural harmony or disharmony. It is the combination of the aesthetic properties of unity, wholeness, proportion, rhythm and tempo on the fictional level and the above properties on the sensory level that underlies the holistic aesthetic experience.

There is something paradoxical in the experience of harmony that is reached at the expense of a character that elicits the spectators' identification, but is sacrificed on the altar of their value system. This paradox reflects the wrong assumption that in the eyes of spectators a character's welfare and the validity of the value system enjoy the same status. The archetypal structures of fictional worlds indicate that this is not the case. Spectators are more concerned by the possible collapse of their own value systems, which afford them a sense of meaning and orientation in the world, and are prepared to sacrifice a character despite possible identification. This is evident when a character fulfills the suppressed wishes of the spectators, which (paradoxically again) arouses anxiety. The implication is that the aesthetic experience takes place in the mind of a socialized spectator, on the borderline between the conscious and the unconscious, and reflects preference for conscious wishes. Only identification with the value system can bring about total harmony in the spectator's psyche.

The archetypal pre-structuration of a fictional world based on archetypal expectations bestows a ritual dimension on the theatre experience.

Since it is structured *a priori* for producing a pre-determined experience, its epistemic value is negligible. The spectators are not expected to learn anything – in contrast to Horace's contention that a play should yield both pleasure and ethical instruction (335) – but to enjoy recurrent experiences of verification of their own value system, usually challenged under extreme circumstances. This indicates that fundamentally the spectator is more interested in an experience of truth than in truth itself. The experience of truth actually reflects the feeling of harmony between the outcome of a fictional action and the archetypal expectations of an audience, conditioned by a synchronic value system. Such a pre-structuration also apples to absurd endings based on the same archetypal expectations: they too have limited cognitive value. The only way of entering a genuine cognitive course is to preclude archetypal expectations on ethical grounds (cf. Chekhov's *The Seagull*).

Structure of the character

In principle, a character can be characterized as wished, including paradoxically; e.g., as a character that is not enacted by an actor in Luigi Pirandello's *Six Characters in Search of an Author*. However, a character is not merely a set of casually related qualities. In archetypal fictional worlds it is subordinated to the poetic and aesthetic structures of an action and to the effect that a synchronic audience is meant to experience. A character thus reflects all the five structural layers suggested above, which contrasts any possible reduction of characterization to a single quality. Subordination also applies to fictional worlds that reverse the archetypal structure, and lead to the experience of the absurd.

Possible fallacies

Each structural layer may lead to a fallacy, if considered as the only or main structural level. The 'mythical fallacy' lies in the assumption that revealing the mythical layer is the ultimate end of play or performance analysis. This is typical of traditional psychoanalytic analysis (cf. Wright: 36). It leads to the absurd conclusion that different fictional worlds based on the same myth (or variations of it) have the same meaning. We should distinguish, therefore, between revealing the ethically neutral mythical layer as a precondition of analysis and seeing it as its ultimate interpretation.

The 'praxical fallacy' lies in viewing the fictional world as structured only by the praxical layer. This is clearly illustrated by Vladimir Propp's *Morphology of the Folktale*, and Étienne Souriau's *Les Deux Cent Mille*

116

Situations Dramatiques, which presuppose that a restricted set of interactive functions is sufficient for determining the structure of a fictional world. Souriau's model, for example, is characterized by a combination of six functions that constitute a fictional action, motivated by a wish to achieve/preclude a goal, and couched in terms of 'seeking', 'opposing', 'helping' and 'receiving a good' (cf. Pavis, 1982: 16). It also offers a thematic list of wishes that can specify such abstract functions. Algirdas. J. Greimas endeavors to unify and generalize Propp's and Souriau's models, and presents them as extrapolations of language's syntactic structure, such as subject and predicate functions, an attempt that is commendable in itself. He suggests a model of six 'actants' (functions), which do not necessarily overlap the actual 'actors' (characters), with each character possibly fulfilling more than one function, and each function possibly being fulfilled by more than one character (Greimas). However, because of overlooking additional structural layers, these praxical models are extremely limited. Elam correctly remarks that Souriau's model 'does seem to deal successfully [only] with structurally simple dramas whose characters are largely determined by their function in the action' (p. 130).

The 'naïve fallacy' lies in seeing the viewpoint of a character as the unique perspective on his world. An example of this is Hegel's interpretation of Sophocles' *Antigone* (1217; cf. 1163, note 1; 1196; & Bradley: 73–5). He suggests that its action revolves around a conflict between two positive motives, based on either state or family values. He disregards, however, that both Antigone and Creon employ these values only to naïvely justify their deeds, and that the chorus (with ironic authority) views this conflict as implementing the gods' will on different grounds (582–625). This fallacy may stem from the widespread wrong assumption that authors are absent in drama, and spectators have no role in categorization; e.g., E. R. Dodds claims that no *hamartia* can be established unless voiced by a character (p. 179).

The 'ironic fallacy' lies in conceiving of the viewpoint of the author/audience as the unique perspective on the fictional world, canceling thereby the ironic gap between it and the naïve layer. Jean-Pierre Vernant, for example, denies the mythical substratum of *Oedipus the King*, while stressing the crucial function of the social notions typical of the fifth-century BC polis, such as 'responsibility' and 'unintentional crime' (pp. 85–111). He even mocks the likelihood that Aeschylus' *Agamemnon* reflects an urge of wives to punish their husbands (*ibid.*: 93). Similarly, Corneille cannot believe that any spectator watching *Oedipus the King* would wish to kill his father and marry his mother (p. 209).

The 'aesthetic fallacy' would lie in ignoring the structural layer of harmony/disharmony. I have not found any clear-cut instance of such a fallacy.

Sophocles' *Oedipus the King*

On the mythical level, this narrative revolves around two actions: murdering a father and marrying a mother. These are most disturbing events, probably because of reflecting drives universally suppressed to the unconscious. On this level, the narrative features abstract characterizations, such as 'son', 'father' and 'mother'; and an abstract action, such as killing and marriage, both devoid of value and aesthetic characterization. Further abstraction would change their nature. It is on this level that these actions are assumedly most meaningful for the spectator.

On the praxical level, at least two motives can be discerned: to avoid fate and to reveal who killed King Laius. The former is implicit in Oedipus' act of leaving Corinth and the latter is made explicit in the play-script. Which is the macro-motive of the entire action? Whereas the latter is crowned with success, and cannot explain the final catastrophe, it is the failure in regard to the former and the correspondent *anagnorisis* that leads to the catastrophe and explains it. This procedure establishes the main motive that structures the macro-action.

On the naïve level, we may assume that Oedipus' endeavor to avoid his twofold fate is conceived of as a positive move from his own ethical viewpoint. Since he was doomed to infringe two deeply-rooted taboos in human culture, we may also assume that Oedipus' decision was probably supported by the synchronic audience, considering that these taboos were established by the gods themselves. However, while Oedipus' realization of forbidden and suppressed drives probably aroused deep anxiety on the spectators' unconscious level, his attempt to avoid their fulfillment probably aroused even deeper concern on the conscious level, due to contrasting their synchronic belief in the gods' authority.

On the ironic level, there is a manifest paradox: the oracle's prediction contradicts taboos imposed by the gods themselves – further problematized by Oedipus' conviction that it is within his wisdom and power to avert the gods' decision, thus questioning their rule. His attitude reveals that he is afflicted by hubris, a particular instance of *hamartia*. Moreover, he views himself as the 'child of Fortune', i.e., the goddess Tyche (1080; cf. Ehrenburg: 69), thus additionally questioning Delphi's authority. This is corroborated by the anxiety that such thoughts arouse in the chorus, when it reacts to similar words of disbelief voiced by Jocasta: 'Why should man fear since chance [fortune] is all in all for him' (977). The chorus even undergoes the experience of the absurd: 'When such deeds are held in honour, / why should I honour the Gods in the dance?' (895–6). These words should be understood as pondering on the possible futility of worshiping the gods. Oedipus' infringement of the two taboos, which are dismissed as guilt in *Oedipus at Colonus*, cannot explain his catastrophe. It is only against the background of an audience that is well-versed in the ancient Greek system of beliefs that Oedipus' endeavor to avoid his fate, supported by his sense of intellectual superiority (Knox) and his belief in Tyche, can be understood as an act of hubris. It is the utmost gravity of this attitude of sheer irreverence that can be balanced only by catastrophe, thus reinstating the logic of the worship of Apollo. From an ironic viewpoint, the paradox is settled: the gods can impose a fate that contradicts their own taboos if they wish. Oedipus, who seemingly complies with firm human values, reveals that he is contravening a fundamental religious dogma and has to face catastrophe.

Oedipus' blindness is a crucial verbal metaphor in this fictional world, which both supports the ironic advantage of the audience and reaffirms the validity of the oracle. The blinding of his corporeal eyes, a stage metaphor, is the natural reaction to his mental blindness, and possibly the beginning of his ascent to genuine 'seeing'.

On the aesthetic level, Oedipus' life is fundamentally disharmonious. He actually contravenes taboos and probably realizes wishes suppressed by the audience, thus challenging their religious beliefs, and yet manages to live in great honor. Thus, only catastrophe can harmonize the expectations of synchronic audiences and restore the validity of their value system. Oedipus is made to discover his true condition by himself. It is even possible that the gods contrived such an action, for establishing it as an existential exemplum. Sophocles thus reveals his endeavor to bring about the experience of harmony on the epistemic, ethical and emotional levels.

8

The Metaphoric Nature of the Fictional Experience

Traditional performance analysis has overlooked a fundamental question: What is the reason for spectators to invest time and money in experiencing fictional worlds that usually differ from their own worlds to a remarkable degree, with differences ranging from the minimal to the extreme, including worlds that reflect principles distinct from those of their real worlds? What is the reason for the spectators' total involvement, usually explained in terms of 'identification', despite inherent difference? These questions, already implicit in age-old theories of drama, presuppose that there are principles that govern the relationship between fictional worlds and spectators, under the assumption that experiencing a performance-text fulfils a crucial function in the economy of their psyches.

A possible answer is that a fictional world is a kind of description of the spectator's psychical state of affairs. On this structural level, 'description' means bestowing form on an amorphous psychical reality through a text couched in a cultural system of signification. Such an answer is based on the analogy between fictional worlds and the worlds crafted by the psyche in dreaming, daydreaming and children's imaginative play (Rozik, 2002a: 247ff).

The problem is that, fundamentally, a fictional world cannot be a literal description of the spectator's world, due to their basic difference. This chapter explores, therefore, the possibility that such a world is experienced as a metaphor of the spectator's world, because this is the only form of description in which apparent difference (improperness), eventually proves utmost adequacy (chapter 3). The principle of 'metaphor', there-fore, possibly is the only principle that can explain the spectator's utmost involvement, despite the said gap (Rozik: 2004).

This chapter aims at showing that (a) the fictional world is a potential metaphor of the spectator's amorphous psychical state of affairs; (b) the

120

metaphoric principle materializes already on the mythical level of the poetic structure in the form of a basic personification; (c) all other structural layers of the fictional world are grafted upon this fundamental personified layer; (d) the principle of expanded metaphor thus applies not only to allegoric fictional worlds, but also to 'praxical' ones; and (e) metaphor is the only principle that can explain the total involvement of the spectators in fictional worlds, because and despite fundamental difference.

Since chapter 4 has expanded on the metaphoric principle, the following remarks are restricted to only aspects relevant to these theses, which are illustrated by relevant analyses of Sophocles' *Oedipus the King* (continuation of chapter 7), and Rina Yerushalmi's dramatization of the biblical narrative of Jephthah's daughter.

The metaphoric principle

The following principles enable the application of the metaphoric principle to the relation between a description of a fictional world and the world of a spectator:

(a) Metaphor is a standard form of description of real or fictional referents, alternative to literal description.

(b) The definition of 'metaphoric' depends on the definition of 'literal'. A description of a referent is literal if the predicate is proper; i.e., is conceived of as a possible predicate of such a subject/referent; and is potentially metaphoric if the predicate is improper.

(c) Since improperness is essential to metaphor, the identification of a case of metaphor requires knowledge of the referent. While the subject of a metaphoric description is literal, as otherwise it could not identify its referent, the predicate must be improper.

(d) In most cases, an improper predicate is meant to generate an associative process meant to evoke a set of common literal modifiers that make sense with the subject on the literal level, and induce referential associations originating in the improper term. These associations are the *raison d'être* and the specific difference of metaphoric.

(e) A common literal modifier is apparently connected to two objects, the one represented by the subject and the other represented by the improper term, which are two potential and alternative sources of referential associations. Conventionally, metaphor prefers referential associations originating in the improper term. Initial improperness is thus only apparent, with the resulting description possibly being most adequate.

121

(f) Reference to the second object is only apparent, as all noun predicates are: after inducing its alternative referential associations it should be overlooked. In metaphor double reference is thus only apparent, and results in single reference.

(g) Because the improper term is needed as the source of alternative referential associations, it is essential to metaphor and its marker. Without the improper term no improperness can be detected and no associative processes set in motion.

(h) Surface structures of metaphor reflect several elliptical processes that may reduce its surface structures to a minimum. Since most missing components, except for the improper term, can be evoked on the grounds of the common deep structure and semantic context, they should be conceived of as 'elliptically present'.

(i) Literal and metaphoric predicates, which have the same modifier in common in its literal capacity and only differ in their referential associations, have different truth conditions.

The expressive nature of fictional worlds

Theatre authors express themselves through fictional worlds; i.e., of worlds of interacting human characters (chapter 7; Frye: 33; 52 & 365–7). In other words, a multiple world of characters expresses the single psyche of an author.

Because theatre authors are represented on stage by interactive characters, which act and reflect their independent viewpoints, and by functional characters that counteract these viewpoints from ironic viewpoints, it follows that they express themselves through *whole* fictional worlds. The notion of 'expression' thus applies to a performance-text in its entirety, because it is only on this level that it *indicates* the author's image/concept of the world. A fictional world, as a whole, is consequently a self-referential description *by* and *of* an author, similarly to a self-referential poem.

It may be conjectured, therefore, that in the process of experiencing a performance-text, the spectator may take over the function of referent. This principle is fully acknowledged in the theory of lyric poetry. The deictic terms of a poem – such as 'I', 'you', 'here' and 'now' – assumedly refer to the poet and the circumstances of his lyric expression. Nonetheless, *because of the abstract nature of these terms, in the act of reading their referential function can be appropriated by a reader, who thus becomes the poem's main referent*. This explains why readers deem such ready-made texts as expressions of themselves, and praise them accordingly.

If the principle of expression adequately describes the relationship between an 'I' poet and an 'I' reader, it can be conjectured that *in theatre a similar substitution of referents by a spectator also takes place.* This substitution is facilitated by the fact that the author of a theatre text, the subject of a theatre expression, is not marked ('0' sign); i.e., there is no obstacle for such a substitution to occur. In principle, there is no need for making a subject explicit, if it is self-understood.

If a fictional world is a description of a single psyche through a multiple world of characters, the spectator's involvement does not regard a single character, but an entire fictional world; i.e., it is a pluri-identification with all its characters, including the ethically good and the depraved. The general appeal of a performance-text lies in its potentially being meaningful for each and every spectator, i.e., being experienced as an adequate overall metaphor. The principles of multiple metaphoric description and substitution of referents replace, therefore, previous theories based on identification with single characters.

The principle of personification

The claim that *a multiple fictional world is a potential metaphor of the spectator's amorphous psychical state of affairs* presupposes that the psyche is somehow split into aspects or components, and that each of them is personified by a character. *'Personification' is a particular kind of metaphor, whose improper source of referential associations is the human sphere.* It thus implies that it cannot be used for description of human beings. Nonetheless, it may aptly describe abstract or spontaneously partitioned components of the human psyche; e.g., in *Everyman* (chapter 3).

It would appear that this thesis adequately describes only allegoric performance-texts, which usually operate the principle of personification. However, in allegory the referents of expanded stage metaphors are mediated by abstract ideas and relations between them; e.g., 'humans should adequately prepare for the journey of death' in anonymous *Everyman*. My claim is, in contrast, that *the metaphoric function of fictional worlds also applies to 'praxical' (non-allegoric) performance-texts.* Such texts are non-mediated descriptions of the psyche through a world of human interacting characters; i.e., 'personification' is the fundamental metaphoric structure that underlies the relation between fictional world and spectator. It refers to and formulates spontaneously partitioned aspects of the psyche, like in dreams. It is on this level that the principle of personification already substantiates the metaphoric thesis.

The principle of personification is by no means foreign to the inborn thinking mechanisms of the psyche. Psychoanalytic theory contends that in dreams the psyche is represented and described by such worlds of characters and their actions, which indicates that each character describes a partial entity/drive of the psyche, such as unconscious suppressed wishes and actions aimed at materializing them. In other words, the 'dream-work' creates fictional worlds that 'express' the dreamer's unconscious (Freud, 1978: 114 & 467–8; cf. Jung: 49). This principle also applies to daydreams (Freud, 1990: 131–41), children's imaginative play and drawings (Rozik, 2002a: 270–92).

Even more to the point is Freud's suggestion that '[t]he psychological novel [. . .] owes its special nature to the inclination of the modern writer to split up his ego, by self-observation, into many part-egos, and, in conse-quence, to personify the conflicting currents of his own mental life in several heroes' (1990: 138). Since this principle is also postulated for daydreaming, it is possible that Freud discovered the inborn mechanism of creation of 'fictional worlds': the expression of a single psyche through a world of characters and their actions. Even real people in dreams, rather than representing themselves, are personified descriptions of intra-psychical entities (1978: 434–5).

No human-like image, however, can be created by an actor on the abstract level of sheer personification. In order to become a concrete source of referential associations an actor should add specific human traits. Personification should, therefore, be conceived of as a basic improper layer of a more complex stage metaphor. *In principle, the more a character resem-bles a human being, the more the principle of personification materializes.* The use of flesh and blood actors adds a concrete dimension to it.

In personification the said apparent improperness (to the psyche) that characterizes metaphor, which eventually proves utmost properness, is already found. However, this only indicates the existence of a potential complex metaphoric relationship. The gist of the metaphoric function of a fictional world resides in its ability to describe a psychical state of affairs through literal modifiers common to such a world and the spectator's world, further modified by the referential associations originating in the experience of an improper fictional world.

The apparent double reference of the performance-text

It would appear that this line of argumentation, in support of the metaphoric function of fictional worlds, leads to a contradiction. If a theatre performance-text is a description of a fictional world, it follows that the latter is the referent of the former. As suggested above, the notion of 'reference' is vital for the understanding of 'metaphor', since improperness cannot be established without knowledge of the referent (chapter 3). The same sentence/text can be either literal or metaphoric depending on the nature of the referent. Therefore, if indeed a performance-text refers to a fictional world, and the latter refers to the spectator's world, a single description would paradoxically refer to two different referents, contradicting thereby the very notion of 'reference' (Searle, 1985: 72–96).

I suggest that only the principle of metaphor settles this paradox, because of conceiving a fictional world as the predicate of a metaphoric relationship between it and the spectator's world. The main function of a predicate is categorization of a referent (Searle, *ibid.*). In metaphor, therefore, reference to a second referent is only apparent and aims at inducing alternative referential associations, and attaching them to a common literal modifier. The moment the improper term provides the expected referential associations, it can be ignored; e.g., in 'John hesitates like Hamlet', reference to Hamlet only aims at activating the character's name as an improper source of referential associations for qualifying John's hesitation. I contend that this metaphoric function also characterizes the relation between the whole fictional world of Hamlet, in the capacity of predicate, and the spectator's psyche. Consequently, while apparently describing and referring to a world, a performance-text actually describes the improper term of a metaphor, which is the source of improper referential associations for the description of the spectator's world, its actual referent; i.e., the metaphoric nature of fictional worlds too transmutes apparent double reference into single reference.

The mechanism of textual metaphor

The function of a fictional world as the improper term of an overall metaphor is proven by the very fact of personification. As suggested above, personification is supported by additional specific human traits, basically differing from those of the spectator, and by being enacted by flesh and blood actors. It is the inherent difference between a fictional world and the world of a spectator that substantiates the metaphoric relation between them. The elements shared by a fictional world and a spectator's world, such as common qualities, drives, motives, actions and viewpoints, should be seen as the common literal modifiers of such an overall metaphor; e.g., the unbridled ambition of Macbeth. In contrast, the elements of difference, particularly the referential associations induced by the unique nature of a fictional world, are the crux of the metaphoric description, whose (unmarked) subject refers to the amorphous psychical state of affairs of the spectator. On these grounds, the predicative relation between a described world and the spectator's psyche satisfies the truth conditions of the predicate 'is a metaphor'. The mechanism of textual metaphor can therefore be described as follows: (a) a fictional world is (subliminally) perceived not as a literal but as a potential metaphoric description of a spectator's world; (b) a performance-text employs or evokes common literal modifiers capable of modifying both a fictional world and the real world of a spectator; (c) these literal modifiers bear alternative referential associations originating not in the world of a spectator, but in a fictional world; and (d) these literal modifiers, modified by referential associations originating in the improper term (the fictional world), lend formulation to the amorphous contents of a spectator's psyche. The metaphoric deep structure of the theatre experience can thus be represented graphically as follows:

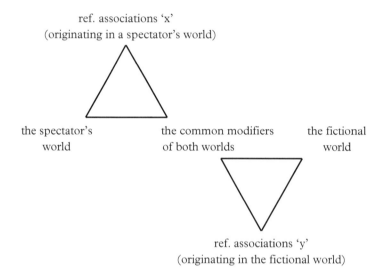

ref. associations 'x'
(originating in a spectator's world)

the spectator's   the common modifiers   the fictional
world   of both worlds   world

ref. associations 'y'
(originating in the fictional world)

As suggested for simpler metaphoric structures (sentence and motif), the deep structure of metaphor determines preference for the referential associations 'y' originating in the improper term: the fictional world.

Since theatre is an iconic medium characterized by imprinting images on matter similar to their models, a performance-text reveals a material reality capable of creating sensory experiences, which may replace sensory recollections induced by verbal metaphor, and thus condition a spectator's perception of a fictional world. It would appear, therefore, that instead of referential associations, a fictional metaphor depends entirely on such an unmediated experience. Furthermore, the pleasure (or displeasure) that a spectator experiences in watching such a text, including effects on the aesthetic level, may also become part of the activated referential associations. Without underestimating such an experience, however, it should be remembered that referential associations are not circumscribed to sensory aspects, but include emotional, ethic, aesthetic and modal aspects as well, all of which can be induced by a fictional world, and not necessarily by the performance-text.

While the metaphoric thesis may apply to both author and spectator, only the latter is the genuine object of a metaphoric fictional description. Whereas for the author the description of a world may be literal, the spectator cannot avoid experiencing it as metaphoric due to the basic differences between these worlds to various extents. Moreover, authors may also create fictional worlds in expectation that they will make sense for spectators, without necessarily subscribing to their truth-value in regard to themselves. Consequently, the craft of an author of a fictional world lies in creating a special kind of artifact, capable of functioning as a potential metaphoric description for a spectator's amorphous being. Spectators intuitively decide whether or not such a potential metaphor aptly describes their inner states of affairs.

Poetic implications

The principle of metaphoric description of the spectator's psychical state of affairs has far-reaching implications in regard to the structure of a fictional world, which is a complex construct that organizes human qualities, motives, actions and viewpoints on several levels (mythical, praxical, naïve, ironic and aesthetic (chapter 7). *Because of being grafted upon the substratum of personification each of these layers becomes an additional layer in the metaphoric buildup of a fictional world.* If the fundamental structural layer of personification did not substantiate the metaphoric thesis posited in this chapter, then all other layers would not be metaphoric either. The metaphoric relationship between fictional world and spectator thus involves all the structural layers of a fictional work, which create a potential overall metaphor of the spectator's psychical state of affairs. This principle applies to all fictional arts, literary or dramatic, such as fiction, cinema, puppet theatre, TV and radio drama. It also applies to play-scripts despite their deficient nature.

Since it is the spectator's concluding experience that determines the nature and structure of a fictional world, within the wide category of 'prestructured theatre experiences', a crucial distinction should be made between experiences of harmony or disharmony (absurdity) with the expectations of synchronic audiences (cf. Esslin: xix). While the former usually aim at reaffirming the value systems cherished by an audience (cf. Hegel: 1195–99 & Bradley: 80) and producing catharsis of anxiety (Aristotle, *Poetics*, VI, ii), the latter aim at refuting them and increasing anxiety. In the terms of the metaphoric thesis, it may be claimed that while *the aim of an archetypal fictional world is to attach a metaphoric predicate of harmony to a description of the spectator's world, absurd fictional worlds strive for the opposite effect.*

An absurdist fictional world reinforces the subversive power of real experiences that contradict the cognitive/ethical system of an audience. Such an overall metaphor of disorder may lead spectators to doubt the validity of their own concepts of the world. However, the mere fact of metaphoric description through a cultural medium may create an aesthetic detachment that enables spectators, in Nietzsche's terms, 'to gaze into the horror of individual existence, yet without being turned to stone by the vision' (1956: 102). Whereas the aim of such a structure is to attach a disharmonious metaphoric predicate to the description of a spectator's world, paradoxically, depending on the initial attitude of the spectator, such an experience may also reaffirm an absurdist viewpoint. Such a possible effect supports the assumption of an existential need for reaffirmation.

Both kinds of fictional structures reflect a predetermined authorial intention, whether to reaffirm or refute held views; therefore, the truth-value of such fictional worlds is negligible (chapter 7). Metaphor itself aims not necessarily at truth, but at an experience of truth. Moreover, the truth or falsity of the connotations of an improper term (a fictional world) is irrelevant to the truth conditions of a metaphor (*ibid.*). For example, whereas the presupposition that rhinoceros are violent animals is false, such an association does not prevent the overall metaphor of Ionesco's *Rhinoceros* from producing an experience of truth, provided that the audience assumes that it is true.

The fact that spectators have a need for recurrent experiences of truth, and invest time and money to expose themselves to metaphoric fictional worlds, indicates that they need constant reassurance from exactly the opposite end: anxiety in the face of chaos. Anxiety is rooted in the inherent non-correspondence between any cultural ideology and real life, which constantly provides reasons for its disproof. Anxiety is rooted in the possibility of harmony being overthrown by malicious or unintentional evil. Both the harmonious and absurdist structures of fictional worlds thus bear witness to this elementary struggle in the psyche.

The fundamental similarity between dreams and performance-texts should be stressed again and again. In both there is a transmutation of the inner world of a dreamer/spectator into a world of human characters and actions; i.e., into a fictional world. For both it is assumed that such a personified world metaphorically expresses/describes the inner world of a dreamer/spectator. The difference lies in that, in contrast to dreams, theatre is capable of mobilizing symbols of culture as barriers against non-ethical (neutral) and anti-ethical threatening forces. Theatre can therefore be conceived of as a socially and culturally-conditioned form of dreaming.

128

On this structural level, the metaphoric principle bears witness to theatre's cognitive function, in affording complex metaphors of an actual or potential human existence. It reveals theatre as a universal laboratory for humans to think about themselves and their potentialities. It may be safely argued, therefore, that the basic function of a fictional art is, unless it aims at the opposite goal, to create appropriate metaphors, which can protect people from anxiety in the face of chaos, thereby affording barriers that enable them to day-dream the dream of culture.

Metaphor in dramatic practice

In principle, a potential metaphoric relation between a fictional world and a spectator's world applies to all fictional experiences and can be illustrated by each of them. Nonetheless, as presupposed for smaller units, there can be improper predications that are simply nonsensical. The main thesis of this chapter is illustrated by pertinent analyses of Sophocles' *Oedipus the King*, and Yerushalmi's dramatization of the biblical narrative of Jephthah's daughter. These examples have amply demonstrated their meaningfulness to audiences.

(A) *Sophocles' Oedipus the King* (continued): Freud claims: 'It is the fate of all of us, perhaps, to direct our first sexual impulse towards our mother and our first hatred and our first murderous wish against our father' (Freud, 1978: 364). A translation of Otto Rank works offers an alternative version to the last phrase: 'our first impulses of hatred and resistance towards our fathers' (Rank: 8). If indeed the referent of the myth of Oedipus is everyman, this narrative cannot be a literal description of the existential human predicament. First, because it is a fictional world, in which Oedipus not only directs his 'first sexual impulse' towards his mother, but actually marries and has children with her (i.e., commits incest). Second, because he not only directs his first 'hatred' or 'resistance' towards his father, but actually kills him (i.e., commits parricide). This could have been a literal and true description only if the actual drives of a child were indeed incestuous and murderous, which is doubtful at the so-called 'Oedipal age'. Assumedly, they have no exact idea of what 'marriage' and 'death' mean. Moreover, 'first sexual impulse' may just mean a child's need for bodily tenderness, symbolized by his mother, and 'first murderous wish' or 'first impulses of hatred' – a metaphoric description of the child's struggle against the imminent invasion of his soul by social values, symbol-ized by his father. An often forgotten fact is that in this myth, Jocasta is as incestuous as Oedipus and Laius, in contrast to his son, is murderous. If indeed this myth maps two of everyman's fundamental and universal unconscious drives, these gaps preclude considering it as a meaningful description of them, unless the principle of metaphor is invoked. Freud definitely failed to perceive that the myth of Oedipus is an unmistakable case of a metaphoric description of the psyche. In any case, the world of Oedipus is not the world of the spectator and a potential metaphoric description is thus established.

Jephthah's daughter welcomes her father. Courtesy of the Itim Theatre.
Photo: Israel Haramaty.

The metaphoric quality of this myth, which describes two elementary attitudes towards parents, is reinforced by the family's royal status and the setting of their story in the nation's remote (or, rather, mythical) past, although it could have been set in any other 'reality'. Following this line of reasoning it can be conjectured that myths or historical narratives featuring aggression or eroticism among family share this basic metaphoric description of psychical drives.

(B) *Yerushalmi's Jephthah's Daughter.* This narrative was dramatized in a scene of Yerushalmi's *Vayomar, Vayelekh* (biblical opening phrases, meaning 'He spoke, He went'), the first part of her ambitious stage version of the Bible. In this scene, the actress recites the biblical text four times, seemingly enacting the storyteller. The entire sequence lasts about ten minutes, each part commencing with 'the spirit of the Lord came upon Jephthah' and ending with 'the daughters of Israel went yearly to lament the daughter of Jephthah the Gileadite four days in a year' (*Judges* 11, 29–40). Initially, the actress enters and kneels down, with her hands leaning on her thighs, and her torso rhythmically bowing as in mourning, while reciting the story for the first time in a laconic and monotonous manner, in tune with the detached attitude of the biblical storyteller. Then, she stands up and remains standing throughout the scene, and accompanies each sentence with a hand gesture typical of the audience's culture, such as raising the right hand, palm extended and toward the main axis of the body, when Jephthah vows his oath. Some of these gestures are imprinted images of typical activities, such as dancing when the daughter welcomes Jephthah 'with timbrels and with dances' (11, 34); and some of them are bodily metaphors, such as the body foundering as if under a heavy load, when Jephthah says 'thou has brought me very low' (11, 35), and crossing her hands on her chest as if in handcuffs at the end of the passage. These gestures are performed in a stylized mode, in a crescendo of volume and pitch in the actress' voice, against the background of a crescendo in the volume and tempo of electronic music. This crescendo also applies to her facial expressions, bodily movements and hand gestures, eventually creating a vertiginous rhythm. The fourth time, against the background of additional lighting effects, resembling lightning, the volume of her voice reaches paroxysm and her bodily movements become a hysterical dance. All these seemingly reflect the storyteller character's growing emotional involvement and intensity, up to total identification with the daughter's suffering. Eventually the actress interrupts the sequence while reciting 'that I may go up and down upon the mountains, and bewail my virginity (11, 37) and adds to the script, "'Then [the spirit of the Lord]"; "And he passed over"; "And [he] vowed"; "Alas, my daughter"; My father!!!' The ending with 'My father', finally confirms the growing suspicion that Jephthah's

131

daughter has gradually appropriated the story from the biblical storyteller. Her continuous dancing, initially associated to her happiness and transport in welcoming her father, and the light-heartedness reflected in her intonation, well after she becomes aware of her fate, is ironically refuted by a sarcastic innuendo that infiltrates her voice and genuinely reflects her profound suffering and desperation. Her dance of happiness thus becomes a dance of death. The scene ends with a fraught total silence of music, dance and words.

In Yerushalmi's alternative interpretation, Jephthah's daughter's individual suffering becomes central. She expresses grief not only for the non-consummation of her femininity and her imminent death, but also, through a combination of sorrow and sarcasm and the sudden change of perspective, creates a subversive image that defies the unqualified authority of her father. This image also constitutes an ironic comment on the way the biblical storyteller ignores her predicament, which, in contrast, the daughters of Israel emphasize in their annual commemoration of her grim fate (*Judges* 11, 40). He also ignores the biblical story of the Binding of Isaac, with its implicit prohibition of human sacrifice. The biblical storyteller is, consequently, exposed as oblivious of divine justice. This scene is thus a subversive statement against the patriarchal ethos reflected in the attitude of the biblical storyteller; i.e., a potential metaphor of the total subordination of women to the patriarchal ethos that governs society until present days. From a wider perspective, it is a potential metaphor of the subordination of the individual to traditional and outdated rules of society, which may promote the involvement of male spectators as well.

Whereas the shared elements between this and spectators' worlds explain their meaningful involvement, the different elements constitute the very source of improper referential associations. The description of the typical Israeli spectator's predicament through this biblical metaphor may induce a sense of living in a biblical patriarchal society, as if nothing has changed since ancient times, and perhaps, encourage a drive for change. The enthusiastic reception of this production, this scene in particular, attests to the meaningfulness of this overall stage metaphor.

9

The Rhetoric Structure of the Theatre Experience

There is an apparent incongruity in viewing a performance-text as both a description of a fictional world and an artifact that aims at a particular effect on an audience. There are, however, well established sets of theoretical notions and expressions that nonetheless refer to various kinds of effect; such as (a) 'reaffirmation' of held views (Hegel: 1195–99), 'defamiliarization of reality' (Shklovsky: 12), 'experience of the absurd' (Esslin: xix) and *'épater le bourgeois'*; (b) promotion of 'conformism', awareness and criticism; and (c) 'catharsis' (Aristotle's *Poetics*: VI, 2) and 'shocking' effects (*ibid.*: XIII, 2). All these terms imply that a fictional world is designed to produce a particular effect on an audience. Since these effects cannot be ignored, it is sensible to explore their mechanisms, regarding this kind of relation between a fictional world and the spectator's psyche; i.e., on the stage-audience structural level.

It would appear that viewing performance-texts in terms of 'description' excludes the notion of 'effect' because descriptions are not supposed to have effects. In contrast, viewing performance-texts in terms of 'action', which implies 'intentions' and 'purposes', allows the possibility of an embedded description. *This apparent incongruity can thus be settled by applying a pragmatic approach, speech act theory in particular.* According to this approach, a verbal description is part of a micro-speech act that is performed with the intention of constituting or changing a state of affairs and the purpose of producing an expected effect. It is sensible, therefore, to apply this principle also to a verbal or iconic description of textual scope: a macro-speech act.

A performance-text is thus a 'macro-speech act', which is performed by an act that indicates the intention of changing a (psychical) state of affairs, and this act embeds a description of a fictional world, on the level of interaction between director and spectator. In other words, the theatre medium not only generates descriptive texts, which can be read and inter-preted by spectators, but also artifacts that can be experienced as acts/actions performed upon them. While 'description' belongs in the sphere of semiotics, notions referring to possible effects belong in the province of rhetoric.

A performance-text fully articulates a description of a (real or fictional) world; but such a text usually does not articulate the intentions and purposes underlying such a description; e.g., affecting and even changing the attitudes of an audience to the injustice in a governmental policy, or the obsolete nature of certain social values. Such intentions and purposes are usually made explicit in comments *about* a production in programs and interviews by directors or performers. In recent years, directors have been obsessed with disproving rooted concepts and attitudes of audiences, as illustrated by productions of modernist and post-modernist productions.

The aim of this chapter is to show that (a) speech act theory settles the apparent incongruence of a performance-text being both a description and an act/action on the director/spectator axis; (b) speech act theory applies to performance-texts on a holistic level; (c) such a text aims more at an experience of truth than at truth itself; and (d) the theatre experience thus reflects a rhetoric deep structure. The following considerations mainly follow Dijk's theory of speech activity. These principles are illustrated through an additional analysis of Yerushalmi's stage interpretation of the biblical Jephthah's Daughter narrative (chapter 8).

The pragmatic nature of speech interaction

Since the nature of real, iconic and fictional verbal interaction were dealt with above (chapter 2), the following remarks are circumscribed to features relevant to the application of speech act theory to the textual level:

(a) A speech act is the perceptible aspect of an action; i.e., its index.

(b) While a verbal description aims at categorizing a state of affairs, a verbal action aims at changing it. A speech act/action is not a description but at most an object of description.

(c) A speech act/action is characterized by two kinds of intentionality: 'intention' ('illocutionary force' in Austin terms), reflected in the nature of an act; and 'purpose' ('perlocutionary effect' in Austin terms), which reflects the expected effects of an act/action (Austin: 95–132; cf. Dijk: 175; Lyons, 1988: 730).

(d) A speech act includes a descriptive sentence (p) that is subordi-nated to the nature of an act; i.e., it is the performance of an action through stating a descriptive sentence.

(e) Speech acts reflect a common deep structure: I, you, performative verb and embedded descriptive sentence, with 'I' being the agent and 'you' its object. Following the course of interaction, the referents of 'I' and 'you' interchange. The performative verb is always in the present indicative (now), which is the only time of an action. The place of performance, which is always 'here', is self-understood. The nature of an act/action (intention) determines how the embedded descriptive sentence should be understood; e.g., as an actual or possible state of affairs.

(f) The same embedded sentence can be used to perform different actions, thus being inherently ambiguous. Its disambiguation depends on concomitant non-verbal indicators that are the only reliable indicators of intention.

(g) Under typical conditions of interaction, a speech act only articulates the embedded sentence, while the performative elements ('I', 'you' and performative verb) are either indicated by non-verbal indicators or self-understood (primary speech acts). These indicators are always explicit.

(h) The specific intention of changing a specific state of affairs is either categorized by a performative verb or by non-verbal indicators. In contrast, the purposes of an act are usually not articulated and their categorization depends on interpretation.

(i) Categorization of intentions and purposes of a previous act/action is a genuine verbal activity and a necessary step prior to reaction, if the intention is to react adequately. A reaction thus features two elements: a categorization of the intentions and purposes of a previous act/action, and a subsequent action, thus opening a new performative cycle.

(j) Being an exchange not of descriptions, but of acts/actions, dialogue is a kind of interaction.

The pragmatic nature of stage/audience interaction

I suggest that a performance-text is an authorial act of textual scope that employs an iconic description of a fictional world to produce an effect on an audience. This thesis presupposes that the theatre medium, which is non-verbal in nature, has the ability to generate descriptions and employ them for performing actions.

It is widely accepted that in theatre there are two axes of communication: the fictional axis (character–character) and the theatrical axis (stage–audience); with the latter describing the former, which is not an axis of communication, but of interaction (chapter 2). I contend that the latter

135

too is not an axis of communication, despite offering a description of a fictional world, but an axis of interaction. It reflects thereby the same principles of speech interaction: the use of a descriptive text for the sake of changing a state of affairs.

Ingarden claims that the same words, voiced by actors on stage, while simultaneously operating on both the axes of character–character and stage–audience, they fulfil different functions: 'Something in them must be different for the spectator and for the represented person [the character]; otherwise the difference between their action on the spectator and that person would be, not only incomprehensible, but impossible' (p. 394). Therefore, '[t]he only difference still possible is in a different ontic character of the words spoken' on stage: whereas the characters 'see the expression of these words as a fact in their common (represented) world', the spectators 'observe the spoken words and the fact of their being spoken only as [. . .] something portrayed by artistic means but not actually existing in the real world' (pp. 394–5). In other words, while on the fictional axis the function of such words is interaction, on the theatrical axis it is a description (a portrayal) of interaction. Moreover, whereas within the fictional world a character speaks them for their effect on another character, on the stage–audience axis they aim at being perceived in their artistic function, so that 'the result will be an aesthetic reaction and, in particular, pleasure or displeasure' (p. 394). In other words, the difference lies in the distinct effect they have on either fellow characters or spectators. However, this insight does not explain all the effects suggested above. The following sections examine the reasons for applying the principles of speech activity to the theatrical experience.

(A) *Descriptive nature of the performance-text*: If the nature of 'speech act' is epitomized in the performance of an act through performing a description, the descriptive condition is satisfied by any iconic medium, theatre in particular. If the description of a fictional world basically means a description of an interaction, a dialogue in particular, the iconic principle is even more adequate than language: while a literary work can describe speech acts by notation of their wording and additional verbal descriptions of their non-verbal indicators, in the linear sequence typical of language, a performance-text can replicate them as complex images, presenting all their components at once like in real life. The notion of 'speech act' can thus be used as a technical term for any description of any scope in any language/medium, if employed for performing an act/action.

(B) *Performative nature of the performance-text*: The main reason for expanding the applicability of speech act theory to theatre performance-texts is that their ultimate aim is to produce predetermined effects on audiences. Notions referring to kinds of effect, such as 'reaffirmation', 'criticism' and 'catharsis' should find their right conceptual frame in action theory; i.e., be understood in terms of directorial 'intentions and purposes'. Whereas a fictional world, in its capacity of description, should be conceived of in terms of 'structural metaphor' and categorized in terms of 'truth' or 'falsity' (chapter 8), in its capacity of act/action it should be in terms of intentional 'success' or 'failure'.

Broadly speaking, the intentions of authors may be either to 'reaffirm' spectators' beliefs or 'challenge' them on the cognitive level; i.e., a performance-text may be a description of a fictional world that is meant to be either in harmony or disharmony with the world image/concept of a spectator, by either supporting or refuting it respectively. The main purposes are probably to induce certain attitudes in audiences, such as conformism, awareness, criticism and even willingness to engage in active struggle. The tragic, comic or grotesque treatment of a fictional world should also be seen as subordinated to such an overall intent. Cathartic or shocking effects, on the other hand, should be seen as the expected effects on the emotional level. Emotional effects naturally accompany the fictional experience on the epistemological level.

It would appear that there is a difference between micro- and macro-speech acts in their manners of indicating their intentions. Whereas the former do so through a performative verb and non-verbal indicators, performance-texts do not articulate them at all. However, the description of a fictional world operates like a primary speech act, in which only the embedded sentence is present in the surface structure, while the performative elements 'I' and 'you' are self-understood, and the intentions and purposes should be conjectured on the grounds of structural interpretation and wider cultural and social contexts.

The equivalence of micro- and macro-speech acts implies that the description of a fictional world by a performance-text is subordinated to the action it is meant to perform. In this sense *a performance-text becomes the natural object of a theory of action that should account for both the descriptive and performative aspects of theatre.*

(c) *Equivalence of agent/director and object/spectator.* The expansion of 'speech act' to denote acts of textual scope, including descriptions of fictional worlds in any language/medium, entails the equivalence of the notions of 'agent' and 'director' on the one hand, and the notions of 'object' and 'spectator' on the other. Moreover, 'speaker' and 'hearer', although widely employed in speech act theory, are inadequate even for verbal speech acts: they do not reflect that speech is not used in language's typical capacity of description but, rather, for the sake of changing states of affairs.

137

It is not speaking and hearing that characterizes them, but 'doing' and being an 'object' of a doing.

The 'I–you' relationship between director and spectator is also taken in turns as in micro-speech acts. Although spectators are not supposed to interact within the boundaries of the fictional world, they do react to performance-texts and, in particular, to directors and performers of texts (actors and designers/makers) by various means such as applause, fame, criticism, recommendation, taking interest in their lives, and even buying tickets for performances by the same artists on subsequent occasions.

(D) *Notion of 'macro-speech act'*: Dijk employs 'global speech act' for a sequence of speech acts that involves the same agent and addressee, and reflects a consistent macro-intention and macro-purposes (1977: 184ff); e.g., Anthony's famous speech in Shakespeare's *Julius Caesar*. It would appear, however, that there is a fundamental difference between Anthony's speech and a performance-text. The former is composed of a series of fairly equivalent and homogeneous speech acts of persuasion (intention), which are performed by the same fictional agent (Anthony) and addressed to the same fictional object (the crowd), and whose unified rhetoric purpose is to bring about a significant change in their attitude to the murderers of Caesar and consequently to himself. In contrast, in a performance-text, actors perform heterogeneous sets of speech acts that describe fictional speech acts with different and even contrasting intentions and purposes. It would appear, therefore, that a performance-text is devoid of unity. Yet, *the interaction between director and spectator does not take place on the level of partial descriptions of speech acts; but on the level of a whole description of a fictional world*. On this level, the entire performance-text is a complex and homogeneous macro-unit, totally different from the micro-units performed by actors or characters. I thus suggest the notion 'macro-speech act' for such a complex unit, regardless of the variety and number of constituent micro-units. Instead of Dijk's 'global speech act', therefore, 'macro-speech act' should be preferred for preserving both the common nature of speech and medium act, and the contrast between 'micro' and 'macro' for the constituent and textual units respectively.

There is thus a basic intentional and structural equivalence between real or fictional micro-speech acts and such macro-speech acts, which reflect the following principles: (a) the intention to change a (psychical) state of affairs; (b) the existence of an embedded description; (c) the meaning of such a description as determined by the overall intention; (d) the aim to produce an effect on the object of the act/action; and (e) the relation between agent/director and object/spectator as a kind of interaction.

138

Rhetoric nature of stage/audience interaction

In principle, although a performance-text may reflect any intention, such as reaffirmation or confutation of held beliefs, persuasion is a precondition for its success. It is sensible to suggest, therefore, that such a text is a particular form of 'rhetoric text', like a political speech, a sermon or a scientific lecture. In these too persuasion is a precondition for the achievement of their ends.

The aim of a rhetoric intention is, however, not to bring about the acceptance of an idea on the grounds of 'truth' in the scientific sense of the term. *The rhetoric approach rather extends the sphere of persuasion to encompass the 'experience of truth', which in most cases does not even partially overlap 'truth' in the above sense.* The aim of a rhetoric act is usually not truth itself, but, rather, the experience of truth. To account for this difference, Aristotle introduced the notion of 'enthymeme', which refers to the mental mechanism by which persuasion is achieved with no necessary commitment to truth (*Rhetoric*: section II, ch. 1, 2; pp. 75ff). In contrast to 'syllogism', *the premises of an enthymematic discourse are not necessarily true, but conceived of as true by a synchronic receiver.* The enthymematic process of persuasion aims at demonstrating that a pre-established conclusion logically follows from the premises accepted by a certain readership/audience. This explains how politicians, while being able to persuade people who accept the "truth" of their conclusions which follow from their shared premises, cannot persuade others who share different ones. *The rhetoric structure of a performance-text thus aims not necessarily at truth but at an experience of truth.*

The 'enthymematic' structure is clearly privileged by authors and audiences. The beliefs of the audience, in comedy and tragedy as well as in farce and melodrama, provide the common ground for the theatre experience to take off. The 'sacred cows' of the community are always tested in extreme situations, whether they are eventually reaffirmed or confuted. Probing held beliefs under extreme conditions produces tension, a euphemism for fear, which is manipulated by all the above-mentioned genres. Such conditions also explain how even reaffirmation of held beliefs can be conceived of as a change in a psychical state of affairs: from initial uncertainty to eventual conviction.

Most dramatic fictional worlds are pre-structured for both anchoring on the accepted views of prospective audiences and bringing about their persuasion. Tailoring fictional worlds in accordance with intentions of persuasion, excludes such performance-texts from the sphere of the search for truth. However, this does not mean that the theatre medium cannot be used for such a purpose. Some kinds of modernist theatre are clear instances of striving to achieve such a goal.

Since most descriptions of fictional worlds are subordinated to rhetoric ends, it is crucial for them to command credibility. Therefore, notions such as Aristotle's the 'probable', the 'credible', the 'necessary' (*Poetics*: IX), the 'possible' and the 'impossible' (*ibid.*: XXV,17); Corneille's the '*vraisemblable*' and the '*croyable*' (pp. 218ff; cf. Burns: 98ff – authenticating conventions) make reference to these aspects of the mechanism of enthymematic persuasion; i.e., to the psychological mechanisms that should be activated (or avoided) for creating an experience of truth. This principle is epitomized in Aristotle's dictum: 'the poet should prefer probable impossibilities to improbable possibilities' (*Poetics*: XXIV, 10). The classicist notion of 'verisimilitude' accounts for the promotion of an experience of truth by not contradicting what is known and/or is assumed as known by an audience (*ibid.*: XV, 1–5). The 'logos' of such fictional worlds is thus subordinated to the enthymematic principle. Nonetheless, although a performance-text manipulates an audience into accept the truth embodied in its fictional world, a spectator is free to be persuaded or not.

From a rhetoric viewpoint, since the effect on a spectator mainly depends on the nature of a fictional world, it may be assumed that its description is an artifact that fundamentally aims at a predetermined effect (cf. *Poetics*: XIII), while reflecting the spectator's mechanism of response (chapter 7). I suggest, therefore, that *the rhetoric structure subordinates all the inner and outer structural layers and that the experience of truth is the ultimate end of a fictional world*. In other words, the overall rhetoric gradually transmutes mythical material into a rhetoric mechanism meant to have a pre-programmed effect on each spectator. If a performance-text is a macro-speech act that aims at affecting spectators, especially their sense of orientation in the world, it follows that all the structural layers, the ironic, the aesthetic, and the metaphoric in particular, are subordinated to the rhetoric aim.

(A) *The ironic experience*: The theatre medium poses a problem for authors who wish to promote an audience's sense of understanding a fictional world better than the characters, what is usually termed 'dramatic irony' (Sedgewick; cf. Styan, 1967: 48ff). The problem lies in that, by virtue of the fictional principle, characters are independent of authors, and conceive of their worlds from their own restricted and biased viewpoints. Nonetheless, directors usually aim at guiding spectators to the appropriate readings and interpretations of performance-texts through functional characters or fictional characters in functional situations (chapter 4). These conventions, which convey more information and/or advantageous conceptual frames, are meant to promote and control the formation of ironic viewpoints in the spectators' minds. I note that while conventions are devices of the theatre medium, their functions affect the understanding of fictional worlds.

I have suggested elsewhere the following features of 'irony': inversion of meaning, super-understanding, ironic contemplation, and ironic pleasure (1992a: 126–43).

(1) *'Inversion of meaning'* means that an ironic text conveys two perspectives, naïve and ironic, which converge on the same referent, the praxical layer, with the ironic viewpoint potentially inverting the naïve one. Whereas the latter is found inadequate, the former fits the referent. The principle of 'inversion of meaning', therefore, requires the knowledge of the fictional referent, as otherwise no sense of discrepancy can be detected. This principle may thus apply to both the unintended inadequacy of the object of irony and the spurious irony of an alleged ironist.

(2) *'Super-understanding'* means that the privileged spectator is accorded the ability to perceive both the naïve and ironic meanings, and prefer the latter (Rozik, *ibid.*: 129; cf. Styan, *ibid.*: 49). While characters' understanding is deemed inferior, the spectator is meant to command a sense of superiority. Although J. L. Styan conceives of 'dramatic irony' in terms of 'super-knowledge', I prefer 'super-understanding' because it is not only a matter of knowledge, but also of superior understanding based on communication between authors and spectators through an additional channel of communication that circumvents the characters. Since each character exhibits its independent viewpoint, there is a need for such an indirect channel. The ironic perspective thus enjoys privileged authority, without necessarily meaning that it is more adequate. The aim is not to impart absolute wisdom, divine or otherwise, but an experience of wisdom. Inversion of meaning is not produced for its own sake but for the sake of ironic superiority (Rozik, *ibid.*: 132–4). The author may refuse ironic superiority by canceling the indirect channel or by using it in contrast to its professed aim (*ibid.*: 135). In such a case, the spectators themselves become the objects of irony.

(3) *'Ironic contemplation'* means that ironic superiority creates a sense of detachment: in contrast to the characters' total involvement in their own world, the spectators are given a kind of freedom in their cognitive and moral considerations. Such a detachment does not exclude possible total involvement on a different level. It rather presupposes it. There is no point in being detached without involvement. This duality characterizes spectatorship.

(4) *'Ironic pleasure'* is a particular kind of pleasure that derives not from fulfillment of drives, reconfirmation of ideas or catharsis, but from the opportunity to experience and enjoy ironic superiority and contemplation, of which human beings are existentially deprived. Therefore, there is nothing more natural than compensating them for this missing faculty.

In contrast to Frye, the notions of '*eiron*' and '*alazon*' (p. 172), based on a pair of comic stock-types mentioned in the *Tractatus Coislinianus* (Cooper: 226), should be redefined in terms of 'subject' and 'object' of irony respectively. Through pre-structuration of a fictional world and ironic conventions, the spectator may become an eiron, unless intentionally deprived. Such a sense of ironic superiority may regard even the cleverest characters (e.g., Oedipus). In archetypal theatre, dramatic irony is thus not only a basic mode of experience, but also crucial for the rhetoric persuasion of the spectator. The possible denial of dramatic irony reveals that it is crucial for absurdist theatre too. As a medium, theatre is capable of producing contrasting experiences.

(B) *The aesthetic experience*: typical aesthetic notions, such as 'whole', 'unity', 'consistency', 'coherence', 'proportion', 'harmony' and 'absurdity' are usually employed to further characterize the ironic layer. In particular, they apply to the cognitive and emotional dimensions of the relation between spectators' expectations and the eventual consequences of fictional worlds; e.g., in structures that are either harmonious with these expectations ('reaffirmation'), particularly in cases of harmony despite disharmony, or eventually disharmonious with them (experience of the 'absurd'). They are also employed for the aesthetic relations among perceptible aspects of a semiotic text, such as the physiognomy of actors and the qualities of costume, set and lighting; and for the possible correspondence between these two levels of the performance-text. This structural layer too is thus crucial in the mechanism of enthymematic persuasion.

(C) *The metaphoric experience*: a fictional world is designed to function as a macro-metaphor of the synchronic spectators' psychical states of affairs, which explains their extreme involvement in the fictional action (chapter 8). The metaphoric principle explains why spectators expose themselves to such descriptions of fictional worlds, which fundamentally differ from their own worlds. In this sense a theatre experience is a confrontation between an amorphous psyche and a metaphoric description of it, as two sides of the same coin. Therefore, as suggested above, reference to a fictional world is only apparent, and the rhetoric aim of a description of a fictional world is to constitute a potential metaphor of the spectator's psychical state of affairs (chapter 8).

In principle, there is no meaningful difference between a literal and a metaphoric description embedded in a macro-speech act, in regard to its rhetoric aim, except for the latter possibly appealing also to unconscious layers and primeval forms of thinking of the psyche. The metaphoric nature of the fictional experience is thus not only compatible with the rhetoric aim, but also probably more efficient.

142

Rhetoric analysis should be made on a synchronic basis, because no definite effect can be envisaged for any possible audience. Such an effect should be conjectured not only on the grounds of universal patterns of response, but also of specific cultural values, which determine audiences' expectations. Rhetoric analysis of macro-speech acts thus complements the contributions of other disciplines, the semiotic and poetic in particular, in elucidating the theatre mechanisms of generating meaning. Therefore, a rhetoric theory of the theatre experience should be developed.

Yerushalmi's *Jephthah's Daughter* (continued)

Yerushalmi's interpretation of this biblical narrative reflects severe criticism of its underlying patriarchal ethos, which constitutes the cultural baggage of typical Israeli spectators, educated in the State system (chapter 8). This baggage consists of the biblical text, which in itself constitutes an interpretation, wrapped up in a wealth of later midrashic and Zionist interpretations.

In *Judges*, the story is told from the viewpoint of an omniscient storyteller, in a matter of fact and detached mode. He condenses a prolonged and probably complex series of events into a few sentences, while quoting a few consequential speeches, out of what must have been a bitter and excruciating dialogue between a sacrificing father and a sacrificial daughter. The attitude of the storyteller definitely mitigates the emotional potential of this narrative. His viewpoint presupposes the validity of the historiographic formula typical of *Judges*: whenever the children of Israel abandon God's ways they are defeated, and only upon their return they are redeemed. The very inclusion of the myth in this book implies that Jephthah's victories substantiate the formula. Moreover, the storyteller avoids any critical comment on the sacrifice, thus indicating that God accepts the judge's declaration that he cannot retract his vow.

Most intriguing is the fact that the biblical storyteller ignores the Binding of Isaac. This narrative is usually interpreted, by ancient sources too, as a testimony of divine aversion to human sacrifice, progeny in particular, and evidence of the biblical ethical superiority over the widespread pagan ritual practice in ancient times. Against this background, God's lack of intervention to save Jephthah's daughter is most conspicuous. Furthermore, the Bible tells the stories of the kings of Judah, Ahaz and Manas'she, who made their sons 'pass through the fire' on the altar of Baal, adopting 'the abominations of the heathens', and were accordingly punished by God (Kings II, 16, 3 & 21, 6 respectively). The fact that Jephthah goes unpunished also contradicts this divine pattern of response.

In stark contrast, the *Midrash* vehemently criticizes Jephthah's deed.

'*Midrash*' is used here for an entire genre of books devoted to the inter-pretation of the *Torah*, also through parables. Although this predominantly Halachic genre does not make reference to the sacrifice of Isaac in this context either, it does criticize the biblical storyteller for ignoring God's rejection of human sacrifice; e.g., 'And the sacred spirit [God] shouts: did I ask you to sacrifice human souls to me? – which I have not announced and not commanded, and did not even imagine?' (Bialik: 82; my trans.); and '[b]ecause Jephthah wished to sacrifice his daughter, she was crying in front of him and said unto him: My father, my father! [the final words of Yerushalmi's text] I came out towards you in joy and you slaughter me! Is it written in the Torah that the children of Israel should sacrifice their own children on the altar? He said: my daughter, I have already vowed' (*ibid*.; my trans.). Moreover, the *Midrash* conceives of the very act of sacrificing his daughter as the actual punishment of Jephthah: since he had promised a human sacrifice, God chanced upon him his own daughter (*ibid.*)

The Zionist interpretation, which maintains inter-textual relations with the previous ones, reflects the ideological intention to promote the Bible not only as a testimony of the glorious past of the nation, free in its own land, but also as the creator of the universal ethos of the prophets, which it bequeathed to humanity. This narrative definitely poses a problem to this ideology too.

In the biblical version she is portrayed as a totally obedient daughter, who accepts her father's decision without reservation, and even assists him in the implementation of his oath. It would appear that the *Midrash* contrasts this interpretation, but despite articulating her own objections, these are also based on *Halachic* principles, thus reflecting a patriarchal ethos. In other words, in these interpretations she is not consulted on matters concerning her own life; i.e., she is not conceived of as an indi-vidual. She is not given even a personal name. Similar considerations apply to the Zionist interpretation, which actually accepts the supremacy of patriarchal national values over individual self-fulfillment and happiness. In the literature of the generation of the War of Independence, the 'Binding of Isaac' motif was employed rhetorically as a metaphor of the sons and daughters' objection to their sacrifice on the altar of the national ideals of their parents.

The common attitude reflected in this tradition is the total supremacy of patriarchal values. It is this attitude that shaped the cultural baggage of most spectators. It is against this interpretive tradition and educational background that the Jephthah's daughter scene in Yerushalmi's produc-tion implies criticism of all previous interpretations. Because of the enthymematic nature of theatre rhetoric, knowledge of the cultural baggage of the spectators is vital.

The abrupt transition from the biblical storyteller's to Jephthah daughter's perspectives, both enacted by the same actress (chapter 8), reflects preference for the viewpoint of a woman, who was traditionally denied any stand in the negotiation between father and God, and whose happiness and life were sacrificed on the altar of obsolete values. Yerushalmi stressed the groundless sacrifice and individual suffering of Jephthah's daughter, rather than the religious and ethical considerations characteristic of the former interpretations. In this production, she also produced a female version of the Binding of Isaac, with the same rhetoric intention.

Yerushalmi advocates Jephthah's daughter's right, and her own, to interpret the narrative from an alternative viewpoint. She coerces thereby the spectator into a revision of the narrative from the viewpoint of anti-patriarchal current values. By emphasizing Jephthah's daughter's suffering in facing her fate, the meaning of this narrative changes from total obedience to a father and fulfillment of an oath to God, into an act of sheer cruelty, undesired by God and humans alike. Fundamentally, this scene equally reflects severe criticism of the storyteller's indifference to human suffering, the *Halachic* attitude of the *Midrash* and the problematic universal approach of Zionism. In contrast to all previous interpretations, Yerushalmi creates a caustic manifesto against deprivation of the daughter's elementary human right to decide her own fate and to consummate her potential femininity and happiness. Her protest is the protest of all those who annually bewail the frustrated virginity of the nameless daughter.

Comparison with the sacrifice of Isaac leads to the conclusion that Yerushalmi's statement transcends the narrow limits of feminist criticism, and reflects a subversive attitude to a culture that has ignored existential human rights throughout millennia. Rendering this narrative from the viewpoint of Jephthah's daughter justifies her decision to cast an actress to voice it, thus defying the biblical (male) storyteller's appropriation.

The fundamental changes in the hierarchy of values in Israeli society in recent years definitely prepared the ground for the spectators to adopt this alternative viewpoint. This scene, consequently, can be seen as a rhetoric macro-speech act aiming at an experience of harmony with spectators' values and expectations. Audiences more than warmly welcomed the Yerushalmi production (cf. Aharonson).

145

10

The Implied Director

The rhetoric structure of the theatre experience presupposes an interaction between a real director and a real spectator. In parallel to this rhetoric structure, *a dialogic structure between an implied director and an implied spectator, which is inscribed in the performance-text, can be discerned.* This twofold structure reflects the overall rhetoric deep structure that generates an actual performance-text. This chapter is devoted to the implied director, and the following chapter to the implied spectator.

Directors may explain their intentions and purposes in programs, interviews or articles. However, although they may excel in their use of the theatre medium, when explaining their own productions directors employ language, a less effective medium for them, and couch their comments in terms of specific and even dated theories. The question is, therefore, how can a director's actual rhetoric intentions be established? I suggest that *they are implicit and inscribed in a performance-text.*

Assumedly, these implied rhetoric intentions are evident in productions based on pre-existing play-scripts, which reflect their own intentions and purposes, albeit on less firm grounds. As suggested above, departures from an established interpretation of a source-text indicate the innovative intentions of a director (chapter 6). I have termed elsewhere this form of re-structuration 'creative interpretation' (Rozik: 2000a). Although such intentions are also implied in productions that are not based on pre-existing play-scripts, it is useful to reveal them in new productions of pre-existing texts, whether play-scripts or other, as this is typical of the current theatre practice.

The aim of this chapter is to show that (a) *there is a fundamental difference between hermeneutic and creative interpretation;* (b) it is the deficient nature of the play-script that necessitates creative interpretation; (c) *directorial interpretation is fundamentally not a form of interpretation, but a form of creativity;* (d) *the mechanism of creative interpretation operates by assigning specific choices to indeterminate traits in a play-script or changing them;* (e)

since creative interpretation is a necessity, the question of legitimacy is super-
fluous; (f) *a creative interpretation establishes new intertextual relations with a*
source play-script and/or previous productions of it; and (g) *departures from a*
source play-script are the main clues for revealing implied directorial intentions.

Hermeneutic vs. creative interpretation

How is it that the same play-script can generate different performance-
texts or, rather, what is the nature of the relationship between these
so-called 'variants' and the source play-script? The notion of 'variant'
betrays the commonplace literary assumption that a play-script is a self-
sufficient work of art, that everything is already formulated or implied in
it, and that its performance only adds a concrete dimension to what is
already in its wording. The complementary commonplace assumption is
that a director only has to be proficient in interpreting a play-script and
materializing its potentialities. Such a theoretical approach allows for
minor differences, on condition that these derive from a faithful and honest
interpretation of a play-script.

In recent years, however, theatre practice has disproved these presuppositions. Directors are usually less interested in play-scripts in their own
right, even if fluent in their various interpretations, and more concerned
with how they can be used for their own purposes. Their intentions are not
to reflect the original perspectives of playwrights, but rather to subordinate
play-scripts to their own images of the world (*weltanschauung*). The same
applies to actors in regard to well-designed characters. For both, a play-
script is a kind of raw material.

Although interpretation of play-scripts and interpretation by directors
and actors reflect different mental activities, the same term 'interpretation'
is employed. People say, for example, 'Peter Brook's interpretation of *A
Midsummer Night's Dream*' and 'Laurence Olivier's interpretation of
Hamlet'. The actual nature of these interpretations implies, however, that
it is not a hermeneutic interpretation that has been performed, but an innovative description of a fictional world/character that has been created.
Awareness of this is made conspicuous through comparison with previous
productions of the same play-script. A clear distinction should be established, therefore, between 'hermeneutic interpretation', which strives to
determine the meaning of a play-script or performance-text, and 'creative
interpretation', which reflects the innovative use of source-texts by a
director, as raw material for reflecting his/her own visions.

'Hermeneutic interpretation' is a reading that takes into account everything
that is explicit or implicit in a text and the possible complementation of the
reader/spectator. In contrast, *'creative interpretation' aims at creating a new*

structural metaphor, reflecting a new vision and an intention to produce a singular effect on an audience through using a pre-existing play-script, its wording in particular, and assigning specific choices to indeterminate traits or changing them; especially, by specifying the non-verbal elements of ambiguous speech acts, the qualities of characters and the definitions of situations, or reassigning them. Such a procedure reflects the original design of a director, who is the ultimate author of a performance-text.

It is the incompleteness of the play-script that both necessitates creative interpretation and explains the variation among productions based on it. Deficiency opens play-scripts to an infinite number of possible re-creations. The only constraint is that any creative interpretation should generate a highly coherent description of a fictional world.

Variation is also discerned in productions that professedly aim at being faithful to their source-text. In this sense even an attempt to closely follow the original design of a playwright is a particular case of creative interpretation. In contrast to Übersfeld, who assumes that it is the play-script ('the written text') that 'governs' the productions it generates (p. 163), the alleged original design is usually no more than a conventionalized reading of a play-script. Current trends indicate that, in most cases, directors deliberately follow this creative form of interpretation. From the viewpoint of culture, the deficiency of play-scripts even proves a great advantage, since it enables accommodation to constantly changing socio-cultural contexts. Paradoxically, *inter alia*, it is their intrinsic incompleteness that enables their universality.

Although creative interpretation usually relies on hermeneutic interpretations of play-scripts, directors mainly approach them as sources of raw material and inspiration. They employ hermeneutic interpretations only for recycling and exploiting play-scripts for the sake of new performance-texts, reflecting their own perspectives. Hermeneutic interpretation, therefore, only assists them in revealing the potentialities of play-scripts, particularly if they have been canonized. *Rather than being a particular form of interpretation, creative interpretation is a particular form of creativity.*

Creative interpretation does not contradict or exclude hermeneutic interpretation but, in fact, the former subordinates the latter. The products of creative interpretation too constitute legitimate objects for hermeneutic interpretation, which complements the creativity embodied in a performance-text. In this sense the process of hermeneutic interpretation of performance-texts is the same as for literary and other works of art. In addition, one should not overlook the possibility of a specific creative interpretation shedding light on an unperceived aspect of a source-text, contributing thereby to the collective interpretive enterprise of a cultural community.

148

Partial justification for the use of 'interpretation' in such a new sense resides in metonymic expansion, based on the assumption that the process of creative interpretation commences with hermeneutic interpretation of a play-script. Further justification may lie in the assumption that traces of a hermeneutic interpretation of a play-script may be found even in an innovative performance-text.

The mechanism of creative interpretation

How do directors combine existing verbal dialogues with sets of additional and/or alternative non-verbal features, thus generating distinct fictional worlds that are coherent, effective and faithfully reflect their own visions? Such a mixture may astonish, due to the difficulty in conceiving how new coherent descriptions of fictional worlds can be thus created. I suggest instead that *a seemingly faithful staging that seeks to express the viewpoint of a playwright, and not that of the director, should be even more astonishing, because it is impossible to imagine a work of art that reflects the viewpoint and sensibility of somebody else.* In fact, *such a combination is possible and even necessary because of the deficient nature of the play-script. Even if the director wishes to achieve an effect similar to the original production of a play-script, for an audience with a different socio-cultural background, innovation is mandatory.*

On such grounds, as suggested above, *the mechanism of creative interpretation proceeds by assigning or reassigning qualities, motives and values to characters, intentions and purposes to verbal and non-verbal acts and definitions of dramatic situations, while also reflecting the values of synchronic audiences*; i.e., through creating a structure of a fictional world based on new premises. *The process of creative interpretation includes, therefore, the following phases: hermeneutic interpretation of a play-script, deconstruction and reconstruction.*

Creative interpretation is usually characterized by disregard of a playwright's stage directions, which are 'directive' speech acts concerning the non-verbal aspects of the possible production of a play-script. Consequently, their addressee is not a readership, but a group of performers. Since in most cases stage directions are scarce or nonexistent, their share in determining the final nature of the dialogue is usually marginal. Since there is disproportion between any number of stage directions and the scope of non-verbal signs performed during a performance, this principle applies even to play-scripts that abound in them, such as Beckett's *Waiting for Godot*. Consequently, the question of whether or not stage directions are observed is fundamentally immaterial. Moreover, productions may differ even if they comply with the stage directions. Casting is also a crucial tool of creative interpretation.

The mechanism of creative interpretation also applies to the manner in which playwrights handle their different sources of narrative materials, such as mythology (e.g., the myth of Oedipus); history (e.g., the life of Julius Caesar); journalistic reports (e.g., Büchner's *Woyzeck*); and previous play-scripts; e.g., Sophocles' *Electra* and Euripides' *Electra* were first performed in 413 BC against the background of Aeschylus' *The Libation Bearers*, first performed in 458 BC. Moreover, any new production of Shakespeare's *Macbeth* employs exactly the same mechanism of creative interpretation as that employed by Shakespeare in regard to the Chronicle of Holinshed. From the perspective of creative interpretation, there is no difference between playwright, director or fiction writer concerning the raw material that inspires a new description of a fictional world.

Fidelity, creativity and legitimacy

A distinction is usually made between a production that is 'faithful' to its source play-script and a production that is innovative and clearly deviant from it or, rather, 'unfaithful'. Such a distinction presupposes that a play-script has a definite meaning to begin with, and that such a meaning constitutes a firm basis in relation to which fidelity or deviation can be determined. This presupposition, which does not distinguish between the literary and the theatrical nature of a play-script, is erroneous (chapter 6). The opposite assumption that a play-script is a theatre text, albeit deficient, thus undermines the distinction between fidelity and deviation, since to various degrees all productions necessarily reflect creative interpretation.

In principle, a production could be faithful if it preserves the play-wright's design in regard to characterization, definition of situations, structure of the fictional world and possible effect on a synchronic audience. However, the deficiency of a play-script precludes definite conclusions, and determines that 'fidelity' can only apply to a particular hermeneutic interpretation of it, whether widely accepted or not, or, rather, to what a director believes is its true hermeneutic interpretation. Therefore, *the so-called 'faithful interpretation' is in fact only a particular case of creative interpretation*, and striving for fidelity is at most an ideal aspiration.

Nonetheless, the mere persistence of this distinction requires a measure of care. A play-script is usually more than a design of the verbal components of an eventual performance-text. In most cases, its dialogues reflect a concept of a fictional interaction, their possible staging and expected effects on a synchronic audience. Moreover, playwrights write for synchronic theatres, with their typical styles and conventions, the traces of which are inscribed in their play-scripts. Therefore, despite deficiency, a play-script should be seen as a kind of text, which may substantially restrict the latitude of creative interpretation. Therefore, despite inherent ambiguity, a play-script usually imposes initial deconstruction prior to recreation.

A staging that reflects a pronounced deviation from a conventional interpretation of a play-script also poses questions of legitimacy. For millennia, such questions have been asked in regard to works that borrowed narrative materials from earlier ones. For cases of extreme borrowing, the term 'plagiarism' used to be and still is employed. The borrowing of an entire dialogue could be seen, therefore, as a proper instance of it. However, as usually posed, the question of legitimacy does not belong in the realm of art, but in the realm of ethics. *From the perspective of theatre, justification for the borrowing of a ready-made dialogue is a matter of artistic necessity, and does not require legitimization.* Consequently, one should not speak in ethical terms such as 'appropriation' and 'plagiarism', but in terms of assimilation within a new, definite, coherent and more complex work of art. Moreover, since the advent and institutionalization of the theatre director, in the sense of author of the performance-text, absolute legitimacy has been bestowed upon such a procedure. Creative interpretation is unanimously welcome, provided that it generates a coherent production and conveys an original vision. Although there is a frequent feeling that directors compel themselves to innovation for its own sake, creative interpretation has generated some highly interesting productions, which have justified this new attitude and rejuvenated the art of theatre.

Creative interpretation also fulfils a crucial role in the preservation of play-scripts for the benefit of human culture. Traditionally, play-scripting has been the only form of preservation of such works. However, creative interpretation, in addition to being a necessity, infuses new life into dated scripts; i.e., it bestows a dimension of relevance upon them, by becoming a means for the expression of directors who reflect their own actuality, current ideas and new perceptions of society and theatre. The universality of play-scripts is indeed a function of creative interpretation.

Creative interpretation and intertextuality

A production that reflects creative interpretation creates potential intertextual relations between it and its source play-script; thus generating a new hermeneutic space. A production that establishes a paradigmatic stage interpretation of a play-script, which shapes the expectations of future audiences, and generates potential intertextual relations with a new production, should also be seen as a source-text. In all cases, the effect of such intertextual relations depends on the audience's knowledge of the source-text.

Furthermore, methodically, *any deviation from a standard hermeneutic inter-pretation of a play-script or an influential production should be seen as a clue for revealing implied directorial intentions.*

Bilha Blum's analysis of Hanan Snir's production of García Lorca's *Blood Wedding* is an excellent example of such intertextuality (Blum). Despite several major departures from the play-script, including Snir's decision to abolish the original woodcutters' scene, what actually changed the meaning of the narrative was the treatment of the concluding song, originally sung by Mother and Bride. In the play-script, ironically, this song places the responsibility for the death of Leonardo and Groom upon the little knife, instead of Mother and Bride. Authorial irony thereby reverses their sense of self-justification, and places the responsibility squarely on faithfulness to obsolete traditional values. In Snir's production, instead, Mother conveyed a sudden awareness of the absurdity of the cycle of violence, thus creating an actualized message for the local audience.

Fischer-Lichte suggests that '[a]n intercultural performance produc-tively receives the elements taken from the foreign theatre traditions and cultures according to the problematic which lies at the point of departure' (1990: 284). She thus implies that such a performance is monocultural, despite adopting elements from a foreign theatre tradition. Brian Singleton problematizes her approach by suggesting that whereas Mnouchkine's *Les Atrides* appears to be an intercultural performance-text, in fact it is mono-cultural based on an intertextual reading (p. 19). He correctly claims that its intertextuality relates more to the internal tradition of the Théâtre du Soleil's engagement with interculturalism (*ibid.*), i.e., more to its 'own generated cultural historical code' (p. 23), than to the elements of Japanese culture used in the production or the Greek origin of the narrative.

Productions of Beckett's *Waiting for Godot*

This section illustrates the application of this model of creative interpreta-tion against the background of intertextuality by a comparative analysis of two productions of Beckett's in the Israeli theatre (Rozik, 2000a).

(A) *The play-script*: Detecting deviations from *Waiting for Godot* is highly problematic because the play-script deliberately withholds crucial information from the reader and, although to a lesser degree, even from the spectator under conditions of performance. Variation among scholarly interpretations is disconcerting too. Although attempts to capture Beckett's own concept of the fictional world are legitimate, the prospects of certainty are slim. The following remarks concern some of its features that have been preserved in most productions:

(1) The fictional world reveals a tendency to *abstract characterization*. There are no indications of collective properties, such as nationality, social class, profession and age, let alone individual ones. Since it also avoids ethical characterization, there is little ground upon which readers can establish attitudes towards the characters. Didi and Gogo occasionally employ Christian terminology, which may confer religious meaning to their predicament, but this is not developed either. Cases of explicit characterization are subsequently contradicted: e.g., Didi's age (pp. 27–28). Godot is not characterized either, but for his white beard (a possible metonymy of God) and name, probably a French diminutive of 'god' (god-ot). Beckett also refrains from explicit characterization of Didi and Gogo's relations, which in some cases convey a sense of intimacy typical of married couples (e.g., pp. 15–16). Pozzo and Lucky's relations are described only in terms of 'master–slave'. His definition of the dramatic situation is reduced to an abstract expectation for 'redemption'. Its nature and the redeemer's identity, however, remain unclear. Beckett also avoids precise descriptions of the characters' costumes, which could have hinted at their social class, occupation or age. They wear rags and hats, and Estragon wears boots, but nothing is indicative. The editor remarks on their bowler hats and characterization as vagabonds that they were probably taken from an early production (p. 33). Beckett provides little information on the place and time of action. The set includes only a mound and a tree, bare of leaves in the first act and a few ones in the second. A stage direction states that the stage enacts 'a country road', with no geographical definition. The only indications of time are that both acts take place during evenings, the second a day after the first, with no historical indication.

(2) The fictional world reveals an *allegoric structure* (chapter 3). There are hints to the effect that the characters represent and describe humankind; i.e., constitute a double or quadruple personification of 'everyman'. For example, when Gogo attempts to guess Pozzo's name – he calls: 'Abel! Abel!' and then 'Cain. Cain! Cain!' Then Gogo remarks: 'He's all humanity' (p. 83; cf. p. 79). The four characters certainly constitute a personification of a specific deconstruction of 'mankind' into constituent abstractions; but it is not at all clear what these are. Interpretations may vary, but any interpretation of a stage allegory must look for its mediating idea (chapter 3).

(3) The overall action embodies an *absurd structure* of archetypal expectation and its frustration: Didi and Gogo are expecting Godot, a symbol of redemption, and their frustration in the first act is repeated in the second. The recurrence of this pattern may induce a sense of a cyclic frustration of the existential expectation for redemption. Lack of characterization on the ethical level, therefore, is probably in detriment of the audience's

involvement in Didi and Gogo's fates, were it not for their naïve and sympathetic nature, and the seriousness that transpires from the text.

(4) The mood is *grotesque*: whereas the comic behavior of the characters indicates the intention to create an object of dramatic irony, the serious substratum reflects the frustration of an existential longing for redemption in its religious sense; e.g., Didi's thoughts about the two thieves who were crucified with Jesus and the one who was saved (pp. 12–13); and the claim implied in Lucky's speech on God's inexplicable behavior toward His creatures:

> *Lucky*: Given the existence [. . .] of a personal god [. . .] with a white beard [. . .] outside time without extension [. . .] who from the heights of divine apathia [. . .] divine aphasia loves us dearly with some exceptions for reasons unknown [. . .] and suffers [. . .] with those who for reasons unknown but time will tell are plunged in torment [. . .]   (pp. 42–3)

Lucky expresses the all too human perplexity at a God who is utterly cut off from mankind and does not conform to any human logic. A grotesque tension is thus created between the implied sense of extreme seriousness of the theme, clearly felt by the audience, and its explicit comic mood; e.g., Gogo's attempt to commit suicide at the end of the second act, when suddenly his trousers 'fall about his ankles' (p. 93); and the use of a tree with a few leaves, a symbol of renewal and hope, for suicide; i.e., an antithetic symbol (cf. Ben Zvi: 145).

Since Beckett withholds definite characterization, definition of situations and specific time and place, it may be conjectured that his intention was to create a fictional reality, on the level of 'every-man', in every-place and at every-time, in his absurd and grotesque every-expectation for every-redemption from every-divinity. In contrast to the sublime–tragic image traditionally connected to the theme of redemption, Beckett presents a comic mirror that derides the spectators' existential expectations, reflecting thereby his own intuition of the grotesque nature of the human condition. This abstract allegory should be conceived of as a ready-made stage metaphor for every-spectator.

(B) *Creative interpretations of Waiting for Godot*: The following comparative and schematic analysis focuses on two productions of *Waiting for Godot*: the Tel Aviv University Theatre production, translated and directed by Edna Shavit, 1966, and the Haifa Municipal Theatre production, translated by Anton Shamas and directed by Ilan Ronen, 1984. While the former was meant to be a faithful production, the latter was a professedly innovative one. These productions preserved most of the aforementioned features of the play-script, including the wording. Therefore, the following comparison focuses on their non-verbal components, under the assumption that they determine the meaning of this wording.

(1) *Characterization*: In the University Theatre production, Didi and Gogo were characterized as vagabonds. The actors were instructed to play in the clownish style 'typical of music-hall, the Marx Brothers or Laurel and Hardy'. This style lent an almost realistic rationale to the characters, originally designed as objects of dramatic irony. It also lent coherence to the grotesque dialogue, under the assumption, even if erroneous, that vagabonds are characterized by clownish behavior.

In the bilingual Haifa Theatre production Didi and Gogo were characterized as Arab builders, speaking Arabic; Pozzo as a Jewish contractor speaking stylish Hebrew; and Lucky as an old Arab slave, against the background of a building site. Pozzo spoke slowly 'so that the workers could understand him'; and they answered him in a quite distorted Hebrew with a heavy Arabic accent, 'as expected from an Arab' (Ronen). Lucky, in contrast, spoke literary Arabic, as befits an Arab intellectual. The boy spoke Arabic. The actors also produced body and hand gestures typical of each local culture. The fact that Arab actors enacted Didi and Gogo and a Jewish actor enacted Pozzo stressed national characterization, a quite common actualizing device in the Jewish Israeli theatre. Didi and Gogo preserved the clownish features, lending a controversial dimension to the new interpretation.

The spectators, Arabs and Jews, were intentionally led to see Didi and Gogo as representing Arab workers, in particular those from the occupied territories, who every morning used to enter the Jewish cities in expectation of a day's work (Ronen). In response to a spectator who argued that the production distorts reality, the Arab actor Makhram Khouri said: 'Go and look at Paris Square in this neighborhood, the Slaves' Square. You will see Arab workers from the Galilee at early dawn offering themselves to the Jewish masters for nothing' (Fuchs; cf. Ronen; and Rapp).

(2) *Set design*: In the University Theatre production the stage was an empty regular lecture hall, with the blackboard in the background, while the furniture was piled up in one of its corners. On the improvised stage (a dais), there was a semblance of a leafless tree constructed of a metal bench that stood on its end, with a leafless branch on top. In the second act, a few leaves were attached to it. The space was lit by the hall lighting. The audience was implicitly requested to overlook that the performance space was not a theatre. Although the set did not comply with the stage directions, it nevertheless conveyed a sense of emptiness and every-place.

In the Haifa Theatre production the set closely followed the stage directions for the spatial organization of the stage; but instead of the tree there stood a pillar of concrete, half cast, the iron skeleton partly protruding, and surrounded by building blocks strewn about, against a gray cyclorama on which a spotlight projected a moon-like image. In the second act, the cast part of the pillar was higher, recalling the growing tree. Spatial similarity emphasized the translation from concept to concept. While describing a building site, this set preserved a sense of emptiness and dreariness. Ironically, while 'construction' was a key ideal of traditional Zionism in its endeavor to bring about the rebirth of the nation, people of another nation currently materialize it.

Vladimir and Estragon in Ronen's *Waiting for Godot.* Courtesy of the Haifa Municipal Theatre. Photo: Morel Defler.

(3) *Costume and props*: In the University Theatre production Didi and Gogo were dressed in shabby tailcoats and bowler hats; Didi in black and Gogo in white worn out trousers. These garments created a contrast between past opulence and actual poverty, fitting their characterization as

vagabonds; i.e., as outsiders of society. Pozzo was dressed in the garments of an English gentleman: riding jacket and trousers, leather boots and a golden fob. He was smoking a pipe. Lucky was dressed in a shabby long overcoat and was tied to Pozzo by a remarkably thick rope.

In the Haifa Theatre production Didi and Gogo were dressed in worn out clothes, typical of Arab builders. They wore caps that emphasized their additional clownish characterization. In contrast, Pozzo was dressed in elegant, clean and pressed garments – a beige suit, a white shirt, sunglasses, and a hat that combined the features of a pith helmet, with its colonialist connotations, and a '*tembel* (silly)' hat, typical of Israeli pioneers. Lucky's load characterized his exploiting master: a surveyor's tripod, a set of scrolled building plans and a briefcase. The attitude of Pozzo to Lucky was characterized by a metaphor of master and dog: he was attached by a dog's collar and a typical surveyor's measuring tape, while Pozzo spurred him on with a whip. In the second act, a harness used by guide-dogs for the blind substituted for the regular collar.

Vladimir, Estragon, Pozzo and Lucky in Ronen's *Waiting for Godot*.
Courtesy of the Haifa Municipal Theatre. Photo: Morel Defler.

(4) *Mood*: The University Theatre production emphasized the comic mood, but preserved a balance with the distressing subtext, thus maintaining the original grotesque tension. The first act was performed as comedy and tragedy alternately, and the second act as farce and melodrama

157

alternately. The parallel alternation within each act and the lowering of acting styles in the second act actually intensified the grotesque tension. The
Haifa Theatre production too preserved the comic mood and grotesque
tension of the play-script. The allusion to the local political reality bestowed
unexpected actualized meanings on some speech acts; e.g., Pozzo's words
to the Arab workers: 'You are human beings none the less. (*He puts on his
glasses.*) As far as one can see. (*He takes off his glasses.*) Of the same species
as myself. (*He bursts into an enormous laugh*) [. . .] Made in God's image!'
(p. 23). This additional level of meaning successfully conveyed the director's criticism of the Israeli arrogance in the Israeli–Arab conflict.

(5) *Intertextual contexts*: Both productions operated two kinds of intertextual relations: between the performance-text and the play-script and
between the former and previous productions of the latter in Israel and
abroad.

Poster of the Hebrew/Arabic production of Ronen's *Waiting for Godot*.
Courtesy of the Haifa Municipal Theatre. Photo: Morel Defler.

158

The Haifa Theatre production could not have been understood by a Jewish audience (80 percent of the verbal text was performed in Arabic), unless they had previously read the play-script, or had seen an earlier production of it. It was quite reasonable to expect some familiarity with a play-script that had become a modern classic. Any previous acquaintance would have generated a universal dimension even for this actualized production. Therefore, the tension between universality and actuality was still preserved, although seemingly missing in this production.

In Nola Chilton's production, at the Acco Festival for Alternative Theatre, 1995, Didi, Gogo and Lucky were enacted by actresses and Pozzo by an actor. Chilton's decision reflected the intertextual intention of focusing criticism on the way men run the world. It was possibly meant to be also a critical statement against Beckett himself for representing humanity exclusively by male characters.

(6) *Structural metaphor*: The University Theatre production actually produced a structural stage metaphor of the grotesque nature of the human condition, following typical interpretations of this play-script. The problem: creating an undignified and ludicrous image of humanity (e.g., as clownish vagabonds) creates an undignified portrayal of humanity in its innermost and most serious craving for redemption. This was probably the intention of Beckett. In contrast, director Shavit claimed: 'The production rejected the usual interpretation of the play-script as conveying a sense of despair. The belief that eventually Godot will come next morning maintains Didi and Gogo's optimism. Godot has messengers! That is, he exists! Godot is a metaphysical entity that nourishes their hope. They perhaps delude themselves, but such a delusion does not contradict optimism.' Paradoxically, despite her peculiar interpretation, in her eyes 'the production was faithful and devoted to the play-script' (Shavit).

The Haifa Theatre production produced a metaphor of expectation for and frustration of national redemption, which can be read in two ways: as concretizing an originally abstract metaphoric predicate, or as actualizing the originally non-specified referent of the metaphor. According to the first reading, the world of the Arab workers was a concrete metaphoric predicate, which could aptly describe only real feelings of national destitution. According to the second reading, the world of Arab builders was one of the possible real situations to which the abstract metaphor could have referred. The latter probably reflects more accurately the director's intention (cf. Ronen). The use of Arab actors the Arabic language and typical garments, which actualized the fictional world's relevance to the current political conflict, is typical of the Israeli theatre. For example, the productions of Euripides/Sartre's *Les Troyennes* at the Habimah Theatre, 1983 (chapter 15); Strindberg's *Miss Julie* at the Haifa Theatre, 1987 (Urian, 1997: 70); and the co-production of

Shakespeare's *Romeo and Juliet* at the Jerusalem Khan Theatre and El Casba el Kuds Theatre, 1994 (*ibid.*: 65).

Ronen's creative interpretation probably lost the universal dimension that characterizes Beckett's play-script. Because of its abstraction, this text creates a ready-made metaphor of any existential expectation of any spectator in any situation, political or otherwise, including the particular expectations of an Arab builder, whether in the shape of a day's work or national independence. In this sense this actualization was superfluous. The production thus removed the original ready-made metaphor from the philosophical sphere and placed it in the restricted context of socio-political criticism. I note that this undignified interpretation definitely counteracted its crude criticism, because the victims were depicted as ludicrous characters.

Assumedly, in any 'faithful' production of this play-script spectators would identify their own existential expectations for redemption and their frustration. Despite possible reduction, the shared message of such productions would probably focus on the ludicrous nature of the perennial belief in the possible intervention of a redeeming and possibly divine entity, despite recurrent frustration. Such a message could have reaffirmed intuitions of absurdity for many a spectator. This message was shared by neither the Haifa Theatre production nor the University theatre, despite the director's claim to utter fidelity. The unique interpretations of both directors, however, coherently conveyed their creative interpretations; i.e., each director was clearly implied in the structures of their different fictional worlds.

11

The Implied Spectator

Until quite recently the question of performance reception had been neglected not only by traditional semiotics, but also by theatre theory in general, except for the Aristotelian notion of 'catharsis' and the Brechtian notion of '*Verfremdungseffekt*' (cf. Pavis, 1982: 70). In recent years interest in reception theory has increased tangibly. This study presupposes that theatre meaning results from the interaction between a performance-text and a spectator, whose contribution is no less crucial than that of the performance-text. The spectators are expected to provide indispensable literacy, associative capacity from their own resources and psychological mechanisms, without which no performance-text makes sense. The text should thus be conceived of as a set of clues for spectators to activate these competences and mechanisms.

In contrast to reception theory, this chapter aims at showing that (a) a basic distinction should be made between 'real spectator' and 'implied spectator'; (b) while the implied spectator reflects by definition all the competences and functions needed for the complementation of a performance-text, the real spectator is restricted in various respects; (c) performance-analysis should focus on the implied spectator, which is part of the deep structure of the fictional world; (d) the role of the implied spectator is characterized by framing, reading, interpreting and experiencing a performance-text; and (e) there is an implied dialogue between an implied director and an implied spectator, which reflects a directorial intuition of the expected real dialogue between a real director and a prospective real spectator.

Real vs. implied spectator

For Iser the 'implied reader' 'embodies all those predispositions necessary for a literary work to exercise its effect – predispositions laid down, not by

161

an empirical outside reality, but by the text itself. Consequently, the implied reader as a concept has his roots firmly planted in the structure of the text; he is a construct and in no way to be identified with any real reader' (1991: 34). Iser establishes thereby a basic distinction between an implied reader and a real one (cf. Marinis pp. 163–64), and claims that the term 'implied reader' 'incorporates both the pre-structuring of the potential meaning by the text, and the reader's actualization of this potential through the reading process' (1974: xii). This term refers, therefore, to the spectator's presupposed meaningful complementation for a text to make sense. Marinis prefers the term 'model reader' (p. 164), coined by Umberto Eco in his *The Role of the Reader*, with quite the same meaning, and applies this model to the theatre spectator: 'The model spectator's competence is nothing more than the idealized competence of the empirical spectator' (Marinis: 168). Gad Kaynar successfully adapts Iser's notion to performance analysis, while also employing the notion of 'implied spectator' (1997; 53ff; cf. 2000).

'Implied spectator' actually stands for the 'role' (in the sociological sense) that a performance-text imposes for its full meaning to emerge. This role is integral to the deep structure of the performance-text. In contrast, *the contribution of real spectators is limited to various extents, reflecting various handicaps, such as partial knowledge of the theatre medium, incomplete cultural baggage and psychological biases and inhibitions.* However, while the implied spectator is by definition manipulated by the implied director, it is the real spectator who actually experiences the performance-text, who can either accept or refuse the required role. I thus suggest that *the implied spectator reflects a directorial speculation regarding the real spectator.*

In contrast to Marinis, the implied spectator's function should not be perceived as a matter of 'filling gaps' or removing 'points of indeterminacy' through 'concretizations', following Ingarden's theory (Marinis: 164). For Ingarden 'points of indeterminacy' are inherent in the 'schematic represented objectivities [characters]' that characterize any work of art as an intentional construct; i.e., in principle, they cannot be totally removed (pp. 246–54; cf. Iser, 1991: 170). However, even if totally removed the reader's complementation is still crucial. Moreover, a performance-text not only prescribes what is required for constructing its meaning, but also may feature restrictions to 'prevent a theoretically infinite proliferation of readings' (Marinis: 168).

Whereas the reading and interpretation by an implied spectator, as a theoretical construct, rest on firm grounds, the actual reading and interpretation by real spectators are essentially personal and, therefore, any claim to objective reading is fundamentally ruled out. In contrast to Iser, unless the aim is ambiguity, it is not the implied spectator that opens a performance-text to multiple interpretations, but the real one (cf. 1991:

37). Due to the communal nature of the theatre experience, i.e., the expectation is that an audience reacts in unison, the structural control of a performance-text is usually much tighter than that of a literary work. Moreover, real reading and interpretation do not depend on the truth of its results, and take place even if the wrong rules and associations are applied. Therefore, *from the viewpoint of performance analysis, it is sensible to focus on the implied spectator, which is integral to the structure of a performance-text.* Performance analysis should be interested in the expected competences, and not if these are realized or not.

It may be conjectured that real directors usually operate an intuition of the nature of their real prospective spectators, which is reflected in the implied spectator, and that their success actually depends on the degree of overlap between them. Sarah Brayant Bertail correctly contends that 'the "performance-text" [. . .] cannot be contained by the actors' or director's intentions, but is also determined by what spectators expect and understand in a historically specific context' (1994a: 95). This implies that a thorough knowledge of the prospective spectator is vital. Carlson's analysis of the opera *The Ghosts of Versailles* is an excellent example of a director who accurately intuited the nature of his prospective audience and successfully manipulated their expectations (2000: 3–9). The implied spectator of this opera indeed reflects the cultural context of this production. Dean Wilcox's analysis of his own reactions to Karen Finley's *The Constant State of Desire* constitutes the analysis of a real spectator. His analysis of her own explanations of this work is the analysis of a real director and, perhaps, also of an implied spectator (1997: 31–7). Having seen only a video recording of the performance and read both the play-script and her explanations in her interview with Richard Schechner (Finley), it is sensible to think that the underlying intention of this work was probably to elicit a sense of guilt in the spectator, and that Wilcox, as a real spectator, accepted the role of the accused. Therefore, in this case, there is a considerable overlap between the implied spectator and the actual reception of her work (Wilcox: *ibid.*).

Roles of the implied spectator

This study assumes that in generating theatre meaning the implied spectator's role is no less crucial than the performance-text itself, and that directors presuppose it. I suggest that *the contribution of the implied spectator consists of the following competences and mechanisms: 'framing', 'reading', 'interpreting' and 'experiencing' a performance-text* (Rozik 2002d). This model is illustrated below by the analysis of certain images in Yerushalmi's *Woyzeck 91*, the Itim Theatre (Yerushalmi). Since a full analysis of this production is provided in chapter 17, the following synopsis is meant to facilitate the reader's orientation.

Yerushalmi's *Woyzeck 91*

Woyzeck 91 basically followed the main action of Büchner's *Woyzeck*, and employed selected excerpts of its dialogue. In a nutshell, Woyzeck is provoked to react to Marie's infatuation with Drum Major and murder her. Yerushalmi added two macro-images, of military might and medical research, rhythmically interwoven with interaction scenes, which developed Büchner's scenes with Captain and Doctor in the original play-script. A group of supernumerary actors, in some scenes dressed in white gowns, created the ambience of a medical school through images of bodily examinations, slide projections of organs and mini-lectures on them; while in other scenes, dressed in army uniforms, they created the ambience of an army barrack, through images of drill, gymnastics and canteen, and, on the vocal level, by the barking of military orders in gibberish. While the soldiers' uniforms did not identify any particular army, the Captain's was reminiscent of a Nazi officer. In the context of the medical school image, Woyzeck was subject to constant experimentation and abused like a laboratory mouse. While Doctor promoted a crude and spurious Darwinist approach, applying the principles of natural selection to the human species, verging on racial violence, Captain voiced slogans advocating a super race in the familiar terms of Nazi ideology. While Woyzeck murdered Marie, his closest soul in the world, Doctor, Captain and their students/soldiers frantically celebrated their criminal complicity in a grotesque banquet. Eventually, Woyzeck died from exhaustion and grief.

(A) *Framing a performance-text*: In recent years, frame theory has had a major impact on understanding the reading, interpreting and experiencing of a particular kind of text. The notion of 'frame' was introduced by Gregory Bateson (1955) and developed by Erving Goffman in his *Frame Analysis* (1975). It is now widely accepted that 'even the simplest communication depends on complex interpretive processes' and that '[t]hese processes [. . .] depend in turn on various kinds of framing' (MacLachlan: 1).

For Goffman, a 'definition of a situation' is the answer to the question 'What is it that's going on here?' (p. 8) A possible answer is: a keyed event such as 'a joke, or a dream, or an accident [. . .] or a theatrical performance and so forth' (p. 10). 'Key' is a central concept in frame analysis, referring 'to the set of conventions by which a given activity, one already meaningful in terms of some primary framework [e.g., a real social event], is trans-

164

formed into something patterned on this activity but seen by the participants to be something quite else [e.g., a theatre event]. The process of transcription can be called keying' (pp. 43–4). In other words, a keyed event should thus be understood as reflecting different rules. Goffman's discussion focuses on the specific principles of organization that govern and determine the rules of interpretation of each domain. Although his interest lies in real human experience (p. 13), his definition applies to experiencing theatre as well.

In considering 'framing' as synonymous to 'perspective', 'schemata of interpretation' (p. 21) and 'frame of understanding' (p. 22), Goffman postulates that it is a precondition for making sense of any event and, by implication, of any text: framing, which determines the rules to be applied, logically precedes reading and interpretation. In particular, a performance-text, prior to its reading and interpretation, needs to be framed as theatre. Following Goffman's theory, after due translation to the terms of this study, I suggest the following model of the framing expected from an implied spectator:

(1) A frame disconnects a discernible unit from its context, like a picture from a non-picture, and distinguishes between 'in-frame' and 'out-of-frame'. By the same token, it re-connects them on the axis of text-context. The frame is neither part of the text nor of the context. It reflects a mental mechanism for positing and delimitating a unit as an object of perception. Such a unit can be discerned on the different levels of organization of a performance-text; e.g., a stage metaphor and a motif. On the textual level, it establishes the limits between a text and its socio-cultural context.

(2) The moment the nature of the 'in-frame' is determined (e.g., 'it is theatre'), the 'out-of-frame' is automatically determined as well (e.g., it is real life). In this sense 'framing' is synonymous with 'categorization'.

(3) The fundamental question of framing is: how do similar events/texts generate different meanings? The answer is that difference depends on domain-categorization, which implies that each frame presupposes the existence of different domains that require the application of different rules. This applies even if the rules are unknown, or there is no agreement on what those are. A typical example is a scene of brutality in street theatre, which may be mistaken by onlookers for a real event (particularly if deliberately designed to produce such an impression). Only a correct framing would determine how it is to be understood and experienced: is it to be just witnessed, actively involved, or watched as a work of art? The implied spectator is thus expected to accept the simple presupposition that a theatre performance is not a real event, but a description of a (fictional) event. Possible confusion between them may be caused by the extension of the principle of similarity to the imprinted matter, typical of theatre. However, because theatre is usually performed on a stage and/or in a

theatre building, these frame such an event as theatre. The existence of such a material frame behaves as a meta-textual operator conveying the meta-message that a distinct set of rules of reading and interpretation applies.

It is not the aim of frame theory to establish the rules that apply in each particular domain. Whereas it attempts to establish the nature and function of domain indicators, it is the task of theatre theory to determine the specific rules applying to performance-texts on their various structural levels. Obviously, such rules are theory-dependent. 'Framing' is thus the establishment of a triadic relationship between a text, a domain category, and a set of rules of reading and interpretation.

(B) *Reading a performance-text*: The notion of 'reading' ('decoding' in traditional terms) should be understood in a wide sense that applies to all systems of signification and communication, including non-verbal ones. It approaches texts according to the rules of their language/medium. 'Reading' and 'text' presuppose each other. 'Text' should be also defined in the wide sense of the entire set of structured verbal and/or non-verbal sentences meant to be read, interpreted and experienced by a reader/spectator. 'Reading' regards the inference of meaning from a 'text'; i.e., the inference of the signified level from the signifier level. Reading is, therefore, a basic competence, complementary to formulating a text ('encoding' in traditional terms). *Reading a performance-text thus presupposes theatre medium literacy.*

'Reading' a performance-text applies up to the level of iconic sentence/icon, which is the most complex structured unit that the any theatre medium generates. It also applies to elliptical sentences that can be made explicit through knowledge of the principles of 'deep structure', rules of 'ellipsis' and 'semantic context'. By merely reading, therefore, the implied spectator remains within the sphere of the basic convention of theatre; namely, the possibility of describing fictional worlds through images imprinted on matter, similar to that of their models, and mediated by language. Since previous chapters have expanded on these matters, the following remarks are confined to the reading competences expected from the implied spectator.

The iconic medium is transparent, in the sense that the principles of similarity, underlying its descriptive sentences/icons, and the mediation of language, enable the spectator to infer their meanings with no need to learn the medium (chapter 1). 'Transparency' applies to most forms of theatre semiosis: regular iconic sentences/icons, real objects on stage and stage metaphors. 'Reading' also regards identification of the direct referents of such sentences/icons. The implied spectator is expected to refer iconic descriptions to fictional entities by deflection of reference (chapter 5).

While the apparent referent of a performance-text is a fictional world, i.e., the set of characters and their actions, its actual referent is the implied spectator.

It would appear that stage metaphors pose a problem, because their predicates are improper imprinted images; however, in addition to metaphor being an inborn form of predication a brain conditioned by language and programmed to use verbal metaphoric predication can apply the very same competence to stage metaphor. Since improperness depends on the nature of a referent, a metaphoric reading presupposes that the implied spectator is able to identify it. Although understanding metaphor depends on interpretation, reading it is a precondition for interpretation, which also regards the elliptical presence of signs in its surface structures; e.g., in a very shocking scene, Woyzeck's penis was milked like a cow for a specimen of his semen. While the metaphoric treatment like a cow was iconically explicit, interpretation was expected to contribute its verbal and non-verbal associations.

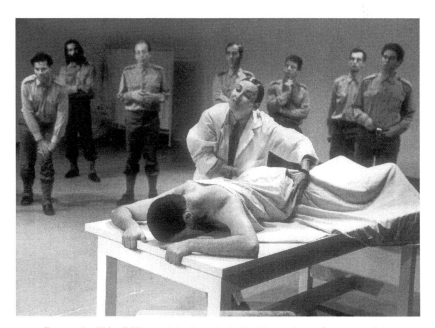

Doctor "milking" Woyzeck in Yerushalmi's *Woyzeck 91*. Courtesy of the Itim Theatre. Photo: Israel Haramaty.

In contrast, stage conventions pose a real difficulty because of departing, at least partially, from the principle of similarity typical of iconic sentences/icons, thus hindering transparency. Conventions, therefore, must be learned, or otherwise grasped. However, while in some conventions transparency is not impaired (medium conventions), in others the meaning of sentences conveyed by them can be inferred from residual elements of similarity and/or their functions in describing a fictional world (chapter 4). Moreover such conventions do materialize the imagistic principle, as otherwise their presence on stage would have been impossible.

(c) *Interpreting a performance-text*: 'Hermeneutic interpretation' presupposes reading a text and conditions its experience. Whereas text-reading presupposes a finite set of semiotic means, and is fully accounted for by them, text-interpretation regards an open-ended domain of images, thoughts and referential associations, mentally evoked or induced by the actual components of a text. Whereas within a real cultural community the reading competence of performance-texts is usually taken for granted, because of the basic transparency of the theatre medium, interpretation is highly dependent on personal competence and cultural baggage. Therefore, even the same production may create different meanings when performed in front of culturally different audiences (Esslin: xv-xvii). A text may prescribe, therefore, its reading by a real spectator, but cannot fully determine its interpretation, which explains individual interpretations. This is not the case in regard to the implied spectator that by definition responds appropriately to all the requirements of a text. Implied interpretation too depends on reading and complements it. It is no less vital to the full generation of theatre meaning than the performance-text itself.

The cardinal contribution of the implied spectator lies, therefore, in its 'implied interpretation', which applies to a variety of expected mental operations that would appear to challenge the assumption that 'intuition' applies to a unified function. However, this assumption is probably correct. Despite diversity, the interpretive function of the implied spectator is indeed one: to provide associations to a performance-text, beyond reading, from its own resources; originating in various domains such as socio-political reality, history, religion and the arts, the theatre in particular, which includes familiarity with original play-scripts, previous performances of them, earlier works of directors and actors, and dramatic genres.

Elam suggests that the meanings generated by 'Bogatyrev's "signs of signs" are what are generally designated *connotations*' (p. 10). Elam defines 'connotation' as 'a parasitic semantic function, [. . .] whereby the sign-vehicle of one sign-relationship provides the basis for a second-order sign-relationship' (*ibid.*: 10–11). In terms of this study: a connotation is not the core signified (denotation) of a sign, but the set of associations that a sign/sentence/icon usually evokes in a given context. For example, a typical costume is a conventional index that, under certain contextual conditions, may evoke connotations originating, for example, in the class, religion and/or nation of its wearer (cf. Bogatyrev, 1986a: 33). Therefore, its iconic replica is read accordingly. The task of the implied spectator is to provide such connotations. I note that 'connotation' applies to both verbal and non-verbal (referential) associations.

Implied spectators are also expected to contextualize what has been read. Several kinds of contextualization can be discerned: (a) intra-textual verbal and non-verbal associations that are evoked/induced within a performance-text itself, e.g., motifs; (b) extra-textual such associations that are evoked/induced by explicit or implicit reference to the actual political and socio-cultural context of a performance-text; and (c) inter-textual such associations that are evoked/induced by explicit or implicit reference to other texts, canonic in particular, including source play-scripts and previous performances of it. Such associations can be either conscious or not.

(1) *On an elementary level*, single iconic signs, sentences or icons may elicit associations of all the above-mentioned kinds in literal and metaphoric descriptions. Whereas literal descriptions may create the wrong impression that interpretation is not necessary, it is obvious that an iconic metaphor requires interpretation; e.g., after Woyzeck's penis was milked for a specimen of his semen, he was eventually held by his feet, head down and arms extended, thus creating an inverted image of crucified Jesus. Such metaphoric and symbolic images of scorn for the sacredness of human life and extreme human suffering are meaningless without interpretation.

A verbal metaphor can be part of the embedded sentence of an imprinted image of a speech act, in which case it should be interpreted accordingly; for example:

Captain: [. . .] You have got a child without the church's blessing, [. . .]
Woyzeck: Sir, God the father isn't going to worry if nobody said amen at the
          poor worm's making. (p. 11)

Since Woyzeck uses 'worm', which cannot literally describe a child, to describe his own 'child', it evokes a set of verbal associations, such as 'vulnerable' and 'worthless', and elicits repulsive referential associations originating in 'worm', which are its crucial aim. These associations totally depend on interpretation.

(2) *On an intermediary level*, 'motif' is an intra-textual principle that organizes partial iconic units into complex semantic clusters, which underlie and explain the experience of a fictional world as a unitary whole. I have suggested elsewhere five elements that characterize the formation and function of such a complex unit: (a) *reiteration* of meaningful units of various scopes, such as plain repetition, synonymy and antonymy; (b) *expansion* of such a semantic cluster beyond the principle of reiteration through additional contextual processes, such as paradigmatic and syntag-

matic associations; (c) *accumulation* of meaning based on recurrence of
tokens of a motif in different intra-textual contexts, in the guise of a
symbolic associative periphery (chapter 5); (d) *spatiality* in the sense that,
in contrast to the temporal nature of accumulation, a motif connects its
various tokens as if coexisting in time, making possible application of its
complex meaning regardless of location, including previous and expected
occurrences; and (e) *functionality* on the level of the entire text, which
enables the interaction of a reduced number of such integrated clusters,
especially in the complex final accords of a description of a fictional world
(Rozik, 1988).

Motifs can be either literal or metaphoric. For example, the sexual act
between Drum-major and Marie, which was metaphorically depicted by a
violent dance in which he wore a horse-skull mask and she was half-naked,
clearly epitomized the play-script's motif of 'animalization' imposed on the
oppressed classes. Another example: in the final banquet, which was an
ironic version of the Last Supper, Woyzeck sat at the end of a huge table,
chaired by the false apostles of modern society (Doctor, Captain and ten
students/soldiers). While a cook dished out spaghetti, Woyzeck was left to
his peas. The banquet degenerated into an orgiastic and grotesque celebration of Doctor and Captain's success in dehumanizing Woyzeck. The
ironic version of this 'Last Supper' image aimed at tearing off their
spurious Christian mask. In particular, this was already hinted at by the
inverted image of the crucified Woyzeck after he had been subjected to
cruel experimentation. These allusions to Christian motifs created an
overall metaphor of betrayal of genuine Christianity's values.

From the viewpoint of reading, a character is a motif in the sense of a
set of qualities and motives reflected in whatever it does. 'Characterization'
also refers to the viewpoint of a character, mainly indicated by the religious,
philosophical or ideological key words that it employs in categorizing its
own world. From the same viewpoint, an overall action is a motif in the
sense of projecting a set of motives and actions on the time axis, predicated
on a character. From the viewpoint of interpretation, a character and its
actions constitute a motif in the sense of organizing both its description
and associative periphery around a fictional entity, human or otherwise.
Characterization is performed on both the naïve and ironic levels; for
example:

> *Marie*: That man! So haunted by everything. – He didn't even stop to look
> at his child. Thinking's wound his mind up like a *watch-spring, it'll
> break* one'v these days.   (p. 6; my italics)

For the implied spectator, Marie's naïve premonition, implied in this
metaphoric description of Woyzeck's eventual fate in terms of a broken
watch-spring, eventually proves right.

Interpretation also regards the adequate characterization from an ironic viewpoint. For example, it would appear that the murder of Marie confirms Captain's naïve assessment of Woyzeck's character: 'you've no sense of virtue. You're not a virtuous man!' (p. 12) However, it proves false from an ironic viewpoint. Whereas Captain speaks in terms of a distorted Christian morality, in Yerushalmi's production too, Woyzeck is the victim of a crude scientific experimentation, fostered by military interest, which brings him to the brink of animality. No wonder, therefore, that he reacts like a cat thrown out of a window (p. 16). The implied spectator is expected to interpret Woyzeck's value characterization from such an ironic viewpoint.

(3) *On the level of a whole performance-text,* the implied spectator is expected to determine the overall meaning of a performance-text. It is expected to conceive of the entire fictional world as generated by an overall structure, which organizes narrative materials through mythical, praxical, naïve, ironic, aesthetic, metaphoric substructures into an overall rhetoric structure, reflecting a directorial intention and possible effects (chapter 9). Such an overall structure reflects an intuition of the archetypal expectations of real audiences, even when frustrating them (chapter 7).

It is the diversity of rules that, as illustrated above, raises the question of whether or not there is a semantic core shared by all specific uses of 'interpretation'. I suggest that the following are its shared features: first, it refers to the expected application of specific rules upon a text as read by an implied spectator. Second, it operates beyond reading, aiming at supplementation of what is not and/or cannot be articulated by the medium. Third, it generates a set of associations, from the implied spectator's own resources, originating in culturally established contexts, which cannot be verified in a scientific sense, and whose validity is supported only by considerations of fullness and coherence. Fourth, the text itself controls such associative processes; i.e., it may accept them, reject them or merely feature constraints that prevent unwished interpretations. Fifth, the semantic contribution of interpretation is crucial and its complementary function is presupposed by all authors.

(D) *Experiencing a performance-text*: The implied spectator is expected to experience a fictional world through a reading and an interpretation. The entire performance-text intentionally aims at evoking a macro-image of such a world, which is the main mechanism that affects the implied spectator in a specific cognitive and emotional manner. The implied spectator is meant to integrate all the structural layers, under the rhetoric structure in particular (chapter 9), meaning that it is supposed to experience a performance-text as a macro-speech act, reflecting a macro-intention (e.g., criticism of held beliefs) and macro-purposes (e.g., subversion), with the implied director being the agent and the implied spectator its object.

The performance-text presupposes not only a set of competences and functions of the implied spectator, but also its image/concept of the world. Its cognitive experience depends, therefore, on the way an aesthetic and metaphoric fictional world impinges on this image/concept; whether it accords with or upsets it. In addition to the experience of dramatic irony, which is most rewarding, the implied spectator is also expected to experience cathartic or shocking effects.

The implied spectator neither receives a ready-made fictional world, nor does it construct its meaning on its own. It is manipulated to contribute to the process of creating such a world, generating its meaning and experiencing it. Only a symbiotic process between performance-text and implied spectator can explain such an implied holistic experience.

In *Woyzeck 91*, Yerushalmi staged a world populated by two marginal characters, Woyzeck and Marie, in stark contrast to her contemporary typical theatre-goers, and two (metonymic) representatives of the military and scientific establishments. She thus created a complex metaphor of victimization of two frail individuals by the totalitarian and criminal alliance of these establishments. For a Jewish audience there was an additional dimension: the combination of images of Nazi militarism and scientific research automatically recalled the Holocaust, and particularly the tragic era of scientific experimentation with human beings, which aimed at the improvement of an allegedly superior race at the expense of an allegedly inferior one. Audiences were certainly familiar with the Nazi application of the principle of 'scientific selection' to humankind, which had proved both iniquitous and disastrous. The Nazi regime, explicitly alluded to by Captain's uniform, was evidently employed as a universal metaphor of such a criminal alliance, which aptly applies to present times.

Woyzeck 91 definitely aimed at manipulating the audience's present fears, aroused by a science at the service of totalitarian and militaristic regimes, such as the reproduction of human clones in infinite numbers and the creation of ever more destructive atomic, chemical and biological weapons. Yerushalmi's implied spectator was expected to conceive of the military and scientific establishments as responsible for Woyzeck's tragic end. It can be claimed, therefore, that in contrast to Büchner's critical intent, Yerushalmi's absurd ending was meant to reaffirm the real audience's values. Indeed, in recent years the bourgeois audience has adopted an anti-establishment stand.

Dialogue between implied director and implied spectator

The 'implied director' is a theoretical construct that reflects what a perfor-mance-text actually features for the sake of generating theatre meaning. The 'implied spectator' too is a theoretical construct that reflects the complementation expected by such a text for theatre meaning to emerge; i.e., its competences and functions. *There is, therefore, a pre-structured dialogue between these two constructs or, to be more precise, a pre-designed mutual complementation.*

It is not only that real spectators are limited in their reading and inter-pretive capacities, but also in their abilities to understand and report their own reactions to fictional worlds, which may involve unconscious layers of the psyche. Their inability to explain their own involvement does not necessarily impinge on their reactions, but does make the results of empir-ical research based on their reports most problematic. In contrast, the analysis of the implied spectator rests on firmer grounds, by definition.

An implied spectator should be rather seen as reflecting a directorial intuition of the prospective real spectator. After all, the latter is the main object of the theatre experience. The actual effect of a performance-text thus hinges on a real director's ability to capture the real spectator's nature, although a full correlation between implied and real spectators is seldom achieved. Real directors may not possess the correct perceptions of real spectators, and expect competences that they may not have. Conversely, although real spectators may feel that they have comprehended and adequately reacted to a certain work, this feeling may be spurious. The advantage in including the implied spectator in performance analysis should not obscure the fact that the actual dialogue only obtains between a real director and a real spectator.

12

A Phenomenology of Theatre

In recent years, it has been suggested that the physical presence of actors on stage marks the limits and limitations of the semiotic approach to theatre, and determines the need for a complementary methodology of research: a phenomenology of theatre (e.g., States). The current theoretical trend thus advocates a fundamental duality of two irreducible elements on stage: text and actors' bodies. According to this approach, bodies on stage enjoy a kind of independence *vis-à-vis* the text inscribed in them, and are experienced in their own right. The traditional semiotic approach focuses, instead, only on the textual nature of the performance-text and totally ignores the actors' bodies. Nonetheless, with no commitment to a limitless application of semiotic methodology, I suggest that actors' bodies fulfil poetic, aesthetic and rhetoric functions, in addition to their semiotic functions, in the inner and outer structures of a performance-text.

In particular, this chapter analyzes and challenges an instance of the so-called 'phenomenological approach', suggested by Bert O. States, who not only supports a 'binocular' semiotic/phenomenological approach, but also subordinates the text to the actor's body. However, although a phenomenology of theatre is possible, and even commendable, such an approach should not be confined to physical presence on stage alone, but to all aspects of a performance-text, including its semiotic substratum.

Focus on the actors' corporeality has undoubtedly led to conceiving of theatre as having more in common with both artistic and non-artistic activities, performed by live people in front of live spectators/onlookers in actual time and space, e.g., a concert, a ballet, a Bar Mitzvah ceremony and a hostage crisis (cf. Schechner: 252–3), than with other dramatic arts such as cinema and TV drama. However, *whereas performativity and unmediated bodily experience are indeed properties of theatre, its fundamental affinity to the latter regards the mechanism of enacting fictional entities* (chapter 5). In any case, no theory of theatre can afford to ignore this dilemma.

This chapter aims at showing that (a) the traditional semiotic approach, which focuses solely on the textual function of the body, is incorrect; (b) States fails to explain the functions of actors' bodies, and even the advantage of his phenomenological approach; (c) actors' bodies fulfil the functions of 'textuality', 'metatheatricality', 'personification', 'characterization' and 'aesthetic effect'; (d) seeing the experience of actors' bodies as the common denominator of theatre and performance art is misleading; and (e) a phenomenological approach should apply to all the elements that have a share in generating theatre meaning.

States' phenomenological approach

In *Great Reckonings in Little Rooms*, States offers theoretical support for the irreducible presence of the body on stage based on a fundamental distinction between two complementary 'modes of seeing':

> It seems to me that semiotics is a useful, if incomplete, discipline. It has become evident to me [. . .] that semiotics and phenomenology are best seen as complementary perspectives on the world and on art. [. . .] If we think of semiotics and phenomenology as *modes of seeing*, we might say that they constitute a kind of *binocular vision*: one eye enables us to see the world phenomenally; the other eye enables us to see it significatively (p. 8; my italics).

Moreover, whereas the interest of the semiotician is restricted to the signs of a performance, the phenomenologist is in search of 'the essence' of things (p. 21). This is an odd observation because, if the object of phenomenological analysis is a text, it is sensible to assume that its semiotic function would not be seen merely as one of its 'possible functions', but as its fundamental one. The following are the main tenets of States' argument:

(A) *Sign-ness vs. thing-ness*: For States, signs 'achieve their vitality – and in turn the vitality of the theater – not simply by signifying the world but by being *of* it' (p. 20). He correctly implies thereby a distinction between two functions of the same objects on stage: (1) qua bearers of the semiotic text they fulfil a descriptive function; and (2) qua performers, the actors' bodies are entities in the real world, independent of the texts that they perform, and may thus attract the spectators' attention as such. However, this distinction, which is meant to support their equal status, i.e., States' 'binocular vision', contradicts the fundamental function of these bodies (1), as otherwise their physical presence on stage would be meaningless.

Following the 'Prague linguists', States considers that from a semiotic viewpoint everything on stage is a sign (p. 19; cf. Veltrusky: 84). He is not aware, however, that even for Bogatyrev these signs are not of the same kind, and are not employed to describe and/or refer to the same world: he suggests that there are 'signs of material things' and 'signs of signs' (1986a: 33). Whereas the latter describe a fictional world (W_1), the former are indexes of the performing mechanism in the real world, including actors (W_0) (chapter 5).

(B) *Sign vs. image*: States suggests a distinction between 'sign' and 'image' (pp. 23ff), which assumedly supports a kind of theatre semiotics that is akin to his approach:

> Unlike the sign, the image is unique and unreproducible (except as facsimile); whereas the sign is of no value unless it repeats itself. [. . .] In other words, the inclination of a sign is to become more efficient, to be read easily. [. . .] In the strictly utilitarian sphere [. . .] the sign gets down to its referential business with as little flourish as possible. (States: 25)

In this context 'sign' is assumedly employed here in a Saussurian sense, and having verbal signs in mind. Words: the more they are used the more efficient they are. Unfortunately, he does not define 'image' that, indeed, in its imprinted version, can be 'unique and unreproducible'. However, these properties do not impinge on its descriptive and referential functions. An iconic sentence/icon, easily recognized and read on the grounds of similarity, 'gets down to its referential business' exactly as any verbal description. Because of language mediation, imprinted images and words are equivalent signs in different systems, with both being equally capable of describing worlds to a high degree of accuracy and non-ambiguity (chapter 1).

(C) *Text vs. reality*: States argues that 'stage images (including actors) do not always or entirely surrender their objective nature to the sign/image function. They retain, in other words, a high degree of *en soi*' (p. 29). For example, it is virtually impossible to entirely subordinate the behavior of an animal that follows 'its own inclinations' to its acting role (p. 32); e.g., when defecating on stage. In such a case, bodies may focus the attention of the audience for their own sake. The same applies to children, because 'they are conspicuously not identical with their characters' (p. 32). Indeed, no audience will accept professional actors who follow their own inclinations on stage. Moreover, animals or children following their own inclinations often elicit laughter in the wrong places. States' examples may lead, therefore, to the opposite conclusion: actors are not expected to focus attention on themselves, which is absurd. This does not entail, as presupposed by States, that a semiotic approach would expect 'identity' between actor and character, which evidently reflects a naturalistic bias. Actor, description of character and character belong in three different ontological spheres.

In contrast to States' examples, the notions of 'text' and 'description' imply 'intentionality'. Whose intentionality? For example, in the annual Passion of Esparragueras (Catalonia), during the Last Supper scene, a dove, trained to appear on stage, hovers about the table and lands exactly on the brim of the Holy Grail in front of Jesus. The impression is breath-taking. The audience responds to this flawless stage metaphor of the Holy Spirit as if it were a miracle. The bird behaves as a professional actor: the dove is 'conspicuously identical' with its character. Obviously, it is not the bird's intentionality, but only a clear indication of directorial intentionality.

(D) *Description vs. illusion*: States contends that real objects on stage, like running water, when not identical with their sign-function 'something indisputably real leaks out of the *illusion*' (p. 31; my italics). For him 'the physical actuality of the actor on stage' is 'the whole phenomenal floor of the theater *illusion* [. . .] which, for the most part, we accept as perceptually given' (p. 34; my italics); i.e., the aim of physical actuality is to create illusion, with the naturalistic set probably being a paradigmatic example. Unfortunately, he does not define 'illusion', which is usually perceived as a perceptual mistake. The notion of 'theatre illusion' indeed implies a spurious sense of identity between stage and fictional world. The problem is that States also views real objects as subverting this illusion. In analyzing the anti-illusionist effect of an object 'obeying its own laws of behavior' (p. 30), such as animals, children, running water and fire, he presupposes that real objects may preclude assimilation within the imagistic (and thus illusionist) nature of a performance. He asks, therefore: '[t]o what extent can these nodes of reality extruding from the illusion any longer be called images or signs?' (p. 34). This is a paradoxical claim because of implying that the same objects may both produce illusion and break it. On the contrary, these 'nodes of reality' may reinforce a sense of illusion, because the unexpected behavior of children and animals is part of the human sense of reality.

In dealing with these 'extruding' examples, States aims at determining 'points at which the floor [of theatre illusion] cracks open and we are startled, however pleasantly, by the upsurge of the real into the magic circle where the conventions of theatricality have assured us that the real has been subdued and transcended' (p. 34). Furthermore, States conceives of theatre as 'intentionally devoted to confusing these two orders of signification' (*ibid.*) and bestows on this confusion the crucial function of constant colonization of the real world:

my thesis here is that the dog on stage is a nearly perfect symptom of the cutting edge of theater, the bite that it makes into actuality in order to sustain itself in the dynamic order of its own ever-dying signs and images. One could define the history of theater – especially where we find it overthrowing its own traditions – as a progressive colonization of the real world. (p. 36)

This 'ontological confusion' allegedly lies at the heart of the theatre experience: it allows the mind 'to oscillate rapidly between the two kinds of perception' (p. 36). The question is, therefore, whether or not such marginal upsurges or, rather, semiotic failures could be seen as indexes of the phenomenal nature of theatre?

In contrast, from a semiotic viewpoint, the notion of 'illusion' cannot be accepted. If the theatre performance is a text, couched in a cultural medium, there exists an ontological gap between stage reality as description of a world and the described (fictional) world. If what is inscribed in the actors' bodies is a descriptive text, the (fictional) referent cannot be identical with it. This existential gap is manifest in that some features of a performance-text cannot be attributed to a fictional world, e.g., stage conventions (chapter 4). If the notion of 'illusion' is an attempt to understand the total involvement of a spectator in the theatre experience, this psychological phenomenon is better explained by the nature of the fictional world and its profound meaning for the spectator (chapter 7). Illusion may be the spurious aim of a specific theatre style, but is not in the nature of theatre.

The twofold similarity on the imagistic and material levels typical of theatre may induce a sense of illusion in a naïve spectator, and a belief that he is experiencing a world, but this would reflect a misapprehension of theatre. Spectators may be taken in by an exceptional similarity to the real world; but it is their sheer amazement that betrays their basic awareness of theatre's theatricality. Apart from naturalistic theatre, most theatre styles stress their own theatricality. A performance-text does not aim at persuading spectators that they are witnessing a world and allowed to sneak a look at it, but rather at presenting a description of a world that is most meaningful to them.

(E) *Defamiliarization:* By coupling his own version of phenomenology with Shklovsky's notion of 'defamiliarization', States actually advocates the subordination of semiotics to phenomenology. Following Shklovsky, who promotes the de-automatization of perception (pp. 12–13), States claims that the purpose of 'the upsurge of the real' is to 'suddenly see the familiar in defamiliarization' (p. 34). By this change of perspective reality regains the interest of the audience and its true nature is reconsidered: 'If the objects of reality depicted in art carry some of their worldly meanings with them – and no one would deny that they do – they are now seen, by a trick of perspective, to have been partially concealed all along *by* the meanings' (p. 22). States' notion of 'defamiliarization' allegedly captures the main function of art, which is to release cognition of reality from the bonds of signification: 'art is a way of bringing us home via an "unfamiliar" route' (*ibid.*). This implies that theatre semiosis is used for being dialectically negated by the experience of the real. Following this logic, meaning is parasitic on the phenomenological nature of theatre (cf. p. 27).

Indeed, it is widely accepted that the price of signification is veiling to a certain extent the true nature of things. Indeed, defamiliarization for the purpose of cognition of the world is undoubtedly an effective procedure, which is shared by the arts and sciences, not to mention philosophy. Not to accept reality as it appears through mediation of *a priori* categories of thought is not only a basic mechanism of thinking, but also reflects a critical attitude to a preconceived reality. Viewing the theatre as a medium, which is an instrument of thinking equivalent to language, supports the contention that defamiliarization can be one of its methods. However, the claim that this mechanism reflects the essence of theatre contradicts its nature as a medium, which by definition may convey any attitude, whether defamiliarizing or not. Not all kinds of thinking are critical. Not all acts of thinking achieve cognitive gains. Thinking cannot be defined by one of its particular forms. It is more sensible to assume that defamiliarization may be achieved, if at all, by the nature of a specific fictional world. Therefore, actors' bodies cannot have a defamiliarizing function in themselves.

Alternative phenomenological approaches

States claims that his study 'is not even a phenomenology of the theater, properly speaking' (p. 1). Craig Steward Walker, who is aware of this disclaimer, has attempted to demonstrate that there is no theoretical justification for considering States' theory as reflecting a phenomenological approach (Walker: 71). Seemingly States' definition of 'phenomenology' is rather sound: 'I use the adjective *phenomenal* in the sense of pertaining to phenomena or to our sensory experience with empirical objects. The adjective *phenomenological*, of course, refers to the analytical or descriptive problem of dealing with such phenomena' (p. 21, note 5). However, *in contrast to States' own 'binocular vision', such a definition leads to a comprehensive approach, which not only includes actors', animals' and children's bodies, but also the semiotic substratum and additional poetic, metaphoric and rhetoric strata.* In addition, States operates a narrow and dated semiotics of theatre; namely, an imperialistic semiotics that excluded crucial disciplines from performance analysis (cf. Marinis: 11). *A phenomenological approach should thus apply to all the elements that have a share in generating theatre meaning.*

In contrast to States, Bruce Wilshire operates a broader 'phenomenology of theatre'. He suggests that Husserl 'endeavored to formulate a method for revealing the meanings of things and events through revealing the structure of their modes of appearing' (p. 11). 'Phenomenological methods, if employed sufficiently flexibly and imaginatively, can disclose essential characteristics of theatre art [. . .] without which the event would not be theatre art. This set of characteristics might be called the "essence of theatre"' (p. 15). 'Phenomenology is [thus] a discipline of the imagination' (p. 12). For example, a performance-text without enacting characters is not theatre anymore.

Following Wilshire's theory, theatre itself can be seen as a tool of phenomenological thinking, because spectators usually confront human nature in an infinite number of variations that enable its better understanding: 'We will regard theatre as a fictive variation on existence, conducted by a community of participants, in which each may surprise every other – as well as himself – with what emerges through their spontaneous interaction and involvement' (p. 17). It is in this sense that theatre is a laboratory that explores the nature of the human experience.

Wilshire's approach is thus incompatible with States' narrow phenomenology of theatre, which focuses only on the actors' bodies, and excludes textual, fictional and spectatorial aspects. No phenomenological approach can be partial. It should cast a wider net. Unfortunately, no phenomenologist approach has produced performance analyses of note. I note that no recent phenomenologist approach has followed Ingarden's magnificent contribution to theatre theory.

Functions of actors' bodies on stage

Bogatyrev claims that the dual perception of actor and text 'affirms that it is impossible to identify the player with the role he plays, that no equation can be made between the actor and the character whom he represents, that the costume and mask and gestures of the actor are only a sign of a sign of the character portrayed by him' (1986a: 48). Moreover, following Veltrusky, the relationship between actor and character is mediated by a descriptive text, a 'stage figure' in his terms, distinct from both (1981: 232). This implies a twofold distinction between (a) the actors' bodies as performers of a descriptive text and a text; and (b) between a text and a described character. No semiotic approach would deny that the corporeality of the actors' bodies is by definition an organic component of the theatre medium. I suggest, however, that *in addition to its descriptive function, corporeality may fulfil other significant functions in the overall structure of a performance-text.* These functions are: 'textuality', 'metatheatricality', 'personification', 'characterization' and 'aesthetic effect':

(A) *Textuality*: actors' bodies on stage should be conceived of in terms of 'acting'; i.e., performing descriptions of characters by imprinting images on their own bodies, carrying these imprinted images, and deflecting reference to characters (chapter 5). As performers of such descriptions actors share this function with other craftsmen, such as carpenters, costume makers and lighting operators, usually not present on stage. As materials for imprinted texts, actors' bodies share this function with other materials used for imprinting images on stage. Whereas all objects on stage enact fictional ones, only actors combine the performing and textual functions on their own bodies.

(B) *Metatheatricality*: the actual experience of actors' bodies, while performing descriptions of characters, indicates the theatricality of a performance-text (Rozik, 2002b). 'Metatheatricality' applies here to whatever constitutes a reference, verbal or iconic, to the theatrical nature of a performance-text, and is usually viewed as an anti-illusionist device. Metatheatricality thus reflects tension between performative and textual aspects within the very same body, as if two different entities coexist within it. This tension can be emphasized or played down at will: e.g. by promotion of interest in an actor's previous roles and offstage life. Different attitudes to this gap may reflect different theatre styles. Without such tension the assessment of an actor's performance as such could not be explained; e.g., applause. Awareness of this tension emphasizes the ontological gap between the performers of a text and a text, and reveals that a performance-text is not a world, but a description of a world; i.e., a cultural construct in line with dramatic texts generated by media that do not feature similarity on the material level.

Carlson addresses the issue of drawing attention 'to the actor at the expense of the stage figure [the description of a character]' (1994: 112), and suggests conceiving of this phenomenon in terms of 'ghosting', a notion of wider application (2004). Ghosting 'is not something created during the theatre experience by the actor, but is dependent upon a specific audience contribution' (1994: 112). He is aware that this may be 'a source of distraction, a valuable tool of interpretation or a source of enrichment and deepened pleasure' (*ibid.*: 113). Ghosting thus fulfils a metatheatrical function.

A metatheatrical effect is also achieved by focusing the spectator's attention on the mechanism of performing a theatre-text; e.g., by revealing the presence of light operators or exposing stagehands in changing a set. The same applies to the presence of projectors, microphones and the like. While this is most effective for an audience familiar with theatre styles that tend to hide this mechanism, such an effect may be lost if perpetuated. The presence of the puppeteers on stage in Japanese *bunraku* is an interesting example, because it discloses the mechanism of performing images and imprinting them on the puppets' bodies. This is performed by two puppeteers dressed in black. *Bunraku* thus reveals that metatheatricality also applies to non-human actors. Japanese audiences accept willingly this convention, without impairing their experience. This procedure may suggest that human actors too harbor a kind of puppeteer within their own bodies.

(c) *Personification*: In contrast to the thematic mode, a fictional world is the expression of a single psyche through a world of characters and their actions (chapter 1). Therefore, it is fundamentally a multiple and complex personification, which is a specific kind of metaphor that draws its associations from the human sphere, of a psychic state of affairs (chapter 3). Since theatre inscribes images of human beings and their behavior on live actors' bodies, stage personification acquires an additional human dimension. In contrast, literature conveys personification through the evocative power of words, and most iconic arts through imprinting their images on materials different from their models, such as paint on canvas, marble and wood (puppets). Personification that is imprinted on human bodies is shared by Cinema and TV drama; therefore, despite lacking the bodily concreteness that characterizes theatre, these arts are closer to theatre than most forms of performance art, because the imprinting of human images on live actors precedes recording.

In other iconic arts too the imprinted matter of an image may acquire a metaphoric function; e.g., in a statue of Socrates, the marble may induce an association of timelessness or eternity originating in the sense of durability attached to this material. Timelessness, which can be assimilated to the image of the philosopher, should be seen, therefore, as a metaphoric connotation of 'marble'. Accordingly, a contrasting sense of ephemeral existence can be achieved by sculpting a human image in ice. Furthermore, the sculpture of a nude woman in white marble may contrast the above connotations, while assimilating others, such as transparency, paleness and beauty. Since this is not always the case, it follows that only under particular conditions, governed by the interaction of a particular image and its imprinted matter, such a phenomenon can take place. Since a performance-text is a personified expression of an author, and offered as a possible personified expression of a spectator, the connotations deriving from the flesh and blood concreteness of actors' bodies are always assimilated within the overall metaphoric image of a fictional world.

The presence of additional objects on stage, which also constitute images imprinted on materials similar to their models, broadens the scope of such a metaphoric function beyond personification, to include 'animalization', 'mechanization' and the like (chapter 3). It follows that a theatre description of a fictional world – on the levels of both image and matter – can be subsumed under total 'metaphorization' of the psyche.

(D) *Characterization*: In order to fulfil its metaphoric task, characterization cannot be circumscribed to the level of abstract personification and requires additional concrete qualities and motives (chapter 8), which are described by words or indicated by characters' actions. In addition, directors may and usually cast actors for their bodily qualities *per se* or for what they represent. In this sense *casting is a central device of creative interpretation, the intention being to integrate personal, including bodily qualities, to characters*: e.g., Bryant-Bertail appropriately analyzes the casting of Jeanne Moreau in the role of the procuress in Vitez' production of Fernando Rojas' *La Célestine*. She suggests that as an actress 'Moreau "carried her own legend" into the production, a legend of a "twentieth-century woman"' (1994b: 102), which explains her casting: 'Vitez intended for Moreau – in his own words "a mythic actress" – to join Célestine and the Whore of Babylon in forming a kind of bridge linking, cities, eras, cultures, and ideologies – an expandable surface upon which to project ostensibly "universal" desire, and a way to magnify *La Célestine* by stretching its spatio-temporal frame' (*ibid.*: 107). His intention was evidently to universalize and actualize the play-script by casting an actress who, not personally, but intertextually represents twentieth-century corruption. The use of *La Célestine* as a metaphor for the twentieth century probably reflects criticism of the negative values in Rojas times, such as carnal love and happiness, having become top positive values in this century. Moreau's physiognomy thus attaches specific connotations to Célestine. Similarly, Wilcox emphasizes the seductive aspects of Karen Finley's own nudity and the frustration of desire that it may elicit (1997: 31ff); i.e., the use of her own body as an integral part of the overall imprinted image. Moreover, features that cannot be integrated should be seen as conventions and thus overlooked.

(E) *Aesthetic effect*: the perceptible nature of a performance-text, as experienced by the spectator, is a possible component of its visual and aural aesthetic organization. Since actors' bodies are part of the signifying level, combining nonmaterial images and matter, they may maintain aesthetic relations with other signifiers on stage, such as symmetry, proportion and harmony of color and form in set, and rhythm and harmony in voiced interaction. It follows, therefore, that the materiality of actors' bodies, together with other stage objects, may induce aesthetic experiences of harmony or disharmony, and beauty or ugliness. Moreover, such experiences may suit or contrast aesthetic configurations on the signified (fictional) level, which can be described in aesthetic terms such as 'wholeness', 'unity', 'harmony' and 'absurdity'. It is the combination of both aesthetic levels that can be integrated within a complex overall metaphoric image of a performance-text.

Most of these functions cannot be subsumed under semiotics and require additional methods of analysis. This list probably does not exhaust all possible functions. It may be concluded, nonetheless, that inasmuch as actors' bodies do not fulfil such functions they are of no interest for performance analysis.

Life Class: a personal experience

During the rehearsals of David Storey's *Life Class*, at the Royal Court Theatre, 1974, I repeatedly experienced the striking presence of the actress' nude body on stage. Most scenes of this play take place in the classroom of an art school, in which a group of male students are drawing from a nude female model. While the teacher is most eager to spread his ideology, which legitimizes doing anything wished, the students interpret his words as a permit to rape the model, which they eventually do, bringing the teacher's credo to the absurd.

Director Lindsey Anderson decided not to wait for the [un]dress rehearsal and asked the actress to rehearse naked from the beginning. His decision was probably meant to create the psychological space needed for the actress, who was not a professional model, to adjust to her role. So, for long hours, she used to stand motionless and speechless on the podium, even while, in his unique style, Anderson commented on every nuance of the acting. In addition to her extremely beautiful body, most striking was her relaxed manner: she did not even dress for coffee breaks and, while remaining nude, she used to chat with us, nonchalantly, a cup of coffee in her right hand, as if this was the most natural thing to do. Her bodily presence could definitely not be ignored. Her nudity unreservedly transgressed the frail borderline between her concrete corporeality (the coffee breaks) and her textuality (being a description of a nude model).

A nude body probably best illustrates the autonomy of the body because, besides attracting attention on its own, it would appear that nothing is inscribed on it. In fact, however, although almost motionless, the actress inscribed images typical of nude models on her own body, and its beauty was completely assimilated into the imprinted image of a fictional model. The beauty of her naked body also accounted for the students' sexual arousal that led to her rape.

Had the model in this life class been enacted by an ugly and wrinkled old woman, attention to the body would probably have been equally powerful, but for different reasons. The rape itself would have acquired a totally different meaning. Probably, it would have motivated spectators into inquiring about the director's intention. One possible explanation could have been convention; after all, actors playing roles which do not match their real age or sex are not rare in theatre. In the case of convention, spectators are tacitly expected to overlook actual discrepancy and focus on the meaning of the enacted images. However, in the case of raping a nude model such a choice is quite inconceivable. Another possible explanation could have been the intention of stressing further the absurdity of the teacher's preaching.

Models usually are beautiful and show a kind of indifference (not necessarily genuine) to people pondering their bodies. A director's choice of an actress with a beautiful body is no different from using a red-haired actor to enact King David, or an adolescent actress to play Juliet. It is most sensible to assume, therefore, that this actress was chosen for the overall image she was able to project, including her beautiful nude body and nonchalant manner, and for its possible integration in the overall meaning of the fictional world.

If the fictional world of *Life Class* is considered as a personification of the perennial struggle between instinctual wish and moral constraint, *the nakedness of the actress, similarly to the dressed images of the students and their undressing images during the rape, lent a further dimension of personification to the overall metaphor.* If the intention was to create a metaphor of abrupt transition from breathtaking beauty to sheer vandalism, on the sensory level, the disheveled body of the actress complemented the image of total chaos on the fictional level. In this sense the aesthetic level too was assimilated within the overall metaphoric image.

The spectators' strong involvement in the action undoubtedly reflected that the conflict between wish and moral constraint was latent in them, and that they found in this fictional world an appropriate metaphor of their psychic state of affairs. Did her nude body defamiliarize the notion of 'nude female body'? Actually, there was nothing unfamiliar about it. Could her nude body on stage have subverted its textual function? My personal impression was that any effect it had on the audience could have been assimilated into the overall meaning of the fictional world. This impression does not contrast the possibility of creating inner tension between corporeality and textuality that, as suggested above, fulfils a metatheatrical function.

185

LIVERPOOL JOHN MOORES UNIVERSITY
LEARNING SERVICES

Focusing on the materiality of a nude body on stage seemingly implies that theatre is closer to nude modeling or striptease (a performance) than to the image of a nude body in cinema or TV drama, which may appear dematerialized because of photographic mediation. In these media, however, the imprinting of images on actors' bodies precedes photography.

Theatre vs. performance art

Theatre is a performative art, in the sense of live actors performing for live audiences. It thus shares its performative nature with other arts, such as music, dance, and performance-art. However, *the fact that their common denominator is the bodily presence of performers, by no means eliminates profound differences between them.* The specific difference of theatre art lies in the existential twofold gap between the describing performers and the descriptions inscribed in their bodies, and between these descriptions and the described characters.

The crucial duality is, therefore, not of body and text, but of imprinting a text and imprinted text, which applies to both human and nonhuman actors. In contrast, although the specific difference of performance art has not been theoretically established as yet, and some of its forms fully or partially employ the theatre medium, its underlying intention is to produce an exclusive sense of actuality, i.e., of self-reference, which is fundamentally foreign to theatre. Even naïve or extremely involved theatre spectators must become aware that they are watching not a world but a description of a world. *By definition, theatre cannot be non-representational* (cf. Carlson, 1990: 3–9).

Is Finley's *The Constant State of Desire* an instance of theatre? She declares: 'I do go into somewhat of a trance because when I perform I want it to be different from acting' (*ibid.*: 154; cf. Balme: 28–9). However, *The Constant State of Desire* includes several stories about male and female victims of unbridled desire, whose character she sporadically enacts, while her consistent *gestus* of accusation, her pervading singsong and trance-like delivery reflect her mediating viewpoint. Her mode of performing is thus akin to oral storytelling, which allows for occasional enacting of characters. She actually enacts a fictional storyteller. In contrast, some works of performance art cannot be related to theatre at all.

Furthermore, within the category of 'art', there is no advantage in distinguishing, between performative and non-performative arts, such as painting and sculpting. In a sense, these are also performative arts: paintings and sculptures are performed, although like set objects put on stage, artists are dissociated from their works, while spectators still participate in generating their meaning. Moreover, viewing the principle of acting as the hallmark of theatre leads to the conclusion that cinema, TV drama and puppet theatre have more in common with it than any other performative art, despite not providing a non-mediated experience of actors' bodies. Therefore, *seeing the experience of actors' bodies as the essential common denominator of theatre and performance art is a fallacy.*

PART III

Examples of Performance Analysis

Actual performance analysis is the cornerstone of the inductive method advocated in this study. Each new performance analysis should lead to the re-examination of theory, including that proposed in this book. It is the constant interaction between established theory and new insights that provides the ground for an ever growing sound theory and effective methodology of theatre. Part III thus contains five examples of performance analysis that both reflect a critique of traditional theory and apply the alternative principles advanced in this study.

13

A Transient Shadow: *A Silent Description of a Speaking Fictional World*

Since the beginning of the twentieth century much has been said and written about theatre being subjugated by the word and about the necessity for its liberation from this bondage. Without necessarily aiming at abolishing the verbal element, a new hierarchy of means dominated by non-verbal concrete images was envisaged (cf. Artaud: 159–84). Concurrently, at the beginning of that century, silent films were produced but, because voicelessness was perceived as a handicap of the new medium, this was rapidly corrected by the invention of the sound track. Regretfully, although silent movies could have been used to explore the potentials of a non-verbal image-dominated theatre, this was not attempted. The idea of a theatre in which the non-verbal image subordinates the word has nevertheless had a crucial impact not only on the practice of theatre, but also on its theoretical perception.

However, if theatre is considered as an art of images imprinted on human bodies, images of speech are not foreign to this principle. Speech acts are non-verbal in nature because of being indexes of actions, and their iconic replicas too are non-verbal by definition (chapter 1). In this sense iconic speech acts should be conceived of as imprinted images of real models, and dialogue as a comprehensive imprinted image of human interaction. Such a conclusion was not envisaged by Antonin Artaud.

Even a superficial survey reveals that silent movies do not describe silent fictional worlds. The moving lips of the actors and other bodily indicators reveal that their silent frames are meant to describe verbal interactions. This apparent incongruence also applies to a theatre production designed after the model of silent film. Therefore, the question is: *how does a speechless performance-text manage to describe and evoke a speaking fictional world?*

191

In other words, *what principles enable the audience to perceive such a gap and fill it in by associatively providing the missing verbal elements*; and, under the assumption that not all verbal elements are used for the sake of fictional interaction, as in some stage conventions, *what happens to the verbal categorization of the fictional world if these elements are missing?*

This chapter explores these questions through the analysis of *A Transient Shadow*, a silent theatre production, designed and directed by Michael Gurevitch at the Khan Theatre, Jerusalem, 1999 (Rozik, 2002c). It focuses on the nature of silent film, the model adopted by the director, only to the extent that it assists this inquiry. The enthusiastic response of the audience clearly indicated that this silent production, although describing a complex fictional world, was manifestly understood.

Reading *A Transient Shadow*

The set featured the front wall of a derelict house, placed back stage, with an entrance door in the middle and flanked by two stone walls. The faded paint on the wall was partially peeling. The set remained unchanged throughout the performance, but for a few changing pieces of furniture in front of it, which characterized various locations, such as a restaurant indicated by a few square tables, a dining room by a large table, and a children's bedroom by two single beds. No furniture denoted outdoors. In the final scene, the stage simultaneously evoked the restaurant (the tables) and the family dining room (the dinner table), visibly indicating that it enacted the space of the mind.

The passing of time was characterized by signs of age, Girl/Woman in particular; e.g., Girl as a child (period I), Girl as a teenager (period II), Girl as a young woman (period III), Girl as a mature woman (period IV) and Girl as an old lady (period V). Age was depicted through typical bodily movements and physical features (e.g., shaky movements and white hair for old age), props and costume (e.g., a red balloon and panties for young age). The scenes were not arranged in chronological order, indicating that the entire action was taking place in Woman's retrospective mind, revealing the logic of events retrieved from memory. Although the child–teenager–young woman and the mature–old woman were the same character at different ages, two actresses enacted them, following a well-established convention, thereby enabling their actual confrontation on stage.

Scene I – *title: Woman returns [restaurant, period IV]*
Old Waiter dozes while seated at a restaurant table. Mature Woman enters carrying a suitcase in her hand. Old Man and Waiter play cards.

Young Man reads a book. She watches them. Young Man recognizes her, because of a ring on her finger. They embrace. Old Man loses the game and leaves in anger. Young Man kisses Woman.

Inferences: The age of Woman and the suitcase frame the scene as her return to a familiar place. The Young Man's way of recognition implies long absence. Although the elderly characters could have identified her, they do not.

Scene II – *title: first memory [restaurant, period I]*
Girl (as baby) and Parents sit at a table. Mother is pregnant. Girl holds a red balloon. Mother dresses Girl in panties. The atmosphere is idyllic. Young Waiter gives Girl a lollipop, serves drinks, plays a gramophone and takes a photo of the family. Magician is captivated by Girl. There is anxiety in his look. Magician performs tricks out of a little magic box, and Girl is fascinated. Girl dances like a doll on a musical box to a baby-like tune. Magician gives her a ring, sends her a pint of beer and gives her a cigarette. She drinks the beer and Parents protest. She smokes. They protest. Eventually, Magician folds a napkin in the shape of a penis. The outraged Parents leave the restaurant.

Inferences: The ring identifies Girl as Woman of Scene I, and thus Old Man is identified as Woman's Father. The entire sequence thus presents Woman's memories from forty-five years ago (program). The young age of Girl, enacted by a child-like adult actress, is indicated by her panties, red balloon and way of dancing.

Scene III – *title: lovers [outdoors, period I]*
Waiter dresses, and then meets Lover. They scrutinize one another, embrace and eventually leave together.

Inferences: a short scene of homosexual attraction and love.

Scene IV – *title: a night in the children's room [children's room, period II]*
Parents put children to bed, while dressing for going out. Brother hugs a teddy bear (Young Man as a child – enacted by the same actor). Each parent clearly shows predilection for the child of the opposite sex. Brother cries and Mother reads him a story. Brother calms down. Left alone, Girl reads him a frightening story. Brother cries. Parents return, calm him down and leave. Girl shows her sex to Brother. He is astonished to find nothing. She looks at his penis. She caresses it. Both are delighted. Shadow (a black actor) passes behind the back door. Girl is fascinated and frightened by him. She returns to bed and Brother joins her. They embrace and fall asleep. Shadow reappears to watch them from back door.

Inferences: in the meantime Mother has given birth to Brother.

193

Children's curiosity indicates the beginning of their sexual life. Girl makes a further step in a first act of real sexuality. Parents' predilection for the child of the opposite sex already reflects sexuality. Shadow's appearance is, therefore, connected to sexuality by contiguity.

Scene V – *title: a shadow passes [restaurant, period III]*
Girl (as teenager) returns from school, throwing her briefcase away. She embraces, and kisses Waiter. She dances with him, no longer as a child. She wants to serve him a meal. Lover enters from inside quite undressed. She realizes that they have been sleeping together. Father enters and regards Lover with contempt. Father leaves. Shadow enters the restaurant and sits down to read a book. She kisses him, and eventually he kisses her. They embrace and leave together.
Inferences: Girl attempts to connect her sexual drive to Waiter. In serving him a meal she follows Mother's model. She reveals that he is gay. Father adds an attitude of contempt for homosexuality. Then she tries Shadow, who now appears in the guise of an intellectual "macho".

Scene VI – *no title [restaurant, period IV]*
Woman with suitcase enters. She looks at Waiter and Old Magician with loving eyes. Old Magician wishes to impress Woman with a cigarette trick, but fails. Woman reveals her identity to Waiter by showing him the ring. He produces a photo (scene II) from his wallet and asks (gesture), if she is the girl of the photo. She confirms and dances her childhood dance. Magician is terrified and leaves in a hurry.
Inferences: Woman reveals an attitude of reconciliation. She accepts Magician, as performer of tricks, and Waiter for what he is. Magician leaves in terror.

Scene VII – *no title [restaurant, period III]*
Girl (as teenager) comes in to collect her briefcase. She is extremely sad and leaves. Lover (dressed in the meantime) tries to embrace Waiter, who refuses. He orders Lover to leave and throws his jacket at him. Lover leaves. Waiter remains anguished.
Inferences: Girl's briefcase connects this scene to scene V. Waiter refuses Lover's love because of social norms, implicitly reflected in Father's and Girl's attitude.

Scene VIII – *title: Shadow returns [outdoors, period IV]*
Shadow appears to Magician in the guise of a blond and seducing black woman. While performing an erotic dance, Shadow undresses to reveal a black male's chest. He then takes off his blond wig and repeatedly punches and kicks Old Magician's body. Shadow also attempts to rob him. All these

assaults happen under Woman's gaze, who chases Shadow off. She helps Magician on his feet and leave together.

Shadow and Magician in *A Transient Shadow*. Courtesy of the Jerusalem Khan Theatre. Photo: Gadi Dagon.

Inferences: Shadow appears to different people in different guises, like a fantasy. Woman discovers that Shadow, who had previously attracted her, is a deceptive thief.

Scene IX – *title: family dinner [family dining room, period III]*

Father returns from work and tries to make love to Mother, while she is setting the table for dinner. She tries to persuade him to stop because of the children. Eventually Father pushes her under the table to suck Father's penis. Brother enters to join the meal. Father pretends that nothing happens. He alternates expressions of sexual crescendo and embarrassed apology. His grotesque behavior culminates in disguised orgasm. To the amazement of Brother, Father utters the only verbal sentence in the performance: 'Where is Mother?' Mother manages to reappear and dinner proceeds as usual. Girl enters, takes off her blouse and leaves wearing only a bra. She is overwhelmed by sadness. Woman watches the scene.

Inferences: This scene portrays bourgeois hypocrisy: while speaking about sex is taboo, frantic oral sex is extremely enjoyed. Girl returns after a traumatic experience with Shadow (after scene V). The title of this scene is ironic.

Father's delight in *A Transient Shadow*. Courtesy of the Jerusalem Khan Theatre. Photo: Gadi Dagon.

Scene X – *title: mirror [the mind, period III]*

Girl (as young woman) in camisole dances while holding a big oblong mirror and staring at it. Brother watches her. Father, Mother and Woman also watch the scene.

Inferences: Girl is pondering her own image, attempting to understand her reflection in the mirror. This is a typical stage metaphor of identity-searching.

Scene XI – *no title [Lover's home, period III]*

Lover alone, half-dressed, hides a knife in his shirtsleeve. He dresses in a tie, a jacket and sunglasses. He goes out in determination.

Inferences: Lover is planning to kill someone. It is unclear who will be the victim.

Scene XII – *no title [the mind, period III]*

Girl in camisole continues dancing with the mirror and pondering her own image (after scene X). Shadow and Brother alternately appear behind the transparent mirror. They struggle. Brother, as a young man, is half-naked. Girl and Brother perform an erotic dance. She kisses him on his mouth. He hesitates. A long piece of cloth, or low curtain, is repeatedly lifted and lowered in between them. When lowered, Brother and Shadow alternately reappear. They engage in erotic foreplay with Girl in turns, until eventually Brother and Girl embrace and lie down in stylized intercourse.

196

Father enters. He is shocked. Girl sneaks off. Father franticly whips Brother with his belt. Mother and Girl enter. Mother puts a suitcase in Girl's hands. Girl leaves. Mother casts a blaming look at Father. She hugs Brother who is lying on the floor.

Inferences: Woman's absence and her late return are explained by Girl's sexual relations with Brother and her expulsion by Mother. The alternation between Brother and Shadow suggests the possible projection of 'shadow' (in the Jungian sense) on Brother. Parents' predilection for a child of the opposite sex is reflected again.

Scene XIII – *title: at Magician's home [Magician's home, period IV]*

Woman helps Old Magician to his home (after scene VIII). In the room there is a big chest similar to his little magic box (scene II). He pours wine, which takes on different colors, red and blue, in each goblet. They drink and dance gently. He leads her to lie down on the chest, caresses her thighs, slides his right hand between them, and takes out a bunch of magician's flowers, which he gallantly offers her. She is overwhelmed. Girl comes out from the chest and dances her childish dance (scene II). Girl pushes Woman towards Magician. Magician kisses Woman on her forehead. He lays his head on her chest, like a child. Girl returns to the chest and closes it on herself. He opens the chest to find nothing but a red balloon (scene II).

Inferences: Girl makes a final choice between Shadow and Magician, by pushing Woman towards the latter: she prefers asexual Magician (the flowers and kiss on the forehead) to the delusion of Shadow's sexuality.

Scene XIV – *title: deep sadness [restaurant, period III]*

Parents are extremely sad. Mother orders and eats in a kind of frenzy. Father does not eat. Lover comes in and tries to impose his love on Waiter, who repeatedly refuses. Father looks at Lover with suspicion. He tries to take Mother out, but she refuses and continues eating. Father and Waiter sit to play cards. Magician comes in, attempts a trick and fails. Lover kisses Father on his mouth (who tries to rub off the kiss in disgust). Lover lowers his trousers, enwraps his hips with a red tablecloth, climbs the table, performs an erotic dance in his underpants, forces Waiter to dance with him and eventually slashes his own veins and dies.

Inferences: Three kinds of expressions of deep sorrow: exaggerated eating, abstention from eating and suicide. Parents' sorrow indicates that this scene takes place after Girl was driven out of home. Waiter too is left to grieve.

Scene XV – *title: last dinner in the family [family dining room, period IV]*

Old Mother is wheeled in to sit at the table. Woman with suitcase enters

197

her childhood's home. She brings flowers. Old Father recognizes and embraces her. Woman embraces Brother. She kisses Old Mother on her head. Initially Old Mother does not recognize Woman. Pregnant Girl emerges from under the table. Old Mother stares at Woman in hatred. Girl leaves. Old Mother faints or dies. She is wheeled out. Woman and Brother embrace.

Inferences: Girl's appearance connects Woman to pregnant Girl in Old Mother's mind. Her pregnancy connects to sexual intercourse with Brother. Woman attempts reconciliation, but is met with hostility. Mother is unable to forgive.

Scene XVI – *no title [family dining room and restaurant, period IV]*
Fully dressed Lover appears behind the rear opening. Waiter hesitates. The gate closes. Waiter decides to reach Lover. The gate reopens, but Lover has disappeared.

Inferences: This scene hints at Waiter's possible alternative choice, but too late. Waiter eventually accepts himself for what he is.

Scene XVII – *no title [family dining room and restaurant, period V]*
Brother with teddy bear and Girl with red balloon enter. Pregnant Young Mother sits at a restaurant table. The atmosphere is idyllic. Young Mother looks happy and with a dreamy gaze. Woman (as a very old lady) is wheeled in to sit at the family table, like Old Mother (scene XV). Old Woman looks at Young Mother. Magician scatters confetti in the air. He kisses Old Woman on her forehead. Shadow enters and tenderly puts his arm around Old Woman's shoulders, kisses her on the mouth and leaves. Parents embrace Girl. Parents retreat while extending their arms to Old Woman, as if drawn by an invisible power. Old Woman is left alone. Behind her, Girl with her red balloon, dances and sings her song. Old Woman listens in wonder. Gradual blackout.

Inferences: The retreating characters probably mean that they escape Old Woman's memory. In her mind, she recapitulates her entire life. She wonders and thinks of how things might have been, had Parents' attitude been different.

This reading could not have been possible unless mastering a semiotic competence.

Interpreting *A Transient Shadow*

The narrative is quite simple and can be recapitulated as follows: Girl, raised in the puritan atmosphere of a bourgeois family, is tempted by natural curiosity to realize her sexual drives and fantasies. Eventually, out of ignorance, she engages in sexual relations with Brother and gets pregnant. Mother banishes her. After many years mature Girl/Woman returns home in an attitude of reconciliation to find that her family has grown old and is devastated. She reconsiders the *personae* of her childhood and youth with loving eyes. She is accepted by Old Father and Brother, but rejected by Old Mother who dies unable to forgive. Back from exile, she demystifies the spell of sex and the magic of adult life, personified in the characters of Shadow and Magician respectively. Eventually, as an old woman, she ponders how things might have been, if she had been raised otherwise. The renewed encounter with her own past was theatrically described through the structural image of a returning person, carrying a suitcase, who relives crucial scenes of her childhood and youth. These scenes were not presented in chronological order, thus reflecting the workings of Woman's memory, and enacted in front of the audience as if they were unfolding before Woman's own eyes, thereby establishing the stage as representing the space of her mind.

In parallel, Waiter initially accepts Lover's wooing, only to reject him later. His rejection is understood against the background of bourgeois values, clearly reflected in Father's gestures of disgust. Eventually, after Lover commits suicide, Waiter too considers how his life could have been otherwise. A structural analogy was thus created between Girl's craving for sexual experience and Waiter's striving to abstain from it, with both contradicting the bourgeois ethos, which eventually was reconsidered. Their parallel catastrophe implied criticism of bourgeois moral values, and suggested that things could have been different had society been more permissive.

This fictional world featured two types of *dramatis personae*: praxical characters, which described human beings (the family and the Waiter–Lover couple), and allegoric characters, which described personified psychical entities (Shadow and Magician). I suggest that the latter should be interpreted in terms of Jungian psychoanalysis.

'Shadow' is the term used by Jung for a specific archetype; i.e., the personification of a suppressed and thus unconscious entity of the psyche: 'Whatever form it takes, the function of the shadow is to represent the opposite side of the ego and to embody just those qualities that one dislikes most in other people. [. . .] the shadow contains the overwhelming power of irresistible impulse' (Franz: 173). Like all archetypes, the shadow is usually projected on real human beings, who become 'imagos'; i.e., bearers of such projections (Jung, 1974: 50). 'Everything that is unconscious is projected' (*ibid.*: 45). The shadow is a manifestation of an instinctual urge in the form of a 'primordial' and 'symbolical image' (Jung, 1969: 67–9; cf. p. 78).

The stress on Shadow's sexual behavior indicates that it was a person-ification of Girl's suppressed sexuality. The problem is that Shadow was enacted by a male actor, while in Jung's theory, '[i]n dreams and myths [. . .] the shadow appears as a person of the same sex as that of the dreamer' (p. 169), and personifies whatever a person suppressed in him/herself (p. 168). Therefore, Shadow suits better Jung's archetype of 'animus'. In his terms, 'animus' is the suppressed element of the opposite sex in a woman's psyche (Franz: 189–95), and is then the female's equivalent of 'anima' in the male's psyche. A woman tends to project her animus, so that it appears to her as the qualities of a real man (cf. *ibid.*: 180). This projection reflects what is unconsciously needed for complementing the unity of her psyche. In other words, the animus is a personification of what an individual woman expects in a man. Therefore, it can take different forms, depending on the unconscious disposition of each woman. Franz claims that '[t]he animus is basically influenced by a woman's father' (*ibid.*: 189). The name 'Shadow' probably reflects the director's personal interpretation of Jung's theory.

Shadow was enacted by a black actor, an obvious stage metaphor, whose black skin possibly reflected the popular association between black males and virility. His concrete body on stage added, therefore, a crucial dimen-sion to this abstract personification. He appeared to Girl in the guise of an intellectual lover. Girl initially projected her animus on Waiter, only to real-ize that being homosexual he was not an apt imago, and then on Brother. Shadow appeared to Magician as a seducing black lady, thus embodying the image of his anima. Shadow performed a kind of striptease act before revealing his male body and assaulting Magician. Under Woman's scrutiny, Shadow appeared as a fraud and thief – two stage metaphors of deceitful nature. Woman then realized that she had been lured by her own psyche into projecting a fraudulent animus on real human beings.

Whereas Magician could be conceived of in terms of 'realistic char-acter', who by coincidence is a customer of the restaurant, he should be seen as an alternative personification of Girl's animus. For a bourgeois girl, Magician clearly personifies the magic associated with male adult life: already in their first encounter (scene II), among his tricks, he offers Girl (as a baby) a mug of beer, a cigarette and a penis-shaped napkin – the symbols of adult male privileges. In contrast to Shadow, however, Magician's behavior was asexual and romantic. He always kissed Girl or Woman on her forehead, a kind of fatherly kiss. Young Girl startled him because he detected her strong sexual drive, and this may also explain why he initially ran away from Woman. In contrast to the ominous nature of Shadow, Magician personified the positive thrill of adult life. The confrontation between these two forms of animus reveals that they were designed as conflicting entities within Girl's psyche.

Woman returns to find Magician as an Old Man. He is no longer dexterous and most of his tricks fail. Whereas for Girl he epitomized the wonder of adult life, for mature Woman its charm had vanished. In retrospect Woman surveys her entire life to reveal that the magic of adult life is just a bunch of tricks and that sexual drives are similar delusions, while accepting her two archetypes with mature understanding: eventually, Woman lets herself to be fondled by Magician, and allows Shadow to kiss her on her mouth. Her acceptance of the psychic entities that had ruined her life implies her 'coming-to-terms' with these archetypal drives within her own 'Self' (Franz: 166), which is 'the totality of the whole psyche' (*ibid.*: 161). This process is the ultimate aim of psychic growth, the 'process of individuation' in Jungian terms (*ibid.*: 160).

The stage personification of two basic archetypes in Girl/Woman's psyche, the disregard of chronological order of the scenes, and her continuous witnessing them fits the workings of memory and indicates that this fictional world was designed as a reconsideration of her entire life, taking place in Old Woman's mind, in the spirit of an expressionist fictional world. The convention of two actresses enacting two major phases in Woman's life also suits the memory structure, and enabled the director to actually confront them on stage as coexisting in time. In her last dream she creates an alternative image of her own life as it could have been, if Parents had accepted her and themselves as they are. The action of Waiter points at the same conclusion. I contend that the above analysis is not a typical psychoanalytical interpretation of a fictional world, but a narrative created on the grounds of a psychoanalytical theory.

An alternative interpretation may be suggested on the grounds of Job's remark: 'because our days upon earth are a shadow' (Job, VIII, 9). In this verse 'shadow' metaphorically alludes to the ephemeral nature of life on earth, a feeling that is probably reflected also in Shakespeare's *Macbeth*: 'Life's but a walking shadow' (V, v, 24), although articulated by a flawed character who flagrantly violates the Christian faith. The same motif is voiced by Segismundo in Calderón de la Barca's *Life is a Dream*: 'What is this life? A frenzy, an illusion, / A shadow, a delirium, a fiction. [. . .] and this life / Is but a dream, and dreams are only dreams' (Calderón, English: 456; Spanish: 1195–200). Experiencing life in terms of 'fleeting nature', in Job's existential sense, may have been the basic association in the director's mind. It indeed suits Woman's sense of contrast between the bourgeois ethos and the fleeting nature of life. Such an intertextual interpretation, while enriching the text, does not contradict the Jungian one.

The rhetoric structure (on the level of relation between fictional world and spectator) revealed a clear didactic intent. This narrative created an overall metaphor of a misdirected bourgeois upbringing. The bourgeois atmosphere of Girl's house was saturated with both sex and total denial, i.e., was characterized as hypocritical, thus depriving Girl of orientation regarding "disturbing" facts of life (scene XI). This bourgeois atmosphere was also plagued by prejudice, as illustrated by Father's attitude to homosexuality. Such a background was probably identified by most spectators as similar to their own. The fictional world implied that the taboo on alluding to sex in front of children exacerbates their sexual curiosity and may lead to catastrophe. The rhetoric intention was thus to promote an anti-bourgeois ethos in the audience. This anti-bourgeois critique was made prominent by Parents' design in the style of silent movies, characterized by jerky bodily movements, which, although partly due to technical reasons, is ludicrous. The connotations of this style cast a grotesque dimension on them, in the first scenes in particular.

This performance-text was a combination of social satire, by citation from the style of silent movies, and a serious description of a process of individual growth, assisted by a set of allegoric characters. The duality was reflected in the transmutation from the initial grotesque style of silent film to the eventual serious style of melodrama. Ironically, during the second half of the twentieth century, this 'anti-bourgeois ethos' was adopted by the bourgeoisie. Therefore, rather than aiming at shocking the audience, this production aimed at reaffirming their critical attitude.

Principles of non-verbal description

This section explores principles that explain how a mute performance-text, such as *A Transient Shadow*, is able to describe and evoke a fictional verbal interaction, thus enabling the audience to associatively provide the missing elements.

In principle, since the same words of a speech act can be part of different actions, depending on intention, it needs additional non-verbal indicators to disambiguate it. These non-verbal indicators of action, which are the most reliable indexes of intention, are facial expression, intonation, body posture and hand gesture. In *A Transient Shadow*, being a silent performance-text, the situation was reversed: spectators were confronted with only non-verbal indexes of acts, and had to deduce possible concomitant words. Because intonation was excluded, and facial expression mainly specializes in reflecting feelings/emotions and attitudes, they had to rely mostly on body posture and gesture. The following are seven principles that enabled the audience to evoke a verbal interaction:

(A) *Inherently non-verbal acts*: There is a wide range of iconic acts that describe and indicate fictional actions, which are actually performed non-verbally; e.g., 'falling asleep' (scene IV), 'kicking a body' (scene VIII) and 'drinking soup' (scene IX). Such non-verbal acts are characterized by instrumental bodily movements, which clearly differ from gestures. In this production the vast majority of acts were non-verbal in nature. This propensity probably characterizes silent movies too. For example, Mother taking Girl away from Magician for preventing Girl from being badly influenced (playing with a penis-shaped napkin) (scene II). A bourgeois family cannot allow itself to expose their young to "obscenity". Such an exposure violates a deeply rooted bourgeois taboo: alluding to sex in front of children. Paradoxically, while Parents' purpose was her "good education", the unfortunate events were definitely the consequence of being abandoned to her immature imagination.

(B) *Symbolic non-verbal acts*: A real non-verbal act is 'symbolic' if it is performed by a gesture that indicates an action through a sign that conventionally conveys a definite meaning, like a word. Such a 'symbolic' gesture is equivalent to the embedded sentence of a speech act. The conventional nature of such a gesture makes the use of words redundant. The same applies to its iconic replica. For example, the upright index finger across the mouth is a conventional gesture that stands for 'silence' or, rather, for the speech act 'I ask/order you to be silent'; e.g., a nurse performing this gesture in a hospital. The difference between request and order depends on additional bodily signs of intensity. In its usual form the performer touches his index finger to his own mouth. In *A Transient Shadow*, Girl performed this gesture on Brother's mouth, while trying to prevent his crying. Since Brother stopped crying, her act proved successful.

(C) *Metonymic non-verbal acts*: Verbal 'metonymy' is an elliptical figure of speech that involves two terms, a present one that evokes an absent one due to their tendency to appear together. Texts employ metonymy, under the safe assumption that the missing term will be evoked, which should be conceived of as elliptically present. Since the elliptic term is an integral component of a text, its absence is noticed, triggering thereby a syntagmatic associative process of complementation. Its evocation is based on various principles of association, such as the part for the whole and the container for the contained (Quintilian: VIII, vi, 17–27). Jakobson correctly suggests that the classical distinction between metonymy and synecdoche should be abandoned, leaving only 'metonymy' for both (pp. 76–82).

Since words and (imprinted) images are equivalent representations, in confronting a non-verbal configuration the spectator is expected to evoke a sentence that is typically associated with it. The inversion of this procedure is hardly possible, due to the fundamental ambiguity of the verbal component of a speech act, which acquires different meanings when accompanied by different non-verbal indexes, thus indicating different actions. For example, in the restaurant (scene II), Mother took the menu and addressed the waiter. She pointed to an item (a hand gesture), and performed a non-verbal configuration of question. The waiter responded by performing a non-verbal configuration of explanation, and she non-verbally agreed. The actors also replicated silent lip movements to indicate that the non-verbal configuration described a speech act. From this non-verbal exchange, it can safely be inferred that she was asking about the meaning of a name or a composition of an item, the explanation was given and she agreed to order it. Although such configurations of non-verbal indicators can only evoke generic kinds of speech acts, in this case these were sufficient. Moreover, a comparison between this sequence in scene II and a parallel one in scene XIV reveals that Mother's behavior has changed from a civilized-bourgeois to an uncivilized, uncontrolled and compulsive way of ordering and eating, which reflects the severe trauma caused by her own decision to expel her daughter.

Another example, Mother sat on Brother's bed, looked at a book, and performed lip movements. From this configuration it was evident that she was reading a story for calming him down before sleep. This is a natural inference, which may apply even if such a situation is seen through a window, or from far away. In this case, the fact that the spectators did not hear the actual story is immaterial too. Many a story can fulfil such a lulling function. It is such an image that was relevant to the narrative. The fact that Brother immediately calmed down and fell asleep indicates that Mother's purpose was crowned with success.

(D) *Metaphoric non-verbal acts*: The image of a non-verbal act is a stage metaphor, if it is improper to a character. Although in stage metaphor the improper term is not a word, but an improper non-verbal image, the metaphoric mechanism of generating meaning is the same (chapter 3). For example, Girl's dancing and watching a big oblong mirror (scenes X and XII) should be conceived of as a potential stage metaphor, because as a partner of dance a mirror is an improper predicate. Moreover, looking into a mirror is a culturally well-established metaphor of pondering one's own identity or soul; i.e., of introspection. While looking at her own image, Girl alternately saw Brother and Shadow. In Jungian terms, their reflection and interchange probably conveyed the idea that both were representations in her own psyche (Franz: 158–229) and that eventually Girl's animus was projected on Brother (the imago).

(E) *Metaphoric hand gestures*: An image of a hand gesture is metaphoric if it is improper to what it is meant to describe (the referential entity) – with the connotations (verbal and referential associations) originating in the improper term. For example, when Father blamed Magician for giving a cigarette to Girl, by performing a facial expression of anger, i.e., a metonymic non-verbal act of blame, he also performed a palm down gesture, showing literally that Girl is short. His intention was, however, to allude to her being young. Since size is an improper description of age – a person can be short and old – this is a potential stage metaphor. The use of indicators of blame together with a metaphoric description of young age creates a composite non-verbal act of blame because of young age.

(F) *Allegoric characters*: A character is allegoric if it is a stage personification of an abstract idea, principle or archetype, and enacted by a flesh and blood actor (chapter 3). Such a character is, therefore, a stage metaphor, whose associations originate in the human sphere. Since allegoric characters too perform verbal or non-verbal acts, their behavior on stage is humanlike and the previous categories apply to them as well. For example: Since Shadow is a personification of Girl's 'animus', in the Jungian sense, its basic metaphoric characterization was 'human' and 'male'; while its appearances – 'black' and 'intellectual youngster' – were additional stage metaphors. The unexpected change from intellectual male to female stripper indicated that Shadow, which reflected the projection of suppressed contents of a psyche, took different forms for Girl's animus and Magician's anima. Woman's discovery that he was a fraud and a thief reflected her eventual recognition of the deceitful nature of her own archetype. The fact that eventually Woman lets herself to be kissed by him indicated reconciliation with her suppressed sexual drives. Similarly, since Magician is an alternative personification of Girl's animus, its basic characterization was 'human' and 'male'; while 'magician' and 'romantic' were additional stage metaphors. In this case too, whereas from Girl's perspective he was a source of wonder, from Woman's mature viewpoint he was a poor illusionist. The fact that eventually Woman lets herself to be caressed by him indicated her reconciliation with the deceiving wonder of adult life.

(G) *Projected titles*: The titles that were projected on the walls flanking the back set, at the beginning of most scenes, would appear to have followed the model of silent movies. However, none of these projections featured a verbal speech, unlike most projections in them. In some cases they framed the circumstances of the retrospective scenes, e.g., 'woman returns' (scene I); 'first memory' (scene II); 'a night in the Children's room' (scene IV); and 'family dinner' (scene IX). In a few cases, they framed the meanings of the scenes, e.g., 'lovers' (scene III); and 'deep sadness' (scene XIV). In others, they pointed at stage metaphors, including

205

allegoric characters, e.g., 'mirror' (Scene X); 'Shadow returns' (as a stripper – scene VIII); and 'at Magician's home' (scene XIII).

The leading question of this chapter was: is it possible to describe a speaking fictional world through a silent performance-text? The above set of principles demonstrates that this is possible. The secondary question was: what happens to the description of a fictional world if the verbal elements, not in the performative but the descriptive capacity, are precluded? In typical performance-texts most imprinted images of speech are employed predominantly for the description of fictional interaction. However, the descriptive function is not altogether absent, but fulfilled by the sentences embedded in speech acts and descriptions by functional characters or interactive characters in functional situations, for the sake of dramatic irony (chapter 4). This function can hardly be fulfilled by a silent performance-text. It would seem to lead to the conclusion that such a text was definitely impoverished, as in typical simplistic melodrama. However, in the case of *A Transient Shadow* such a conclusion does not apply, because the suggested principles, the allegoric characters in particular, lent a dimension of interpretation from an ironic viewpoint that should not be underestimated. In other words, despite being silent, this was a very complex production, which conveyed a clear critical message that was fully understood and warmly welcomed by the audience. After all, the typical *gestus* of modern bourgeoisie is the apparent criticism of bourgeois values.

14

Suz/o/Suz *by La Fura dels Baus: Theatre at the Borderline*

Demarcation of boundaries between theatre and non-theatre, performance art in particular, is not only a theoretical concern. In recent years, the perception of this art has been vitiated by an over-expanded notion of 'theatre'. This chapter aims at suggesting and illustrating a boundary between theatre and performance art; the latter usually characterized as 'non-mimetic' or 'non-representational' theatre. A distinction is imperative, because texts generated by different systems of signification and communication require different reading competences.

The following discussion is conducted against the background of Schechner's notion of 'performance', which probably reflects more an ideology than a systematic theory of theatre (p. 68ff). He employs 'performance' in a sense that definitely differs from its usual sense in the context of theatre, and blurs the boundaries not only between it and performance art, but also between it and other performative arts, such as music, ballet and declamation. It also blurs the boundaries between theatre and non-artistic performative activities, such as a soccer game, a circus performance and a Bar Mitzvah ceremony (Rozik, 2002: 165–84). However, it is difficult to conceive of such events as germane to a theatre performance, despite being capable of producing memorable experiences, dexterously designed to arouse admiration or fear, and even to produce catharsis. Although theatre is obviously a performative art, this does not entail any additional property in common with other performative endeavors. In contrast, Schechner's notion of 'actual' can be employed to clarify the distinction between theatre and non-theatre.

Performance art is not only possible, but in recent years has become an acknowledged fact. Although culture is not always inclined to grant artistic

207

status to all performative activities, some of them reveal dimensions usually attributed to certain arts, such as employing a medium, conveying a message, constituting an overall metaphor and producing aesthetic and rhetoric effects. While the intuition is that performance art fundamentally differs from theatre, the question arises as to how to theoretically distinguish between them? This distinction is possible due to theatre's unique descriptive nature, characterized by the principle of 'acting'. *Whereas performance art usually attempts to create real events, enacting them is the fundamental principle of the theatre medium* (chapter 5).

This chapter aims, therefore, at showing that (a) *theatre shares performativity with other cultural activities, but it is not only an 'actual', it is also a description*; and (b) *an actual art, based on the performance of non-representational activities by live performers in front of live spectators, without being theatre, is possible*. These theses are illustrated through an analysis of *Suz/o/Suz*, by the Barcelona based company La Fura dels Baus.

The notion of 'performance'

Schechner suggests the term 'performance' in a new sense for a set of highly diversified events, such as sport, play, game, theatre, dance, music (sacred or secular) ritual and social intercourse (pp. 6 & 252–3). Since this set includes an amazing array of 'human activities', what is contrasted to 'performance' should also be determined. Indeed, he explicitly excludes 'productive work' (*ibid.*: 9), implying that work is not a performance, particularly if not watched by others.

The crux of Schechner's notion of 'performance' is the relation between performer and onlooker/spectator. He defines 'performance' as 'an activity done by an individual or group in the presence of and for another individual or group' (*ibid.*: 30). He is aware that such a definition not only expands, but also narrows down the entire set, excluding some forms of play, games, sports and ritual. Yet he still insists on its centrality: 'Even where audiences do not exist as such – some happenings, rituals, and play – the function of the audience persists' (*ibid.*). From this basic relationship of live performer/spectator Schechner derives his model of 'performance' as a social activity at a given time and place, and patterned as a sequence of 'gathering/performing/dispersing' (*ibid.*: 168).

Schechner's definition of 'performance' should be distinguished from two well established senses widely employed in the study of art and theatre: (a) the execution of a work of art, which otherwise only enjoys potential existence in the form of script or score; and (b) a doing through a verbal ('performative' verbs) or non-verbal act, in the context of pragmatics and action theory. In theatre studies, sense (a) is usually applied to 'enacting' a play-script on stage (chapter 5), and sense (b) to acts/actions on both the descriptive or fictional levels (chapter 2). In this sense I have employed the latter also for the level of interaction between performance-text and spectator (chapter 9). All these senses are relevant to the field of this study and should be kept as distinct categories of thought, i.e., as homonyms.

Schechner's definition certainly seizes a set of social circumstances, shared by all the particular forms under 'performance'. However, although it may be useful for sociological purposes, close scrutiny reveals that this notion focuses on aspects that can tell us very little about the nature of the activities embedded in such social circumstances. Furthermore, such a definition is both too broad – it also applies to instrumental activities such as witnessing an auction or a trial – and too narrow – it excludes artistic activities such as cinema and puppet theatre, due to its insistence on 'live performers', despite their strong affinity to theatre.

Schechner postulates two abstract properties, 'entertainment' and 'efficacy', whose combination in various proportions allegedly generate the different kinds of performance (*ibid.*: 120–4; cf. Rozik, 2002a: 172ff). However, although these properties may remove some difficulties in the intricate ritual-theatre relationship, it hardly contributes any insight into the unique nature of other embedded activities, such as children's play, games and sports, not to speak of theatre and ritual themselves.

In his theatre practice with the Performance Group, Schechner aimed at emphasizing the 'performers-to-spectator interaction (as opposed to character-to-spectator interaction)' (p. 82). He attempted to do so by various means, before, during and after the performance of a play, such as interrupting acting, moving throughout the premises, repeating scenes and the like, as well as predetermining aspects of gathering and dispersing. His explicit aim was to create 'tension' between performative and fictional components of the performance: 'I try to establish non-story-telling time as an integral part of the whole performance scheme, while clearly separating this time from the drama' (*ibid.*: 173). This was done for promoting a 'critical attitude' to the play (*ibid.*: 83), probably in Brecht's spirit (*ibid.*: 118).

There is no theoretical problem in seeing that a 'theatre performance', in the sense of enacting a fictional world (sense 'a'), is embedded in a sequence of 'performance', in the sense of a comprehensive social event, and in increasing tension between them, which exists in any case. Indeed, the social aspects of performance are shared by theatre and some kinds of non-theatre. The problem resides in viewing Schechner's 'performance' as having any explanatory power within the domain of theatre itself.

The notion of 'actual'

In Schechner's view, 'performance' implies 'being an actual'. He suggests five properties that define 'actuality': '(1) *process*, something happens *here* and *now*; (2) *consequential, irremediable*, and *irrevocable* acts, exchanges or situations; (3) *contest*, something is *at stake* for the performers and often for the spectators; (4) *initiation*, a *change in status* for participants; (5) space is used *concretely* and *organically*' (p. 51). All these properties should be seen as reflections of being in the sphere not of description, but of real action in 'the world'. The term 'actual' thus conveys its usual meaning.

Schechner makes a clear distinction between the 'Aristotelian' approach to art and his own: '[a]n Aristotelian artwork lives a double life. It is mimetic in the Platonic sense, but it is also itself. [. . .] Art always "comes after" experience; the separation between art and life is built into the idea of mimesis. It is this coming after and separation that has been so decisive in the development of western theater' (*ibid.*: 38). In other words, for Schechner what he calls 'Aristotelian' art is both an actual and a representation; i.e., is characterized by a fundamental duality. He also claims that there is also another kind of art which is 'non-mimetic' or, rather, exclusively an 'actual': '[i]n non-mimetic art the boundaries between "life" and "art" – raw and cooked – are blurry and permeable' (*ibid.*). The alleged implication is that 'actuality' and not mimesis is the quintessence of performing art. In principle, I suggest that this distinction is sound, but the gap between these arts is so deep that it cannot be bridged by the notion of 'performance' in Schechner's sense. For reasons suggested above, 'description' should be preferred to 'representation' (Introduction), and that *mimesis* in the sense of imitation of life should not be seen as a common denominator of iconic arts, which may use iconicity to describe worlds partly or utterly different from the real one; e.g., science fiction (chapter 1).

Schechner illustrates his thesis by Alan Kaprow's *Fluids* (1967). Kaprow describes his own work as follows:

> a single event done in many places over a three-day period. It consists simply in building huge, blank, rectangular ice structures 30 feet long, 10 feet wide, and 8 feet high. The structures are built by people who decide to meet a truck carrying 650 ice blocks per structure. They set this thing up using rock salt as a binder – which hastens melting and fuses the block together. The structures are to be built (and were) in about 20 places throughout Los Angeles. If you were crossing the city you might suddenly be confronted by these mute and meaningless blank structures which have been left to melt. Obviously, what's taken place is a mystery of sorts. (Kaprow, 1968; quoted by Schechner, *ibid.*: 36)

Such an event can indeed count as an example of pure performance, in the sense of 'actual', because it is a sequence of actions performed by real people, while watched by other real people here and now, with neither use of a certain established medium, nor descriptive intent.

Schechner, however, ignores that in this context his category of 'actual' bears two senses and is applied on two different levels: (a) the performance of a series of real acts with no intention of description; and (b) the performance of acts/actions by living performers for watching spectators. Kaprow's ice structure is an actual on both accounts. The question is whether or not theatre can also be an actual on both these accounts? If a theatre performance is defined in terms of description generated by the theatre medium, the answer is negative by definition: *if there is no description, there is no theatre* and, therefore, a theatre performance can be an actual only in the second sense (b). The moment there is reference to a fictional world, as in the performance of Brecht's *Mother Courage* by the Performance Group, there is acting and description. In such a case, the only possibility, as suggested by Schechner himself, is to create tension between 'actuality' and the described world: 'even in aesthetic theater something approaching actuality has been sought for by making the performer the "author" of his/her own actions or "visible" side by side with the character in a Brechtian way' (*ibid.*: 118). In a theatre performance, however, 'actuality' in sense (a) cannot be put in tension, because it does not apply to it by definition.

'Actuality' through doing things with no intention of description was probably what Michael Kirby had in mind when coining the term 'nonsemiotic performance' (Carlson, 1990: 3–9). However, as Carlson perceives, Kirby is not aware of the iconic elements in his own *Double Gothic*. Carlson correctly contends that in the description of his own production Kirby refers to images, such as blindness and thunder, that can only be understood on 'representational' (descriptive) grounds (1990: 3ff). Moreover, Carlson demonstrates that Kirby also confuses between 'conveying a message', in the regular thematic sense, and semiosis.

Schechner also suggests the notion of 'transformational' acting, which is the projection of actuality onto the level of acting. Transformational acting incarnates 'in a theater place what cannot take place anywhere else. [. . .] a theater is a place where transformations of time, place, and persons (human and non-human) are accomplished' (p. 166). He believes in a kind of performer who does not play [enact] a character but plays himself; e.g., '[s]tand-up comics play aspects of themselves. Disclosure is the heart of the comic's art' (*ibid.*: 50). Stand-up comedy, however, is not necessarily theatre: it is a kind of verbal art that exhibits and enhances the verbal dexterity and sharp perspective of the artist himself; i.e., it is basically only an actual. Although it may display verbal or iconic descriptions of real people, as objects of satire for example, this is typical of oral storytelling too. The latter may be conceived of as a precursor of theatre, but is a non-theatrical verbal art (Rozik, 2002a: 151ff). Furthermore, Schechner's belief is paradoxical in the sense that in such cases no transformation necessarily takes place, while the performance still is a self-referential actual.

Like Ernest T. Kirby, Schechner views the shaman as a prototype of 'transformational' acting: 'Understanding actualizing means understanding both the creative condition and the artwork, the actual. Among primitive peoples the creative condition is identical with trances, dances, ecstasies; in short, shamanism' (p. 41). The shaman is indeed transformed: he enters such a state for confronting real spirits and performing a cure, which is meant to be 'effective' in *actual* terms. The question is, however, whether or not the basic duality (performing and describing) that characterizes acting can be found in trance or ecstasy? Since in performing a ritual the shaman and his patient are part of the real world, the answer is negative. Although he does produce images that characterize his "art", like in performing real acts, these are self-referential. Even if his skills are attributed to spirits, the effects remain self-referential to them (chapter 5). The entire act is therefore an actual and, therefore, only self-referential (Rozik, 2002a: 69–89).

Like Kirby, Schechner views '[a]thletes, like circus performers, display their skills. The rules of games are designed to show prowess, quick judgment, finesse and grace, speed, endurance, strength and teamwork' (*ibid.*: 50; cf. Kirby, 1974: 5–15). None of these artists, however, enact a character and deflect reference. Conversely, as suggested above, the exhibition of skills is purportedly meant to project an improved image of the performers themselves; i.e., to be a self-referential actual. In other words, they do not describe anything and there is nothing in their displays beyond what is done and achieved (chapter 5). Furthermore, circus performers take pride in not being actors, and insist that their doings are real acts (Carmeli); i.e., their acts are not transformational. In contrast, actors can enact circus performers.

The notion of 'transformational acting' may apply, if at all, to a few restricted theatre styles; perhaps to Stanislavsky's method and its followers. Such a theatre style may be possible, but is definitely not a necessary condition. Moreover, if the notion of 'transformation' implies that in any sense the actor 'becomes' the character he portrays, it is fallacious. Therefore, 'transformation' does not impinge on the intrinsic duality of acting. As mentioned above, Schechner accepts the possibility of such a duality in art. The question is, again, whether or not the notion of 'performance' can bridge between pure actual art and theatre. *Theatre shares performativity with other cultural activities, but it is not only an 'actual', it is also a description.*

Performing an action vs. enacting an action

In contrast to Schechner's notions, a fundamental distinction should be made between 'performing an action' and 'enacting an action' (chapter 5). While 'performing an action' reflects the intention of changing a state of affairs in the real world (sense b), 'enacting an action' reflects the intention of describing and evoking such an action in a fictional world (sense a), which by virtue of deflection of reference should be understood as an action performed by a character (sense b).

'Enacting an action' is characterized by a fundamental triadic nature: the 'actual' performance of descriptive acts within the real time and space of actors and spectators, the 'textual' nature of the description imprinted on the actors' bodies, and the 'fictional' nature of the described acts, whose supposed existence does not pertain the actors' and spectators' real time and space. These are three aspects of the very same behavior. Since in theatre the principle of similarity also applies to the imprinting matter, in some cases it may be difficult to distinguish between 'performing an action' and 'enacting an action', particularly in street and even naturalistic theatre. However, the distinction is a prerequisite of appropriately reading, interpreting and experiencing theatre.

Whereas Schechner's notion of 'actuality' can explain some aspects of theatre art, there is little advantage in the all-inclusive notion of 'performance'. A pure actual performance may generate meaning, although assumedly in a different way. Investing a great deal of effort in a purposeless and eventually melting away construction, such as *Fluids*, may create a meaningful and adequate metaphor of life for performers and onlookers alike. Being a metaphor of life is not, however, a distinct feature of art. Even real events, which are not works of art, may be experienced as metaphors; e.g., a tempest or a soccer match. Constructing such a pile of ice cubes is an 'actual' because it is a sequence of acts performed by people for other people to watch, in obvious social interaction, and aimed at producing a meaningful experience, but devoid of descriptive intent. On such grounds, depending on definitions, it should be conceived of as a work of performance-art. *Theatre and performance-art (in this sense), however, have little in common.* Since art is not necessarily defined by the use of a descriptive medium, the theoretical possibility of pure actual art should be considered.

Suz/o/Suz by La Fura dels Baus

I contend that the performance of *Suz/o/Suz* is not a piece of theatre, but of performance art, an actual in Schechner's sense. The following analysis relates to the performance at the Belilius Hangar, a huge and empty indus-trial space, in Jerusalem, on 23 May 1993 (Rozik, 1996c). The nature of this acting space was not supposed to affect the nature of the performance: in Madrid, for example it was performed in a funeral parlor.

(1) While the spectators gather, a few musicians on stage, dressed in loin-cloths, water pouring on their heads, are playing drums, electronic guitars and barrels full of water, and performing vigorous and ecstatic music that induces a sense of mystery and even anxiety. Scattered on the vast floor are several constructions that look like primitive machines, with no observable function, produce deafening noise that adds to the sense of alarm. Smoke is in the air.

The audience at *Suz/o/Suz*. Courtesy of La Fura dels Baus. Photo: Gol.

(2) Suddenly, performers dressed in black and white slowly descend on ropes from the ceiling, while undressing. When on the floor, only loincloths covering their nudity, they annoy the spectators by thrusting tires and mine-like objects or brandishing battery-operated electric saws at them in a threatening manner. One performer pushes a supermarket trolley, carrying a crouching bald performer into the surrounding spectators who retreat in terror. Wherever they go, another 'danger' appears, with the intention being to frighten them, while music and light magnify this effect. Some spectators leave the hangar. Eventually, the performers leave the performing space.

214

Weird contraption in *Suz/o/Suz*. Courtesy of La Fura dels Baus. Photo: Gol.

(3) The lights dim. The musicians then play extremely noisy music to gibberish 'words'. The spectators gather around them in an attempt to calm down. Suddenly, all the lights go off producing real panic. When the lights are lit again, primitive wagons loaded with raw organs of animals and buckets of (fake) blood are wildly driven into the space. The performers bite the raw flesh, spit the scraps and throw the blood-like liquid at the spectators, who, frightened and deeply disgusted, flee in every direction. Some people in the audience cry and some cover their eyes. One lady vomits. Eventually, wagons and performers leave the space.

(4) A transition to a more comfortable atmosphere that is marked by calm music. Suddenly, performers enter brandishing geometrical frames in flames. Then two wagons enter, each of them carrying a huge cubic aquarium full of water and a naked performer immersed in it, in a sitting position, and breathing through a pipe. The wagons stop at opposite corners of the hangar, and the spectators crowd around them. Two more performers, each one on a small wagon, with a torch in his hand, is driven to an aquarium. Each one climbs it and, while seated on its brim, starts pestering the immersed performer with a stick. Each thrust is marked by a change of the water's color. Then each 'victim' goes into a 'fetal' posture and the 'intruder' immerses himself in the aquarium and rubs

215

raw vegetables on the victim's mouth. Eventually, the latter floats motionless face down. The wagons are taken away.

Pestering an immersed performer in *Suz/o/Suz*.
Courtesy of La Fura dels Baus. Photo: Gol.

(5) A musical interval. Performers enter the main space on wildly driven wagons. Also a tub full of water carrying a happy performer is driven in. They fling flour-like powder at the audience who, again, retreat hysterically from both the wagons and the powder. The performers pour buckets of water on each other. More performers join the 'water/powder battle'. The spectators are caught in between and get a fair share of the mixture. Some spectators actually struggle with performers trying to avoid it. Eventually, the 'battle' comes to an end and the performers leave the space.

(6) Music. Two platforms are pushed in. On each one, two performers engage in hanging a third one from a metal construction. One is hung in a horizontal position and the other in a vertical one. On both platforms, the hanging performers start annoying the hung ones: they swing them, smear their bodies with paint, crush raw vegetables or water melons on them, and thrust fire, water and white powder at them, while the entire scene is shrouded in heavy smoke and whirling straw. The 'victims' are hung by their feet, and intensely embraced and kissed. The hung performers are brought down and laid motionless on the platform. All the performers now look extremely dirty, covered with a mixture of paint, smoke, water, straw and crushed vegetables. The music dwindles and the lights dim. Spectators wonder whether or not the performance is over. After a while there is an ovation.

The entire performance reflects a clear intention to avoid a description of a (fictional) world, in the sense of 'enacting' characters and actions. Although the performers imprinted images on their own bodies, these images evidently did not deflect reference, but were self-referential (chapter 5). Some actions were probably read and interpreted by the audience in terms of 'similarity', e.g., the machines, the 'fetal' postures in the 'aquarium' and the pseudo 'crucifixions' and 'death'. More than a requirement of the text, however, such interpretations would have reflected the bewilderment of the spectators who desperately sought for any clue that could have enabled them to make sense of the experience. The performance itself possibly rejected such readings. For example, the machine-like constructions defied recognition as specific machines, being monstrous composites of various machines, greatly damaged, rusty and evidently devoid of definite function; the immersed performer in the aquarium was seated under water and breathing through a pipe in a cubic, not even round, womb-like aquarium; and the hanging did not allude to a crucifixion, because it was not performed on a cross or a pole, with nails, but on a scaffolding structure, with ropes. In principle, only images imprinted on matter similar to their models and deflecting reference to a world constitute a theatre description.

Some doings could have been recognized and categorized on a more elementary level: e.g., 'dragging tires', 'biting raw flesh', 'spitting scraps at the audience', or 'smashing water melons'. However, there is a fundamental difference between categorization of doings on such a level and the description of a world by imprinted images of doings.

Critics too looked for any possible clue for the purpose of interpretation; e.g., it was suggested that these are the children of a 'post-urban civilization' in search of their ritual sources, possibly undergoing a rite of initiation (Perez Cortillo); or that 'the embodiment of the dark instincts that overpower a cultural man and dictate his rebellion against the tyranny and futility of objects' (Benach; my trans.). However, although such interpretations reflect genuine attempts to construe this event as a kind of theatre text, there is nothing in the performance to support an image of a 'post-urban civilization' or a 'rebellion against tyranny'. Some objects could have been read as metonyms of modern life ('tire', 'supermarket trolley' and 'electric saw') and contrasted to metonyms of primitive life (wearing loincloths and eating raw flesh), with the text possibly being interpreted as conveying the banal 'message' that 'post urban' people will behave like animals and culture will eventually return to primitive brutality. However, such a reading too does not lead to a coherent interpretation; even the biting of raw flesh and spitting it at the audience cannot be perceived as images of primitivism on any known grounds.

Whatever the interpretation, the crucial test is whether or not this performance reflects the intention to 'create' or, rather, describe fictional characters, actions and situations. In *Suz/o/Suz* no character can be identified, not even at a minimal level of characterization. In the program's words, 'La Fura dels Baus is not trying to tell anything specific. The only thing needed to germinate history and legend is to posit a human being.' Even if it is assumed that acting refers here to humanity on the abstract level of 'everyman', there is little to support such a contention too.

The only principle that lends inner logic to the entire sequence is that the performers are engaged in performing a set of real acts or, rather, actuals whose main purpose is to induce negative feelings in the audience, particularly fear and disgust. The following sequences are given in the order they occur in the performance. Three sequences are meant not to be watched by the audience, but to directly affect them: (i) dragging objects into them; (ii) spitting raw flesh and pouring blood-like liquid on them; and (iv) flinging water and white powder at them. The two other sequences – the aquarium (iii) and the hanging (v) – although interaction takes place among the performers themselves, indirectly it aims at the same effect. The performers cancel thereby the existential boundary between a description of a world and the world of the audience. The company sees itself in terms of 'theatre of friction', a term that betrays direct action on spectators (Benach). Consequently, while contending that *Suz/o/Suz* is theatre is contrary to reason, assuming that it is a sequence of actual actions that avoid description is not.

La Fura dels Baus not only avoids acting but also the use of language. At most, they engage in gibberish. Even the name of the production has no meaning: '[the name] *Suz/o/Suz* is meaningless. We simply liked the word' (Gimenez; my trans.). In their attitude to language the influence of typical but erroneous interpretations of Artaud's writings is very clear. In their own words: 'We wished to understand culture in a more open manner, and not only restricted by language' (Perez Cortillo; my trans.).

The fact that *Suz/o/Suz* is highly powerful and effective in producing fear and disgust is not indicative of theatricality, because in order to produce such feelings there is no need for a theatre text. Fear and disgust can be achieved by real actions too. The fact that this production induces emotions of fear and, therefore, may even be conducive to a cathartic experience, does not support that it is theatre, because various real events may trigger the cathartic mechanism; e.g., a soccer match or a rescue from a mine explosion. The fact that this sequence is scripted and carefully rehearsed does not support its theatricality because many real events are so devised, as Goffman clearly demonstrates in *The Presentation of Self in Everyday Life* (1955). The fact that this sequence is performed in a 'specialized' space does not support its theatre nature because various types of real actions are performed in such spaces, such as a courtroom.

Suz/o/Suz shares with theatre the actuality of the social circumstances of performance and the actuality of live performers performing in front of a live audience. It differs from theatre, however, in avoiding the enactment of an action; i.e., its description. If indeed there is no acting involved in *Suz/o/Suz*, any attempt to read it as a theatre performance-text is preposterous. Moreover, even it only features mere doings, the audience is entitled to ask for their underlying intentions and purposes, as for regular real actions; i.e., 'actual' art should be matched by 'actual' reception.

The behavior of the performers of *Suz/o/Suz* may be considered 'transformational' in the sense that it involves the performers' bodies and the spectators' psyches in extreme experiences. However, this too indicates that their performance was not meant to enact characters, but to be self-referential. Some critics argued that the performance conveyed a sense of ritual: the actors were dressed as aborigines and employed vehicles, machines and materials (water, blood, fire) which could be reminiscent of primeval forms of worship. In the program's words: 'Earth, fire, air, music set the place for the specific actions of the performers, who do no so much *act* as *invoke, perform ceremonies, accomplish acts*' (my trans.). Indeed, ritual is self-referential, and therefore it is not theatre (Rozik, 2002a: 3–28). However, no real element of ritual could be detected and, at most, *Suz/o/Suz* resembled one of these artificial attempts to recreate ritual properties in modern theatre. In this context, Schechner's remark is very relevant: 'When artists, or their audiences, recognize that these staged "rituals" are mostly symbolic activities masquerading as effective acts, a feeling of helplessness overcomes them. So-called "real events" are revealed as metaphors' (p. 118). Kaprow's '*Fluids*' too was probably experienced as a metaphor.

In the spirit of Ernest Kirby, the company claims a peculiar ancestry: 'We come from the streets, like the jongleurs of the middle ages, or the 'happening' of the seventies, or the revival of popular traditions in the sixties' (Perez Cortillo; my trans.). However, these predecessors too engaged not in theatre, but in actual actions, and were thus self-referential. La Fura dels Baus attracts its audiences because of its ingenuity and display of tremendous energy, which undoubtedly indicates its fundamental intention, as in true performance art, to focus on the performers' doings and not on what they may enact.

In distinguishing between theatre and 'performance art' the main difficulty resides in theatre's inscription of images of human beings on human bodies. Nonetheless, this distinction is essential. For instance, the same act of biting raw meat and spitting its scraps can be construed differently, depending on whether it is framed in the context of performance art or theatre acting. In the first case, it will be understood as the performance of the act in itself, and in the second, as an enactment of a fictional act. The specific difference is thus the descriptive nature of a theatre performance-text. Two criteria of distinction can be suggested: (a) considering the frame or, rather, domain markers; e.g., whether it is performed in a theatre building or found place functioning as such a space or not, which in the case of this production is insufficient; (b) considering the advantage of each interpretation: e.g., whether spitting raw meat on an audience serves a descriptive purpose or not, which in this case is decisive. In addition, it is quite evident that a performance such as *Suz/o/Suz* aims at a very low common denominator of any possible gathering: at responses of instinctual fear and disgust, without requiring or expecting any theatre competence from the spectator. Therefore, the hypothesis that *Suz/o/Suz* is not theatre, but an instance of 'actual art', is to be preferred.

Consequently, in principle, *an art based on actual performance and non-mediated interaction with spectators is possible.* This requires a thorough reexamination of the notion of 'art', which exceeds the scope of the present study. My intuition is, however, that there is no reason why additional arts cannot be based on such a principle. No definition of art actually requires either the use of a language/medium or acting. In light of the above considerations, reexamination of some well established arts, such as music, abstract ballet and abstract art, for which the use of terms such as 'code' and 'medium' can only be metaphoric, may prove fruitful. For example, the ecstatic music of *Suz/o/Suz* too is a clear instance of actuality.

To conclude, the all-inclusive notion of 'performance', in Schechner's sense, tells very little about each encompassed art, and cannot bridge the gap between theatre and performance art.

15

Habimah's The Trojan Women: *A Ready-made Metaphor of Unjustified War*

The Israeli theatre reveals a clear tendency to prefer fictional worlds that bear on the present rifts and antagonisms in the fabric of Israeli society and the political situation, the Israeli–Palestinian conflict in particular. This proclivity is reflected in productions not only of original, but also of ingeniously actualized classical play-scripts.

This chapter explores this type of actualization through an analysis of the Habimah (Israel's National Theatre) production of Sartre's *Les Troyennes* (1983), an adaptation of Euripides' *The Trojan Women*. I suggest that *the universality of this play depends on its renewed actualization, which presupposes a constant creative re-interpretation of its narrative*. I also propose several principles that may explain how *the tragic fate of the Trojan women, once a metaphor of the actual political situation in fifth-century Greece, was transmuted into an apt metaphor of the absurdity of war in general, and for the Israeli wars in particular*. Like Euripides' original play-script and Sartre's adaptation, the Habimah production conveyed a severe critique of warlike policy.

The following analysis is carried out as an accumulative intertextual interaction and creative interpretation among four texts: the Homeric sources, Euripides' first dramatization in *The Trojan Women*, Sartre's adaptation in *Les Troyennes*, and the Hebrew production of Sartre's adaptation. The focus is on the non-verbal elements of the Habimah production that transmuted a pre-existing wording into a metaphor of political actuality.

Euripides' *The Trojan Women* and its Homeric sources

Homer's *The Iliad* (c. ninth century BC) narrates the Trojan War, which took place c. 1184 BC, but does not include a description of the fall of the city that put an end to the ten-year siege. This episode is provided in Virgil's *The Aeneid*, Book II (70–19 BC), whose detailed account includes the legendary wooden horse episode, missing in *The Iliad* (cf. Camps), although existing in other Homeric sources. However, no known source that could have been available to Euripides relates the tragic fate of the royal women. Euripides may well have been inspired by other Homeric sources, but probably invented the entire action of the play by filling in several gaps in the saga, in the spirit of creative interpretation. The desperate predicament of these women was indeed a plausible development in a world ruled by the Greek laws of war, sanctioning that all defeated warriors should be killed and all the women taken in slavery.

Euripides staged *The Trojan Women* in 415 BC, in the historic context of the Peloponnesian Wars. He plausibly had in mind the cruel punishment of the neutral Island State of Melos, a previous year, for not joining the Athenian confederacy, and the preparations for the unprovoked expedition to conquer Sicily. He found in the ancient legend of Troy an obvious metaphor of the atrocities perpetrated by the Athenian forces in Melos: all the male citizens were slaughtered and all the women and children enslaved (Thucydides: V, 106).

Euripides probably presupposed that his contemporary audience, inclined to see in this Homeric narrative a token of the heroic past of the nation, would strongly react to his description from the viewpoint of the defeated enemy, the women in particular. He may have assumed that the fate of those unfortunate women would induce a sense of identification and compassion that could outweigh the hatred of the enemy, and instigate animosity toward the prospective unjustified war in Sicily.

While highlighting the women's sublime sufferings, he also revealed the vile and *barbarian* demeanor of the Greek conquerors. Within the context of Euripides' other plays, it is evident that the heroic aura emanating from the Homeric tradition was a suitable target for his criticism. Moreover, he combined this attitude with severe criticism of contemporaneous notions of divinity, rooted in the Homeric ethos. Although there was no hint to actuality, he probably believed that the spectators would intuitively understand the fictional world as a metaphor of the actual political situation. His manner of presenting the Greek heroes and gods indicates the intention to shock the naïve sectors of the audience. His subsequent prosecution by the Athenian authorities corroborates the success of his endeavor.

Euripides' mechanism of criticism is most conspicuous in regard to the gods, who are presented not only in their conventional anthropomorphic guise, but also in their all too "human" weaknesses. In the typical structure of his plays, (e.g., *Bacchae* and *Hippolytus*), the human characters show a kind of dignity and ethical standard, which the gods fail to emulate (cf. Vellacott: 163 and Thucydides: V, 104–5). Hecuba, the focal victim of Athena's wantonness, is more majestic and sublime than the goddess herself. Euripides insinuates that, if victory depends on the whimsical nature of the gods, the fate of the victors could just as easily be that of the defeated. He implies that the inhabitants of Melos had put their trust in their gods, just as the Trojans had done in theirs, and that the gods had let them down (Vellacott: *ibid.*). The Athenians, therefore, could have been subjected to a similar reversal. The gods are also shown in their cruel and capricious nature by stressing the disproportion between the gravity of human offences and the magnitude of divine punishment, which presupposes a more sophisticated notion of divinity, which is usually attributed to the playwright. The main object of his criticism was not divinity itself, but people's absurd notions of divinity.

Euripides' mechanism of self-criticism confronts his audience with their suppressed intuitions and anxieties, particularly based on experiences contradicting their notions of divinity and heroism, which life provides in abundance. The typical attitude of a society at war is characterized by attempts to de-humanize its enemies, which range from depicting their alleged monstrosity to merely ignoring their shared humanity. Whereas the suffering of any victims of war, particularly women and children, is likely to spontaneously elicit pity and fear, Euripides' attempt to promote human involvement in their fates was assumedly meant to re-humanize them. This attitude reflects the intention to create a conflict between spurious national identification and genuine human compassion in the spectators' minds.

By the same token, Euripides de-humanized the Greek heroes by stressing their anti-heroic nature; for example:

Talthybius: You shall be slave to Odysseus, lord of Ithaca.
Hecuba: Oh no, no!
   [. . .] To be given as slave to serve the vile, that slippery man,
   right's enemy, brute, murderous beast,
   that mouth of lies and treachery, that makes void
   faith and things promised
   and that which was beloved turns to hate. (277–86)

Despite his ill-famed and cunning character (cf. Sophocles' *Philoctetes*) and the troubles awaiting him on his way home, the implied audience knows that Odysseus will survive and live with faithful Penelope happily ever after. The anti-heroic nature of the Greek is conspicuous not only in their victimization of defenseless women, but also in their murder of an innocent child:

Hecuba: [. . .] What shall the poet say,
what words will he inscribe upon your monument?
Here lies a little child the Argives killed, because
they were afraid of him. That? The epitaph of Greek shame. (1188–91)

The killing of Astyanax is actually justified by Hecuba's own hope that he 'might grow to manhood and bring back [. . .] something of our city's strength' (701–3). However, by describing it as a token of Athenian fear, Hecuba's irony undermines the alleged masculine heroism of the Greeks. Their gratuitous cruelty towards women and children justifies Andromache's oximoron: 'Greeks! Your Greek cleverness is simple barbarity' (764). Whereas contemporaneous Athenians used to rank the Trojans as 'barbarians' and themselves as a cultured nation, *The Trojan Women* reflects Euripides's intention to reverse this pejorative categorization. The 'barbarian' metaphor is most aptly predicated on the Greeks due to the sheer disproportion between the trivial reasons for the War of Troy and the wholesale slaughter of all male adults and the enslaving of all women and children (367–69). Menelaus' hesitant attitude toward Helen indicates that he still is under her spell, which is an additional instance of the Greeks' anti-heroic nature, and forecasts her return to royal power. Even Agamemnon's sacrifice of his daughter Iphigenia, for the purpose of the "great cause", and Athena's spurious sense of justice, were probably perceived in this absurd light.

Euripides certainly did not condemn war altogether, clearly distinguishing between defensive war and what in present days would have been called a 'colonial' war:

Cassandra: Though surely the wise man will forever shrink from war,
yet if war come, the hero's death will lay a wreath
not lustreless on the city. The coward alone brings shame. (400–2)

War is evil; but, if imposed on Athens, glory should be bestowed upon its defenders.

Through the Trojan metaphor – in its anti-heroic sense – Euripides aimed at denouncing the warmongering policy of the Athenian authorities. By alluding to the capricious nature of war – for even the gods cannot guarantee success – and by showing the suffering of the defeated, Euripides probably hoped to expose the planned conquest of Sicily as a risky enterprise. He possibly expected to reverse the trend of support for this policy and thus the course of contemporary events.

Hecuba and Astyanax in Freytag's *The Trojan Women*. Courtesy of the
Habimah National Theatre. Photo: Amon Schneider.

Although Euripides could have shown suffering Greek mothers and
children in a previous defeat, this could have elicited uncontrollable fear,
not to mention feelings of outrage and fanatic patriotism. In contrast,
focusing on the sufferings of the enemies' mothers and children could have

226

compelled the real audience to subliminally and perhaps aesthetically envisage the possibility of their own defeat, and consider the absurdity of such a dangerous game. This is presented by Euripides as a viable course of events in the words of Poseidon, who comments on Athena's whimsical 'change of sympathy' (67). Euripides' audience may well have been prepared to devote their lives to a just and inevitable war, but not necessarily to a militarist adventure. Empathy with the enemy is used here to force the audience into reconsidering their own attitude to colonial wars, and even their own pseudo-patriotic feelings. Euripides targets his harsh criticism at the Homeric tradition by contrasting the implied spectators' pride in the heroic past of their nation with the familiar anti-heroic nature of their troops and the suffering inflicted on their helpless enemies. He possibly meant not only to shock the real spectators, but to actually change their attitude to colonial wars.

Sartre's adaptation: *Les Troyennes*

In writing *Les Troyennes*, Sartre probably had in mind the success of a previous production of the classical play-script (in the faithful translation by Jacqueline Moatti) for audiences who were in favor of negotiating with the FLN (Front de Libération Nationale), during Algeria's war of independence (Pingaud: 6). This success possibly encouraged Sartre to adopt Euripides' self-critical viewpoint. Sartre did not make explicit reference to France and Algeria, which indicates that his intention was to create an abstract metaphor of absurdity, applicable to any war. The fact is that the war in Algeria ended in 1962, and *Les Troyennes* was produced by the Théâtre National Populaire and premiered at the Théâtre du Palais de Chaillot, Paris, in 1965.

Sartre closely followed Euripides in adopting the main action and the serious and sublime tragic mood and, particularly, the victims' perspective. He also stressed the intolerable anthropomorphic nature of the gods and the unbearable dependence of humans on their sheer 'capricious' (p. 21) and evil (p. 122) nature. 'Les Dieux qui apparaissent dans *Les Troyennes* sont à la fois puissant et ridicules. D'un côté, ils dominent le monde: la guerre de Troie a été leur oeuvre. Mais vu de près, on s'aperçoit qu'ils ne se conduisent pas autrement que les hommes et que, comme eux, ils sont menés par de petites vanités, de petites rancunes' (Pingaud: 7). Moreover, suffering is shown to befall the human characters because of insignificant conflicts between the gods themselves; e.g., Poséidon and Pallas (p. 14). Not only from an ironic viewpoint are the Olympian gods devoid of genuine divinity, but also from the characters' naïve perspectives. In Hécube's words: 'Troie n'a pas été conquise, / Les Troyens n'ont pas été vaincus, / Une déesse les a livrés, / perfide et rancuneuse comme une femme' (p. 62).

However, Sartre could not have attacked pagan beliefs. Whereas Euripides wrote for spectators who could not see beyond the horizons of paganism, Sartre wrote for an audience nurtured in the tradition of Christian monotheism, profoundly rooted in the French culture, including the French classicist theatre. At most, some spectators may have adopted a post-Christian agnosticism or even an atheist stand. He understood that for eliciting a critical response, similar to that intended for the ancient Athenian audiences, he had to introduce fundamental changes in the play-script (Pingaud: 4).

In order to preserve the characters' naïve attitude to their gods intact, Sartre had to find a way to present them in a form meaningful to his implied spectator. The French Classicist theatre adhered to the teachings of the Catholic Church in presenting the pre-Christian gods as demonic powers, thereby fundamentally changing their status in the divine hierarchy, and the positive characters as intuitive critics of Pagan theology and prophets of the true God. For example, Thésée and Aricie's severe criticism of the gods' cruelty in Racine's *Phèdre* (1612–16), and Dymas' quotation of Oedipus' premonition in Corneille's *Oedipe* (1988–94): 'Ne voyons plus le ciel après sa cruauté: / Pur nous venger de lui dédaignons sa clarté. / Refusons-lui nos yeux, et gardons quelque vie / Qui montre encore à tous quelle est sa tyrannie' (1991–1994).

The paradox of gods behaving in contrast to purer concepts of divinity and still being granted sway over the world, which they run absurdly, was left unsolved by Euripides, who contented himself with rational criticism of paganism, without suggesting a theological alternative. Christianity solved this paradox by conceiving of the pagan world as not yet redeemed by the Messiah and left to the mercy of evil forces. Sartre followed this tradition in conceiving of the pagan gods as embodiments of evil. In addition, he followed another French tradition without contradicting the former: conceiving of them as personified projections of negative psychic energies that cause chaos in the world. Such an attitude can be found already in *The Trojan Woman*:

Hecuba: [. . .] since Aphrodite is nothing but the human lust,
(989–90)

In *Les Troyennes*:

Hécube: Quand les hommes deviennent fous d'amour
ils ne reconnaissent pas leur folie
et lui donnent le nom d'Aphrodite.

(p. 102)

Hécube not only denounces the absurdity of the gods' rule, but also dares to doubt their very existence ('S'il est un Dieu,' [p. 114]) and immortality, and even dares to challenge them: 'Eh bien! foudroyez moi!' (p. 121).

Hécube not only bitterly criticizes the gods – verging on heresy – but also envisages divine justice. Whereas in its criticism of paganism, *The Trojan Women* reflects an intuition of a more accomplished notion of divinity, unthikable within the framework of the Homeric tradition, *Les Troyennes* obviously preached to the converted. Nonetheless, if Sartre's criticism is conceived of as a stage metaphor, it may well apply to monotheism: 'Euripide se sert ainsi de la légende pour faire apparaître, [. . .] en opposant seulement les mythes les uns aux autres, les difficultés d'un polythéisme auquel son public ne croit déjà plus. Le monothéisme échappe-t-il à cette condamnation? (Pingaud: 7–8). By thus alluding to monotheism Sartre reverted to Euripides' criticism of current religious beliefs.

Sartre's main criticism focused on colonial war. Typically, people engaging in a war believe in their eventual victory and anticipate its benefits, such as ruling over other nations and lands, and expanding their own national economy. By reversing the meaning of the Homeric narrative, Sartre reflected his belief that war is absurd in nature, because it is as cruel for the victorious as for the vanquished: 'La guerre, nous savons aujourd'hui ce que cela signifie: une guerre atomique ne laissera ni vainqueurs ni vaincus. C'est précisément ce que toute la pièce démontre [. . .] J'ai préféré laisser à Poséidon le mot de la fin' (Pingaud: 6–7): 'Faites la guerre, mortels imbéciles, [. . .] Vous en crèverez. Tous' (p. 130). The Trojan war thus becomes an appropriate metaphor of this insight too. Both Euripides' and Sartre's metaphors equally apply to the Peloponnesian, Algerian and any other colonial war.

Having in mind the colonial wars of the twentieth century, Sartre too stressed the paradox in the extreme cruelty of the so-called more "civilized" cultures:

Andromaque: Hommes de l'Europe,
vous méprisez l'Afrique et l'Asie
et vous nous appelez barbares, je crois,
Mais quand la gloriole et la cupidité
vous jettent chez nous,
vous pillez, vous torturez, vous massacrez.
Où sont les barbares, alors?
Et vous, les Grecs, si fiers de votre humanité,
Où êtes-vous? (p. 81)

By attributing 'barbaric' demeanor to the Europeans, Andromache denounces the purported cultural superiority and acculturative mission of colonialism, typical of modern imperialism too. Sartre implies that from a humane viewpoint the conquerors were more barbarians than the conquered and, morally speaking, they brought about their own defeat through relinquishing their own humanity. The implication is that there is no justification whatsoever for colonialist war. The only possible justification for war resides in the very opposite: the defense of a country against colonialism, i.e., defense of the natural right to freedom:

> *Cassandre*:   Gloire aux défenseurs de la patrie.
>   Mais les autres, les conquérants,
>   Ceux qui font une sale guerre et qui en meurent,
>   leur mort est plus bête encore que leur vie. (p. 51)

The notions 'défenseurs de la patrie' and 'sale guerre' are the fictional equivalents of 'justified' and 'unjustified' war, typical political terms in the twentieth century. Sartre transformed thereby *Les Troyennes* into an explicit anti-colonialist manifesto.

On the personal level, slavery is worse than death. It is the loss of the natural right not only to freedom, but also to dignity. Therefore, the natural reaction to slavery, even if hopeless, is rebellion. In a gesture that is meant to command the admiration of the spectator, Hécube performs a desperate act of asserting her human dignity:

> *Hécube*:   portez-nous, chiens, tirez-nous,
>   poussez-nous de force,
>   Nous n'irons pas de notre plain gré
>   vers l'exil et l'esclavage.
>   (on les entraîne. La scène reste vide un instant.) (p. 125)

This act prefigures her eventual suicide, probably known to Euripides' audiences from Homeric sources. It also echoes Hécube's own challenging the gods (p. 121). Her rebellion thus becomes a metaphor not merely of struggle against colonialism, but mainly against any kind of order that one nation may impose upon another.

War is controlled by demonic, irrational and unpredictable forces, as capricious as Athena herself, the unreasonable goddess of reason (p. 21). The moment the initiative of war is taken, these demonic energies rule of the world. Following Hécube's (and the ironic) line of interpretation, the gods' rule is in fact a kind of indulgence in human amoral drives. Namely, since human beings wage war, they are responsible for letting loose these energies. The crux of absurdity lies in that no divinity exists to counteract these drives. Left to humans, the world is a chaotic world. It is man-made absurdity.

The harmony of peace contrasts the absurdity of war. The chorus describes the day when the Greeks appeared to have left Troy, and only the wooden horse remained on the beach, as their happiest day: 'c'est la paix' (p. 61) and what followed, as the saddest one: 'C'était la guerre' (p. 62).

Sartre followed Euripides in many respects, especially in adopting the perspectives of the enemies' suffering women – a seemingly disloyal attitude – for confronting the spectators not only with their own suppressed fears, but also with their suppressed sense of compassion, and shock them. Nonetheless, *Les Troyennes* is in fact a new fictional world, reflecting creative interpretation. It embodies a different dramatic structure, which culminates in Hécube's moral victory and, consequently, in achieving a different effect on the implied audience. In her parallel rebellion against gods and heroes she is a living manifesto for the natural human right to freedom and dignity, with rebellion being the appropriate response to imposed rule. Sartre generalized his criticism to the extent of condemning the rule of the world, based on whatever religion or philosophy. The impotency of theologies, whether pagan or monotheistic, in their endeavor to bestow sense upon the world, stresses the responsibility of humans for their own fate. Sartre perceived the narrative of the Trojan women as an apt metaphor of the inherent absurdity of the human condition.

Habimah's production of *Les Troyennes*

Sartre's *Les Troyennes* was translated by Eli Malka, directed by Holk Freytag, and premiered on 19 February 1983. The set and costume, designed by Angelica Edingen, and the music, composed by Ofer Schlachin, played a major role in conveying this actualized creative interpretation. Initially, this production hinged on equating the Greek troops with the Israeli forces occupying the West Bank and the Gaza Strip, and the Trojan women and children with refugee Arab women and children. However, while still rehearsing the Lebanon War broke out (June 1982), which drastically changed the political constellation and the way this ancient metaphor was received by the audience.

Before this war, a widespread perception was that the IDF (Israel Defense Force) presence in the occupied territories was imposed upon Israel by the unwillingness of the Palestinians to negotiate peace. In contrast, the vast majority of the public, of theatregoers at least, immediately reacted to the Lebanon War as a political adventure and a gross national mistake. Whereas prior to this war public controversy would have focused on the validity of the analogy between the local political situation and those referred to by Euripides (Melos and Sicily) and Sartre (colonial

231

war), this turn of events favored the transmutation of the same production into an unquestionably fitting metaphor. The war, officially justified by considerations of national security, was widely perceived as the result of a fanciful plan to solve the problem of guerrilla infiltration and force peace upon Lebanon and, therefore, as causing unnecessary suffering, particularly to the Lebanese civilian population. Both the enemy propaganda and the Israeli media encouraged criticism by extensive and prominent coverage of the dead and wounded Arab women and children. Only the extreme right-wing was shocked by the allusion. Although it was clear that the massacres in the Lebanese villages of Sabra and Shatilla (16–17 September 1982) had not been perpetrated by the IDF, these events exacerbated a general sense of discontent with governmental policy. Paradoxically, although the Habimah production employed exactly the same mechanism of self-criticism operated by Euripides and Sartre – presenting the war from the viewpoint of the vanquished and eliciting sympathy for their suffering – the eventual result was different. Whereas the implied spectator was expected to be shocked, most real spectators expressed profound agreement with the critical message.

The Habimah production preserved the original dialogue, the absurdist structure of the play-script. However, although retaining the original identities of Greek and Trojan characters, it added clear non-verbal allusions to the Israeli–Arab conflict through costume, set, sound and body language:

(A) *Costume*: most of Trojan women were attired in long black robes and shawls, reminiscent of both classical and Bedouin garments. They carried shabby old-fashioned suitcases and bundles, as if tied up in a hurry, typical of refugees in flight. The Greek soldiers wore light khaki uniforms, badges, army boots and guns of various kinds that, although not typical of the IDF, were meant to be perceived as such. The uniform of Menelaus, the only general on stage, with its exaggerated display of military paraphernalia, such as badges, medals and binoculars, verged on the grotesque. Helen, in an iron and glass cage illuminated by neon light, with flowing blond hair, was attired in a sexy tight blue dress and high-heeled shoes, reminiscent of whores in a red light district. Astyanax, in modern blue shirt, pants and designer sneakers, resembled a typical Western (and Israeli) middle-class boy. His dead body, wrapped in a bloodstained white sheet, probably suggested the blurring of national identity in death.

(B) *Set*: On an initially bare stage, the women were engaged in building a few tents, with wooden sticks and scraps of cloth, in clear allusion to refugees preparing for sheltering in a makeshift refugee camp. The floor was covered with sawdust, which created a cloud of dust whenever stepped upon. The set was equally ambiguous: although it did not replicate any local refugee camp, whether in the occupied territories or other countries, it alluded to such a camp.

A makeshift refugee camp in Freytag's *The Trojan Women*. Courtesy of the
Habimah National Theatre. Photo: Amon Schneider.

(c) *Sound*: there was a background sound of diving jet bombers and electronic noise. The music was a combination of flute and electronic tunes, the former alluding to oriental motifs. There was also a scene of typical oriental drumming.

(d) *Body language*: using elements of posture, gesture and intonation, the actresses indicated a typical oriental behavior. In a mute scene, a soldier engages in meticulously disassembling, cleaning and reassembling his gun, in the typical manner of the IDF.

In a 12-minute long and powerful opening mute scene, Freytag's own creation, dispassionate soldiers were brutally pushing refugee women, carrying bundles and suitcases, onto the desolate set; the women were erecting tents, fighting each other for any available scrap of cloth, to the tune of an oriental melody (Weitz). Under the inspiration of Sartre's heroic final accord, Freytag devised a new end for Hecuba: she tied herself up and attempted to pour petrol over her head, from a typical military jerrycan, and set herself alight. Eventually, while the entire set was being destroyed, she was brutally dragged off the stage: a non-verbal image of humiliation and devastation of human life that epitomized the gestus of the production: heroism despite suffering.

The combination of these non-verbal elements, foreign to the original design, created a new referent for the ancient metaphor. Freytag maintained an apparent dual reference to both ancient Greek and Israeli/Palestinian women, particularly by dual characterization of the same garments. While the allusion to Greece remained the metaphoric predicate, the allusion to the local conflict explicitly indicated its new referent. All the structural components of the metaphor thus coexisted on the very same stage. The apparent dual reference was resolved into a single one (chapter 8).

In contrast to Euripides and Sartre, who avoided any textual clue to their intended referents, and relied on their implied and real audiences' ability to identify them, Freytag stressed such clues; and for his indirect, but well calculated actualization, he was heavily criticized. In the ensuing discussion, which reached the Knesset (the Israeli Parliament) in December 1983, the right wing was furious. A religious member attacked the Habimah Theatre for offending 'the basic values of Judaism'. Yoseph Lapid, then a prominent journalist and the chairman of the National Broadcasting Authority, sarcastically noted that the play should have been performed at a PLO conference in Algeria (Handelsaltz). The attempt to discredit the production as a mere piece of anti-patriotic propaganda favoring the enemy had probably been the fate of the first production of *The Trojan Women* in ancient Greece too.

Freytag's actualization was problematic also due to his German nationality, which for many critics evoked an analogy to Nazi Germany. For example, in Khava Novak's words:

> I do not know whether or not it was sensible for a German director to stress so vehemently this analogy on the stage of the National Theatre. No doubt that his own personal associations reflect his own national feelings of guilt. If there is any sin here, this resides in the attempt to attribute Nazi brutality and cruelty to people living in this area, in this land, in the present. (Novak; my trans.)

While explicitly rejecting any possible analogy between Nazis and Israelis, Novak implies that the brutal extermination of those who are defined as 'enemy' on racist grounds is only appropriate to Nazi Germany, and not to a nation that defends its natural right to exist. The use of 'Nazi' for any kind of army or police brutality, even for internal affairs, is quite frequent in the heavily loaded Israeli political discourse.

Sartre characterized Talthybius as the prototype of the civilized soldier, who shares in perpetrating the most ignominious crimes. Freytag combined contrasting images of his gentle behavior and shocking cruelty;

e.g., Talthybius, wearing an IDF-like uniform, bore Astyanax on his shoulders, or played ball with him, thus creating images of fatherly love; and yet he participated in his horrible murder, while finding justification in that he was merely fulfilling orders. In both the French and Israeli contexts, this excuse too was reminiscent of the Nazi officers' self-defense at the Nüremberg trials and Adolph Eichman's trial in Israel. It was this allusion to a possible analogy between the IDF with the Nazi army that explains more than anything else the passionate reaction of some Israeli spectators. Audiences could have accepted the analogy Greece/Israel, but could not accept the analogy Nazi Germany/Israel.

'Actualization' is a typical self-imposed aim of the Israeli theatre. Many productions of classic plays reflect a tendency to relate their fictional worlds to political actuality, whether rifts within Israeli society (e.g., the production of *Tartuffe* at the Haifa Municipal Theatre, 1985, in which Tartuffe was portrayed as an ultra-Orthodox Jew – Urian, 1994: 137–41); or the Israeli–Arab conflict (e.g., the production of Beckett's *Waiting for Godot* at the Haifa Municipal Theatre, 1985, in which Vladimir and Estragon were portrayed as Arab builders and Pozzo as a Jewish contractor – Urian, 1996: 62–3) (chapter 11).

For Euripides the absurdity of war was an instance of the absurdity of established beliefs. The Habimah production, magnifying Sartre's rhetoric intent, further marginalized the religious theme and subordinated it to the criticism of national oppression. Freytag probably felt that, for an Israeli audience, criticism of such beliefs was not an item on their agenda, and made Sartre's adaptation almost exclusively relevant to the Israeli–Arab conflict. This procedure certainly gained in establishing strong referential connections with the immediate concerns of the audience, but probably lost in conveying the universality of the message: the absurd nature of religious beliefs and war in general. Euripides chose the most senseless war he could have found in his own cultural tradition for criticizing both humans and gods: a war in which the victors spent ten years of their lives in avenging the abduction of a single morally weak woman; they killed and were killed in the thousands; and they suffered even more upon their triumphal return. By employing the description of this war as a metaphor of any war Sartre shows that wars are inherently unnecessary, unjust and, in short, absurd.

Euripides unknowingly created an all-purpose metaphor. The universality of *The Trojan Women* is clearly demonstrated by the ability of its mechanism of self-criticism to apply to any warlike policy, opening the way to constant creative reinterpretation. One need only mention the intertextual relations between the texts by Homer, Virgil, Euripides, Sartre and Freytag. The peoples entangled: Greece and Troy, Greece and Melos-Sicily, France and Algeria, Israel and the Palestinians, and Israel and

Lebanon. The religions involved: Paganism, Christianity, Judaism and Islam; and indirectly, an association accidentally introduced by the national identity of the director, Nazi Germany and the rest of Europe, the Jews and the Gypsies in particular. Not to mention many other productions of the play-script, referring to similar conflicts under different circumstances (cf. Bryant-Bertail, 2000). In all cases, in order to elicit an audience response similar to that expected by Euripides, the referent of the Trojan metaphor needed to be continually re-actualized, which does not imply that the actual referent is to be made explicit in the text. Rather, it can be spontaneously evoked by any audience, as demonstrated by Euripides, and possibly by Sartre. Universality is not an intrinsic quality of a play-script, but is achieved by continuous re-creative interpretation.

16

Robert Wilson's H.G.: *Non-Theatrical Space as Stage Metaphor*

It is typical of modern and postmodern theatre to perform in 'found spaces' that 'had not been designed for theatre performances, whether palace, village clearing or quarry' (Mackintosh: 83). In some cases, it is customary to integrate the connotations of such a space into the overall meaning of a fictional world. Ariane Mnouchkine chose a *cartoucherie* (a munitions factory) for housing her theatre because 'it has been built to house creations, productions, works, inventions, and *explosions!*' (quoted by Mackintosh: 86) Her reason applies to all her productions in this space. This chapter, in contrast, focuses on the connotations of a specific found space in the context of a particular performance-text.

Usually, an established theatre space functions in a dual capacity: as a functional space in which a theatre event can take place and as a real place that enacts a fictional place; i.e., deflects reference to it like any human or non-human actor (chapter 5). A non-theatrical space may add a further dimension: due to its nature and/or usual function, its connotations can be incorporated to the overall meaning of a fictional world in a metaphoric capacity.

This chapter focuses on this phenomenon through an analysis of *H.G.*, commissioned and produced by Artangel and directed by Robert Wilson in conjunction with sound and light architect Hans Peter Kuhn, produced in London, 1995 (Rozik, 1998c). This production was conceived by its authors in terms not of 'theatre', but of 'installation', a category that seems adequate because there were no live actors, no characters and no apparent action. I contend, nonetheless, that *H.G.* is an instance of theatre; and that there is an advantage in reading, interpreting and experiencing it as such, because: (a) *the absence of human characters, enacted by human actors, was justified by the fictional circumstances;* (b) *the spectators were meant to enact the characters of the narrative;* (c) *the non-human components of the stage-text enacted objects in various worlds;* (d) *the real time of spectator's experience enacted several fictional times;* and (e) *the non-theatrical space in which it was produced enacted several fictional places.* A crucial condition for correctly considering an installation as an instance of theatre is the applicability of the principle of 'acting', in the sense of deflection of reference (cf. Kreuder).

The main question here is: were the connotations of the found space integrated into the overall meaning of the performance-text? This chapter aims at showing that in *H.G. the found place was employed as a key metaphor in the description of the fictional world.*

Reading *H.G.*

H.G. was produced in London's Clink Street Vaults, underneath the ruins of the Clink, once a medieval prison, situated beneath the railway arches in the proximity of Southwark Cathedral. In these damp, dark and ill-illuminated vaults, Wilson and Kuhn installed a sequence of tableaux.

The spectators entered in small groups through a very low door and walked these vaults in a predominantly fixed although not obligatory order, and were expected to watch or, rather, experience their exhibits. Most of these were static objects, displayed in harmony with the size and shape of each vault, and only a few included moving elements. The scenes and their possible order are mapped and numbered in the following diagram (the scenes have been named for the sake of convenience):

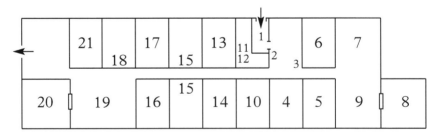

(0) *Entrance* through a low wooden doorway with the initials H.G. engraved on a small brass plaque.

(1) *The dinner scene*: a Georgian candle-lit dining room apparently abandoned in the midst of a lavish dinner. There are fresh flowers, burning candles, goblets with wine, plates with leftovers and napkins strewn about. On the table: bone china, silver-plated cutlery and miniature decorative

sphinxes. Around it: heavily decorated mahogany furniture and display-cabinets with valuable china. On the walls: medical diagrams of the human body (the muscles and the digestive system), a decorative mirror on a black cloth and portraits of Elizabeth I and several noblemen. In the fireplace: an extinguished fire. An unseen clock is ticking loudly. All suggests that this is the house of a well-to-do and cultivated gentleman with an interest in science, history and travel; and that the meal was interrupted under sudden and unexplained circumstances.

Dinner scene in Robert Wilson's *H.G.*. Courtesy of Artangel.
Photo: Stephen White.

(2) *The Times scene*: in a very dark passage, in an ill-illuminated and small niche there is a stuffed rhino's head and an old exemplar of *The Times* dated 1895.

(3) *The fob watch scene*: in the same passage, in another ill-illuminated small niche, behind a heavy iron door, there is a fob watch with the engraved initials H.G. At the end of the passage, the spectators can choose to go either right or left; but two guides, standing under a dim light-bulb, suggest that they go left first.

(4) *The cat scene*: in very dark vault, watched from behind an iron barrier, a single ray of light, which scans the darkness every few seconds, reveals square wooden pillars and a stuffed yellowish cat frozen in a pounce.

(5) *The silhouette scene*: in another very dark vault, watched from behind

an iron barrier, a dim purple light reveals a rear red brick wall looking like a back street alley. After getting used to the darkness, made heavier by the illuminated background, wooden pillars and a very low ceiling is discerned; and then the faint silhouette of a man, first sitting and then walking very slowly, also becomes visible.

(6) *The mummy scene*: in a big vault, a human mummy lies on the floor on its back under a shaft of light. A few colored stones, wall debris and a metal hip flask with the initials H.G. are scattered around. Under another beam of light a severed hand (made in plaster) is suspended from the ceiling. The strong light from both projectors starkly contrasts the surrounding darkness of the vault and the entire warren.

Mummy scene in Robert Wilson's *H.G.*. Courtesy of Artangel.
Photo: Stephen White.

(7) *The hospital scene*: in several intercommunicating vaults, arranged as a hospital wing, there are twenty-four iron beds arrayed in six rows at regular intervals with freshly laundered and neatly tucked in off-white sheets and khaki blankets. They make the impression of an abandoned military hospital. In square holes, between the beds, steel buckets filled with (fake) blood are illuminated by feeble light-bulbs suspended from the ceiling. The entire space is damp. Old documents are scattered on the floor and some are about to fall in from a square opening in the ceiling. A sequence of single notes is struck on a far-off piano, against the background of a sound resembling the noise made by scratching a microphone.

Hospital scene in Robert Wilson's *H.G.*. Courtesy of Artangel.
Photo: Stephen White.

(8) *The rainforest scene*: a sunlit rainforest glade with fluttering foliage and singing birds, watched from behind a barred dungeon-like window in the previous vault, is colored in the background by slightly purpled light. There is a sense of idyllic atmosphere, which is in stark contrast to the gloomy image of the hospital, from within which this encapsulated paradise is observed.

(9) *The medical office scene*: at other end of the hospital vault, there is a typical off-white desk and an office chair. On the desk there is a Medical Officer of Health's report, a tobacco box with the initials H.G. and an unsharpened red pencil. The report charts the death toll of the influenza epidemic in 1919, with the mortality figures of the first week of April in various European cities. Reference is thus made to the great post-war 'flu epidemic. On the desk an old wireless is broadcasting German propaganda. Besides the desk, there is a luxurious pair of leather riding boots and a whip, very carefully arranged on the floor and poorly illuminated by a 20-watt light-bulb.

(10) *The portraits scene*: in the next huge dark vault, also supported by square wooden pillars, water is dripping from the ceiling. Dusty and discarded 17th century-type portraits, partially covered by cobwebs and/or sawdust, are strewn about on the floor, with the water dripping on them. The pictures are damaged beyond repair and feeble bulbs light them from

241

the ceiling. Among them, there are a white and thin iron ladder reaching the ceiling; a few red bricks, some of them piled and some scattered about, a big garden gnome, with a gray beard and a red hat and, near the exit, a small Christmas tree and a hammer stained with (fake) blood beside it.

(11) *The violin scene*: in a long and very dark vault, watched from behind an iron barrier, in total silence, a violin tune, as if played by a novice, is heard. After getting used to the darkness some faraway unrecognizable shapes are discerned. Spectators try to guess. The guesses seldom coincide.

(12) *The green glass scene*: on the walkway, there is a box with bottle debris of thin greenish glass in various shades, slightly lit from underneath.

(13) *The universe scene*: in an attic of a huge vault, watched through a square opening in the middle of a wooden deck, which is very well-lit, a big bluish globe with the continents painted by a childish hand, hanging among cotton wool clouds, can be seen. In the distance, another bluish globe with no drawings hovers above. Steps on the wooden floor are heard.

(14) *The aquarium scene*: in a dark medium-size vault, there is an oblong brick pillar, about two meters high, which supports a medium size aquarium containing a live weird legged fish and a small bottle with (fake) blood on its bottom. A strong jet of air is being injected into the water. In total silence, a mysterious and very low-pitched whistling, against the background of a kind of chatter, is heard.

(15) *The soft drink cans scene*: in between two small vaults, on both sides of the walkway, there are two huge piles of used and extremely battered soft drink cans. Yellow bulbs light both sides.

(16) *The grave scene*: in the next dark vault, the floor changes into a soft and black earth-like soil. At the entrance, on the left-hand side, there is a perfect conic pile of white gravel and a 20-watt light-bulb hangs from the ceiling exactly above its tip. On the right-hand side, a black square grave-like cavity, with white gravel on its bottom and lit by a purple light. At the left end, a black ramp descends towards a barred iron door. A very low-pitched German chatter is heard in the background. The atmosphere is very calm. Near the exit, on a small shelf, beyond reach, there is a goblet (possibly a Holy Grail) filled with (fake) blood.

(17) *The temple scene*: in a huge, fully lit and white painted vault, watched from behind a small and barred window, a formation of high and massive Doric columns looking like the ruins of an ancient Greek temple can be seen. One of the columns and some scattered debris are on the ground; and arrows are suspended overhead as if in flight, against the background of a Mediterranean deep blue sky. The background music is reminiscent of a Church.

242

Temple scene in Robert Wilson's *H.G.*. Courtesy of Artangel.
Photo: Stephen White.

(18) *The sphinx scene*: in a very small vault, a disproportionately large Egyptian sphinx made of plaster, can be seen from behind a narrow opening between two semi-opened heavy iron doors, joined by a heavy iron lock. Plaster waste is scattered around. The sphinx looks like the result of an intentional effort to create a cheap imitation of the real thing. The light is white and sharp.

243

(19) *The shoes scene*: in a huge L-shaped vault there is a display of a huge assembly of used shoes of all kinds, in all possible sizes and for any gender, age, social status and activity, including skates, flippers and shod artificial legs. The shoes are arrayed in perfect order and labeled by numbers. In their midst, there is a very heavy and ornate table, one of its legs leaning on a lit light-bulb. Again, the space is lit by feeble light-bulbs hung from the ceiling, some of which rest on the floor. A background of electronic sound recalls a sailing ship.

(20) *The dinosaur scene*: in a huge dark vault, watched from behind an iron barrier in the previous L-shaped vault, there is a shape, which is very difficult to identify, but reminisces a huge dinosaur. The light is predominantly green. The same background electronic noise as in the previous scene, being the same space, is heard.

(21) *The rabbit scene*: in a huge well-lit vault, watched from behind a narrow and barred window, on a high pedestal against the back wall, a big white rabbit puppet stands on its rear feet, presiding like an idol. The floor is covered by large corrugated sheets of transparent plastic. A background electronic noise is reminiscent of a machine.

(22) *Exit to the street.*

On the legitimacy of interpretation

Wilson warned against any attempt to look for a definite interpretation of *H.G.*. When asked about the principles that underlie this work, he postulated the inadequacy of looking for its 'correct' meaning: 'If you try to make too much sense of it, you'll miss the experience of it' (quoted by Jackson). In his interviews, he consistently contrasted meaning to experience, and described his work as only 'a sequence of images that are structured, as a sequence of spaces and experiences' (quoted by MacRitchie). It would appear, therefore, that the entire work was made for the spectators to go through, contemplate, freely associate, experience and at most construct their own meanings: 'You willingly enter into the *fictional world* that is created for you and employ your imaginative powers to make sense of it. [. . .] You may start to put the clues together and invent a story connecting the images, though you don't have to and there isn't a "right" or "wrong" solution' (Bayley; my italics).

Postmodern ideology does not ignore, however, the existential proclivity of people to seek a definite meaning in a text, which assumedly reflects an authorial intention. It rather presupposes such a propensity and possibly promotes texts that intentionally preclude its gratification; thus enabling and even encouraging different individual readings. The problem with this approach lies in that, rather than offering a ready-made expression that the spectator can adopt or reject, it diverts responsibility from the artist to the non-artist and may result, therefore, in a poor or misinformed interpretation. Moreover, such an anti-objective-meaning stance does not rule out the author's own existential tendency, even if unconscious, to reflect a unitary intention and create a coherent meaning. Even ambiguity is a definite meaning. Consequently, to oppose any attempt at making sense of a text may be an honorable ideological position, but does not necessarily apply to actual works of art, which are intentional doings by definition. Whether meaning is declared pre-established or not, therefore, unitary meaning should be presupposed, and any attempt to ascertain the meaning of *H.G.* is legitimate.

An attempt at interpretation

Several clues point at H. G. Wells' *The Time Machine* as the backbone allusion of the installation. The initials 'H.G.' are inscribed or engraved on various objects, such as the street door, the hip flask, the fob watch and the cigarette case – probably the belongings of the missing host from the interrupted feast. The dinner scene clearly alludes to the opening chapter of his book, in which the host explains the principles of time-travel to his guests. Moreover, the exemplar of *The Times* is dated 1895, which is the year of publication of Wells' book. The production of *H.G.* can thus be conceived of as a centenary celebration of this event.

From such a perspective, walking the vaults of the Clink can be understood as a spatial metaphor of time-travel and several images as illustrating the various destinations in such a time-journey. Under the assumption that the point of departure is the dinner scene, (i.e., London, 1895), the inclusion of images from both the preceding and the following centuries may create the impression of traveling backwards and forwards into the past and the future. In chronological order the stations are: Prehistory (the dinosaur scene), Ancient Egypt (the sphinx scene), Ancient Greece (the temple scene), English seventeenth century (the portraits scene), First World War (the hospital scene) and twentieth-century Western Culture (the soft drink cans, the shoes and the rabbit scenes). Although this order is not preserved, in the typical manner of human memory, warren-walking is correlated to time-travel and both become comprehensive metaphors for the scrutiny of the history and possible future of human culture from a subjective viewpoint.

In Wells' novel, in concluding his explanation of time-travel principles, the host claims that time is the fourth dimension, and that we move constantly through time by memory and imagination (Dorment). Indeed, whereas history is conceived of as an objective record of the human species, memory and imagination are the tools of subjective history. In this sense, *H.G.* is not only an account of the cultural development of *homo sapiens sapiens*, but also, and perhaps mainly, a subjective attempt to understand and assess the human world through images that are stored in an individual memory. In regard to making sense of the world we live in, history and personal memory are two sides of the same coin.

This journey into the meaning of human culture thus also becomes a journey into the depths of the human psyche. The traveling mind searches for its inner images that prove to be a mixture of the real and the imagined, originating in the present or the past, in history or childhood, which is the past of the individual. The mind records the past thorugh motionless images, as if time has been frozen and spatialized.

I suggest that this shift in understanding 'time/space-travel' from being a literal description of an imaginary adventure to being a metaphor of the perennial human endeavor to understand one's own existence and creativity, by searching both human history and its reflection in the depths of the psyche, is a precondition for making sense of *H.G.*. The spectators are expected to intuit this shift from time to space and from the latter's objective dimensions to mind and, in experiencing the sequence of images, to become mind-travelers themselves. They are also expected to explore the installation as a metaphor of their own searching minds.

The various cultures are mostly represented by non-verbal metonyms, which clearly induce a sense of decay and regression. The ancient Greek colonnade is in ruins and the suspended arrows in the air (a static image of flying) can be interpreted as the victory of barbarism over culture. The seventeenth-century portraits, which are damaged beyond repair, may indicate neglect of their artistic values. The crude plaster cast of the sphinx reflects a deliberate attempt to convey a sense of cheap and careless imita-tion of one of the wonders of ancient civilization. Twentieth-century culture is represented by the worship of the rabbit, the universal metaphor and symbol of (animal) sexual excess, and the piles of dilapidated soft drink cans can be interpreted as symbols of a consumers' non-cultural culture. This motif of 'decay' and 'regression' clearly has a cumulative effect, which is conducive to a sense of disappointment with humankind whose culture, embodied in symbols of worthlessness, is in a constant process of decline.

Following the equivalence between history and personal memory, through recurrent reference, the death of culture is clearly paralleled to individual death, with the mummy and the grave scenes probably being its central images. Moreover, the end of the First World War is illustrated by the absurd image of a hospital that has succeeded in being cleaned to immaculateness and arrayed to perfection through sheer redundancy; i.e., by its total "success" in increasing the death toll. War and disease are shown thereby as allies in a perennial battle against humankind. The empty shoes at the end of the journey correspond to the empty beds of the hospital and the statistics of the flu epidemic. Objects divorced from their human occupants become additional images of death.

There are recurrent images of human blood out of its natural vessels: in the steel buckets of the hospital, which is thereby attributed the metaphoric dimension of a slaughter-house; on the blood-stained hammer (the portraits scene), which is thereby presented as an instrument for murdering human beings and/or works of art; and in the blood-filled bottle on the bottom of the aquarium: blood out of its natural container, the human body, also symbolizes death. Consequently, individual death becomes a metaphor of a dying culture and vice versa.

'The roomful of labeled and discarded shoes near the end of *H.G.*, which is not found in *The Time Machine*, induces a sense of extreme sadness for loss and endless extermination, which reinforces the tenor of Wells' concluding page, where the narrator describes how the Time-traveler 'thought but cheerlessly of the Advancement of Mankind, and saw in the growing pile of civilization only a foolish heaping that must inevitably fall back upon and destroy its makers in the end' (Cork). This sense of pessimism permeates the entire text of *H.G.*: 'Working exactly a century after those words were published, Wilson probably sees every reason to adopt Wells' prescient pessimism' (*ibid.*). The inaccessible Holy Grail, in which the holy wine is believed to transmute into the real blood of the Savior (the grave scene), probably conveys a (metaphoric) sense of unattainable redemption.

The warren – a found-space metaphor

Several descriptions have been suggested for the found-space in which the entire installation had been arranged, such as 'subterranean' or 'cavernous labyrinth', 'derelict cellars' and 'vast warren of subterranean vaults'. All these are not only adequate literal descriptions for this set of dark and damp interconnected vaults, but also apt metaphors of the tortuous psychological 'path' that the mind follows in its attempts to search its own uncharted lands (cf. Cork). Time-travel is not only transmuted into a spatial journey, but also embodied in a labyrinthine stage metaphor of a journey into the depths of the psyche: a panoramic subjective view of the past, present and future from the viewpoint of an individual consciousness.

This overall metaphor of consciousness in search of hidden meaning is particularly reinforced by the darkness of the warren, and further emphasized by the dim lighting throughout the premises. Within such an interpretative framework, the light-bulbs become additional metaphors of

247

the limitations of the mind in searching its own depths. The only shaft of light in the installation illuminates a mummy, which is probably meant to convey the vividness of awareness of death – also a stage metaphor.

Moreover, most of the exhibits have to be watched from behind small windows, semi-closed doors, narrow apertures and bars (the watch, cat, silhouette, violin, universe, temple, sphinx, dinosaur, and rabbit scenes). In the context of the suggested overall metaphor, these should be interpreted as peering into recondite corners of the psyche. The rainforest, which is watched from the hospital, attains the meaning of a wishful dream: from a concrete (literal) symbol of death (the empty hospital) and the depths of human misery, a window opens up on a paradisiacal landscape, embodied in a concrete (metaphoric) symbol of growth and life. These images also reinforce both a sense of peering into the hidden and, perhaps even the forbidden, and a sense of being obstructed in the search for knowledge and happiness. It is an image of an exploration without a hope of discovery, let alone scientific truth. Darkness, feeble light, small openings and iron-made obstacles metaphorically epitomize the futility of humankind's attempts to understand the world that it has created itself.

Although the entire sequence of images could have been staged in any possible space, the choice of the Clink vaults was crucial in shaping *H.G.*. Speaking about the incubation stage, after the work was commissioned, Wilson remarked: 'I had no idea what to do. I didn't know whether it should be indoors or out, in a park or a factory building or someone's house. I went through a catalogue of locations and found this. You don't really need to do very much with the space. I let the rooms talk to me' (quoted by Ratcliffe).

The search for the meaning of human culture is described in terms of both 'time-travel' and 'space-walking' through a kind of labyrinth, in almost total darkness, with views partially obstructed by iron bars, doors and windows and thus beyond reach. These images add a dimension of meaning that is missing in the scenes themselves and conveyed by the skillful use of this particular space: setting out on the innermost journey is experienced as entering a labyrinthine warren in which darkness and physical obstacles prevail. As often as consciousness has been described as a searching light in the dark depths of the psyche, darkness has been used as a metaphor of its limited understanding. The metaphoric struggle between feeble light and pervading darkness aptly describes the futile attempt of consciousness to make sense of human existence and culture. In this sense the former use of the Clink vaults as a prison can be seen as an additional metaphoric dimension. The dark warren which apparently is no more than a neutral space for the various settings, thus becomes a central metaphor in *H.G.*. It adds, moreover, an aesthetic dimension in lending the entire work a sense of wholeness and unified meaning.

What is the difference between staging a production in a theatre or in a non-theatrical found space? Since the last century the use of non-theatrical spaces for theatre purposes has become customary. In theatre the stage is not only functional in providing the space for the theatre performance to take place, but also in enacting a fictional place (1994e: 88). These are also true for a non-theatrical space. The difference resides in that the deliberate choice of such spaces attests to a function that a regular stage cannot fulfil: the generation of improper referential associations, and their attribution to a fictional world, unless a production deals with the theme or motif of theatre, as in Luigi Pirandello's *Six Characters in Search of an Author* or used as a metaphor in Shakespeare's *Macbeth* (V, v, 24–8). In the case of *H.G.*, walking the Clink vaults adds a metaphoric dimension that could have not been attained in a theatre building, because of providing additional verbal and referential associations that originate in the found place as an improper term. It also attests to the theme's ability to evoke and assimilate such connotations; namely, the additional associative periphery of an acting space can be activated and integrated only by the thematic elements of a performance-text. In *H.G.*, the spectators are also meant to experience the Clink vaults by enacting the mind travelers themselves, and their actual feelings become additional sources of referential associations.

The metaphoric function of the Clink vaults would have been the same whether *H.G.* was a theatre performance or an installation. However, in this case (a) *the absence of live human characters in the performance-text, enacted by human actors, was justified by the thematic predominance of non-human images*; (b) *the spectators were meant to enact the time travelers*;(c) *the non-human images of the text were meant to enact images of past and future cultures*; (d) *the real time of the spectator was meant to enact several historical times*; and (e) *the real warren was meant to enact several geographic places*. The Clink vaults should be seen, therefore, not merely as a neutral found-space for the production, but as an integral part of its overall metaphoric meaning. This may explain what Wilson meant by 'I let the rooms talk to me.'

17

Yerushalmi's Woyzeck 91: *Intention in Creative Interpretation*

One of the most difficult tasks of interpretation is probably to establish implied directorial intentions and purposes. Assumedly, accounts by directors are not necessarily valid and, indeed, they are often conspicuously inadequate. For determining such intentions and purposes, therefore, performance-texts are the only reliable objects of inquiry. The following sections apply an inter-textual method of interpretation that aims at conjecturing such implied directorial intentions and purposes reflected in a performance-text.

This method consists, first, *in presupposing an intertextual relation between a target performance-text and its source play-script*; second, *in identifying deviations of the former from the latter;* and third, *in conjecturing the 'intentions' and 'purposes' of an implied director on such grounds*. In a generative manner, such a conjecture should explain all the said deviations. By implication, the set of preserved elements too indicates specific intentions and purposes. It may be claimed, therefore, that the set of all choices is indicative of an implied director's design.

As suggested above, a performance-text is a rhetoric macro-speech act (in a wide semiotic sense) that reflects a macro-action on the level of implied director/implied spectator relationship (chapter 9). In this sense, specific intentions and purposes lend unity to a performance-text and should be conjectured on the grounds not only of specific directorial choices, but also of a thorough knowledge of the values and beliefs attributed to an implied spectator, and through it to a prospective real audience.

The problem is that deviations from a play-script can be detected only against the background of a (widely accepted) interpretation of it, which, being a fundamentally incomplete text, cannot provide any sort of certitude (chapter 6). This claim should be qualified because in many a play-script there exist more textual clues that constrain possible interpretations than theoretically envisaged (Rozik, 1993a: 118–20). Moreover in writing a play-script, a playwright assumedly has a concept of its meaning, its possible performance, and its potential effect on a prospective audience. These are reflected in the particular use of the theatre medium, conventions in particular, and the structure of the fictional world. Therefore, the validity of conclusions that can be drawn through a method of analysis that presupposes its incomplete nature should not be underestimated. Yet due to its nature, total certitude about a playwright's design beyond a learned but never verifiable intuition is ruled out. It is only on such shaky grounds that deviations from a source play-script can be detected.

But this does not imply that a performance-text is exempt from incertitude. Even if it is assumed that it is fully articulated in the theatre medium, and that analysis of its described fictional world is made on firmer grounds, relative indeterminacy still obtains. It is an inherent property of texts and, therefore, hermeneutic interpretation is a necessary complement of reading. The difference resides in either providing the sufficient information for a hermeneutic interpretation to take place or not.

This intertextual method is illustrated here by relating Yerushalmi's *Woyzeck 91*, The Cameri Theatre, 1991 (Yerushalmi), to Büchner's *Woyzeck*. The method presupposes that play-script analysis should precede performance analysis. Quotations are from the English translation of Büchner's *Woyzeck* (1991).

Büchner's *Woyzeck*

The play-script ends in an atrocious act: Woyzeck murders Marie, his mistress, the mother of his child, his only close human being on earth. Notwithstanding, the motivation of this act and its definite meaning are uncertain. It would appear that Woyzeck punishes her for betraying him with Drum-major. However, Woyzeck's contemplative, reflective and poetic nature bestows a profound religious and tragic meaning on his deed, and despite his low characterization, questions such a simplistic interpretation. The murder conveys a sense of protest against a world that has gone astray and a humanity that has forsaken God's image.

Since the playwright did not establish a definite end, Woyzeck's fate is not clear either. There are substantial differences between the two original drafts, each one supporting different possible ends, thus generating different fictional worlds. There are three possible ends: (a) trial and legal execution of Woyzeck, following the journalistic source of the play (Büchner, 1991: viiiff); (b) suicide by drowning in the lake in the draft

251

adopted by the English translation (scene xxiii); and (c) affliction with a sense of guilt and loneliness in the draft adopted by the Hebrew translation (cf. *ibid.*: xxi–xxvi). The playwright did not opt for the end reported in the journals, and none of his creative ends conveys the sense of completion typical of most dramatic structures. In fact, from a thematic perspective, Woyzeck's specific fate is of marginal importance.

Woyzeck is a private who is well-aware of his place in the military and social hierarchy. In front of his superiors he appears extremely submissive, and all abuse him. Among his equals, however, he reveals a feverish quest for meaning; in Marie's terms: 'Thinking's wound his mind like a watch-spring, it'll break one'v these days' (p. 6; cf. p. 14). Despite difficulty in articulating his thoughts, he is highly inquisitive, enjoys an acute sensibility and a kind of poetic language (cf. Steiner: 279ff). Through Biblical quotations, he conveys a sense of imminent doomsday, akin to Büchner's own vision.

Marie's characterization, in contrast, hinges on sheer sexuality and procreation. She takes pride in that (p. 9), and is intensely attracted by Drum-major, equally motivated: 'Christ, I'm going to fill your belly full to drum-majors, sire a whole damn stable of them' (p. 16). The animal metaphors used for their description, such as 'ox' and 'lion', convey not a sense of love, but of affinity between sexuality and animality. While from a bourgeois viewpoint Marie's child is 'illegitimate', for her he is a source of happiness: 'After all, you're only the child of a whore, unlucky thing; 'nd your wicked face just fills your mother's heart with joy' (p. 5). Such a bond does not depend on moral values.

Woyzeck's attitude to Marie is not characterized in terms of love. He provides for her and their child, but does not even look at him (p. 6). Reflecting a spurious Christian ethos, Captain remarks: 'You've got a child without the church's blessing', and Woyzeck answers: 'Sir, God the father isn't going to worry if nobody said amen at the poor worm's making. The Lord said "Suffer little children to come unto me"' (pp. 11–12). He implies thereby that almighty God does not bother with such trifles.

Although Woyzeck's attachment to Marie is disrupted by her infatuation with Drum-major, he actually reacts to Captain who reveals her betrayal and actually incites him to take vengeance (p. 20). Woyzeck fears the loss of his only good on earth: 'Captain, I'm a poor man – I've nothing but her in the world. Please don't make jokes, sir' (*ibid.*). Marie is Woyzeck's 'poor man's lamb' (cf. II Samuel, 12, 1–15) He could have lived with betrayal (scene 4) and accepted her for what she was, like Jesus' attitude to Mary Magdalene; but he cannot stand further dispossession.

At a crucial moment, Woyzeck is exposed to Captain's military–chivalric ethos that, in contrast to true Christianity, assumes that honor can be restored only by death. Killing for reasons of honor is a military specialty. His pretended ethos is thus refuted by his own act of provocation. Woyzeck attempts to fight back at Drum-major, but fails (p. 27). He murders Marie in a state of ecstasy, by repeatedly stabbing her, as if performing a ritual (p. 33). He does not react to her unfaithfulness in the usual sense. He washes her body frantically, a symbol of purification of body and soul.

From Captain's perspective Woyzeck lives with no sense of virtue. In his defense, he claims that virtue is something that the poor cannot afford (p. 12). This may allude to the close affinity between poverty and the Christian ethos. Captain's attitude clearly deviates from the teachings of genuine Christianity. Moreover, the mere presentation of alleged Christian values by an army officer, rather than a more representative alternative such as a priest, suffices to make him the object of the implied spectator's irony. Captain is a hybrid of a spurious preacher and a phony romantic poet.

Doctor represents a different set of values. When Woyzeck urinates against the wall 'like a dog' (p. 13), he rebukes him not in moral terms, but on behalf of an alleged philosophic ethos: 'Man is free, Woyzeck. Man is the ultimate expression of the individual urge to freedom' (*ibid.*). In other words, man is free in nature. Whereas Doctor advocates a quintessential gap between human and animal; he conceives Woyzeck's behavior as consummating the rule of nature, like an animal. While Doctor appears to be motivated by the search for truth, his conclusions are predetermined: he believes that the human will is the essential difference, and his experiments are expected to "demonstrate" this thesis. Therefore, in his eyes, Woyzeck does not refute his theory but, rather, as an abnormal phenomenon, he disqualifies himself for scientific purposes (p. 14). In his pompous pseudo-scientific style, Doctor asks: 'If, gentlemen, I take [. . .] this cat and I throw it out of the window what will be its instinctive behaviour relative to his centre of gravity?' (p. 16) However, when the cat bites and runs away, a further indication of its 'catlike' nature, he refuses to accept the facts and comments: 'Animals have no scientific instincts' (p. 17). In other words, allegedly, both Woyzeck and the cat are 'unscientific', an adjective that cannot be attributed to the world, but only to a method of inquiry. Facts cannot be refuted by theories. Doctor's theory is vitiated by an idealistic pre-judgment.

In contrast to Doctor's blindness, Woyzeck is super-tuned to the world. Whereas Doctor looks at bodily parameters such as pulse, body temperature and muscle contraction, Woyzeck endeavors to reach beyond immediate sensory phenomena. He even attempts to draw Doctor's attention to what lies behind the world of appearances: 'Have you ever seen nature inside-out, Doctor? [. . .] When the world gets so dark you have to feel your way round it with your hands, till you think it's coming apart like a spider's web' (p. 14). But Doctor replies: 'Woyzeck, You've a beautiful aberratio mentalis partialis of the second order' (p. 15). Doctor's pseudo-scientific experimentation is thus contrasted by Woyzeck's poetic sensibility. Doctor's ludicrous characterization lends ironic advantage to Woyzeck's candid and straightforward nature.

In viewing Woyzeck as an accessory of his pseudo-scientific search, Doctor betrays his amoral values. He does not consider that Woyzeck deserves care simply because of being a human being. Instead, he imposes on him a perilous diet of peas merely to explore the borderline between the human and the animal. When Doctor asks Woyzeck to 'wiggle' his ears, he attempts to establish the minimal conditions for human nature to persist: 'There you are, gentlemen, another case of progressive donkeyfi-cation' (p. 17). His anger at any "non-human" gesture reveals his belief that under no circumstances will humanity be lost and that the existential gap with the animal world is unbridgeable.

Doctor is a pre-figuration of the modern dehumanized scientist, the result of a process that culminated in Nazi medical research. Like Captain, Doctor stresses Woyzeck's abnormality. By ironic reversal, Woyzeck becomes a genuine specimen of human nature in his existential refusal to comply with any attempt at reduction on ethical or cognitive grounds. Woyzeck proves human in both his strengths and weaknesses. He is subjected by Captain and Doctor to a process of regression from human to animal nature and, contrary to their expectations, they expose not only that humans are also part of nature, but also that extreme poverty and suffering dehumanizes them. Whereas in killing Marie Woyzeck fulfils Captain's ethical expectations, these rather reflect on the latter's own animal nature. Captain and Doctor, two personifications of the bourgeois distortion of Christian values, consistently weaken Woyzeck's humanity and lead him to commit the crime. If they attempt to throw him out of the window, they should not be surprised that he bites.

What is the implied perspective from which Captain and Doctor are perceived as objects of dramatic irony? Although Woyzeck himself implies an alternative standard, it is the task of Showman at the fair to establish such a viewpoint. Being an outsider of established society lends realistic motivation to his function. He caricatures Doctor by presenting a horse that supposedly enjoys human understanding: 'this animal you see before you [. . .] is a member of all the learned societies and, what's more, a professor at our university' (p. 7). In other words, the horse is an animal that, from the opposite end, is tangential to the borderline between the animal and the human realms and, ironically, questions thereby the ideal-istic attitude that endorses an existential gap between them. The horse thus mirrors Doctor's ludicrous attempt to show, to his own learned audience, a human who by regressive means can only be tangential to this boundary.

Whereas Doctor attempts to demonstrate that even under the most severe conditions this borderline cannot be breached, Showman attempts to demonstrate the opposite. While serious research is not his trade, mockery is. Woyzeck and the horse get too dangerously close to one another for an idealistic taste. Both diverge from their own basic nature, while having something essential in common: nature. Contrary to bourgeois expectation, both evacuate (defecate and urinate) in public (something that 'is not done') and declare thereby the priority of their natural needs. Woyzeck's urination thus reflects Doctor's failure, and forebodes the murder of Marie.

Showman quite explicitly establishes an alternative viewpoint. 'The message is: Man, be natural. You were fashioned out of dust, out of sand, out of mud – would you be anything more than dust, sand, mud?' (p. 8). In other words, humans cannot avoid the materiality of their own bodies. Woyzeck is part of nature and any attempt to demonstrate that ethos prevails under conditions of extreme starvation and suffering is bound to fail. The implication is that humanity and dehumanization cannot coexist.

Captain too becomes the object of Showman's ironic perspective. He presents a monkey as the highest achievement of culture, a result of '[a]rt improving on nature' (p. 6). The monkey is also supposed to have crossed the borderline between the animal and human realms and reached the rank of soldier, which is declared the lowest degree of humanity: 'our monkey's a soldier. – Not that that's much. Lowest form of animal life in fact' (p. 6). The ironic innuendo that pervades the entire scene is most poignantly expressed by 'a voice sung', a personification of Death:

On earth is no abiding stay,
All things living pass away –
No-one, no-one says me nay. (p. 6)

This piece of Silenus' wisdom is a reminder that man is dust, part of cyclic nature and bound for death; and that this existential truth is absolute.

The fair thus constitutes an interpretive stage metaphor. People who come to the fair to entertain themselves by watching freaks of nature are prepared to pay for watching the animal in the human and vice versa. While Doctor allegedly seeks the truth, Showman deliberately exploits curiosity and pokes fun at science. The scientific interest in Woyzeck, far from being a reflection of divine wisdom, thus proves a pretentious version of sheer curiosity and an object of irony. The fair is thus an ironic stage metaphor of the bourgeois ideology.

Showman, however, is not a straightforward reflection of Büchner's attitude. It is the interaction between the images of army/science and fair that conveys his viewpoint. Beyond this, the ultra-serious moralistic attitude of the implied playwright is perceived, which can be put as follows:

humanity can be neither extricated from nature nor reduced to pure spirituality; therefore, it cannot prevail under conditions of extreme deprivation, dispossession and constant humiliation. Consistent disregard of fundamental human needs necessarily undermines human nature.

The play-script is not confined to the social meaning of Woyzeck's action, but also aims at its religious implications. Büchner designed Marie following the model of the remorseful Mary Magdalene. Like the saintly prototype, Marie too is haunted by compunction and frequently cries; she even quotes Magdalene's description in Luke 7, 38: 'And she stood at his feet behind him weeping, and began to wash his feet with tears and did wipe them with the hairs of her head, and kissed his feet and anointed them with ointment' (p. 30). She also quotes the story of the adulterous wife in John 8, 3–11: 'And the scribes and the pharisees brought unto him a woman taken in adultery, and set her in the midst . . . And Jesus said unto her, Neither do I condemn thee. Go, and sin no more' (p. 29). Both passages reflect the early Christian view that even a prostitute and an adulterous woman are entitled to forgiveness and redemption. It would appear that Woyzeck, who shows affinity to the teachings of the Church, and by implication can be seen as modeled on the image of Jesus, should have pardoned Marie; but he pays no heed to her regret. The murder can thus be viewed as a purposeful deviation from the Biblical narrative. However, against the background of his religious characterization, the murder should be understood as an act of rebellion of a forsaken man.

In Woyzeck's view the poor have no chance in any of God's worlds: 'If we went to heaven I expect they'd put us to work on the thunder' (p. 12). Poverty is thus viewed as an absolute and transcendental fate, as an indication that the world is under absurd rule. Therefore, whoever is responsible for human poverty cannot be a true Christian, and a world of extreme poverty cannot be said to be a world of God. During the action Woyzeck clearly undergoes a fundamental change: from Christian belief to heresy. Giving his sister's cross and his mother's holy picture to Andres (p. 30) should be understood not as a mere execution of his will before death, but as an act of rupture with his own religious upbringing and faith. He leaves these symbols of belief to Andres, knowing well that it is not he who is about to die: 'When the carpenter collects his shavings for the box, no-one knows whose head'll lie on them' (*ibid.*). It is rather that something has died within himself. The murder thus becomes a sign of a final rift with the world and its alleged God.

Only because Woyzeck is made to undergo the experience the absurd, can the absurdity of the murder be understood. More than punishing Marie, he feels that he has been victimized by social and divine order and, therefore, revolts against them. It follows that the playwright's own criticism of this order is precisely conveyed by both Woyzeck's change of religious attitude and the act of murder. At this point the ironic perspective of Showman and the serious one of Woyzeck converge to express Büchner's discontent. In his view, the bourgeois version of established Christianity has become anti-Christian and the world of God – the world of Satan.

The play-script is structured as a morality play. This is most evident in the *dramatis personae* that personify typical ideas and attitudes, thus reflecting the way the playwright maps the human world. Woyzeck is confronted with Doctor and Captain who represent two basic and reductive bourgeois attitudes, and both are caricaturized, which is a statement of criticism in itself. By reversal, Woyzeck, initially the object of irony, eventually personifies the critical attitude of the playwright.

The main difference between *Woyzeck* and a medieval morality play resides in the inversion of structure and refutation of the values accepted by the implied spectator. As in the traditional morality play, Büchner attempts to 'teach' the implied spectator a new fundamental truth that, in this case, is meant to overthrow conventional truisms; i.e., rather than reinforcing the audience's faith, the play strives to undermine it. Moreover, in contrast to the medieval morality play, the values at stake only pretend to be Christian. Büchner leads Woyzeck to do exactly the opposite of what Jesus would have done, while deriving justification from the very same tradition. In this sense, although in an inverted version, Woyzeck is a reincarnation of crucified Jesus, a modern Christ in the *Via Dolorosa* of the dispossessed.

Woyzeck is characterized as a natural poet–philosopher–prophet who is haunted by the feeling that 'the time is out of joint' (*Hamlet*: I, v, 189). His predicament should be conceived as a dramatization of an inner struggle among various constituents of the human soul. If all the elements of the human psyche, which are personified in other characters, are separated from Woyzeck, as in *Everyman*, only the personification of a humiliated and dispossessed is left. He is personified humanity in a dehumanized world; a subversive and modernist 'everyman'.

Yerushalmi's *Woyzeck 91*

Against the background of the previous interpretation, and under the assumption of an intertextual relation between these two texts, Yerushalmi's production *Woyzeck 91* is examined as a set of choices preserving and departing from the fictional world of the source play-script (Rozik: 2000b).

Yerushalmi directed *Woyzeck 91* for three years, showing her work to the public 'in progress', in three series of performances. The present analysis refers to a performance-text from the second series in 1991–92, at Beith Zionei America, Tel Aviv (for synopsis see chapter 11). Initially, she employed Ada ben Nakhum's Hebrew translation, which closely followed that by Shimon Zandbank, but the final dialogue was a free adaptation.

Like its source intertext, *Woyzeck 91* dramatizes the despicable murder of Marie. Both texts aimed at an absurd outcome because, from an ironic viewpoint, both killer and victim are characterized as innocent characters. Moreover, both put the murder in the context of Doctor and Captain's dehumanizing motives that exacerbate its absurdity.

The performing area was a large rectangular space. The audience, seated on a scaffolding amphitheatre, occupied approximately half of it, while the rest, in the shape of a large flat square at floor level, was left for the acting. The almost empty stage – featuring only a skeleton, a cart, a white screen, two white tables and two slide-projectors – created the visual image of a hospital ward or a classroom in a medical school. In some scenes, Doctor (played by an actress) and the students wore typical white gowns. This image was complemented by scientific lectures, examinations, and slide projections of bodily organs.

In other scenes, the same actors created the image of an army barrack (hall, square or canteen). The tavern scene in the play-script was relocated to the army canteen. In these scenes Doctor and students wore military uniforms that did not identify any particular army. Throughout the performance, in contrast, Captain wore a uniform reminiscent of a Nazi officer. Being a working private, Woyzeck wore army fatigues and a cap down to his ears, which lent an expression of stupidity to his face. The image of an army was also conveyed by the characters' routines, on both the physical level (drill, gymnastics, karate exercises and marching to the sound of drums) and the vocal level (military-like orders in gibberish). Both dividing and connecting the spoken scenes, the soldiers marched in straight lines and turned at right angles, following an invisible grid, thereby creating images of masculinity and military might.

Although the combination of academic and military images could be explained in naturalistic terms, as soldiers engaged in military research, it actually conveyed a sense of criminal complicity between military aggressiveness and scientific experimentation. Woyzeck, as the victim of this alliance, was ab-used as a laboratory mouse; e.g., in a very shocking scene his penis was milked for a specimen of his semen (chapter 11). This joint image thus created a non-naturalistic or, rather, thematic space.

The conjunction of academic and military images was rhythmically interwoven with action scenes, originating in the play-script. Although the dialogue was drastically abridged, the natural order of the narrative and its component scenes were basically preserved. Yerushalmi kept the most effective bits of dialogue either for their relevance to the action or their poetic beauty. Other scenes fulfilling interpretive functions were also preserved, but subordinated to the new theme and concept of the fictional world. Their original location in the play-script was quite disregarded.

In general, Yerushalmi preserved the original characterization, but nuanced the nature of the relations between Woyzeck and Marie, and between Marie and Drum-major. Whereas in regard to Woyzeck Marie initially produced images of human tenderness and warmth, in the company of Drum-major she projected images of sheer eroticism and violence. Marie was clearly seen to be caught in the mesh of human instincts verging on animality.

Liora Malka addresses the paradoxical combination of tenderness and brutality in Woyzeck's attitude to Marie in the murder scene of *Woyzeck 91*, which leaves 'a touching yet shocking impression' (p. 29). While Woyzeck was caressing Marie's face with one hand, with the other he stabbed her. Malka observes that the murder scene is the only intimate moment in the performance-text against the background of other violent scenes. She correctly contends that this duality is rooted in the nature of human intimacy, and that the production manipulates the concept of 'intimacy' that the spectator brings to the event (p. 37). How does this paradoxical scene contribute to the overall meaning of the performance-text? It probably reflects the human/animal duality to which Woyzeck is driven by criminal abuse.

Woyzeck's fate, which is not fully determined in the play-script, was recreated by Yerushalmi through a puppet show performed in the lobby/bar during the interval. This show hinted at the ending of the story as reported in contemporary newspapers that, supposedly, had inspired Büchner: the execution of the murderer. In this interlude, puppets in the guise of skeletons enacted Woyzeck and Marie. A storyteller, in showman's garments and accompanied by an accordionist, related the story in mocking recitation, while the skeletons mimed the narrative, including sexual intercourse, until Woyzeck's decapitation. This addition reinforced the morality play nature of the source play-script. The contrast between the upsetting action and the frivolity and black humor of Showman was probably meant to produce a grotesque effect.

Yerushalmi probably hinted at this ending for avoiding the ambiguity that characterizes both Büchner's own versions. The performance-text actually ended with Woyzeck washing his hands, possibly at the lake, and subsequently collapsing onto the long white table placed downstage, while projecting an image of defeat and helplessness, before dying. The nurse washed his body, just as he had washed Marie in the play-script, and covered it with a white sheet, as in a Jewish burial ritual. The image of 'washing his hands' was probably not meant to evoke Pontius Pilate's plea of innocence; an association that is difficult to expect from Israeli spectators, because the Jewish tradition associates washing the hands and the dead not with protestation of innocence but with purification.

This performance-text marginalized the motif of 'Christian belief'. Particularly interesting was the omission of allusions to Mary Magdalene and the adulterous woman. Although this omission could be explained by the Jewish unfamiliarity with these narratives, in fact, Israeli drama abounds in allusions to the New Testament. Yerushalmi too created a striking Christian image: Woyzeck under the scrutiny of students/soldiers was held head down and arms stretched, in an image of an inverted crucified Jesus (chapter 11).

An inverted image of Crucified Jesus in Yerushalmi's *Woyzeck 91.*
Courtesy of the Itim Theatre.

Whereas the drill images could have been perceived as illustrations of Woyzeck's military milieu, the addition and interpolation of several mini-lectures constituted a major departure from the play-script and thus offered a firm indication of Yerushalmi's intentions and purposes. These lectures, in plain scientific prose, seasoned with Latin terms, were excerpts from medical textbooks. They stressed the academic image, and their proliferation indicated their central thematic function. They were given either by Doctor or students at her request, and illustrated by slides projections on the wall. They focused on anatomical and physiological aspects of bodily organs and even psychological 'mechanisms' were explained in physiological terms. They reflected a 'positivist' ideology: the belief that the human being is a wonderful mechanism that can be fully understood only by a no less wonderful science, and a profound admiration for the wisdom embodied in evolution, crowned by the ascent of man.

Doctor, Captain and Soldiers/students in Yerushalmi's *Woyzeck 91*.
Courtesy of the Itim Theatre. Photo: Israel Haramaty.

The themes of these mini-presentations were: peas and genetics (Mendel), the heart, the female and male organs of reproduction, natural selection and evolution, human will vs. nature, insemination, the skeleton, the neural system, feelings, dreaming, pain, the mind, digestion, blood circulation, the thumb and index finger in human evolution, and the brain. Whereas in some cases the connection between lecture and dramatic action was not at all clear, in others it could be easily detected; e.g., the presentation on the urinary system was next to Woyzeck's urination on the wall, and the lecture on the blood system to the murder scene. However, beyond such obvious links, a deeper relation could be perceived: the ironic disproportion between the human being, perceived as a wonderfully designed machine, and Woyzeck's lot, which attested to the inability of scientific methodology to account for human nature. Description in terms of hormones, for example, could hardly explain the human warmth emanating from Woyzeck's disposition toward Marie.

261

Captain, Soldier/student and Heart in Yerushalmi's *Woyzeck 91*.
Courtesy of the Itim Theatre. Photo: Israel Haramaty.

The main objective of these presentations was to place evolution at the focal point of the production. The theory of evolution was proposed 22 years after Büchner's death in 1837: Darwin published his *On the Origins of Species* in 1859 and *The Descent of Man* in 1871. The same applies to Mendel, who published his findings in genetics, based on his experimentation on peas, in 1866. Yerushalmi disregarded historical facts and created a new fictional world, in which the motif of evolution comes to the fore and the motifs of poverty and religion became marginal.

In Yerushalmi's interpretation of the original fair scene, a half-naked soldier represented the march of evolution by walking the length of the long table placed in front of the audience, while miming a gradual transmutation from ape to human being. This was performed in front of students/ soldiers, who donned masks of professors, in the image of Albert Einstein, while speaking Hebrew with a heavy German accent. When the march came to an end, they asked the ape/man to demonstrate his ability to kill people. Miming a soldier – the 'lowest form of animal life' (p. 6) – he fired a machine-gun at the audience. The alleged ascent of man, the accomplishment of "glorious" evolution, was thus reduced to mere caricature.

In contrast to Büchner's Doctor, who views nature as the enemy of man, Yerushalmi's Doctor was a champion of nature and its wonderful mechanism of evolution. All the mini-lectures reflected a sense of admiration for the achievements of 'natural selection' in ensuring the dominance of humankind as the superior species. Ironically, this superiority in the natural world was achieved precisely by the human ability to produce ever deadlier weapons.

The mini-lecture on evolution was followed by a dance of the academic/military group who performed a series of contorted images of sexual intercourse. The mixed couples interchanged every few seconds until eventually men were dancing with men and women with women. The ironic innuendo was clear: while evolution proceeds by mechanisms of procreation and is indifferent to the values of monogamy and faithfulness, homosexual couplings totally upset the evolution formula, because of disconnecting sexuality from procreation, and thus from evolution. Homosexual and lesbian relations, therefore, undermine Doctor's fascination for the wisdom embodied in evolution in its relentless drive to improve species through natural selection.

Subsequently, the group crowded around Marie and Drum-major, who performed a highly erotic and violent dance. She was half-naked and he was wearing a horse skull mask, probably symbolizing animal sex and death. Similarly to the previous dance, the distortion of the sexual images and the music reflected a grotesque design, probably also meant to undermine Doctor's fascination.

The centrality of the 'evolution' theme indicates that intention was, first, to update the image of science typical of Büchner's days, and recreate the play-script in terms accessible to a modern audience; second, to denounce the criminal partnership between science and militarism in the application of scientific selection to the human sphere; and third, to manipulate fears that can be aroused by science at the service of military ends and totalitarian regimes. In her research, Doctor implied the possibility of pushing evolution a step further, in an attempt to create a race of supermen. Synchronously, Captain spoke of a super-race in Nazi terms. The combination of images of scientific research and Nazism was meant to recall the tragic era of scientific experimentation with human beings, which aimed at the improvement of an allegedly superior race at the expense of an allegedly inferior one. For any synchronic audience, the Nazi application of 'scientific selection' to the human sphere, an aberration of Darwinism, had proved both criminal and disastrous.

This performance-text revealed a clear tendency to lend a grotesque character to the fictional world through the comic treatment of some of its most dreadful scenes. This was most conspicuous in the mute scenes, added by Yerushalmi to the play-script. For the end of the performance Yerushalmi designed a banqueting scene: at one end of the long table in front of the audience, a cook dished out spaghetti. While all engaged in eagerly eating them, Woyzeck was left to his peas. While Doctor, standing on the table, lectured on the organs of digestion, Captain indulged in nostalgic reminiscences of his childhood. The scene developed into a series of distorted images of eating spaghetti, which gradually changed into a contorted dance to a grotesque tune, which brought the grotesque mood to paroxysm.

The scene ended with a duet by Doctor and Captain in which they bluntly expressed their views. Whereas Doctor praised man as the jewel in the crown of evolution, Captain, riding skates, indulged in a series of totalitarian slogans; e.g., 'All people should unite to create a single soul, a single thought, a single will, for the sake of materializing the objectives of humanity'; 'Do not forsake the flag that was bestowed upon us by God'; and 'It is the willingness to die for mankind that makes our country immortal.' In their contrapuntal duet, while Doctor proclaimed the greatness of the human being, Captain made science subservient to the annihilation of human creatures. Eventually, the voice of Captain predominated, thereby creating an image of final subordination of science to militarism; i.e., to the basest animal drives. All sang a (fictional) national anthem. The image of defeated Woyzeck dying on the table thus became a metaphor of the sacrifice of humankind on the altar of this evil alliance.

From a rhetoric perspective, both Büchner's and Yerushalmi's texts were acts of criticism or, rather, protest against the outbreak of absurdity in the world. However, although both texts point at the same agents of abuse – the scientific and military establishments – their specific objects of criticism were totally different. Whereas Büchner aimed at denouncing human exploitation on the grounds of class and religious ideologies, Yerushalmi aimed at exposing the criminal complicity of the scientific and military establishments in undermining humankind's well-being. Unfortunately, the last centuries have experienced this dreadful complicity. Paradoxically, humans themselves collude against humanity. Irony is thus cast on the idea of evolution itself. Essentially, humankind remains in the animal kingdom.

On the level of the expected effect on the audience, while Büchner intended his criticism to shock contemporary bourgeois audiences, Yerushalmi's criticism could have been willingly adopted by an Israeli or any other contemporary audience. In contrast to the play-script, which clearly aimed at refuting opinions and attitudes conceived as truisms by its implied reader/spectator, the purpose of this performance-text was to bring about the reaffirmation of opinions and attitudes already valid for it. Whereas Büchner aimed at an experience of absurdity, Yerushalmi intended an experience of harmony with held beliefs. The reaffirmation of an absurdist attitude is certainly more complex and problematic, since it does not satisfy the human existential longing for total order.

Assumedly, however, that there is some kind of comfort in reaffirmation itself.

Yerushalmi subordinated both preserving and diverging choices to the theme of criminal complicity between science and militarism and the negation both theories of scientific selection and totalitarian ideologies. This directorial decision resulted in a new interpretation of the original narrative; i.e., in a new fictional world. Could the same conclusions have been reached if departures of *Woyzeck 91* from the play-script had been ignored? In principle, this is possible. Nonetheless, this albeit circuitous procedure provides independent evidence with respect to the possible intentions and purposes of an implied director, thus offering a useful tool for confirming or refuting conclusions reached by intuition or other means of analysis. Although typical real spectators are usually not expected to rely on inter-textuality, unless the source play-script is well known to them, the implied spectator is familiar with it by definition. It should be remembered, however, that although implied intentions and purposes are assumed for any work of art, their precise determination remains a matter of interpretation forever.

18

Methodological Conclusions

The aim of this study is to propose a theory of theatre and a method of performance analysis. This theory suggests a limited set of major principles that explain the generation of theatre meaning through the specific encounter between a performance-text and an implied spectator. While endorsing the basic premises of traditional theatre semiotics in regard to the textual nature of the theatre performance, it also partly supports the criticism leveled at it during the last decades for overlooking additional and vital principles that structure such texts, the (implied) spectator's crucial contribution to the generation of theatre meaning in particular. An attempt has also been made to provide an appropriate method of performance analysis, capable of coping with the complexity of the performance-text.

Against the background of the fundamental function of the theatre medium in generating theatre meaning, without which any further structuration is precluded, this theory suggests additional poetic, aesthetic, and rhetoric structural strata. The performance-text thus reflects a complex deep structure, of which the semiotic stratum is, albeit vital, only one of its components. Each stratum thus requires a particular method of research. It also analyzes the crucial interaction between implied director and implied spectator in providing vital associations and psychical mechanisms for theatre meaning to emerge.

The notion of 'theatricality' applies to the use of the theatre medium, in the sense of imprinting images on matter similar to their models, mediation of language and deflection of reference, for the purpose of describing fictional worlds; i.e., for producing theatre works of art. The implication is that the theatre medium can also be used in other arts (e.g., opera, cinema and TV drama) and non-artistic domains (e.g., advertising).

The complexity of the performance-text poses an enormous difficulty and challenge for any method of performance analysis, because the overall

266

structure determines the function of all the subordinated sub-structures, while each structural level determines the functions of all their component units. However, in contrast to some theories, and despite complexity, this study reflects a profound belief that a method of performance analysis is not only viable, but also beneficial in revealing the theatre mechanisms of generating meaning.

Aims of performance analysis

Different aims of performance analysis result in different methods. In recent years, various aims have been suggested or implied, such as (a) synthesis of a performance-text's meaning based on prior analysis, and as the latter's natural complement; (b) preservation of productions for future generations through accounts by scholars who have actually watched them live; and (c) reconstruction of unknown performance-texts, based on scanty verbal descriptions in secondary verbal sources, clues in play-scripts and/or limited graphic documentation. All these aims are valid, viable, and probably fulfil vital functions in the discourse of a cultural community.

In contrast, this study set a different aim, without belittling the importance of others: the understanding of theatre's mechanisms of generating meaning and its particular way of thinking and communicating thinking. Comprehension of these mechanisms is a precondition for directors to create efficacious performance-texts, and for spectators to read, interpret and experience them. Obviously, these mechanisms are perceived and mastered intuitively by directors and spectators; otherwise the achievements of theatre art throughout the millennia would be inconceivable. There is a need, however, for a methodology to constantly probe such intuitions. I suggest that a generative theory and a sound method of performance analysis can and should derive from this aim.

The achievement of any of these aims presupposes analysis and requires the translation of performance-texts into language, which is the common meta-language of culture in general and scholarship in particular (cf. Rokem, 2000: 1). It may be argued that although this is a widespread practice, it is difficult to see the point of translation and analysis, since the uniqueness of a work of art lies in the specificity and perfect combination of all its elements, which is impaired by them. Nonetheless, since people usually do not communicate or interact through the theatre medium, and due to the extreme complexity of the performance-text, translation and analysis are justified and even mandatory for integrating theatre experiences into the discourse of a cultural community. Do translation and analysis enable a better understanding of the theatre medium and theatre

267

art? A performance analysis, whose aim is to explore the singularity of thinking through experiencing theatre performances, does.

Means of performance analysis

The Performance Analysis Working Group, of the International Federation of Theatre Research, was established with the explicit intention to produce a sound method of performance analysis. It set three fundamental conditions for each specific analysis: a theoretical focus, a personal experience and the use of a video recording, which I fully implemented in my own analyses (chapters 13–17). In addition, I suggest three additional conditions: an abridged account of an entire performance-text, an intuition of the structure and meaning of the whole text, and an independent performance analysis.

(A) *Theoretical focus*: This condition reflects a rejection of intuitive analyses of performance-texts, and a commitment to scientific analysis. Furthermore, it implies criticism of traditional semiotics in its attempts to suggest methods arrived at by deduction from pre-existing theories. Instead, it advocates a method based on induction from a body of specific performance analyses and constant negotiation with pre-established principles; i.e., it reflects the intention to employ analyses of specific performance-texts to probe pre-existing and widely accepted theories, rather than using such texts to illustrate them, and to suggest alternative principles if and when necessary.

As suggested above, the object of performance-analysis is to reveal the principles that explain the generation of theatre meaning, through semiotic, poetic, aesthetic and rhetoric structural principles. These principles, even if arrived at inductively, should always be employed critically, and their validity verified constantly. For example, from a semiotic perspective, it would appear that performance-texts are transparent; i.e., that they can be read intuitively, because of the principle of similarity underlying iconicity. However, performance analysis shows that this principle does not apply to all forms of theatre semiosis, such as real objects on stage and stage conventions. A critical approach should thus lead to a continuous reformulation of theatre theory (chapter 1).

Unfortunately, while presupposing the validity of theory, strict scientific analysis is usually considered too demanding, requiring excessive learning effort. The current tendency is, therefore, to prefer intuitive analysis. However, there is no contradiction between intuitive and scientific analysis. Due to the utter complexity of performance-texts, intuitive analysis should not be dismissed altogether, and theoretical competence should be employed for verification of its conclusions. Sheer intuition should be left to the real spectator.

(B) *Personal experience*: Performance analysis should be conducted on the basis of a personal experience because, first, the non-mediated experience of a trained scholar is more acceptable than generalizations such as 'the audience is', 'the spectators react' and the like, usually employed without much foundation. The typical notion of a 'real' audience or 'spectator' is a cultural construct influenced by conventional concepts, usually based on journalistic or scientific sociology. Although scholars are actually real spectators, they are closest to the implied ones in satisfying the expected competences and psychical mechanisms of performance-texts. Moreover, they should train themselves to explore the nature of the implied spectator, also a textual construct, reflecting what is required for a performance-text to make sense. The study of a real audience should be left to reception analysis (chapter 11).

Second, the introspective examination of a trained scholar should be employed for probing forms of empiric research based on questionnaires addressed to real spectators. There is no reason for preferring responses of untrained spectators, even if surveyed in large groups, because the theatre experience may also involve unconscious contents.

Third, a scholar's personal experience should serve as a corrective for either a scientific or intuitive analysis of a performance-text, which relies on secondary sources, such as journalist critiques. In general, personal experience makes a crucial difference between performance analysis, in the sense of this study, and historic reconstruction of performances, based on scanty descriptions and/or documentation.

(C) *Use of video recording*: The use of a recording of a performance-text for a performance analysis, against the background of the persistent criticism against it, requires explanation. Fischer-Lichte correctly notes that the main problem of the performance-text is its ephemeral nature (pp. 171–2); therefore, there is a need for an appropriate correlate (notation or video) for verifying the conclusions of any analysis. Although a video recording is certainly a poor substitute of the real thing, in conjunction with (usually repeated) personal experiences it can become a useful tool. While personal experience may provide dimensions that cannot be reproduced by a video recording, the latter can preserve features that have been forgotten or simply overlooked. Therefore, under no circumstances should a performance analysis be conducted solely by means of either video or personal experience. If a video recording is the only object of analysis, one enters the realm of reconstruction with all its limitations. Since personal experience has its limitations too, it is the combination of both that is rewarding. In the last years, growing experience in performance analysis reveals that video recording has become an indispensable tool of research.

(D) *Abridged account*: If the aim of a performance analysis is to understand the specific mechanism of generating theatre meaning, its reader should not be expected to have experienced a performance of the production under scrutiny. Moreover, in order to facilitate an understanding of the way a scholar arrived at certain conclusions, and enable an independent assessment of the analytical procedure, a reader needs to know what actually happened on stage; i.e., the context of the specific components that have been analyzed. Each performance analysis should include, therefore, an abridged description of an entire performance-text (cf. Rokem, 2000: 1). Additional graphic materials, such as photos and diagrams, can also contribute to the fulfillment of this function. Rokem correctly contends that a performance analysis aims at 'the theoretical implications in view of possible application to other works' (*ibid.*).

(E) *Intuition of structure and meaning*: Because of its highly complex structure, a full analysis of all the mechanisms of a particular performance-text is an enormous enterprise, and tantamount to reconsideration of an entire theory. Needless to say, the scope of a single article precludes such an analysis. Moreover, if the aim is to understand all possible mechanisms of generating meaning, which assumedly recur in many a performance-text, a full analysis is also superfluous. Therefore, each analysis of a performance-text should focus on a single mechanism, while examining whether it supports an established theoretical principle or challenges it; and whether it should be redefined or replaced. Moreover, due to the structural complexity of a performance-text, the description of fictional worlds in particular, and the structural dominance of the overall structure, which determines the hierarchical contributions of its components, focus on a single principle requires at least an intuition of its whole structure and meaning, including its possible effect on a particular implied spectator (chapters 10 and 11).

It may be assumed, therefore, that, logically, the design of a performance-text starts from the ultimate impact planned for an implied spectator, which is a construct that reflects a real author's intuition of a real audience (chapter 11). Accordingly, a performance analysis too should start from a scholarly intuition of the ultimate effect planned for a specific implied audience. Partial analysis can also be used to support such an intuition, or reveal that it should be replaced by another.

(F) *Independent performance analysis*: If the intention of the analysis of a performance-text is to trigger an inductive theoretical momentum, there is no point in relying on previous critiques and/or analyses of it. This reservation also applies to all the relevant secondary sources, including generalizations about the playwright, director, style and period. A performance analysis should, therefore, be conducted prior to any exposure to other sources. Moreover, an independent analysis should be used to probe pre-established generalizations, and secondary sources can be used subsequently to check conclusions arrived at independently. Generalizations should be based solely on a substantial body of performance analyses, but under no circumstances employed in a deductive manner. At most, deductive procedures should be used as possible theses among others. All generalizations should be re-examined continuously and used, if at all, critically.

The disciplines of performance analysis

The aim of a performance-text is to describe a (fictional) world and affect thereby an (implied) spectator, who shares in generating its meaning; and the aim of performance analysis is to understand the mechanisms that enable directors to achieve their ends, and spectators to experience theatre artifacts. The disciplines relevant to performance analysis are, therefore, determined by the complex structure of the theatre experience. The notion of 'structure' applies on three levels, which in order of decreasing dominance are: the outer relationship between performance-text and spectator, the inner structure of a fictional world, and the semiotic structure of the theatre medium.

(A) *The outer structural level*: The relation between a fictional world and an (implied) spectator is the dominant structural level, because it reflects the ultimate intentions and purposes of an (implied) director. Performance-texts reveal a rhetoric deep structure, of the enthymematic kind, because of their underlying intention is to persuade spectators and affect their perceptions of the world (chapter 9). Therefore, all the structural layers – the ironic, aesthetic and metaphoric in particular – are subordinated to this rhetoric intent.

Rhetoric analysis should be made on a synchronic basis, because any definite effect can be envisaged not for any possible implied or real audience, but only for a specific one. Such an effect should be conjectured not only on the grounds of universal patterns of response, but also of specific established values and cultural baggage that determine the spectators' expectations and contributions.

Whereas the rhetoric intentions underlying descriptions of fictional

271

worlds are usually not articulated in performance-texts, they are implied in the specific enthymematic structures that generate fictional worlds; e.g., the intention of criticizing held views and even changing the attitudes of an audience in regard to a particular social, political or religious issue (chapter 10). Determination of macro-intentions and purposes is a matter of structural interpretation.

The relevant discipline on this level should be a particular version of rhetoric, which is appropriate to theatre studies, developed in the context of speech act theory. Such a discipline should be able to cope also with the ironic, aesthetic and metaphoric sub-structures that also operate on the outer structural level of relation between performance-text and audience. I note that 'irony' and 'metaphor' were already central topics in classical rhetoric. Theories of non-verbal irony and metaphor of textual scope, and a specific version of rhetoric capable of dealing with non-verbal texts, theatre performances in particular, should be developed (chapters 8 & 9).

(B) *The inner structural level*: The study of structures of fictional worlds should definitely not be seen as an exclusive privilege of literary theory. Since described fictional worlds are a vital component of the overall rhetoric mechanism of a performance-text, performance analysis should also engage in the analysis of them. A fictional world is definitely designed to fulfill its rhetoric function on the outer structural level.

On this level, the most relevant discipline is poetics, in the sense of a theory of the structures of fictional worlds. As suggested above, a fictional world features a five-layered structure, each layer superimposed upon the other. In order of decreasing dominance, these are: the aesthetic, the ironic, the naive, the praxical and the mythical, with each layer requiring different principles of analysis (chapter 7). Whereas the mythical and praxical layers, which are ethically neutral, are revealed by stripping off key terms and sentences that connect actions to specific cognitive/ethical systems, such as religions, philosophies and ideologies, the ethical naïve and ironic layers require focus on these terms, whether voiced by the characters themselves (naïve) or by functional characters (ironic), with the latter bestowing meaning on the former. The dominant nature of the aesthetic layer on this level requires the development of a specific version of theatre aesthetics (chapter 7).

(C) *The semiotic level*: A fictional world, structured by poetic principles, requires a language/medium for its description and communication. On this level, the notion of 'structure' applies to the system of signifieds of the theatre medium. This system is mediated by language, which is the main repository of abstractions in any human culture, and is structured to the extent that language in itself is. The notion of 'structure' also applies to iconic syntax, which is also mediated by the syntax of language (chapter 1).

The notion of 'analysis' presupposes the possible segmentation of performance-texts. A crucial task of a method of performance analysis is, therefore, to establish the principles of segmentation and suggest the means for their application. It is on the level not of the iconic sign, but of the iconic sentence/icon that segmentation for performance analysis should be carried out (chapter 2). The iconic sentence is the most complex unit that the theatre medium can generate, and the basic unit of the description of a fictional world. An icon is a configuration of iconic sentences, mediated by verbal nouns. Since a fictional world is a set of characters and their interaction, the typical iconic sentence is a description of a verbal or non-verbal act/action (chapter 2).

In theatre, iconic sentences may be either literal or metaphoric (chapter 3) and either transparent or mediated by stage conventions (chapter 4). Such iconic sentences are descriptions of (fictional entities) through deflection of reference (chapter 5).

The relevant discipline on this level is semiotics, in the sense of a general theory of signification and communication, theatre semiotics in particular. Since the aim of performance analysis is to understand the principles through which this medium generates theatre meaning, a method of performance analysis presupposes first and foremost mastery of this medium (chapters 1–6).

(D) *Intertextual relations*: The relation between a pre-existing play-script (source-text) and a performance-text (target-text) based on it should be conceived in terms of 'intertextuality' (chapter 6). It follows that performance analysis should also take into account play analysis, especially if the play-script is known to the audience.

Play-scripts too are texts generated by the theatre medium, although notated only through language (chapter 6). Therefore, from a theatrical viewpoint a play-script is a deficient text because it lacks the non-verbal indicators that determine the nature of each speech act, thus precluding analysis of dialogue, in the sense of verbal interaction, on firm grounds. Since in every production of a play-script the verbal component usually remains unchanged, it is clear that the non-verbal components condition the specific nature of a verbal interaction. Therefore, whereas performance analysis should pay special attention to these non-verbal components, from a theatrical viewpoint, play analysis must reflect awareness of the fundamental indeterminacy of play-scripts.

Directors create innovative performance-texts by presupposing new premises that, although generating the same wordings, change the nature

273

of verbal interactions and thus the nature of fictional worlds. Due to the intertextual relations between performance-texts and play-scripts, detection of directorial choices – i.e., what has been preserved, changed or added – provide vital clues to directors' intentions and purposes (chapter 6).

Since both play-scripts and performance-texts are generated by the same theatre medium, despite the anomaly of the former, the relevant disciplines of such an intertextual analysis are basically the same. I suggest that the analysis of intertextual relations between a diachronic target performance-text and a source play-script should be based on previous separate synchronic analyses of them. Such relations entail that play-analysis is of utmost relevance to theatre research.

(E) *Implied dialogue director/spectator:* The deep structure of a performance-text reveals a dialogue between an implied director and an implied spectator (chapter 11). Since the implied director is a construct, reflected in the specific choices of a real director for the description of a fictional world, the relevant disciplines are semiotic, poetic, aesthetic and rhetoric, including the study of creative interpretation. Accordingly, since the implied spectator too is a construct, defined by the actual competences and mechanisms required for reading, interpreting and experiencing a performance-text as expected, the relevant disciplines are the same, including the study of hermeneutic interpretation. 'Hermeneutic interpretation' presupposes the competence of providing the relevant associative elements from the implied spectator's own resources. The implied spectator's 'experience' presupposes its cognitive, ethical and emotive competences. For an implied director, the presupposition of such competences constitutes a kind of theatre technology or, rather, a set of intuitions regarding the way fictional worlds affect real spectators (chapters 10 & 11).

Since real directors usually declare their intentions through language, which is not necessarily their privileged medium, and these intentions are usually couched in dated theories of theatre, it is the scholar's task to rephrase them in updated theoretical terms. Since performance-texts do not necessarily materialize every directorial intention, and such declarations may be misleading, an additional task should be to employ them critically; meaning that only against the background of a prior performance analysis should such explanations be accepted or not. Under no circumstance should such comments be used deductively to explain a performance-text, but at most as theses among others. They should be first and foremost an object of inquiry, and not necessarily their means.

(F) *Phenomenology:* A phenomenology of theatre is a possible discipline, but only on condition that it applies to all aspects of the theatre experience (chapter 12).

Excluded Disciplines

Whereas performance-analysis should attempt to understand the interaction between implied director and implied spectator, which is embodied in a performance-text, the study of the dialogue between real director and real spectator requires a set of different disciplines, such as psychology and sociology. Accordingly, the study of the actual experiences of real spectators, under synchronic socio-cultural conditions, should be left to reception analysis, which operates similar disciplines. In principle, therefore, reception analysis should be excluded from performance analysis.

Nonetheless, performance analysis should be regarded as the background against which real reception should be examined. It is indeed sensible to determine first the expectations presupposed by a performance-text, and then examine on such grounds whether real spectators live up to them or not, because the actual theatre experience is theirs. In any case, no analysis should confuse considerations regarding the implied director and spectator with considerations regarding the real ones.

Theories of directing should also be excluded because they deal with extra-textual processes. In contrast to Nordmann's approach, directorial accounts of instructions given to actors too should not be part of performance analysis, unless conceived as conjectures among others (1994). In performance analysis only what is actually in the performance-text counts. For similar reasons, performance analysis should exclude theories of acting and focus instead not on the inscribing function of actors, but on the inscribed text; i.e., on the textual functions of bodies and objects on stage. In performance-analysis directors' actual choices and actors' actual behavior on stage only matter. These constitute the text the real spectators are meant to read, interpret and experience.

Historiography should be excluded because it applies to actual theatre experiences and to larger extra-textual contexts, such as historical, social and cultural processes. It thus operates additional disciplines. Performance analysis should, however, provide the basic tools for a sound historiography also in the future (cf. Rozik, 1997: 2)

Criticism of performance-texts should be excluded because it involves subjective considerations of real spectators, critics in particular. Moreover, there is a tacit understanding that there is no point in suggesting scientific criteria for the evaluation of theatre productions because for any one criterion used for praising a work, there are plenty of examples that materialize the same criterion without enjoying the same value. The question is whether or not, while avoiding entering the field of criticism, it is possible to develop a descriptive method that provides an inkling of what is lost and what is attained by a certain creative interpretation of a play-script, whether canonic or not. For example, it may be felt intuitively that a performance-text does not reveal a sound reading of a play-script, or employ adequate means for materializing a director's declared intentions and purposes. A clear distinction between the descriptive and the evaluative approaches is possible in this respect too.

Is there any sense in attempts to suggest typologies of performance-texts? In 'Beyond Style: Typologies of Performance Analysis' Christopher Balme appropriately problematizes typologies suggested by Pavis and Hans T. Lehmann through showing that they reflect twentieth-century trends at most. He correctly implies thereby that such a typology should take into account the entire theatre tradition. In any case, no typology should be used deductively for explaining the mechanisms of a specific performance-text. Each performance analysis should be primarily conducted on its own. Furthermore, a genuine typology of performance-texts should be based on a substantial body of particular performance analyses.

The above qualifications do not reflect criticism of other fields of research; rather they ratify and help define their particular charters.

The study presented in this volume is a preliminary phase in the development of a sound theory of the performance-text and an effective method of performance analysis. None of its assumptions and conclusions should be taken for granted. Each new performance analysis should lead to their re-examination.

List of Cited Works

Aeschylus (1968) *Agamemnon*. Trans. R. Lattimore. In D. Grene and R. Lattimore (eds.), *Greek Tragedies*, Vol. 1. The University of Chicago Press [1947].

—— (1972) *The Libation Bearers*. Trans. R Lattimore. In D. Grene and R. Lattimore (eds.), *Greek Tragedies*, Vol. 2. The University of Chicago Press [1953].

Ahronson, Sharon (1998) 'Allusions to Contemporary Israel – The Bible According to Rina Yerushalmi'. *Theatron*, 1; 60–73 (Hebrew).

Anonymous, *Everyman*. In S. Barnet, M. Berman & W. Burto (1962) *The Genius of the Early English Theatre*. New York and Toronto: Mentor; 71–94.

Argyle, Michael (1984) *Bodily Communication*. London: Methuen [1975].

Aristophanes (1974) *The Frogs*. In *The Wasps*, etc. Trans. D. Barrett. London. Penguin.

Aristotle, (1951) *The Poetics*. In S. H. Butcher (ed. and trans.), *Aristotle's Theory of Poetry and Fine Arts*. New York: Dover [1894].

—— (1991) *The Art of Rhetoric*. Trans. H. C. Lawson-Tancred. London: Penguin Books.

Arnott, Peter (1971) 'Convention versus Illusion'. In *An Introduction to the Greek Theatre*. London: Macmillan [1959]; 1–14.

Arrabal, Fernando (1976) *Picnic in the Battlefield*. Trans. B. Wright. In *Plays*, Vol. 2. London: John Calder. [1961]

Artaud, Antonin (1964) 'Lettres sur le Langage'. In *Le Théâtre et son Double*. [France]: Gallimard; 153–84.

Austin, J. L. (1980) *How to Do Things with Words*. London: Oxford University Press [1962].

Balme, Christopher (1997) 'Beyond Style: Typologies of Performance Analysis'. *Theatre Research International*, 22, 1; 24–30.

Barca, Calderón de la, *see* Calderón.

Bateson, Gregory (1955) 'A Theory of Play and Phantasy'. *Psychiatric Research Reports*, 2; 39–51.

Bayley, Claire (1995) 'Robert Wilson's *HG* Frees us from the Tyranny of Conventional Theatre'. *Independent*, 20 September.

Beardsley, Monroe C. (1958) 'Theories of Metaphor'. In *Aesthetics*. New York: Harcourt; 134–44.

Beckett, Samuel (1959) *Krapp's Last Tape*. London: Faber and Faber [1958].
—— (1970) *Waiting for Godot*. London: Faber [1956].
—— (1970) *Happy Days*. London: Faber and Faber [1963].
Benach, Joan-Anton (1986) 'Los Bárbaros de la Era Post-Industrial'. *La Vanguardia*. Barcelona: 23 Enero; 37.
Bentley, Eric (1967) *The Life of the Drama*. New York: Atheneum.
Ben-Zvi, Linda (1986) *Samuel Beckett*. Boston: Twayne.
Bialik, H. N. and Ravnitsky, Y. H. (eds.) (1960) *Sefer Ha'agada*. Tel Aviv: Dvir (Hebrew).
Birdwhistell, R. L. (1972) *Kinesics and Context*. Philadelphia: University of Pennsylvania Press [1970].
Black, Max (1962a) 'Metaphor'. In Joseph Margolis (ed.), *Philosophy Looks at the Arts*. New York: Scribner; 218–35.
—— (1962b) *Models and Metaphors – Studies in Language and Philosophy*. Ithaca, N.Y.: Cornell University Press.
—— (1988) 'More about Metaphor'. In A. Ortony (ed.), *Metaphor and Thought*; 19–43.
Blum, Bilha (1997) 'Interaction of Style and Meaning in Drama and Performance'. *Theatre Research International*, 22, 1; 63–69.
Bogatyrev, Petr (1986a) 'Semiotics in the Folk Theater'. In L. Matejka and I. R. Titunik (eds.), *Semiotics of Art* [1976]; 33–49.
—— (1986b) 'Forms and Functions of Folk Theater'. In L. Matejka and I. R. Titunik (eds.), *Semiotics of Art* [1976]; 51–56.
Bradbrook, M. C. (1979) *Themes and Conventions of Elizabethan Tragedy*. London, New York, Melbourne: Cambridge University Press [1935].
Bradley, A. C. (1965) 'Hegel's Theory of Tragedy'. In *Oxford Lectures on Poetry*. London: Macmillan; 69–95.
Brecht, Bertolt (1982) *The Threepenny Opera*. Trans. J. Willett & R. Manheim. London: Methuen; 179–205.
—— (1987) 'A Short Organum for the Theatre'. In John Willett (ed. & trans.), *Brecht on Theatre*. New York: Hill and Wang & London: Methuen [1964]; 179–205.
Breuer, Lee (1988) *The Gospel at Colonus*. A video recording.
Brušák, Karel (1986) 'Signs in the Chinese Theater'. In L. Matejka and I. R. Titunik (eds.), *Semiotics of Art* [1976]; 59–73.
Bryant-Bertail, Sarah (1994a) 'Foreword'. *Theatre Research International*, 19, 2; 95–96.
—— (1994b) 'Woman and the City: The Semiotics of Embodiment'. *Theatre Research International*, 19, 2; 99–110.
—— (2000) '*The Trojan Women a Love Story*: A Postmodern Semiotic of the Tragic'. *Theatre Research International*, 25, 1; 40–52.
Büchner, Georg (1982) *Woyzeck*. Trans. Sh. Zandbank. Tel Aviv: Or Am. (Hebrew).
—— (1991) *Woyzeck*. Trans. J. Mackendrick. London: Methuen [1979].
Burns, Elizabeth (1972) *Theatricality – A Study of Convention in the Theatre and in Social Life*. London: Longman.
Calderón de la Barca (1959) *Life is a Dream*. Trans. R. Campbell. In Eric Bentley

(ed.), *The Classic Theatre, Six Spanish Plays*, Vol. III. New York: Doubleday.

Camps, W. A. (1979) *An Introduction to Virgil's 'Aeneid'*. Oxford University Press [1969].

Carlson, Marvin (1990) *Theatre Semiotics – Signs of Life*. Bloomington and Indianapolis: Indiana University Press.

—— (1994) 'Invisible Presences – Performance Intertextuality'. *Theatre Research International*, 19, 2; 111–117.

—— (2000) 'The Ghosts of Versailles'. *Theatre Research International*, 25, 1; 3–9.

—— (2004) *The Haunted Stage*. Ann Harbor: The University of Michigan Press [2001].

Carmeli, Yoram S. (1988) 'Billy's Wig – Acting versus the Performance of the Real in a British Circus'. *Assaph – Studies in the Theatre*, 4; 93–109.

Cassirer, Ernst (1953) *Language and Myth*. Trans. S. K. Langer. New York: Dover.

Chekhov, *see* Chehov.

Chehov, Anton. (1960) *The Seagull*. Trans. by E. Fen. In *Chehov's Plays*. Harmondsworth, Middlesex: Penguin [1954].

—— (1960) *The Cherry Orchard*. Trans. E. Fen. In *Chehov's Plays*. Harmondsworth, Middlesex: Penguin [1954].

Chomsky, Noam (1966) *Cartesian Linguistics*. New York: Harper and Row.

—— (1968) *Syntactic Structures*. The Hague: Mouton [1957].

Cirlot, J. E. (1973) *A Dictionary of Symbols*. Trans. J. Sage. London: Routledge & Kegan Paul [1968].

Cooper, Lane (1924) *Tractatus Coislinianus*. In *An Aristotelian Theory of Comedy*. New York: Harcourt, Brace; 224–26.

Cork, Richard (1995) 'Escape? All in the Fullness of Time'. *The Times*, 20 September.

Corneille, Pierre (1964) 'Les Trois Discours sur le Poème Dramatique'. In R. Mantero (ed), *Corneille Critique*. Paris, Buchet/Chastel [1960]; 167–260.

—— (no date) *Oedipe*. In Maurice Rat (ed.) *Théâtre Complet de Corneille*. Paris: Garnier; Vol. III.

Damasio, Antonio R. (1994) *Descartes' Error*. New York: Grosset/Putnam.

Dijk, Teun A. van (1977) *Text and Context*. London & New York: Longman.

—— (1980) *Macrostructures*. Hillsdale, New Jersey: Erlbaum.

Dodds, E. R. (1988) 'On Misunderstanding the *Oedipus Rex*'. In Erich Segal (ed.) *Oxford Readings in Greek Tragedy*. Oxford University Press; 177–88 [1983].

Doležel, Lubomír (1989) 'Possible Worlds and Literary Fictions'. In S. Allen (ed.), *Possible Worlds in Humanities, Arts and Sciences: Proceedings of the Nobel Symposium 65*. Berlin & New York: Walter de Gruyter; 221–242.

—— (1998) *Heterocosmica – Fiction and Possible Worlds*. Baltimore and London: The Johns Hopkins University Press.

Dorment, Robert (1995) 'Doing Time in the Clink'. *The Daily Telegraph*, 13 September.

Eco, Umberto (1977) 'Semiotics of Theatrical Performance'. *TDR*, 21, 1 (T 73); 107–17.

—— (1980) *The Role of the Reader – Explorations in the Semiotics of Texts*. Bloomington: Indiana University Press [1979].

Ehrenberg, Victor (1954) *Sophocles and Pericles*. Oxford: Basil Blackwell.
Elam, Keir (1980) *The Semiotics of Theatre and Drama*. London and New York: Methuen.
Erlich, Victor (1965) *Russian Formalism, History – Doctrine*. London, The Hague & Paris, Mouton.
Esslin, Martin (1961) *The Theatre of the Absurd*. Garden City, New York: Doubleday.
—— (1992) *The Field of Drama*. London: Methuen [1987].
Euripides (1968) *Hippolytus*. Trans. D. Grene. In D. Grene and R. Lattimore (eds.), *Greek Tragedies*, Vol. 1. The University of Chicago Press [1942].
—— (1972) *The Trojan Women*. Trans. R. Lattimore. In D. Grene and R. Lattimore (eds.), *Greek Tragedies*, Vol. 2. The University of Chicago Press [1958].
—— (1972) *Electra*. Trans. E. Townsend Vermeule. In D. Grene and R. Lattimore (eds.), *Greek Tragedies*, Vol. 2. The University of Chicago Press [1959].
—— (1974) *Medea*. In *Medea and Other Plays*. Trans. Ph. Vellacott. Hardmondsworth, Middlesex: Penguin [1963].
Finley, Karen (1988a) *The Constant Sate of Desire*. TDR, 32, 1; 139–51.
—— (1988b) 'A Constant State of Becoming – An Interview by Richard Schechner'. *TDR*, 32, 1; 152–158.
Fischer-Lichte, Erika, Riley, J. & Gissenwehrer, M. (eds.) (1990a) *The Dramatic Touch of Difference: Theatre, Own and Foreign*. Tübingen: Narr Verlag.
—— (1990b) *The Semiotics of Theater*. Trans. J. Gaines and D. L. Jones. Bloomington and Indianapolis: Indiana University Press [1983].
Foucault, Michel (1966) *Les Mots et les Choses*. Paris: Gallimard.
Franz, M. L. von (1969) 'The Process of Individuation'. In Carl G. Jung, *Man and his Symbols*. Garden City, N.Y.: Doubleday [1964]; 158–269.
Freud, Sigmund (1978) *The Interpretation of Dreams*. Trans. J. Strachey. Harmondsworth, Middlesex: Penguin [1953].
—— (1990) 'Creative Writers and Day-dreaming'. Trans. J. Strachey. In *Art and Literature*. London: Penguin [1953].
Friel, Brian (1990) *Dancing at Lughnasa*. London – Boston: Faber & Faber.
Frye, Northrop (1957) *Anatomy of Criticism*. Princeton, New Jersey: Princeton University Press.
Fuks, Sarit (1984) 'Godot and the Palestinian Problem'. *Ma'ariv*, 30 November (Hebrew).
Gadamer, H. G. (1975) *Truth and Method*. Trans. J. Weinsheimer & D. G. Marshall. New York: Seabury Press.
García Lorca, Federico (1969a) *Blood Wedding*. In *Three Tragedies*. Trans. J. Graham Lujan and R. L. O'Connel. Harmondsworth, Middlesex [1961].
—— (1969b) *The House of Bernarda Alba*. In *Three Tragedies*. Trans. J. Graham Lujan and R. L. O'Connel. Harmondsworth, Middlesex [1961].
—— (1969c) *Yerma*. In *Three Tragedies*. Trans. J. Graham Lujan and R. L. O'Connel. Harmondsworth, Middlesex [1961].
Gimenez, Maritza (1988) 'No nos Interesa la Trascendencia'. Venezuela, 30 Marzo; 37.
Goffman, Erving (1959) *The Presentation of Self in Everyday Life*. London: Penguin.

—— (1975) *Frame Analysis*. Harmondsworth, Middlesex: Penguin.

Gregory, R. L (1970) *The Intelligent Eye*. New York, St. Louis, San Francisco: McGraw-Hill.

Greimas, Algirdas J. (1983) *Structural Semantics: An Attempt at a Method*. Lincoln: University of Nebraska Press.

Hall, Edward T. (1963) *Proxemics – A Study of Man's Spatial Relations*. International University Press.

Handelsaltz, Michael (1993) 'Actuality on the Stage', *Ha'aretz*, 14 April (Hebrew).

Hartshorne, Charles & Weiss, Paul (eds.) (1965) *Collected Papers of Charles Sanders Peirce*. Cambridge, Mass.: Harvard University Press.

Hauser, Arnold (1958) *Philosophy of Art History – Conflicting Forces in the History of Art: Originality and Conventions*. New York: Knopf.

Hegel, G. W. F. (1975) *Aesthetics*. Trans. T. M. Knox. Oxford: Clarendon Press.

Herman, Vimala (1995) *Dramatic Discourse – Dialogue as Interaction in Plays*. London and New York: Routledge.

Honzl, Jindřich (1986a) 'Dynamics of the Sign in the Theater'. In L. Matejka and I. R. Titunik (eds.), *Semiotics of Art* [1976]; 74–93.

—— (1986b) 'The Hierarchy of Dramatic Devices'. In L. Matejka and I. R. Titunik (eds.), *Semiotics of Art* [1976]; 118–27.

Horace (1972) *On the Art of Poetry*. Trans. T. S. Dorsh. Harmondsworth, Middlesex: Penguin [1965].

Ibsen, Henrik (1961) *Hedda Gabler*. Trans. U. Ellis Fermor. In *Hedda Gabler and Other Plays*. Harmondsworth, Middlesex: Penguin [1950].

—— (1966) *A Doll's House*. Trans. R. Farguharson & E. Marx Aveling. London: Dent.

Ingarden, Roman (1973) *The Literary Work of Art – An Investigation on the Borderlines of Ontology, Logic and Theory of Literature* (with an Appendix on the Functions of Language in the Theater). Trans. G. G. Grabowicz. Evanston: Northwestern University Press.

Ionesco, Eugène (1958) *The Chairs*. Trans. D. Watson. In *Plays*, Vol. I. London: Calder.

—— (1958a) *Amédée*. Trans. D. Watson. In *Plays*, Vol. 2. London: Calder and Boyars [1958].

—— (1958b) *The New Tenant*. Trans. D. Watson. In *Amédée, The New Tenant, Victims of Duty*. New York: Grove Press.

—— (1959a) *Rhinoceros*. Trans. D. Watson. In *Plays*, Vol. 4. London: Calder and Boyars [1958].

—— (1959b) *Macbett*. Trans. D. Watson. In *Plays*, Vol. 9. London: Calder and Boyars [1958].

—— (1970) *Exit the King*. Trans. D. Watson. In *Plays*, Vol. 5. London: Calder & Boyars.

Iser, Wolfgang (1990) *The Implied Reader*. Baltimore and London: The Johns Hopkins University Press [1974].

—— (1991) *The Act of Reading – A Theory of Aesthetic Response*. The Johns Hopkins University Press. Baltimore and London [1978].

Jackson, Kevin (1995) 'Now at a Prison near You'. *Independent on Sunday*, 10 September.

Jakobson, Roman (1956) 'Two Aspects of Language and Two Types of Aphasic Disturbances'. In R. Jakobson and M. Halle, *Fundamentals of Language*. The Hague: Mouton; 53–82.

Jung, Carl G. (1969) *Man and his Symbols*. Garden City, N.Y.: Doubleday [1964].

—— (1974) *Dreams*. Trans. R. F. C. Hull. Princeton, N.J.: Princeton University Press.

Kaprow, Alan (1968) 'Extensions in Time and Space – An Interview with Richard Schechner. *TDR*, 12, 3; 153–59.

Kaynar, Gad (1997) 'The Actor as Performer of the Implied Spectator's Role'. *Theatre Research International*, 22, 1; 49–62.

—— (2000) '*A Jew in the Dark*: The Aesthetics of Absence – Monodrama as Evocation and Formation of "Genetic" Collective Memory'. *Theatre Research International*, 25, 1; 53–63.

Kirby, Ernest T. (1974) 'The Shamanistic Origins of Popular Entertainments'. *The Drama Review*, 18; 5–15.

—— (1975) *Ur Drama – The Origins of Theatre*. New York: New York University Press.

Kirby, Michael (1982) 'Nonsemiotic Performance'. *Modern Drama*, XXV; 105–11.

Knights, L. C. (1933) *How Many Children Had Lady Macbeth?* Cambridge: The Minority Press.

Knox, Bernard (1966) *Oedipus at Thebes – Sophocles' Tragic Hero and his Time*. New Haven and London: Yale University Press [1957].

Kobialka, Michal (1994) 'Topography of Representation'. *Theatre Research International*, 19, 2; 118–33.

Kosslyn, Stephen M. (1995) *Image and Brain*. Cambridge, Mass.: MIT Press [1994].

—— (1996) 'Introduction'. In M. S. Gazzaniga (ed.), *The Cognitive Neurosciences*. Cambridge, Mass.: MIT Press; 959–61.

Kowzan, Tadeusz (1968) 'The Sign in the Theatre'. *Diogenes*, LXI; 52–80.

—— (1975) *Littérature et Spectacle*. Le Haye & Paris: Mouton.

Kreitler, Shulamit and Kreitler Hans (1972) *Psychology of the Arts*. Durham, N.C.: Duke University Press.

Kreuder, Friedmann (2000) 'Theatre as a Medium of Recollection – Klaus Michael Grüber's and Antonio Recalacati's *Rudi* Installation (1979)'. *Theatre Research International*, 25, 1; 64–73.

Krook, Dorothea (1969) *Elements of Tragedy*. New Haven & London: Yale University Press.

Langer, Susanne K. (1976) *Philosophy in a New Key*. Cambridge, Mass.: Harvard University Press [1942].

Leech, Geoffrey N. (1983) *Principles of Pragmatics*. London and New York: Longman.

Levinson, Stephen C. (1987) *Pragmatics*. Cambridge University Press [1983].

Lewis, David K. (1986) *Convention – A Philosophical Study*. Cambridge, Mass.: Harvard University Press [1969].

Lope de Vega Carpio, (1959) *Fuenteovejuna*. Trans. R. Campbell. In Eric Bentley (ed.), *The Classic Theatre*, Vol. III. New York: Doubleday.

—— (1965) 'The New Art of Writing Plays in this Age'. In B. H. Clark, European Theories of the Drama. New York: Crown [1945].

Lorca, *see* García Lorca.

Lyons, John (1969) *Introduction to Theoretical Linguistics.* Cambridge University Press [1968].

—— (1981) *Language Meaning and Context.* Bungay: Fontana.

—— (1988) *Semantics.* Cambridge University Press, Vol. 2 [1977].

Mackintosh, Ian (1993) *Architecture, Actor & Audience.* London: Routledge.

MacLachlan, Gale and Reid, Ian (1994) *Framing and Interpretation.* Melbourne University Press.

MacRitchie, Lynn (1995) 'Clinks of Light'. *The Guardian,* 7 September.

Malka, Liora (2000) 'A World without Intimacy'. *Theatre Research International,* 25, 1; 29–39.

Marinis, Marco de (1993) *The Semiotics of Performance.* Trans. Áine O'Healy. Bloomington and Indianapolis. Indiana University Press [1982].

Matejka, Ladislav & Titunik, Irwin R. (eds.) (1986) *Semiotics of Art.* Cambridge, Mass.: MIT Press [1976].

Matejka, Ladislav (1986) 'Postscript – Prague School Semiotics'. In L. Matejka and I. R. Titunik (eds.) *Semiotics of Art* [1976]; 267–90.

Miller, Arthur (1985) *Death of a Salesman.* Harmondsworth, Middlesex: Penguin.

Molière (1957) *Tartuffe.* Trans. M. Bishop. In *Height Plays by Molière.* New York: The Modern Library.

—— (1957) *The Versailles Impromptu.* Trans. M. Bishop. In *Height Plays by Molière.* New York: The Modern Library.

—— (c. 2001) *Don Juan.* Trans. R. Wilbur. San Diego: Harcourt.

Molina, Tirso de, *see* Tirso.

Muir, Kenneth (ed.) (1973) 'Holinshed'. In Shakespeare, *Macbeth.* The Arden Shakespeare [1962]; 164–81.

Mukařovsky, Jan (1978) *Structure, Sign and Fiction.* Trans. J. Burbank & P. Steiner. New Haven & London: Yale University Press.

—— (1986a) 'Art as Semiotic Fact'. In L. Matejka and I. R. Titunik (eds.), *Semiotics of Art* [1976]; 3–9.

—— (1986b) 'Poetic Reference'. In L. Matejka and I. R. Titunik, *Semiotics of Art* [1976]; 155–63.

Nietzsche, Friedrich (1956) *The Birth of Tragedy.* Trans. F. Golffing. Garden City, N. Y.: Doubleday Anchor.

—— (1998) *Human, All Too Human.* Trans. R. J. Hollingdale. Cambridge University Press [1986].

Nordmann, Alfred (1994) 'The Actor's Brief: Experiences with Chekhov'. *Theatre Research International,* 19, 2; 134–42.

—— & Wickert, Hartmut (1997) 'The Impossible Representation of Wonder: Space Summons Memory'. *Theatre Research International,* 22, 1; 38–48.

Novak, Chava (1983) 'The Israeli Shock in Confronting *The Trojan Women*', *Davar,* 28 February (Hebrew).

Nunn, Trevor (1978) *Macbeth* (theatre production with Ian McKellen and Judi Dench), Royal Shakespeare Company. Thames Video. A video recording.

Ortony, Andrew (ed.) (1988) *Metaphor and Thought.* Cambridge: Cambridge University Press [1979].

Pavis, Patrice (1982) *The Languages of the Stage – Essays in the Semiology of the Theatre.* New York: Performing Arts Journal Publications.
—— (1996) *Dictionary of the Theatre – Terms, Concepts and Analysis.* Trans. Ch. Shantz. University of Toronto Press.
Peirce, Charles Sanders (1965) In Ch. Hartshorne and Paul Weiss (eds.) *Collected Papers of Charles Sanders Peirce.* Cambridge, Mass.: Harvard University Press.
Perez Cortillo, Moises (1985) 'La Fura dels Baus, Africa esta Adentro'. *El Publico,* Madrid, Setiembre; 8–9.
Pfister, Manfred (1993) *The Theory and Analysis of Drama.* Trans. J. Halliday. Cambridge University Press [1988].
Pingaud, Bernard (ed.) (1965) 'Propos' (an interview with Sartre). *Bref,* Février; *see* Sartre, *Les Troyennes.*
Pinter, Harold (1968) *A Slight Ache.* In *A Slight Ache and Other Plays.* London: Methuen [1961].
Pirandello, Luigi (1985) *Six Characters in Search of an Author.* Trans. J. Linstrum. London: Methuen [1979].
Plato (1970) *The Republic.* Trans. P. Shorey. Cambridge, Mass.: Harvard University Press & London: Heinemann; Book X.
Plautus (1972) *The Prisoners.* In *The Pot of Gold and Other Plays.* Trans. E. F. Watling. Harmondsworth, Middlesex: Penguin [1965].
Polanski, Roman (1971) *Macbeth.* A film.
Propp, Vladimir I. (1968) *Morphology of the Folktale.* Trans. L. Scott. University of Texas Press.
Quintilian (1976) *Instituto Oratoria.* Trans. H. E. Butler. Cambridge, Mass.: Harvard University Press and Heinemann [1920].
Racine, Jean (1961) *Phaedra.* Trans. R. Lowell. In E. Bentley, *The Classic Theatre,* Vol. IV. Garden City, N.Y.: Doubleday.
Rank, Otto (1964) *The Myth of the Birth of the Hero and Other Writings by Otto Rank.* New York: Vintage Books [1932].
Rapp, Uri (1985) 'Ambiguous Bonds', *The Jerusalem Post,* 25 January.
Ricoeur, Paul (1965) *De l'Interprétation.* Paris: Seuil.
Rokem, Freddie (1994) 'What, has this thing appeared again tonight?' *Theatre Research International,* 19, 2; 143–47.
—— (1995). 'Theater Semiotics'. *Semiotica,* 106 (1–2); 187–96.
—— (2000) 'Foreword'. *Theatre Research International,* 25, 1; 1–2.
Ronen, Ilan (1997) '*Waiting for Godot* as Political Theater'. In Lois Oppenheim (ed.), *Directing Beckett,* Ann Arbor [1994]; 239–49.
Ross, Alf (1968) *Directives and Norms.* London: Routledge & Kegan Paul.
Sadock, Jerrold (1988) 'Figurative Speech Acts and Linguistics'. In A. Ortony (ed.), *Metaphor and Thought;* 46–63.
Saltz, David Z. (1991) 'How to Do Things on Stage'. *The Journal of Aesthetics and Art Criticism,* 49, 1; 39–45.
Sartre, Jean Paul (1965) *Les Troyennes.* In Euripides, *Les Troyennes.* Paris: Gallimard.
Saussure, Ferdinand de (1972) *Cours de Linguistique Générale.* Paris: Payot.
Schechner, Richard (1988) *Performance Theory.* New York & London: Routledge, [1977].

Searle, John R. (1975) 'The Logical Status of Fictional Discourse'. *New Literary History.* 6, 2; 319–32.

—— (1979) 'What is a Speech Act?'. In J. R. Searle (ed.), *The Philosophy of Language.* London: Oxford University Press [1971]; 39–53.

—— (1985) *Speech Acts.* Cambridge University Press [1969].

—— (1986) *Expression and Meaning.* Cambridge University Press [1979]

—— (1988) 'Metaphor'. In A. Ortony (ed.), *Metaphor and Thought*; 92–123.

Sebeok, Thomas A. (1975) 'Six Species of Signs: Some Propositions and Strictures'. *Semiotica*, 13, 3; 233–60.

Sedgewick, G. G. (1948) *Of Irony, Especially in Drama.* Toronto, University of Toronto [1935].

Serpieri, Alessandro et al. (1981) 'Toward a Segmentation of the Dramatic Text'. *Poetics Today*, 2 (3), 163–200.

Shakespeare, William (1973) *Macbeth.* K. Muir (ed.). London: Methuen.

—— (1973) *Othello.* M. R. Ridlley (ed.). London: Methuen.

—— (1980) *Romeo and Juliet.* B. Gibbons (ed.). London: Methuen.

—— (1982) *Hamlet.* H. Jenkins (ed.). London: Methuen.

Shevtsova, Maria (1997) 'Sociocultural Analysis: National and Cross-cultural Performance'. *Theatre Research International*, 22, 1; 4–18.

Shklovsky, Victor (1965) 'Art as Technique'. In L. T. Lemon & M. J. Reis (eds. & trans.), *Russian Formalist Criticism: Four Essays.* Lincoln, Nebraska, University of Nebraska Press; 5–24.

Singleton, Brian (1997) 'Receiving *Les Atrides* Productively: Mnouchkine's Intercultural Signs as Intertexts'. *Theatre Research International*, 22, 1; 19–23.

Sophocles, (1968a) *Oedipus the King.* Trans. D. Grene. In D. Grene and R. Lattimore (eds.), *Greek Tragedies*, Vol. III. The University of Chicago Press [1942].

—— (1968b) *Antigone.* Trans. W. Wyckoff. In D. Grene and R. Lattimore (eds.), *Greek Tragedies*, Vol. I. The University of Chicago Press [1942].

—— (1968c) *Philoctetes.* Trans. D. Grene. In D. Grene and R. Lattimore (eds.), *Greek Tragedies*, Vol. III. The University of Chicago Press [1942].

Souriau, Étienne (1950) *Les Deux Cent Mille Situations Dramatiques.* Paris: Flammarion.

States, Bert O. (1985) *Great Reckonings in Little Rooms.* Berkeley, Los Angeles, London: University of California Press.

Steiner, George (1961) *The Death of Tragedy.* London: Faber & Faber.

Strindberg, August (1960) *Miss Julia.* Trans. P. Watts. Harmondsworth, Middlesex: Penguin.

Styan, J. L. (1967) *The Elements of Drama.* Cambridge: Cambridge University Press [1960].

Suz/o/Suz by La Fura dels Baus. A video recording by the Israeli Broadcasting Authority.

Synge, John M. (1960) *The Playboy of the Western World.* New York: Vintage Books [1904].

Thucydides (1906) *The History.* Trans. B. Jowett. New York: Tandy-Thomas.

Tirso de Molina, (1959) *The Trickster of Sevilla.* Trans. R. Campbell. In Eric Bentley (ed.), *The Classic Theatre*, Vol. III. New York: Doubleday.

Todorov, Tzvetan (1978) *Symbolism and Interpretation.* Ithaca, N.Y.: Cornell University Press.

Törnquist, Egil (1994) 'Comparative Performance Semiotics: The End of Ibsen's *Et Dukkehjem | A Doll House'. Theatre Research International,* 19, 2; 156–64.

Tractatus Coislinianus, *see* Cooper, Lane.

Turner, Victor (1982) *From Ritual to Theatre.* New York: PAJ Publications.

Übersfeld, Anne (1999) *Reading Theatre.* Trans. F. Collins. University of Toronto Press.

Urian, Dan (1994) 'The Stereotype of the Religious Jew in Israeli Theatre'. *Assaph – Studies in the Theatre,* 10; 131–154.

—— (1997) *The Arab in Israeli Theatre.* Trans. N. Paz. Amsterdam: Harwood.

Vega Carpio, Lope de, *see* Lope.

Vellacott, Philip (1975) *Ironic Drama – A Study of Euripides' Method and Meaning.* Cambridge University Press.

Veltrusky, Jiří (1964) 'Man and Object in the Theater'. In Paul L. Garvin (ed. and trans.) *A Prague School Reader on Esthetics, Literary Structure, and Style.* Washington, D.C.: Georgetown University Press; 83–91.

—— (1986a) 'Dramatic Text as a Component of Theater'. In L. Matejka and I. R. Titunik (eds.) *Semiotics of Art* [1976]; 94–117.

—— (1986b) 'Basic Features of Dramatic Dialogue'. In L. Matejka and I. R. Titunik (eds.) *Semiotics of Art* [1976]; 128–33.

—— (1981) 'The Prague School Theory of Theater'. *Poetics Today,* 2, 3; 225–35.

Vernant, Jean-Pierre and Vidal-Naquet Pierre (1988) 'Oedipus without the Complex'. In *Myth and Tragedy in Ancient Greece.* New York: Zone Books.

Virgil (1991) *The Aeneid.* Trans. D. West. London: Penguin.

Vries, Ad de (1976) *Dictionary of Symbols and Images.* Amsterdam: North Holland.

Walker, Craig Steward (1997) 'Reckoning with States on the Phenomenology of Theatre'. *Dramatic Theory and Criticism,* XI, 2; 65–83.

Weitz, Shoshana & Avigal, Shoshana (1986) 'Cultural and Ideological Variables in Audience Response: The Case of *The Trojan Women,* Tel Aviv, 1982–83'. *Assaph – Studies in the Theatre,* 3; 7–42.

Wilcox, Dean (1997) 'Karen Finley's *Hymen'. Theatre Research International,* 22, 1; 31–37.

—— (2000) 'The Defamiliarization of a Significant Phenomenon'. *Theatre Research International,* 25, 1; 74–85.

Willett, J. (ed. and trans.) (1987) *Brecht on Theatre.* London, Methuen [1957].

Wilshire, Bruce (1982) *Role Playing and Identity – The Limits of Theatre as Metaphor.* Bloomington: Indiana University Press.

Wright, Elizabeth (1987) *Psychoanalytic Criticism – Theory in Practice.* London and New York: Methuen [1984].

Yerushalmi, Rina (1991) *Woyzeck 91,* The *Itim* Ensemble. A video recording.

Works pertinent to performance analysis by Eli Rozik

(1988a) 'On the Apparent Double Reference of Theatrical Texts'. *Degrés,* 6, 56; f 1–20.

(1988b) 'The Interpretative Function of the "Seagull" Motif in Chekhov's *The Seagull*. *Assaph – Studies in the Theatre*, 4; 55–81.

(1989a) 'Theatrical Speech Acts – A Theatre Semiotics Approach and the Theory of Theatrical Communication'. *Kodicas/Code*, 12, 1–2; 41–55.

(1989b) 'Stage Metaphor'. *Theatre Research International*, 14, 1; 50–70.

(1990) 'Towards a Methodology of Play Analysis – A Theatrical Approach'. *Assaph – Studies in the Theatre*, 6; 43–69.

(1991) 'The Common Roots of Dreams and the Theatre'. *Assaph – Studies in the Theatre*, 7; 75–102.

(1992a) *The Language of the Theatre*. Glasgow: Theatre Studies Publications.

(1992b) 'Plot Analysis and Speech Act Theory'. In G. Deledalle (ed.), *Signs of Humanity – L'Homme et ses Signes*. Berlin: Mouton de Gruyter; 1183–91.

(1992c) *Elements of Play Analysis*. Tel Aviv: Or Am, (Hebrew).

(1992d) 'Theatrical Conventions'. *Semiotica*, 89, 1&3; 1–23.

(1993a) 'Categorization of Speech Acts in Play and Performance Analysis'. *Dramatic Theory and Criticism*, VIII, 1; 117–32.

(1993b) 'The Functions of Language in the Theatre'. *Theatre Research International*, 18, 2; 104–14.

(1994a) 'Lady Macbeth: in the Making of a Tragic Hero'. *Essays in Poetics*, 19, 2; 45–61.

(1994b) 'Stage Metaphor: With or Without – On Rina Yerushalmi's Production of *The Chairs* by Ionesco'. *Theatre Research International*, 19, 2; 148–55.

(1994c) 'The Notion of "Reference" – A Key to the Nature of the Theatrical Experience'. *South African Theatre Journal*, 8, 1; 24–43.

(1994d) 'Poetic Metaphor'. *Semiotica*, 102, 1&2; 49–69.

(1994e) 'Neutral Space/Time and "Literary" Theatre'. *Assaph – Studies in the Theatre*, 10; 85–98.

(1996a) 'Iconicity or *Mimesis*: Reading *Semiologie du Théâtre* by Tadeusz Kowzan'. *Semiotica*, 108, 1&2; 188–97.

(1996b) 'Multiple Metaphorical Characterization in *Le Roi se Meurt*'. *Nottingham French Studies*, 35, 1; 120–131.

(1996c) 'Theatre at One of its Borderlines – Reflections on *Suz/o/Suz* by La Fura dels Baus'. *Theatre Annual*, 49; 92–104.

(1997) 'Foreword'. *Theatre Research International*, 22, 1;1–3.

(1998a) 'Ellipsis and the Surface Structures of Verbal and Nonverbal Metaphor'. *Semiotica*, 119 – 1&2; 77–103.

(1998b) 'The Performance-text as a Macro Speech Act'. *South African Theatre Journal*, 12, 1&2; 73–89.

(1998c) 'Non-Theatrical Space as Metaphor – Some Speculations on H.G., an Installation by Hans Peter Kuhn and Robert Wilson'. In Ernest W. B. Hess-Lüttich, Jürgen E. Müller and Aart van Zoest (eds.), *Signs & Space / Raum & Zeichen*. Tübingen: Gunter Narr; 224–35.

(1998d) 'Playscript and Performance: The Same Side of Two Coins – Play Analysis from the Viewpoint of Performance Analysis'. *Gestos*, 26; 11–24.

(1999a) 'Interaction or Communication'. *Semiotica*, 123 – 1&2; 115–31.

(1999b) 'The Corporeality of the Actor/Actress Body: The Boundaries of Theatre and the Limitations of Semiotic Methodology'. *Theatre Research International*, 24, 2; 198–211.

(1999c) 'Word as Image : The Dramatic Arts as Test Case'. *Gestos*, 14, 28; 11–27.

(2000a) 'Creative Interpretation in Theatre'. In Nurit Yaari (ed.), *On Interpretation in the Arts*. Tel Aviv University, Assaph Book Series; 189–220.

(2000b) 'Intention and Purpose in Rina Yerushalmi's *Woyzeck 91*'. *Theatre Research International*, 25, 1; 10–28.

(2000c) 'Speech Act Metaphor in Theatre'. *Journal of Pragmatics*, 32; 203–18.

(2000d) 'The Pragmatic Nature of Theatrical Discourse: The Performance-text as a Macro Speech Act'. *Journal of Literary Semantics*, 29; 123–34.

(2000e) 'Is the Notion of "Theatricality" Void?' *Gestos*, 30; 11–30.

(2001) 'Segmentation of the Theatrical Performance-text'. *Semiotica*, 135, 1–4; 77–99.

(2002a) *The Roots of Theatre – Rethinking Ritual and other Theories of Origin*. Iowa City: University of Iowa Press.

(2002b) 'Acting: The Quintessence of Theatricality'. *Substance*, 31, 2&3; 110–124.

(2002c) 'A Silent Theatrical Production Representing a Speaking Fictional World: Analysis of *A Transient Shadow*'. *Theatre Research International*, 27, 1; 78–96.

(2002d) 'Framing, Decoding and Interpretation: On the Spectator's Vital Role in Creating Theatrical Meaning'. *Gestos*, 17, 34; 9–27.

(2002e) 'The Jephthah' Daughter Narrative – Breaching Models in Yerushalmi's *Vayomar, Vayelekh*'. *Motar*, 10; 43–50. (Hebrew; English version forthcoming).

(2004) 'Theatrical Experience as Metaphor'. *Semiotica*, 149, 1–4; 227–96.

(2005) 'From the Innate Image-making Capacity of the Brain to a Redefinition of the Iconic Arts, the Theatre Medium in Particular'. In Klaus Sachs-Hombach (ed.), *Bildwissenschaft – Zwischen Reflexion and Anwendung*. Keln: Herbert von Halem.

Index

absurd, **114**
acting, 12, 78–101
action theory, 35, 137, 208
actual art, 208, 212–13, 219–20
actualization, 18, 100, 160, 162, 222,
    234–5
Aeschylus, 117, 150
aesthetic layer, **114**
Aharonson, Sharon, 145
alazon, 142
allegory, stage, **58–61**
allusion, 101, 158, 170, 232–5, 245, 260.
ambiguity 41, 94–95, 100, 151, 162, 176,
    203, 245, 259
archetypal, **14**
Argyle, Michael, 37
Aristophanes, 58
Aristotle, 107–12, 127, 133, 139–40
Arnott, Peter, 96
Arrabal, Fernando, 61
Artaud, Antonin, 191, 219
Austin, J. L., 4, 35–7, 40, 51, 92, 134

Bateson, Gregory, 164
Beardsley, Monroe C., 49
Beckett Samuel 59–60, 100, 149, 152–4,
    159–60, 235
Bentley, Eric 8, 87
Ben Zvi, Linda, 100, 154
Birdwhistell, R. L., 37
Black, Max, 49–50
Blum, Bilha, 152
body language, 37, 76, 232–3
Bogatyrev, Petr, 3, 8–10, 13, 16–17, 28–29,
    82, 168, 176, 180
Bradbrook, M. C., 64, 69, 71
Bradley, A. C., 113, 117, 127
Brecht, Bertolt, 3, 75, 161, 209, 211
Breuer, Lee, 98
Bryant Bertail, Sarah, 6, 183, 236
Büchner, Georg, 150, 164, 172, 251–2,
    255–9, 262–4
bunraku, 182

Burns, Elizabeth, 64, 76, 140

Calderón de la Barca, 75, 201
Carlson, Marvin, 4, 17, 22, 28, 81, 84, 163,
    181, 186, 211
Cassirer, Ernst, 3, 23
catastrophe, 71, 108–11, 114, 118–19, 199,
    202
catharsis, cathartic, 15, 108–10, 114, 127,
    133, 137, 141, 161, 207
character, functional, 70–1, 74, 96, 98,
    113, 122, 140, 206, 272
character, interactive, 70–1, 76, 122, 206
Chekhov, Anton, 35, 45–7, 62, 74–6, 81,
    116
chorus, 66–8, 71–5, 93, 117–18, 231
cinema, 29, 88–9, 101, 106, 127, 174, 182,
    186–7, 209, 266
circus, 57, 89, 207, 212
classicism, 73, 76, 140, 228
comedy, 111, 139, 157, 211
comic mood, 154, 157–8
contiguity, 21, 43, 64, 87, 194
convention, basic, **27**
convention, stage, **32**
Cooper, Lane, 142
Corneille, Pierre, 73, 76, 111, 117, 140,
    228
cultural baggage, 112, 143–4, 162, 168,
    271

Damasio, Antonio R., 24–5
deconstruction, 30–1, 149–53
defamiliarization, 3, 15, 133, 178–9, 185
deflection of reference, **71–82**
deixis, 40
Dijk, Teun van, 35–6, 38, 91, 134, 138
Dodds, E. R., 117
Dole el, Lubomír, 14, 31, 53
dramatic irony, **113**

Eco, Umberto, 83, 87, 162
eiron, 142

289

Elam, Keir, 11, 13, 29, 36, 65, 82, 107, 117, 168
ellipsis, **50**
enthymeme, **139**
Erlich, Victor, 2–4
Esslin, Martin, 8, 57–8, 114, 127, 133, 168
Euripides, 73, 75–6, 100, 109, 150, 159, 223–37
Everyman, 59–60, 75, 123, 129, 153, 218, 257

facial expression, 8, 11–13, 37–9, 92, 131, 202, 205
fallacy, literary, **105**
farce, 115, 139, 157
fictional layer, **106**
fictional mode, 106.
Finley, Karen, 163, 183, 186
Fischer-Lichte, Erika, 4–5, 7–9, 11, 13, 22, 27, 30, 44, 152, 269
Foucault, Michel, 94
frame, framing, **161–6**
Franz, M. L. von, 199–201, 204
Freud, Sigmund, 23–4, 110–11, 124, 129
Friel, Brian, 98
Frye, Northrop, 14, 106, 122, 142
Fura dels Baus, La 18, 207–21

Gadamer, H. G., 94
García Lorca, Federico, 59, 61, 73–5, 152
generative theory, 1, 267
gesture, **37**
ghosting, 81, 181
Goffman, Erving, 86–7, 164–5, 219
Gregory, R. L,. 24
Greimas, Algirdas J., 117
Gurevitch, Michael, 192–206
grotesque mood, 58, 264

hamartia, 108, 113–4, 117–18
hand gesture, **37**
Hauser, Arnold, 64
Hegel, G. W. F., 113, 117, 127, 133
Honzl, Jindrich, 10–11
Horace, 116
hubris, 109, 118–19

Ibsen, Henrik, 73, 101
icon, **42**
iconic sentence, **42**
iconic sign (Peirce), **21**
iconicity, **22**
illocutionary force, 35, 134
illusion, 2, 12, 28, 85, **177–8**, 201, 205
image, imprinting, **25**
image, mental, 25, 30, 61
imagistic thinking, 23, **22–7**

imitation, **22**
impersonation, 8, 87
implied director, **146ff**
implied reader, **161**ff
implied spectator, **161**ff
imprinting, **25–30**
improper, **31**
index, **21**
Ingarden, Roman, 4, 12, 39–40, 92–4, 98–9, 136, 162, 180
installation, 18, 237–8, 245–249
Intercultural, 152
interpretation, creative, **147**ff
interpretation, hermeneutic, **147**
intertextuality, **99–101**
intonation, 5, 11, 36–9, 47, 92, 132, 202, 233
Ionesco, Eugène, 31, 45, 48, 55, 59–60, 63, 101, 109, 112, 128
ironic layer, 112ff
irony, dramatic, **113**
Iser, Wolfgang, 16, 161–2

Jakobson, Roman, 3, 203
Jung, Carl G., 23, 124, 197, 199–201, 204–5

Kaynar, Gad, 162
Kirby, Ernest T., 88–9, 212, 220
Kirby, Michael, 28, 211
Knights, L. C., 93
Knox, Bernard, 119
Kobialka, Michal, 22
Kosslyn, Stephen M., 24–5
Kowzan, Tadeusz, 4, 8, 11, 27, 43
Krook, Dorothea, 113

Langer, Susanne K., 24–5
language mediation, **26**
Leech, Geoffrey N., 35, 38
Levinson, Stephen C., 35
Lewis, D. K., 64
linearity, linear, 45, 52, 136
literacy, medium, **19**
literary fallacy, 93, 97–8, 105
logos, 111, 113–14, 140
Lope de Vega Carpio, 73, 75
Lorca, Federico García, see García
Lyons, John, 35–7, 64, 92, 134

MacLachlan, Gale, 164
Malka, Liora, 259
Marinis, Marco de, 4–8, 13, 15–16, 27, 89, 162, 180
Matejka, Ladislav, 13
melodrama, 45, 81, 111, 139, 157, 202, 206

metaphor, speech act, 56ff
metaphor, stage, **31**
metatheatricality, 17, 175, 181–5
metonymy, stage, 63, 83
Miller, Arthur, 74
mimesis, **22**
Molière, 29, 71, 75, 83
motif, **169–70**
motivation, **21**
Mukarovsky, Jan, 3, 7, 9, 14
mythical layer, **110**
mythos, 111

naïve layer, **112**
Nietzsche, Friedrich, 23, 128
nonmimetic, **22**
non-representational, 186, 207–8
nonsemiotic performance, 28, 211
Nordmann, Alfred, 81–2, 275
norm, 76, 93
notation, 90, 92, 96, 136, 269

ostension, 83

pace, 5, 115.
paratheatrical, 88–9
Pavis, Patrice, 1–2, 4–5, 7–9, 13, 16, 22,
    42, 97, 114–17, 161, 276
Peirce, Charles S., 4, 9, 21, 28, 35, 61, 64
performance art, 18, 86–8, 175, 182,
    186–7, 207–8, 213, 220–1
performance-text, **27**
performative art, 78, 86–8, 186–7, 207
performative verb, 36–41, 44, 46, 135–7,
    208
performative nature, 35, 37, 40, 56, 88–9,
    136
perlocutionary effect, 35, 47, 134
personification, **123**
Pfister, Manfred, 97–8
phenomenology, 4, 16–17, 174–5, 178–80,
    274
pictorial, pictoriality, 45, 52, 76, 115
Pinter, Harold, 61
Pirandello, Luigi, 116, 249
plagiarism, 151
Plato, 30, 210
Plautus, 73
play analysis, 90,95–6, 101, 105, 273
play, imaginative, 23, 106–7, 120, 124
possible worlds, 14, 84
praxical, **61**
praxical layer, **111**
production, **98**
Propp, Vladimir I., 116–17
proxemic, 37
puppet theatre, 79, 88, 106, 127, 187, 209

Quintilian, 203

Racine, Jean, 71, 74, 113, 228
radio drama, 88, 127
Rank, Otto, 129
read, reading, **7**, **19**, **166**
reaffirmation, 15, 114, 128, 133, 137–9,
    142, 264–5
reception analysis 269, 275
reconstruction, 149, 267, 269
referential association, **50**
representational, 89, 211
rhythm, **114**
Ricoeur, Paul, 62, 94
Rokem, Freddie, 6, 267, 270
Ross, Alf, 76

Sadock, Jerrold, 43
Saltz, David Z., 43
Sartre, Jean Paul, 18, 100, 159, 227–36
Saussure, Ferdinand de, 3, 21, 64
Schechner, Richard, 81, 86, 89, 99, 163,
    174, 207–13, 220–1
Searle, John R., 35, 49–50, 67, 87, 92, 125
Sebeok, Thomas A., 9, 21
Sedgewick, G. G., 69, 140
segment, basic, **42**
segmentation, 8, 11, 34–5, 39–47, 273
semiotics, charter, **6**
sentence, iconic, **42**
Serpieri, Alessandro, 40–1, 46
Shakespeare, William, 41, 73–5, 101, 111,
    138, 150, 160, 201, 249
shaman, 89, 212
Shevtsova, Maria, 6
Shklovsky, Victor, 3, 133, 178
shocking effect, 15, 108–9, 133, 137, 172,
    202, 223, 227, 231
similarity, **22**
Singleton, Brian, 152
Sophocles 38, 62, 71, 73–5, 117–21, 129,
    150, 224
Souriau, Étienne, 116–17
speech act, **35**
speech act theory, 15, 35, 56, 133–7, 272
speech act, macro-, 15, 137–8, 140, 142–5,
    171, 250
stage directions, **149**
stage figure, 84, 180–1
States, Bert O., 4, 6, 17, 30, 81, 94–5,
    174–80
Steiner, George, 252
Strindberg, August, 159
structure, **105**
Styan, J. L., 69, 140–1
style, **76**
substitution, 58–61, 123

Index

symbol, **21**
symbol, stage, **61**
symmetry, 53, 183
Synge, John M., 73
syntax, iconic, 52, 273

tempo, **115**
text, **34, 91**
theatricality, **266**
thematic mode, 182
thinking, **23–5**
Thucydides, 223–4
Tirso de Molina, 75
Todorov, Tzvetan, 62
Törnquist, Egil, 101
Tractatus Coislinianus, 142
tragedy, 74, 108–9, 115, 139, 157
tragic mood, 227
trance, 186, 212
transparency, medium, 64, 166–8, 182,
    268, 273
TV drama, 29, 88–9, 174, 182, 186–7, 266

Übersfeld, Anne 4, 8, 13, 97–8, 148
universality, 18, 22, 148, 151, 159, 222,
    235–6
Urian, Dan, 159, 235

Vellacott, Philip, 224
Veltrusky, Jirí, 3, 9, 11–13, 17, 82, 84, 97,
    176, 180
Verisimilitude, 140
Vernant, Jean-Pierre, 117
viewpoint, **112**
Virgil, 223, 235

Wilcox, Dean, 163, 183
Wilshire, Bruce, 4, 106, 180
Wilson, Robert, 18, 237–49
Wright, Elizabeth, 116

Yerushalmi, Rina, 18, 48, 53, 121, 129–34,
    143–5, 163–73, 250–65